Translated Documents of Gre

Robert K. Sherk, Editor

VOLUME 6

The Roman Empire: Augustus to Hadrian

The Roman Empire: Augustus to Hadrian

EDITED AND TRANSLATED BY
ROBERT K. SHERK

Professor of Classics, State University of New York at Buffalo

CAMBRIDGE
UNIVERSITY PRESS

Published by the Press Syndicate of the University of Cambridge
The Pitt Building, Trumpington Street, Cambridge CB2 1RP
40 West 20th Street, New York, NY 10011–4211, USA
10 Stamford Road, Oakleigh, Melbourne 3166, Australia

First published 1988
Reprinted 1989, 1993, 1994

Printed in Great Britain by Athenæum Press Ltd, Gateshead, Tyne & Wear

British Library cataloguing in publication data
The Roman Empire: Augustus to Hadrian. –
(Translated documents of Greece and Rome; v. 6).
1. Rome – History – Empire, 30 B.C.–284 A.D. – Sources
I. Sherk, Robert K. II. Series
937'.07   DG275

Library of Congress cataloguing in publication data
The Roman Empire: Augustus to Hadrian, edited and translated by
Robert K. Sherk.
      p.   cm. – (Translated documents of Greece and Rome: v. 6)
Includes index.
ISBN 0 521 33025 4. ISBN 0 521 33887 5 (pbk)
1. Rome – History – Empire 30 B.C.–284 A.D. – Sources.
II. Sherk, Robert K. (Robert Kenneth)
II. Series Translated documents of Greece and Rome
(Cambridge, Cambridgeshire): v. 6.
DG275.R65 1988
937'07–dc 19   87–24204 CIP

ISBN 0 521 33887 5 paperback

WD

Translated Documents of Greece and Rome

SERIES EDITOR'S INTRODUCTION

Greek and Roman history has always been in an ambivalent position in American higher education, having to find a home either in a Department of History or in a Department of Classics, and in both it is usually regarded as marginal. Moreover, in a History Department the subject tends to be taught without regard to the fact that the nature of the evience is, on the whole, very different from that for American, English, or French history, while in a Classics Department it tends to be viewed as a 'philological' subject and taught by methods appropriate to Greek and Latin authors. Even on the undergraduate level the difference may be important, but on the graduate level, where future teachers and scholars, who are to engage in original research, are trained, it becomes quite clear that neither of these solutions is adequate.

One problem is the standard of proficiency that should be required in Greek and Latin – both difficult languages, necessitating years of study; and few students start the study, even of Latin, let alone Greek, before they come to college. The editor recognizes that for the student aiming at a Ph.D. in the subject and at advancing present knowledge of it there can be no substitute for a thorough training in the two languages. Nevertheless, it is possible to extend serious instruction at a high level to graduate students aiming at reaching the M.A. level and to make them into competent teachers. It is also possible to bring about a great improvement in the standard of undergraduate courses not requiring the ancient languages – courses that instructors themselves usually find unsatisfactory, since much of the source material cannot be used.

In order to use this material, at both graduate and serious undergraduate levels, the instructor must, in fact, be able to range far beyond the standard authors who have been translated many times. Harpocration, Valerius Maximus, and the *Suda* are often necessary tools, but they are usually unknown to anyone except the advanced scholar. Inscriptions, papyri, and scholia can be baffling even to the student who does have a grounding in the ancient languages.

It is the aim of the series to supply that need – which colleagues have often discussed with the editor – for translations of materials not readily available in English. The principal historical authors (authors like Herodotus, Thucydides, Livy, and Tacitus) are not included; they are easy enough to find in adequate translations, and the student will have to read far more of them than could be provided in a general source-book. References to important passages in the works of those authors have been given at suitable points, but it is assumed that the instructor will direct the student's reading in them. While doing that reading, the student will now be able to have at his side a comprehensive reference book. Occasionally a passage from an otherwise accessible author (not a main historical source) has been included, so that the student may be spared the temptation of failing to search for it. But most of the material collected in this series would be hard for him to find anywhere in English, and much of it has never been translated at all.

Such translations of documentary sources as exist (and there are some major projects in translation among them, e.g. in the field of legal texts, which are intended to be far more than source-books for students) tend to be seriously misleading in that they offer continuous texts where the original is (so often) fragmentary. The student cannot be aware of how much actually survives on the document and how much is modern conjecture – whether quite certain or mere guesswork. This series aims at presenting the translation of fragmentary sources in something like the way in which original documents were presented to the scholar: a variety of type fonts and brackets (which will be fully explained) have been used for this, and even though the page may at first sight appear forbidding to one unaccustomed to this, he will learn to differentiate between text and restoration and (with the instructor's help and the use of the notes provided) between the dubious, the probable, and the certain restoration. Naturally, the English can never correspond perfectly to the Greek or Latin, but the translation aims at as close a correspondence as can be achieved, so that the run of the original and (where necessary) the amount surviving can be clearly shown. Finer points of English idiom have deliberately been sacrificed in order to produce this increased accuracy, though it is hoped that there will be nothing in the translation so unnatural as to baffle the student. In the case of inscriptions (except for those with excessively short lines) line-by-line correspondence has been the aim, so that the student who sees a precise line reference in a modern work will be able to find it in the translation.

Translation is an art as well as a science; there are bound to be differing opinions on the precise interpretation and on the best rendering of any given passage. But there is always room for improvement, and a need for it. Suggestions and corrections from users of the series will always be welcome.

The general editor sincerely hopes that the present volume will make a major contribution to raising the standard of ancient history teaching in the U.S.A. and, indeed, wherever English is the medium of instruction, and that it will help to convey to students not fully proficient in Greek or Latin, or even entirely ignorant of those languages, some of the immediacy and excitement of real (as distinct from textbook) history. Perhaps some will be encouraged to develop their skill in the two languages so as to go on to a fuller understanding of the ancient world, or even to professional study of it.

State University of New York at Buffalo R.K.S.

CONTENTS

Contents

Contents

Contents

Contents

Contents

VOLUME EDITOR'S INTRODUCTION

With the victory of the Caesarian faction the old Republican politics were dead, replaced by the cult of personality in the figure of the emperor. Men of ambition and talent looked in new directions for the realization of their hopes, and Caesar Augustus showed them the way: careers in service to the state in a variety of positions. The Empire was something totally new, a synthesis of the past but at the same time a new beginning, a melting-pot of nations and peoples. Its sheer mass can be overwhelming when one attempts to describe it from top to bottom, from its beginning to the final transformation. The literary sources, of course, remain the bedrock on which our knowledge of it stands: Tacitus, Dio Cassius, Suetonius, Velleius Paterculus, Plutarch, Josephus, and others for the early Principate. Every student and historian must estimate their respective values and use their contents. Other writers like Juvenal, Martial, Pliny, Fronto, Aelius Aristeides and many others add much of historical importance. Knowledge of Greek and Latin is vital for penetrating the spirit of the Greco-Roman world or unlocking the exact meaning of certain passages or phrases of the extant literature. Of course, all the major figures of that literature have been translated into English and most other European languages to make their information more readily available. Even so, such translations have need of commentaries to bridge the cultural gap of different worlds. Apart from these obvious literary sources there are huge amounts of documentary material that have been preserved on stone or other media. Many hundreds of thousands of inscriptions in Latin and Greek allow us to examine these historical snapshots of almost every aspect of the Empire, and the papyri add more tens of thousands of documents to the inscriptional collection. The present source-book offers a selection of the historically most important of all such documents. Its purpose is not to take the place of modern standard histories or the major historians like Tacitus or Dio, but to support and fill out the pictures they present. Although the major Greek and Roman historians do not appear in this volume, passages from certain other writers like Pliny the Elder, Orosius, Jordanes, Eutropius, and others have been included. Even with omission of the major authors the selective process has also forced the omission of large amounts of documentary material. The general test applied to documents for inclusion has been their value in illustrating the major events or institutions of Roman imperial history: administration, foreign policy of the central government, imperial cult, wars, etc. The *cursus honorum* of a senator or equestrian is included, for example, only if some part of it reveals more than mere passing notice of his various posts. Some unusual piece of information must be present. Thus, much has given way to the larger issues.

Part II on Society in the Roman World speaks for itself, concerned as it is with everyday life. Just as much a part of that ancient world as the emperors and administrators were the people of Italy and the provinces struggling to find their places in the new world: local nobles, the religious communities, the working classes at large, entertainers, actors, athletes, doctors, slaves, farmers, and all the rest.

Each document is accompanied by references to the major literary sources – where applicable, of course – followed by a short bibliography of those works which the editor feels are authoritative or valuable. The notes are not meant to be exhaustive, merely serving as an aid for the proper understanding of the text. For the reign of Augustus there is an overlap with Volume 4 of this series (*Rome and the Greek East to the Death of Augustus*), and therefore some of the documents in the present volume (Nos. 2, 12–13, 15, 25) have been taken from that work, and the *Res Gestae* of Augustus have been given in full. The division of the material emperor by emperor in Part I allows a chronological organization that the editor considers essential in a book that deals with historical events from Augustus to Hadrian, but for obvious reasons it cannot always be followed rigidly. Certain documents cannot be dated precisely, or sometimes their very nature extends beyond a particular year. However, within each group of emperors an effort has been made to keep chronological sequence. And in Part II it would have been pointless to attempt a chronological arrangement.

When the reader wishes to compare a translation with the original text, care must be taken to use only that text which is marked by an asterisk, for the advance of knowledge and new discoveries frequently require slight and sometimes great changes in the older editions. The asterisk denotes the particular text used in making the present translations.

G. W. Bowersock graciously gave me the benefit of his great learning and judgment by reading each of the entries. He made many suggestions and saw to it that a number of recently discovered documents were brought to my attention. And Dr Thomas Banchich compiled part of the index. It is a pleasure to thank them both publicly.

ABBREVIATIONS

Abbott–Johnson, *Municipal Administration*	F. F. Abbott and A. C. Johnson, *Municipal Administration in the Roman Empire* (Princeton 1926)
AÉ	*L'Année Épigraphique*
AJAH	*American Journal of Ancient History*
AJP	*American Journal of Philology*
Alföldy, *Social History*	G. Alföldy, *The Social History of Rome* (Totowa, NJ 1985)
Alföldy, *Tarraco*	G. Alföldy, *Die römischen Inschriften von Tarraco* (Berlin 1975)
ANRW	*Aufstieg und Niedergang der römischen Welt*
Ant. Class.	*L'Antiquité classique*
Balsdon, *Life and Leisure*	J. P. V. D. Balsdon, *Life and Leisure in Ancient Rome* (London 1969)
BCH	*Bulletin de Correspondance Hellénique*
BGU	*Berliner griechische Urkunden (Ägyptische Urkunden aus den Königlichen Museen zu Berlin)* (Berlin 1895–)
Birley, *Fasti*	A. R. Birley, *The Fasti of Roman Britain* (Oxford 1981)
BMC	*British Museum Catalogue* (the word following denotes the specific volume)
Bosch, *Quellen*	E. Bosch, *Quellen zur Geschichte der Stadt Ankara im Altertum* (Ankara 1967)
Bowersock, *Augustus*	G. W. Bowersock, *Augustus and the Greek World* (Oxford 1965)
Bruns[7]	C. G. Bruns and T. Mommsen, *Fontes Iuris Romani Antiqui* (seventh edition by O. Gradenwitz, Tübingen 1909)
Brunt, *Manpower*	P. A. Brunt, *Italian Manpower (225 B.C.–A.D. 14)* (Oxford 1971)
CAH	*Cambridge Ancient History*
Cavenaile, *CPL*	R. Cavenaile, *Corpus Papyrorum Latinarum* (Wiesbaden 1958)
CIG	A. Boeckh, *Corpus Inscriptionum Graecarum*
CIL	*Corpus Inscriptionum Latinarum*
CIRB	*Corpus Inscriptionum Regni Bosporani*
CRAI	*Comptes rendus de l'académie des inscriptions et des belles-lettres*
Duncan-Jones, *Economy*	R. Duncan-Jones, *The Economy of the Roman Empire* (Cambridge 1974)
Eck, *Staatliche Organisation*	W. Eck, *Die staatliche Organisation Italiens in der hohen Kaiserzeit* (Munich 1979)
Economic Survey	*An Economic Survey of Ancient Rome* (in five volumes, Baltimore 1933–)

Abbreviations

Ehrenberg–Jones, *Documents*[2]	V. Ehrenberg and A. H. M. Jones, *Documents Illustrating the Reigns of Augustus and Tiberius* (second edition, Oxford 1955)
FGrHist	F. Jacoby, *Die Fragmente der griechischen Historiker* (Berlin and Leiden 1923–)
FIRA	*Fontes Iuris Romani Antejustiniani* I–III (Rome 1941–3)
Garzetti, *Tiberius to Antonines*	A. Garzetti, *From Tiberius to the Antonines* (London 1974)
Goodyear, *Annals*	F. R. D. Goodyear, *Tacitus: The Annals* I (Cambridge 1972)
Gordon, *Album*	A. E. Gordon, J. S. Gordon, *Album of Dated Latin Inscriptions* (4 parts in 7 volumes, Berkeley and Los Angeles 1958–65)
Gordon, *Epigraphy*	A. E. Gordon, *Illustrated Introduction to Latin Epigraphy* (Berkeley, Los Angeles and London 1983)
Griffin, *Nero*	M. T. Griffin, *Nero. The End of a Dynasty* (London 1984)
Halfmann, *Senatoren*	H. Halfmann, *Die Senatoren aus dem östlichen Teil des Imperium Romanum bis zum Ende des 2. Jahrhunderts n. Chr.* (Göttingen 1979)
Head, *Historia Nummorum*	B. V. Head, *Historia Nummorum* (second edition, London 1911)
Henderson, *Hadrian*	B. W. Henderson, *The Life and Principate of the Emperor Hadrian* (London 1923)
Hengstl, *Griechische Papyri*	J. Hengstl, *Griechische Papyri aus Ägypten* (Munich 1978)
Humphrey, *Circuses*	J. H. Humphrey, *Roman Circuses* (Los Angeles 1986)
I. Cret.	*Inscriptiones Creticae*
I. Ephesos	*Die Inschriften von Ephesos* (Bonn 1979–)
IG	*Inscriptiones Graecae*
IGLS	*Inscriptions grecques et latines de la Syrie* (ed. Jalabert and Mouterde)
IGRR	*Inscriptiones Graecae ad Res Romanas Pertinentes* (ed. Cagnat)
I. Ital.	*Inscriptiones Italiae*
I. Kyzikos	*Die Inschriften von Kyzikos*
ILAfr	*Inscriptions latines d'Afrique*
ILS	*Inscriptiones latinae selectae* (ed. Dessau)
I. Olympia	*Die Inschriften von Olympia* (ed. Dittenberger and Purgold)
IOSPE	*Inscriptiones Antiquae Orae Septentrionalis Ponti Euxini Graecae et Latinae* (ed. Latyschev)
JEA	*Journal of Egyptian Archaeology*
JOAI	*Jahreshefte des Oesterreichischen Archäologischen Instituts*
Jones, *Studies*	A. H. M. Jones, *Studies in Roman Government and Law* (Oxford 1960)
Jones, *Emperor Titus*	B. W. Jones, *The Emperor Titus* (London 1984)
JRS	*Journal of Roman Studies*
Kienast, *Augustus*	D. Kienast, *Augustus: Princeps und Monarch* (Darmstadt 1982)
Lepper, *Parthian War*	F. A. Lepper, *Trajan's Parthian War* (Oxford 1948)
Levick, *Colonies*	B. Levick, *Roman Colonies in Southern Asia Minor* (Oxford 1967)
Magie, *RRAM*	D. Magie, *Roman Rule in Asia Minor* (Princeton 1950)

Mattingly, *BMC*	H. Mattingly, *Coins of the Roman Empire in the British Museum* (London 1923–)
Maxfield, *Military Decorations*	V. A. Maxfield, *Military Decorations of the Roman Army* (London 1981)
McCrum–Woodhead, *Documents*	M. McCrum and A. G. Woodhead, *Select Documents of the Principates of the Flavian Emperors* (Cambridge 1961)
MDAI(A)	*Mitteilungen des Deutschen Archäologischen Instituts (Athenische Mitteilungen)*
MÉFR	*Mélanges d'Archéologie et d'Histoire de l'École française de Rome*
Mellor, *Roma*	R. Mellor, ΘΕΑ ΡΩΜΗ. *The Worship of the Goddess Roma in the Greek World* (Göttingen 1975)
Millar, *Emperor*	F. Millar, *The Emperor in the Roman World* (Ithaca, NY 1977)
Mitteis, *Chrestomathie*	L. Mitteis and U. Wilcken, *Grundzüge und Chrestomathie der Papyruskunde, Zweiter Band, Zweite Hälfte* (Leipzig and Berlin 1912)
Moćsy, *Pannonia*	A. Moćsy, *Pannonia and Upper Moesia* (London 1974)
Moretti, *IGUR*	L. Moretti, *Inscriptiones Graecae urbis Romae* (Rome 1968–)
OCD²	*Oxford Classical Dictionary* (second edition)
O. Fay.	Fayûm Ostraka, published by B. P. Grenfell, A. S. Hunt, and D. G. Hogarth, *Fayûm Towns and their Papyri* (London 1900) pp. 320ff.
P. Brem.	*Die Bremer Papyri*, ed. by U. Wilcken (Berlin 1936)
PBSR	*Papers of the British School at Rome*
Peek, *GVI*	W. Peek, *Griechische Vers-Inschriften* (Vol. I, Berlin 1955)
P. Fay.	B. Grenfell, A. S. Hunt and D. G. Hogarth, *Fayûm Towns and their Papyri* (London 1900)
Pflaum, *Carrières*	H.-G. Pflaum, *Les Carrières procuratoriennes équestres sous le haut-empire romain* (Paris 1961)
Pflaum, *Cursus Publicus*	H.-G. Pflaum, 'Essai sur les cursus publicus sous le haut-empire romain' in *Mém. présentés à l'Acad. des Inscr. et Belles-Letters 14*, 189–391 (Paris 1940)
PIR²	*Prosopographia Imperii Romani*
P. Lon.	*Greek Papyri in the British Museum*, ed. by F. G. Kenyon and H. I. Bell (London 1893–1917)
P. Oslo	*Papyri Osloenses*, ed. by S. Eitrem and L. Amundsen (Oslo 1925–)
P. Oxy.	*The Oxyrhynchus Papyri* (London 1898–)
Price, *Rituals*	S. R. F. Price, *Rituals and Power: The Roman Imperial Cult in Asia Minor* (Cambridge 1984)
RÉG	*Revue des Études Grecques*
Reinmuth, *Prefect*	O. W. Reinmuth, *The Prefect of Egypt from Augustus to Diocletian* (Beiheft 34 of *Klio*, 1935)
Reynolds, *Aphrodisias*	J. Reynolds, *Aphrodisias and Rome* (London 1982)
Reynolds–Perkins, *IRT*	J. M. Reynolds and J. B. Ward Perkins, *The Inscriptions of Roman Tripolitania* (London 1952)

Abbreviations

Rhein. Mus.	*Rheinisches Museum*
RIB	*The Roman Inscriptions of Britain*
Rostovtzeff, *SEHRE*	M. Rostovtzeff, *The Social and Economic History of the Roman Empire* (second edition by P. M. Fraser, Oxford 1957)
Roxan, *Diplomas*	M. M. Roxan, *Roman Military Diplomas 1954–1977* (London 1978); *Roman Military Diplomas 1978 to 1984* (London 1985)
SB	*Sammelbuch griechischer Urkunden aus Ägypten*, ed. by Preisigke and Bilabel
SBAW	*Sitzungsberichte der Akad. der Wissenschaften in Wien, Phil-hist. Klasse*
SEG	*Supplementum Epigraphicum Graecum*
Sherk, *Municipal Decrees*	R. K. Sherk, *The Municipal Decrees of the Roman West* (Buffalo 1970)
Sherk, *RDGE*	R. K. Sherk, *Roman Documents from the Greek East* (Baltimore 1969)
Sherk, *TDGR* 4	R. K. Sherk, *Translated Documents of Greece and Rome* (Vol. IV: *Rome and the Greek East to the Death of Augustus* (Cambridge 1984)
Sherwin-White, *Citizenship*[2]	A. N. Sherwin-White, *The Roman Citizenship* (second edition, Oxford 1973)
SIG[3]	*Sylloge Inscriptionum Graecarum* (third edition)
Smallwood, *Documents Gaius*	E. M. Smallwood, *Documents Illustrating the Principates of Gaius, Claudius and Nero* (Cambridge 1967)
Smallwood, *Documents Nerva*	E. M. Smallwood, *Documents Illustrating the Principates of Nerva, Trajan and Hadrian* (Cambridge 1966)
Smallwood, *Jews*	E. M. Smallwood, *Jews Under Roman Rule* (Leiden 1976)
Speidel, *Roman Army Studies*	M. Speidel, *Roman Army Studies* (Amsterdam 1984)
Stein, *Moesien*	A. Stein, *Die Legaten von Moesien* (Budapest 1940)
Stein, *Präfekten*	A. Stein, *Die Präfekten von Ägypten in der römischen Kaiserzeit* (Bern 1950)
Strobel, *Untersuchungen*	K. Strobel, *Untersuchungen zu den Dakerkriegen Trajans* (Bonn 1984)
Syme, *Danubian Papers*	R. Syme, *Danubian Papers* (Bucharest 1971)
Syme, *Roman Papers*	R. Syme, *Roman Papers* (Vols. I–II edited by E. Badian, Oxford 1979; Vol. III ed. A. R. Birley, Oxford 1984)
Syme, *Roman Revolution*	R. Syme, *The Roman Revolution* (Oxford 1939)
Syme, *Tacitus*	R. Syme, *Tacitus* (Oxford 1958)
TAM	*Tituli Asiae Minoris*
TAPA	*Transactions of the American Philological Association*
Taylor, *Divinity*	L. R. Taylor, *The Divinity of the Roman Emperor* (Middleton 1931)
Tcherikover–Fuks, *CPJ*	V. A. Tcherikover and A. Fuks, *Corpus Papyrorum Judaicarum* (3 vols., Cambridge, Mass. 1957–64)
Weaver, *Familia Caesaris*	P. R. C. Weaver, *Familia Caesaris* (Cambridge 1972)
Webster, *Army*	G. Webster, *The Roman Imperial Army* (London 1969)
West, *Corinth*	A. B. West, *Corinth*, Vol. III, Part II: *Latin Inscriptions* (Cambridge, Mass. 1931)

Abbreviations

Wilkes, *Dalmatia*	J.J. Wilkes, *Dalmatia* (Cambridge, Mass. 1969)
Wilcken, *Chrestomathie*	L. Mitteis and U. Wilcken, *Grundzüge und Chrestomathie der Papyruskunde, Erster Band, Zweite Hälfte* (Leipzig and Berlin 1912)
Yadin, *Bar-Kokhba*	Y. Yadin, *Bar-Kokhba* (New York 1971)
ZPE	*Zeitschrift für Papyrologie und Epigraphik*
ZSS	*Zeitschrift der Savigny Stiftung*

SYMBOLS

( )   indicate explanatory addition to the text.

[ ]   enclose letters or words that no longer stand in the text as it survives, but have been restored by modern scholars.

< >   enclose letters or words thought to have been accidentally omitted on the original document.

[[ ]]   enclose letters or words that were deliberately erased in ancient times.

{ }   enclose apparently superfluous letters or words.

| indicates the end of a line in an inscription.

|| indicate the beginning of every fifth line in an inscription.

/   indicates the end of a line of verse.

//   indicate the beginning of every fifth line of verse.

*   indicates the text on which the translation of an inscription or papyrus here given is based.

v   indicates a vacant letterspace on the original document.

vv   indicate that there is more than one letterspace vacant on the original document.

vacat   indicates that an entire line or a space between entire lines was left vacant.

LACUNA   indicates that a portion of the document is missing.

Italics   indicate that only a part of the original word is extant on the document.

Spelling

Most of the personal and place names are transliterated directly. However, the names of Greek and Roman authors as well as individuals are given in their familiar English or Latin spelling, and certain place names, more familiar to readers in a Latin spelling, are retained in that spelling, regardless of the language of the document. Latin names will regularly appear in their Latin spelling for the same reason, but the more unusual Greek names will be transliterated. To many 'Aetolia' is more familiar than 'Aitolia', while 'Cibyra' would be no more enlightening than 'Kibyra'. Still, I have not followed a rigid set of rules.

PART I
THE IMPERIAL GOVERNMENT
IN WAR AND PEACE

AUGUSTUS
(27 BC–AD 14)
IMPERATOR CAESAR AUGUSTUS

Titles: AUGUSTUS (January 16, 27 BC)
PONTIFEX MAXIMUS (12 BC)
FATHER OF HIS COUNTRY (2 BC)
HOLDER OF THE TRIBUNICIAN POWER: received
it for the first time in 23 BC and it was renewed annually on
July 1 (thus I–XXXVII)
CONSUL: for the 7th time in 27 BC, then in 26 (VIII),
25 (IX), 24 (X), 23 (XI), 5 (XII), 2 (XIII)

Death: August 19, AD 14.

The *consules ordinarii* under Augustus

BC		
27	Imp. Caesar Divi f. VII	M. (Vipsanius) Agrippa III
26	Imp. Caesar Divi f. Augustus VIII	T. Statilius Taurus II
25	Imp. Caesar Divi f. Augustus IX	M. Iunius Silanus
24	Imp. Caesar Divi f. Augustus X	C. Norbanus Flaccus
23	Imp. Caesar Divi f. Augustus XI	A. Terentius Varro Murena
22	M. Claudius Marcellus Aeserninus	L. Arruntius
21	M. Lollius	Q. Aemilius Lepidus
20	M. Appuleius	P. Silius Nerva

19	C. Sentius Saturninus	Q. Lucretius (Cinna?) Vespillo
18	P. Cornelius Lentulus Marcellinus	Cn. Cornelius Lentulus
17	C. Furnius	C. Iunius Silanus
16	L. Domitius Ahenobarbus	P. Cornelius Scipio
15	M. Livius Drusus Libo	L. Calpurnius Piso Frugi (Pontifex)
14	M. Licinius Crassus Frugi	Cn. Cornelius Lentulus (Augur)
13	Ti. Claudius Nero	P. Quinctilius Varus
12	M. Valerius Messala Barbatus Appianus	P. Sulpicius Quirinius
11	Q. Aelius Tubero	Paullus Fabius Maximus
10	Africanus Fabius Maximus	Iullus Antonius
9	Nero Claudius Drusus	T. Quinctius Crispinus (Sulpicianus)
8	C. Marcius Censorinus	C. Asinius Gallus
7	Ti. Claudius Nero II	Cn. Calpurnius Piso
6	D. Laelius Balbus	C. Antistius Vetus
5	Imp. Caesar Divi f. Augustus XII	L. Cornelius Sulla
4	C. Calvisius Sabinus	L. Passienus Rufus
3	L. Cornelius Lentulus	M. Valerius Messalla Messallinus
2	Imp. Caesar Divi f. Augustus XIII	M. Plautius Silvanus
1	Cossus Cornelius Lentulus	L. Calpurnius Piso (Augur)

AD

1	C. Caesar	L. Aemilius Paullus
2	P. Vinicius	P. Alfenus Varus
3	L. Aelius Lamia	M. Servilius
4	Sex. Aelius Catus	C. Sentius Saturninus
5	L. Valerius Messalla Volesus	Cn. Cornelius Cinna Magnus
6	M. Aemilius Lepidus	L. Arruntius
7	Q. Caecilius Metellus Creticus Silanus	A. Licinius Nerva Silianus
8	M. Furius Camillus	Sex. Nonius Quinctilianus
9	C. Poppaeus Sabinus	Q. Sulpicius Camerinus
10	P. Cornelius Dolabella	C. Iunius Silanus
11	M'. Aemilius Lepidus	T. Statilius Taurus
12	Germanicus Caesar	C. Fonteius Capito
13	C. Silius A. Caecina Largus	L. Munatius Plancus
14	Sex. Pompeius	Sex. Appuleius

The standard work on the consular lists for the empire is A. Degrassi, *I fasti consolari dell' impero romano*, Rome 1952 (new edition forthcoming by W. Eck), in which the *consules suffecti* will also be found. The suffect consulship, whereby the *consules ordinarii* held office for only the first few months of each year and were then replaced by another pair, became a regular institution.

1   Calendar entries for Augustus.
Extracts from local Italian calendars.[1] [Latin]

A: January 13, 27 BC. Fasti Praenestini. Ehrenberg–Jones, *Documents*[2] p. 45; *I. Ital. XIII 2 p. 113.

That a crown of oak-leaves be placed [above the door of the house of

Imperator Caesar] Augustus | [was decreed by the senate, because] he *restored* [the Republic] | to the Roman People.[2]

B: January 16, 27 BC. Fasti Praenestini. Ehrenberg–Jones, *Documents*[2] p. 45; *I. Ital.* XIII 2 p. 115.

Imperator Caesar was called [Augustus] in his own [consulship] for the 7th time and Agrip[pa for the 3rd time (27 BC)].

C: October 12, 19 BC. Fasti Amiternini. Ehrenberg–Jones, *Documents*[2] p. 53; *I. Ital.* XIII 2 p. 195.

Festival (was held) in accordance with a decree of the senate, | because on this day Imperator Caesar Augustus, back from the overseas provinces, | entered the city, and the Altar of Fortune Who Brings Back was set up.[3]

D: December 15, 19 BC. Feriale Cumanum. Ehrenberg–Jones, *Documents*[2] p. 55; *I. Ital.* XIII 2 p. 279.

On this day the Altar of Fortune Who Brings Back was dedicated, who brought Caesar back [from the] overseas provinces. Public prayer (made) to Fortune Who Brings Back.

E: July 4, 13 BC. Fasti Amiternini. Ehrenberg–Jones, *Documents*[2] p. 49; *I. Ital.* XIII 2 p. 189.

Festival (was held) in accordance with a decree of the senate, because on this day the Altar | of Augustan Peace in the Campus Martius | was set up | in the consulship of (Tiberius Claudius) Nero and (P. Quinctilius) Varus (13 BC).[4]

F: March 6, 12 BC. Fasti Praenestini. Ehrenberg–Jones, *Documents*[2] p, 47; *I. Ital.* XIII 2 p. 121.

Festival (was held) [in accordance with a decree of the senate, because on this day] Imperator Caesar Augustus [was made] pontifex | *maximus* in the consulship of (P. Sulpicius) [Quir]inius and (Gaius) Valgius (Rufus) (12 BC). The duoviri[5] | for [this reason make sacrifice] and the people wear garlands and abstain from work.

G: February 5, 2 BC. Fasti Praenestini. Ehrenberg–Jones, *Documents*[2] p. 47; *I. Ital.* XIII 2 p. 119.

Festival (was held) in accordance with a decree of the senate, | because on this day Imperator Caesar Augustus, pontifex | maximus, holding the tribunician power for the 21st time (2 BC), consul for the 13th time, | was called father of his country by the senate and the Roman People.[6]

H: August 20, AD 2. Fasti Antiates. Ehrenberg–Jones, *Documents*[2] p. 51; **I. Ital.* XIII 1 p. 328.

Sacrifice (made) in honor of the dead Lucius Caesar.[7]

I: February 21 or 22, AD 4. Fasti Verulani. Ehrenberg–Jones, *Documents*[2] p. 47; **I. Ital.* XIII 2 p. 165.

[Sacrifices (made) in honor of the dead] Gaius Caesar.[7]

J: June 26, AD 4. Fasti Amiternini. Ehrenberg–Jones, *Documents*[2] p. 49; **I. Ital.* XIII 2 p. 187.

Festival (was held) in accordance with a [decree] of the senate, because on this day [Imperator Caesar] | Augustus *adopted* as his | son [Tiberius Caesar, | in the consulship of] (Sextus) Aelius (Catus) [and (Gaius) Sentius (Saturninus) (AD 4).][8]

K: January 27, AD 6. Fasti Praenestini. Ehrenberg–Jones, *Documents*[2] p. 46; **I. Ital.* XIII 2 p. 117.

The temple [of Castor and Po]llux was dedicated.[9]

L: September 17, AD 14. Fasti Amiternini. Ehrenberg–Jones, *Documents*[2] p. 52; **I. Ital.* XIII 2 p. 193.

Festival (was held) in accordance with a decree of the senate, because on this day | divine honors to the deified Augustus | were decreed by the senate | in the consulship of Sextus Appuleius and Sextus Pompeius (AD 14).

1   The old Italian calendars not only listed the days on which the courts were open and on which business could be conducted, but they also gradually came to include other matters, such as lists of magistrates and records of triumphs and similar events of interest to the local towns and cities.
2   Cf. *Res Gestae* 34 (below, No. 26).
3   Cf. the *Res Gestae* 11.1 (below, No. 26).
4   Cf. the *Res Gestae* 12.2 (below, No. 26).
5   The duoviri were the executive magistrates of Praeneste.
6   Cf. the *Res Gestae* 35 (below, No. 26). On the significance of the title see A. Alföldi in *Museum Helveticum* 11 (1954) 133ff.
7   See the honors decreed to Gaius Caesar (below, No. 19).
8   Velleius Paterculus 2.103.3–4.
9   Ovid, *Fasti* 1.705ff.

2   Legal decision by Augustus and Agrippa, and a governor's letter to Kyme. 27 BC (for the legal decision).

Marble stele broken at the bottom, damaged on the right and left, decorated with a festoon of ivy at the top, Kyme in Asia on the Aeolian coast. The inscription is in three parts: A (in Greek) is a legal decision by Augustus and M. Agrippa (27 BC); B (in Latin) is a letter (of unknown date but later than A) from the governor of Asia to the city of Kyme; C (in Greek) is a translation of the Latin letter of the governor.

H. W. Pleket, *The Greek Inscriptions in the 'Rijksmuseum van Oudheden' at Leyden* (Leiden 1958) no. 57 (+ photograph); *SEG* XVIII 555; *RDGE 61; H. Engelmann, *Die Inschriften von Kyme* (Bonn 1976) pp. 46ff.

Pleket, *op. cit.* pp. 49–66; K. M. T. Atkinson, *RIDA* 7 (1960) 227–72 (+ photograph); V. Arangio-Ruiz, *Bullettino del Istituto di Diritto Romano* 64 (1961) 323–42; W. Kunkel, *Studi in Onore di Emilio Betti* II (Rome 1962) 591–620; J. H. Oliver, *GRBS* 4 (1963) 115–22; *RDGE* pp. 315–20; F. Millar, *The Emperor in the Roman World* (London 1977) 317–18; N. Charbonnel, *RIDA* 26 (1979) 177–225.

A. Greek

Imperator Caesar, son of the god, Augustus [--][1] | (and) [M]arcus Agrippa, son of Lucius, consuls *v* [---.[2] | If] there are any public or sacred places in the cities [---][3] | of each city of the province (?),[4] and if

5   there are or will be *any* [dedica‖tions][5] belonging to these places, [nobody] | is to remove or buy (them) or take them as [mortgaged property | or] gift. Whatever has been *taken away* from those places | [or] bought and given as a gift, [whoever may be in charge of the] | province is to see to it that these are restored to the *public* or sacred [account (?)][6]

10   ‖ of the city, and whatever may have been given [as legal secur‖ity,][7] he is not to use this in his administration of justice. *vv* |

B. Latin

[-][8] Vinicius, proconsul, sends greetings to the magistrates of Cyme. Apollonides, son of Lucius, from No[race, | your citizen,] came to me and showed that the temple of Liber Pater[9] was by *title* | *of sale* possessed

15   by Lysias, son of Diogenes, of Tucalla, [your] citizen, ‖ and that *when* the worshippers wished to restore to their god the sacred property, according to the order of Au[gu‖s]tus Caesar, by paying the price which is inscribed on the temple, | *it was withheld* (?)[10] by Lysias. I wish you to see to it that, if such is the case, Lysias| accepts the price which [has been] put on the temple and restores to the god the *tem‖ple and* that there be

20   inscribed on it 'Imperator Caesar, son of god, Augustus rest‖ored it'. But [if] Lysias denies what Apollonides *de|mands*, let him give sufficient bail (to appear) where I will be.[11] That Lysias *prom|ises* (bail) meets [more (?)] with my approval(?).[11]

C. Greek

In the prytany of Phanites,[12] *vv* [-] Vinicius sends greetings to the magistrates of Kyme. A[pol|lonid]es (son) of Lucius of Norake, your
25   citizen, ‖ [came to me] and showed that the temple of Dionysos was by *title* [of sale] possessed by Lysias (son) of Diogenes of [Tukal|la, your citizen,] and that when [the worshippers] *wished* | [---]

1   Perhaps uninscribed? Pleket: 'for the 7th time (?)', i.e. in his seventh consulship (27 BC). Augustus had been consul with Agrippa in both 28 and 27 BC. Atkinson: 'for the 7th time'. Charbonnel: 'imperator for the 7th time', which is too long for the space.

2   Pleket: '[ordered (or) wrote]'. Atkinson: '[wrote]', likewise Charbonnel. Oliver and *RDGE* leave blank, but note the possibilities of '[said]' or '[determined]' or '[ordained]' among others. Oliver and Kunkel believe some word had been used which pointed to a *lex data*, i.e. some kind of a charter.

3   Pleket: '[or in the surrounding area]' etc. Arangio-Ruiz: '[or throughout the] territory of each city', translating the word *eparcheia* as 'territory' instead of 'province'. Oliver: '[when] these localities fall [within the jurisdiction of the] prefecture [protecting] each city's [interests]' (his own translation). Charbonnel: 'in the cities [belonging to a religious guild or] to a city of each province'.

4   The Greek *eparcheia* would normally mean 'province', but Oliver equates it with 'prefecture' or 'domain': *GRBS* and *AJP* 93 (1972) 195. Arangio-Ruiz takes it loosely as 'territory', which is hardly possible. The word 'each' here is grammatically ambiguous, for it could govern either 'province' or 'city'.

5   Atkinson: '[properties]'. Kunkel: '[ornaments]'.

6   Pleket: '[places]', from which they had been taken.

7   Atkinson: '[in this manner]'.

8   Pleket: '[Lucius]', i.e. the consul of 33 BC who became the governor of Asia in 28–27 or 27–26 BC, approved by Syme in *JRS* 45 (1955) 159. Likewise Kunkel, Arangio-Ruiz, and Charbonnel. But Atkinson, with hesitation, believes he was Marcus Vinicius, the consul of 19 BC.

9   I.e. Dionysos.

10   First suggested by Oliver. Pleket punctuates and restores differently: 'and since the worshippers wanted to restore the sacred objects to the god, as Augustus Caesar has ordered, after having paid the price written on the temple of Liber Pater by Lysias, I wish that you see to it that', etc. (Pleket's translation).

11   In saying 'where I shall be' Vinicius refers to his annual circuit of Asia to hold court. At this point in the text there is disagreement about punctuation and restoration, although Pleket correctly saw the intent, explaining (p. 59) that 'whatever the exact wording of this part of the text may have been, its meaning seems to be fairly clear. Lysias must give security to Apollonides, if he opposes Apollonides' claim; afterwards the proconsul himself will devote his attention to settling the affair.' Pleket then suggests: 'But if Lysias opposes the claim which Apollonides makes, that Lysias promise bail to him, with guarantee that he will present himself where I shall be --.' Atkinson, with different punctuation and restoration: 'But [if] Lysias objects, let him hand over as security for his appearance in court the property which Apollonides demands. I approve [of your] sending Lysias to wherever I shall be [sc. holding the assize].' Kunkel added the restoration '[more]'.

12   This phrase introduces the Greek translation of the letter of Vinicius and, thus, uses the local method of dating.

3   Augustus refuses freedom to Samos. Soon after 27 BC (?).

Marble block from the great archive wall of the theater in Aphrodisias in Karia. [Greek]

Reynolds, *Aphrodisias*, Document 13 (photograph).

Reynolds, *op. cit.* pp. 104–6; R. Bernhardt in *Historia* 29 (1980) 190ff.

vv Imperator Caesar, son of the god Iulius, Augustus[1] wrote to the Samians beneath their petition.[2] | You yourselves can see that I have given the privilege of freedom to no people except to the (people) of the |[[Aphrodisians]][3] who in the war took my side and were made captives because of their goodwill towards us. | For it is not right to bestow the greatest privilege of all without purpose and without cause. I || am of goodwill toward you and would be willing to favor my wife who is zealous in your behalf,[4] but | not to the point of breaking my custom. For it is not the money I care about which you pay into our tax (system), | *vv* but I am not willing to have the most valued privileges given to anyone without a reasonable cause.

1 The word 'Augustus' is transliterated here. Since it is usually translated as 'Sebastos', Reynolds believes it was added here by someone at Aphrodisias some-time after the document had been received or had become known in Aphrodisias. If true, it might mean that the document had been issued prior to 27 BC (when Octavian received the title 'Augustus'), but G. W. Bowersock (*Gnomon* 56 (1984) 52) argues for a date 22–19 BC and Badian (*GRBS* 25 (1984) 157ff.) for 31 BC.
2 When the imperial secretariat in Rome received *libelli* ('petitions') addressed to the emperor, the answer was usually 'written below' it. For the procedure see Millar, *Emperor* 480.
3 Erased. The full name was Aphrodisias-Plarasa.
4 Livia in known to have had connections with Samos in the past; Habicht in *MDAI(A)* 75 (1960) 104ff.; *IGRR* IV 982–4.

4   Senatorial and imperial provinces. Reign of Augustus.

Strabo 17.3.25 (C 840). Cf. Dio 53.12–15.

G H. Stevenson, *Roman Provincial Administration* (New York 1939) Ch. 4; Syme, *Roman Revolution* 326–30; G. W. Bowersock in *Rheinisches Museum* 108 (1965) 283–5; F. Millar in *JRS* 56 (1966) 156–66.

The provinces have been divided sometimes in one way, at other times in another, but at present they are as Caesar Augustus has arranged them, for when his country granted him the foremost position of leader-ship and he was made responsible for war and peace for life, he divided the entire empire into two parts:[1] he designated one part to be his own, the other to be the People's; his own was to be whatever areas had need of a military garrison, i.e. the barbarian areas and those near to tribes not yet conquered, or those that were wretched and hard to cultivate, so that, because they lacked everything but fortifications, they would rebel and become disobedient; to the People was to belong the rest (of the empire), whatever of it was peaceful and easy to rule without weapons. He divided each of the two parts into many provinces, his part being called Caesar's, the other part the People's. To the provinces of Caesar he sends (his own) governors and administrators, dividing the countries sometimes in one way and at other times in another, and administering them according to the need of the times, and to the provinces of the People it is the People who send (their own) praetors or (pro)consuls.[2] And these latter provinces are also separated into different parts when advantage dictates it. His arrangement in the People's provinces was to make two of them consular: Libya (Africa), those parts of it subject to the Romans, except for a part formerly subject to (King) Juba and now subject to Ptolemaios, his son; and Asia, this side of the Halys River and the Taurus Mountains, except for the Galatians and those tribes subject to (King) Amyntas, and (except for) Bithynia and the Propontis. And he made ten (of the People's) provinces praetorian, throughout Europe and the adjacent islands: Hispania Ulterior, as it's called, the parts around the Baitis River and the Anas; Narbonese Gaul; third, Sardinia-Corsica; fourth, Sicily; fifth and sixth, the part of Illyricum next to Epirus, and Macedonia; seventh, Achaia <with> Thessaly and Aetolia and Akarnania and certain tribes of Epirus, which are <not> included within the boundaries of Macedonia;[3] eighth, Crete-Cyrene; ninth, Cyprus; tenth, Pontus-Bithynia along the Propontis. Caesar controls the rest of the provinces, to some of which he sends men of consular rank to govern them, to others men of praetorian rank, and to still others men of equestrian rank.[4] Kings and dynasts and dekarchs are and always were in his area of control.[5]

1 Strabo refers to the arrangements made in 27 BC.
2 Caesar's provinces are the so-called imperial provinces governed by *legati Augusti pro praetore* ('legates' or deputies 'of Augustus with pro-praetorian power'). The People's provinces are the so-called senatorial provinces administered by the senate.
3 Recent investigation has shown that the received text of Strabo, here and elsewhere, is very bad and often requires emendation. Accordingly, when Bowersock surveyed the history of Roman Thessaly, he found that Strabo's account here of Achaia was in need of correction. His emendations, followed here in translation, seem to be necessary. Cf. Dio 53.12.4.
4 Equestrian governors were called *praefecti* or *procuratores*.
5 I.e. the so-called client-kings.

5 Illyricum and Thrace under Augustus.

A: *I. Ital.* XIII 1 p. 87 (Fasti Triumphales for 27 BC); Ehrenberg–Jones, **Documents*[2] p. 35. [Latin] The campaign of M. Licinius Crassus in the Thrako-Getic war of 29–28 BC. Cf. Livy, *Per.* 134–5; Florus 2.26; Dio 51.23–7. **B**: *ILS* 8810; **IG* II[2] 4118; Ehrenberg–Jones, *Documents*[2] 190. [Greek] Statue base broken into two parts, Athens. **C**: *Epitome de Caesaribus* 1.7. **D**: *ILS* 8965; Ehrenberg–Jones, **Documents*[2] 43a; A. Degrassi, *I. Ital.* XIII 3.9. [Latin] Inscription in honor of M. Vinicius (?), consul of 19 BC. Small, badly damaged fragment from Frascati, near Tusculum. For the campaigns of Vinicius: *Res Gestae* 30.2 (below, No. 26); Dio 53.26.4; Florus 2.24; Velleius Paterculus 2.96 and 104. **E**: A. D. Keramopoullos in **Archaiologikè Ephemerís* 1932, p. 3 of the Arch. Chronika; Ehrenberg–Jones, *Documents*[2] 268. [Latin] Small fragment found near Amphipolis. Cf. Dio 54.20.3 (where 'Lucius Gaius' seems to be a mistake for 'Lucius Tarius'): see Stein, *Moesien* 13 n. 3. **F**: *I. Ital.* XIII 2.115 (Fasti Praenestini for January 16, 9 BC); Ehrenberg–Jones, **Documents*[2] p. 45. [Latin] **G**: *CIL* XIV 3606; **ILS* 921; Ehrenberg–Jones, *Documents*[2] 200. Large marble tablet found in front of a monument of the Plautii, Tibur. [Latin] AD 9. Cf. Velleius Paterculus 2.112.4; Dio 55.34.4–7 and 56.12.1–2. **H**: Ehrenberg–Jones, **Documents*[2] p. 54. [Latin] AD 12. **I**: *IGRR* I 654. Small fragment from Callatis in Moesia. [Greek]

C. Patsch in *SBAW* 214 (1933) 1, pp. 69–122; R. Syme in *JRS* 24 (1934) 113ff. (*Danubian Papers*, Ch. 3); *idem* in *CAH* 10.355–8 and 364–81; Stein, *Moesien* 10ff.; Wilkes, *Dalmatia* 46–77; Moćsy, *Pannonia* 21–40; Chr. Danov in *ANRW* 2.7.1.120–34.

A. Ehrenberg–Jones, *Documents*[2] p. 35 (27 BC)

Marcus Licinius, son of Marcus (and) grandson of Marcus, Crassus, proconsul,[1] (triumphed) over Thrace and the Getans on the fourth day before the Nones of July (July 4)

B. *IG* II[2] 4118, Athens

vv The People *vv* | (dedicate this statue to) Marcus Licinius, Marcus' | son, Crassus, proconsul | and imperator, for his excellence | and good-will.

C. *Epitome de Caesaribus* 1.7

The Getic peoples and the Bastarnians he (Augustus) attacked and compelled by warfare to (seek peace).

D. Ehrenberg–Jones, *Documents*[2] 43a, Frascati

[--- Marcus Vini]cius[2] [---, | consul, quindecimvir] of sacred affairs, [--- | legate with pro] praetorian power of Augustus Caesar in
5   [Illyricum, | the first (?)] across the Danube River [to --- || -- the --]ian and Bastarnian army [--|---] and he put to flight the Cotini, [the --|---] and the Anartii [---|-- of A]ugustus [----].

E. Keramopoullos in *Archaiologikè Ephemerís* **1932, p. 3, Amphipolis**

Under Imperator Caesar, | son of the deified, Augustus | and for Lucius
Tarius Rufus,[3] holding pro | praetorian power, ‖ the Legion Tenth
Fretensis | built this bridge.

F. Ehrenberg–Jones, *Documents*[2] **p. 45 (under 9 BC)**

Tiberius Caesar *entered* [the city] from Pan[nonia with an ovation].[4]

G. *ILS* 921, Tibur

Marcus Plautius, son of Marcus (and) grandson of Aulus, | Silvanus,[5] |
consul (2 BV), septemvir for religious banquets. | To him has the senate
5 decreed triumphal ornaments ‖ because of his actions in Illyricum, |
done so well. | His wife Lartia, daughter of Gnaeus. | Aulus Plautius,
son of Marcus, | Urgulanius | lived nine years.

H. Ehrenberg–Jones, *Documents*[2] **p. 54 (under AD 12)**

Tiberius Caesar rode a triumphal chariot because of victory over
Illyricum.

I. *IGRR* I 654, Callatis

[The People] (dedicate this) to Publius Vinicius [----,] commander[6]
(and) *patron* [---]

1 This Licinius Crassus is the consul of 30 BC (*PIR*[2] L 186) and grandson of that
   Licinius Crassus who joined in the First Triumvirate. He was proconsul of
   Macedonia in 29 BC: for his campaigns there see F. Papazoglu, *The Central Balkan
   Tribes in Pre-Roman Times* (Amsterdam 1978).
2 The identification with the consul of 19 BC is generally accepted: R. Syme in *Classical
   Quarterly* 27 (1933) 142ff. (*Danubian Papers*, Ch. 2), in *CAH* 10.366–7, and in *Historia* 11
   (1962) 147 (*Roman Papers* II 532).
3 Tarius Rufus (consul suff. 16 BC) was well-known among the officers trusted by
   Augustus during and after Actium. He may have been given an important mission
   in the north about 17 BC.
4 See R. Syme in *Phoenix* 33 (1979) 314ff. (*Roman Papers* III 1203ff.).
5 When the Dalmatians and Pannonians rose in their great revolt of AD 6 M. Plautius
   Silvanus brought reinforcements from the east to the Balkans: Velleius Paterculus
   2.112.4; Dio 55.34.6 and 56.12.2
6 The Greek noun used here is unique. Some would understand it to mean 'proconsul',
   others take it as 'praetorian legate' of a legion. Publius Vinicius was consul in AD 2.
   Clues to date of operations are in Velleius Paterculus (2.101.3), and Velleius himself
   in 1 BC had been tribune of the soldiers 'in Thrace and Macedonia' under P. Silius
   and Publius Vinicius. Cf. Syme in *AJP* 99 (1978) 50 (*Roman Papers* III 1093).

6   General repair of main highways in Italy. 27 BC.

Inscription on the arch over the Via Flaminia in Ariminum. [Latin].

*CIL XI 365; *ILS* 84; Ehrenberg–Jones, *Documents*[2] 286. Cf. Suetonius, *Augustus* 30; *Res Gestae* 20.5 (below, No. 26).

See G. H. Stevenson in *CAH* 10.205; M. H. Ballance in *PBSR* 19 (1951) 79ff.; W. Eck, *Staatliche Organisation* 25 and 28.

The senate and [Roman] People | (dedicate this arch) [to Imperator Caesar, son of the deified, Augustus, imperator for the seventh time,] | consul for the seventh time (27 BC) and designated for the eighth time, the *Via Flaminia* [and the rest of the] | most famous roads of Italy having been repaired by his plan [and at his expense.]][1]

1 Suetonius (*Augustus* 30) reports that Augustus repaired the Via Flaminia as far as Ariminum at his own expense, but that he then asked winners of triumphal ornaments to do the same for the other roads by using their 'booty' money.

7   Augustus and the imperial cult.

I. The West. A: *CIL* XIII 1541; *ILS* 7041; Ehrenberg–Jones, *Documents*[2] 120. Marble tablet, Divona Cadurcorum in Aquitania. [Latin] B: Mattingly, *BMC* I, No. 548; Ehrenberg–Jones, *Documents*[2] 119. Sestertius from mint of Lugdunum (10–6 BC?). Photograph: D. Fishwick in *ANRW* 2.16.2, opp. p. 1248. C: *CIL* XII 4333; *ILS* 112; *FIRA* III 73; Ehrenberg–Jones, *Documents*[2] 100. Inscribed marble altar, re-ingraved in second century AD, Narbo in Gallia Narbonensis. AD 12–13. [Latin] See Taylor, *Divinity* 282 and E. Champlin in *Chiron* 11 (1981) 239–64. Photograph: *ANRW* 2.3, opp. p. 848. D: P. Raveggi in *Notizie degli Scavi di Antichità* 14 (1938) 5–7 (+ photograph). Altar of marble with relief of a Lar (spirit of ancestor) and inscription above, near Cosa in Etruria. [Latin] E: *CIL* XI 3076; *ILS* 116. Stone found on the Via Flaminia. [Latin] F: *CIL* X 1613; Ehrenberg–Jones, *Documents*[2] 110. [Latin] Puteoli.

II. The East. A: Mattingly, *BMC* I, No. 705. Tetradrachm. Temple of Roma and Augustus at Pergamum. See Mellor, *Roma* 140–1; Price, *Rituals* 56. B: *IGRR* IV 975. Inscription probably from the architrave of the temple of Roma and Augustus (so G. Dunst in Mellor, *Roma* 61 n. 220) at Samos. [Greek] See Mellor, *Roma* 138–40. C: A. Laumonier in *BCH* 58 (1934) 300, No. 3 (+ photograph); Ehrenberg-Jones, *Documents*[2] 114. Marble stele, Alabanda in Caria [Greek] D: *IG* II[2] 3173. Epistyle of Pentelic marble from the temple of Roma and Augustus at Athens, from the Acropolis. Soon after 27 BC. [Greek] E: R. Hodot in *The J. Paul Getty Museum Journal* 10 (1982) 166 (+ photograph). Marble stele damaged at top and broken off at bottom, Cumae in Asia Minor. [Greek] See Hodot, *op. cit.* 165–80 and J. and L. Robert in *RÉG* 96 (1983) 132–8 (*Bulletin Épigraphique* No. 323).

I. The West

A. *ILS* 7041, Divona in Aquitania

Marcus Lucterius, | son of Lucterius Sene|cianus, Leo[1] | has held all the
5 || offices in his ci|ty, and is a priest of the altar | of Augustus at the
10   con|fluence of the Arar (Saone) | and Rhodanus (Rhone. || The com-

munity of the Cadurci | because of his good service | has set up (this monument) at public expense.

B. Mattingly, *BMC* I, No. 548, sestertius from mint at Lugdunum

(Obverse, head of   CAESAR, PONTIFEX MAXIMUS
Augustus, Laureate)

(Reverse, altar at   ROMA AND AUGUSTUS
Lugdunum in middle)

C. *ILS* 112, Narbo

(A. On the front face of an altar) When Titus Statilius Taurus | and Lucius Cassius Longinus | were consuls (AD 11), on the 10th day before the Kalends of October (September 22), | to the divine majesty of

5 Augustus a vow ‖ was undertaken by the people of Narbo|nese (Gaul) in perpetuity: | May it be good, favorable, and fortunate for Imperator Caesar, | son of the deified, Augustus, father of his country, pontifex maximus, holding the tribunician power | for the 34th time (AD 11),

10 and for his wife, children, and clan, and for the senate ‖ and Roman People, and for the colonists | of the colony of Iulia Paterna Narbo Martius who have obligated themselves forever to his divine majesty's | worship. The people of Narbone|se (Gaul) have set up an altar at Narbo in the forum, | at which each year on the 9th day before the

15 Kalends of October (September 23), on which day ‖ an age of happiness produced him as the whole world's | ruler,[2] three Roman Knights | from the people and three freedmen shall sacrifice an animal indi|vidually, and for the colonists and inhabitants, to | supplicate his divine majesty,

20 they shall provide incense and wine ‖ at their own expense on that day. And on the 8th day before the Kalends of October (September 24) | they shall likewise provide incense and wine for the colonists and inhabitants; | and on the Kalends of January (January 1) incense and wine | shall they also provide for the colonists and inhabitants; also on the 7th day | before the Ides of January (January 7), on which day for

25 the first time his command ‖ over the whole world was begun,[3] with incense | and wine shall they make supplication and individually shall they sacrifice an animal, | and for the colonists and inhabitants shall they provide incense and wine | on that day as well; | and on the day before the Kalends of June (May 31), because on that day, when Titus

30 Statilius ‖ Taurus and Manius Aemilius Lepidus were consuls (AD 11),[4] | he reconciled the judgments | of the people with those of the decurions, | they shall sacrifice an animal | individually and shall pro-

35 vide incense and wine, to ‖ supplicate his divine majesty, for the

colonists and | inhabitants. | And from these three Roman Knights [and three] | freedmen [---]

(B. On the right face of the altar) [The people] of Narbonese (Gaul) have dedicated this *altar* | of the divine majesty of Augustus [---|---|---]
5   by the laws which are written below. ‖ Divine majesty of Caesar Augustus, father of his country, when to you | on this day I will give and dedicate this altar, | with these laws and within these lim|its will I give and dedicate it which here | today openly I will have declared is the
10   foun‖dation of this altar and its inscriptions: | if anyone wishes to clean, decorate, or | repair it – which he does | for a public service – it shall be
15   right and lawful; or if | anyone makes a sacrifice of an animal ‖ and does not bring the additional sacrifice, | nevertheless it shall be (considered as) properly done; if | anyone wishes to give a gift to this altar and to en|rich it, it shall be permitted, and the same | law shall exist for it as
20   for the altar; ‖ other laws for this altar and inscriptions | shall be the same as for the altar | of Diana on the Aventine. With these la|ws and within these limits, just as | I have said, in regard to this altar on behalf
25   of Imperator ‖ Caesar Augustus, father of his country, pontifex maxi|mus, holding the tribunician power for the 35th time (AD 12), (on behalf of) his wife, children, and his clan, | the senate and the Roman People, the colonists | and inhabitants of the colony of Iulia Paterna Narbo Martius, who have obligated themselves in perpetuity to his
30   divine majesty's | worship, ‖ I give and dedicate it that you (Caesar Augustus) may be willing | to be propitious (toward us).

D. *Notizie degli Scavi di Antichità* **14 (1938) p. 5, near Cosa**

[To Imperator Caesar,] son of the deified, Augustus, pontifex maximus, | (this altar was dedicated by) Quintus Lucretius Eros Murdianus (and) Lucius Volumnius Eros, | masters and priests of the deified Augustus.[5]

E. *ILS* **116, on the Via Flaminia**

To the Genius of Augustus | and Tiberius Caesar, to Juno Livia (this has been dedicated by) Mystes, freedman.

F.   Ehrenberg–Jones, *Documents*[2] **110, Puteoli**

[Lucius C]alpurnius, son of Lucius, built this temple to Augustus with its ornaments out of his own funds.

II. The East

A. Mattingly, *BMC* I, No. 705, tetradrachm

(Obverse, head of Augustus, bare)	IMPERATOR FOR THE 9th TIME, HOLDING THE TRIBUNICIAN POWER FOR THE 5th TIME (19 BC)
(Reverse, temple with six columns on podium of five steps)	(On the entablature) ROMA AND AUGUSTUS. THE ASSEMBLY OF ASIA.[6]

B. *IGRR* IV 975, Samos

The People (dedicate this temple?) to the goddess Roma and to Imperator Caesar, son of a god, god Augustus.

C. *BCH* 58 (1934) 300, Alabanda

[The] People again have honored with | great honors and have dedi-
cated (this monument) to | Aristogenes (son) of Meniskos (grandson)
5   of Aristog|enes, hereditary priest of the Health and ‖ Safety of
Imperator Caesar | and the Sun, a great-minded man, | in piety and
justice out|standing, a benefactor of his city, | a high-priest in his home-
10 land ‖ of Roma and Augustus | Caesar, a man who in the greatest and
most sum|ptuous manner has performed his religious duties [----]

D. *IG* II² 3173, Athens

The People (dedicated this temple) to the goddess Roma and
Au[gus]tus Caesar when the Hoplite General[7] | was Pammenes (son) of
Zenon of Marathon, priest of the goddess Roma | and Augustus Savior
on the Acropolis, when the priestess of Athena | Polias was Megiste
5   daughter of Asklepiades of Halieus. ‖ In the archonship of Areios (son)
of Dorion of Paianieus.[8]

E. Hodot in *The J. Paul Getty Museum Journal* 10 (1982) 166, Cumae

The strategoi made the motion and three (of them),[9] chosen by lot, put
it down in writing: Asklapon | (son) of Dionysios, Hegesandros (son) of
Herakleides, Athenagoras (son) of Dionysios; also the secre|tary of the
People, Heraios (son) of Antipatros. *vv* | Whereas Kleanax (son) of
5   Sarapion and natural (son) of Philodemos, our prytanis,[10] ‖ with ances-
tors well-born on both sides of the family and with unsurpassable |
acquiescence toward his country in love of glory, has done many great
things continuously throughout his lifetime for his ci|ty, giving in to no
opportunity for the omission of care for his people, | conducting his

civic life to the best advantage of his city both | in word and deed, as a
10 result of which in the present circumstances of his ‖ love for glory,
worthy of a prytanis, not only (?) has a panegyric by the people at
present testified | in his behalf, but also the gratitude of the people has
responded to his many official acts with decrees in the past, | namely,
as priest of Dionysos Pan|demos[11] he discharged his religious duties
for the mysteries founded by the city, | (paid) the expenses incurred for
15 the penteteric organization of the mysteries, when ‖ the proportion of
the expenses showed his impressive love for glory and his pi|ety, having
taken the initiative to assume the office all by himself and having
in|vited, by general announcement, citizens and Romans and residents
and foreigners to a ban|quet in the precinct of Dionysos and having
entertained them sumptuously, organizing the fea|st year after year,
and, when celebrating the wedding of his daughter, he held a banquet
20 for the multitude ‖ – for these reasons, the people, remembering and
discerning his good deeds, forgot none of his other activities | to which
they had grown accustomed; *v* and for this reason also | the prytanis
Kleanax is worthy of praise and honor, (namely) that he became the
father of a handsome son, | took thought for the boy's education in
letters, and furnished the people | with a man worthy of his family,
25 Sarapion (by name), a protector and helper, one who in many ‖ ways
has already displayed zeal toward the city by his own manly deeds, | *v*
a father-loving man to whom this epithet ought to be added officially, |
a man who is witness for his | father also by public decree for all time;
for all these reasons | the people approve of the prytanis Kleanax and
30 praise him for his continuous preservation ‖ of good will toward the
people; all his duties at present as prytanis he has performed, | on the
one hand, on New Year's Day,[12] with sacrifices to the gods in the ances-
tral manner, and he has distributed | sweet wine to everyone in the city,
put on the spectacles sumptuously, and has made the | sacrifices for
prosperity in the ancestral manner and has entertained sumptuously in
the Town | Hall for several days many citizens and Romans, and, on the
35 other hand, he has made the sacrifices ‖ for the dead on the customary
day in the ancestral manner and distributed | porridge of milk and flour
to all the freemen and slaves in the city, and in the (Festival of) the Lark
| he took the initiative and all by himself invited by proclamation the
citizens and Romans and residents and foreigners | to dinner in the
Town Hall, and he performed the Tossing Ceremony[13] in the same
fashion as the other | prytaneis did (in the past), and he conducted the
40 Processions of the Laurel;[14] to the priests and ‖ to the victorious
athletes and to the magistrates and to many of the citizens he gave a
banquet; | and in the Games of Augustus conducted by (the Assembly)
of Asia[15] he conducted, just as he announced, the | sacrifices and

festivities, sacrificing oxen to Imperator Caesar Augustus and to | his two sons[16] and to the other gods, after which he also held a feast, having [summoned,[17] in the] | agora by proclamation, Greeks and Romans and
45 residents and foreigners; ‖ and he performed this public service [---] and completed the other rites [----] – for (all) these reasons (therefore), it has been decreed by the Boule and the People: to crown him [at the Dionysiac Festival by the] | altar of Zeus after the sacrifice and amid all [-----] | (etc.)[18]

1 Lucterius Cadurcus is mentioned often by Caesar in his *Gallic Wars*: 7.5.1 and 7.1–8; 8.30.1 and *passim*. For the priesthood of the altar of Augustus at the confluence of the Arar and Rhodanus Rivers see D. Fishwick in *ANRW* 2.16.2, 1204ff. For the altar itself: R . Turcan in *ANRW* 2.12.1, 607–44.
2 September 23 was the birthday of Augustus.
3 The *Feriale Comanum* (*I. Ital.* XIII 2 p. 279) records that on January 7 Octavian 'for the first time took up the fasces'.
4 Lepidus was *consul ordinarius* and later replaced by the suffect consul Longinus.
5 These masters and priests of Augustus (*magistri Augustales*) formed a religious association: R. Duthoy in *ANRW* 2.16.2, 1287ff.
6 This Assembly (or League) of Asia had taken the initiative in honoring Augustus and had then established a cult of Roma and Augustus with a temple at Pergamum. See Taylor, *Divinity* 146 and cf. Suetonius, *Augustus* 52, and Dio 51.20.7–8.
7 In this period the Hoplite General was the principal civic magistrate in Athens. 'Caesar' is inscribed over an erased 'Savior'.
8 The archon Areios can be placed in the period 27/6 to 18/17 BC.
9 As interpreted by the Roberts. Hodot thinks the redaction was done by three commissioners.
10 The prytanis at Cumae was a magistrate possessing important civil and police powers.
11 Pandemos ('of all the people') is a hitherto unknown epithet for Dionysos. It was usually reserved for Zeus or Aphrodite.
12 This phrase permits us to date the present document after 9 BC, for it was then that the birthday of Augustus (September 23) was taken as the beginning of the new year in the province of Asia: Sherk, *TDGR* 4, No. 101. And since Gaius and Lucius Caesar are still alive (line 43), the date of the document must be prior to the death of Lucius in AD 2 and the death of Gaius in AD 4. Hodot narrows it to the period 2 BC–AD 2.
13 As explained by the Roberts, this ceremony is similar to one practised by the Romans: see *ILS* 5074–7 and L. Friedlaender, *Darstellungen aus der Sittengeschichte Roms*[9], Vol. II (Leipzig 1922) p. 17 (English translation, Vol. II, 15). It consisted of throwing fruit and other delicacies to the crowd in acts of generosity.
14 These processions were very common in the Greek world, and particularly in the cult of Apollo.
15 See n. 6.
16 Gaius Caesar, eldest son of Agrippa and Julia, was the grandson of Augustus and adopted by him. He died in AD 4. Lucius Caesar, second son of Agrippa and Julia and also adopted by Augustus, died in AD 2. See also below, Nos. 18–19.
17 Restored by the Roberts.
18 The text continues on to line 52, outlining further honors for father and son, but in an increasingly mutilated form.

8   The Cantabrian campaign in Spain. 26–25 BC.

Orosius, *Against the Pagans* 6.21.3–11. Cf. Florus 2.33.48–60; Dio 53.25.5–8 and 53.26.1–5.

R. Syme in *CAH* 10.343–4; *idem* in *Legio VII Gemina* (León 1970) 83–107 (*Roman Papers* II 825–54); F. Diego Santos in *ANRW* 2.3.531–6.

Therefore Caesar (Augustus) pitched his camp in the area of Segisama and with three armies seized almost all Cantabria. (4) When his troops had been long worn out with nothing to show for it and had been often drawn into danger, he finally ordered his fleet to be moved in from the Aquitanian bay over the ocean, with the enemy unsuspecting, and its troops brought ashore. (5) Then at last the Cantabrians under the walls of Attica were engaged in a mighty battle and in defeat fled to Vinnius, a mountain most secure for them by its very nature, where by siege and hunger they were almost reduced to the point of annihilation. Then the town of Racilium, resisting with great strength for a long time, was finally captured and destroyed. (6) In addition, the more remote parts of Gallaecia, which are filled with mountains and forests and are bounded by the ocean, were subdued by the legates Antistius and Firmius[1] after many great campaigns. (7) Mt Medullius, poised over the Minius River and on which a huge multitude of people had taken refuge, was surrounded by them with siege-works, a fortified ditch 15 miles long. (8) When that group of men, wild and savage by nature, came to know that they were unable to withstand the siege and were not capable of sustaining the war, they agreed to a compact of suicide out of their fear of slavery. Almost all killed themselves, as if in rivalry to do so, by fire, sword, and poison. (9) The Astures pitched their camp by the Astura River and would have overcome the Romans by their great plans and their strength, if they had not been betrayed and stopped. When they attempted suddenly to destroy three legates, who had their legions divided into three camps in three equal groups, their plan was detected by betrayal on the part of their own men. (10) Afterwards, they withdrew from the war and Carisius[2] defeated them, but only with considerable Roman casualties. Some of the Astures escaped from the battle and fled to Lancha. When (Roman) soldiers were preparing to attack the surrounded city with fire, the general Carisius succeeded in keeping his men from firing the city and also induced the barbarians to surrender voluntarily. He took great pains to leave the city intact and unharmed as a witness to his victory. (11) The mark of honor that Caesar (Augustus) obtained from the Cantabrian victory was this: he ordered at that time the gates of war to be closed and barred. Thus, at that time, the second time because of Caesar and the fourth after the founding of Rome, Janus was closed.

1 Gaius Antistius Vetus (cos. 30 BC) was the governor of Hispania Citerior. 'Firmius'
   is Gaius Furnius (cos. 17 BC), on whose appearance here see Syme, *op. cit.* 835.
2 He is Publius Carisius, governor of Lusitania at this time, of praetorian rank: *PIR*[2] C
   422.

9   Military expeditions deep into Africa. 25–20 BC.

A: Pliny, *Nat. Hist.* 6.181.2. B. Pliny, *Nat. Hist.* 5.35.6.

R. K. Sherk in *ANRW* 2.1.538–9.

A. Pliny, *Nat. Hist.* 6.181–2

These towns have come to public attention as far as Meroe,[1] of which
at present almost none still exist on either side (of the Nile). It is at any
rate certain that uninhabited country was recently reported there by
praetorian soldiers sent by our Leader Nero under a tribune for the
purpose of exploration, when in the midst of the rest of his wars he was
thinking of one against Ethiopia. However, Roman arms reached that
area in the days of the deified Augustus under the command of Publius
Petronius, of the equestrian order and the prefect of Egypt.[2] He captured their towns, the only names of which we found we will give here
in order: Pselchis, Primi, Bocchis, Forum Cambysis, Attenia, and
Stadissis, where the Nile plunging on with a roar affects the hearing of
the local inhabitants. He also plundered Napata. The farthest he
advanced from Syene was 870 miles.

B. Pliny, *Nat. Hist.* 5.35–6

Toward the desert of Africa, which we have said is beyond Syrtis Minor,
lies Phazania, where we have subjugated the Phazanian tribe and the
cities of Alele and Cilliba, and also Cydamus of the region of Sabrata.
Beyond these a long mountain range extends from east to west, called
by our men Black Mountain in accordance with its nature, similar to
one burned out or ignited by the rays of the sun. Beyond it is the desert,
then Thelgae, a town of the Garamantes, and then Debris with its
spring pouring out boiling water from the middle of the day to the
middle of the night and then for the same number of hours freezing
cold until midday, and then most famous Garama, capital of the
Garamantes: all of these were overwhelmed by the Roman arms of
Cornelius Balbus, who was granted a triumph in a foreigner's chariot,
the only one of all (so honored), and given full rights of a Roman
citizen. He was born in Gades, and Roman citizenship had been given
to him as well as to his uncle, Balbus.[3]

1 Cf. *Res Gestae* (below, No. 26), Ch. 26.

2 'Publius' is his correct praenomen, despite Dio (54.5.4): see R. S. Bagnall in *Yale Classical Studies* 28 (1985) 85ff. His Ethiopian expedition is also described by Strabo (17.820–1) and Dio (54.5.4–6). The mutilated remains of a papyrus (*P. Mil.* 40) portray a campaign against Ethiopians that might be the one by our Petronius: see S. Jameson in *JRS* 58 (1968) 71–84.
3 Both men were called Lucius Cornelius Balbus: *PIR*[2] C 1331. The younger Balbus held the triumph in 19 BC. The uncle had been a prominent figure in the Civil War and was consul in 40 BC.

10 Peace on the eastern frontier. 18–17 BC.

A: Mattingly, *BMC I, No. 10 (+ photograph); Ehrenberg–Jones, *Documents*[2] 26. Denarius of 18 BC. Mint of Rome. B: Mattingly, *BMC I, No. 427 (+ photograph); Ehrenberg–Jones, *Documents*[2] 27. Aureus of 18–17 BC. Spanish mint. C: Mattingly, *BMC I, No. 18 (+ photograph); Ehrenberg–Jones, *Documents*[2] 28. Denarius of 18 BC. Mint of Rome. D: *Res Gestae* (below, No. 26), Ch. 29.2

Cf. Dio 54.8.1 and 9.4–5; Suetonius, *Augustus* 21 and *Tiberius* 9; Velleius Paterculus 2.94.

Relations between Rome and Parthia under Augustus: see J. G. C. Anderson in *CAH* 10.254–65; N. C. Debevoise, *A Political History of Parthia* (Chicago 1938) 136ff.; Magie, *RRAM* I 475–6 and 482–6; M.-L. Chaumont in *ANRW* 2.9.1.73ff.; Kienast, *Augustus* 282–4.

A. Mattingly, *BMC* I, No. 10. Roman denarius of 18 BC

(Obverse, head of Liber) TURPILIANUS, TRIUMVIR OF THE MINT[1]

(Reverse, Parthian, bare-headed, holding out in his hand a military standard with an attached flag marked X.) CAESAR AUGUSTUS. THE STANDARDS RECOVERED.[2]

B. Mattingly, *BMC* I, No. 427. Aureus of 18–17 BC. Spain

(Obverse, head of Augustus, bare) SENATE AND PEOPLE OF ROME TO IMPERATOR CAESAR AUGUSTUS, CONSUL XI, TRIBUNICIAN POWER VI.

(Reverse,   CITIZENS AND MILITARY STANDARDS
triumphal   RECOVERED FROM THE PARTHIANS.[3]
arch, on
which are a
quadriga
and
standing
figures)

C. Mattingly, *BMC* I, no. 18. Denarius. Mint of Rome

(Obverse,   TURPILIANUS, TRIUMVIR OF THE MINT
head of Liber)

(Reverse,   CAESAR SON OF THE DEIFIED.
Armenian   ARMENIA CAPTURED.
king wearing
tiara and long
robe, kneel-
ing and hold-
ing out both
hands in
submission)

D. *Res Gestae* of Augustus: see below, No. 26, Ch. 29.2

1 Very little is known of Publius Petronius Turpilianus.
2 Cf. *Res Gestae*, below, No. 26, Ch. 29 with note.
3 Dio (54.8.1) reports that King Phraates sent back to Augustus the military standards
   along with Roman captives.

11   The Secular Games of Augustus.[1] 17 BC.
Extracts from a huge inscription on many large white marble blocks
that once were part of a great monument, Rome. [Latin]

CIL VI 32323, lines 50–7 and 90–166; *ILS* 5050; *FIRA* I 40; G. B. Pighi, **De Ludis
Saecularibus*[2] (Amsterdam 1965) lines 50–7 and 90–166 (+ photographs, also in
Epigraphica 3 (1941) 1ff.). Cf. *Res Gestae* (below, No. 26) Ch. 22.2; Zosimus, *New History*
2.1ff.; Virgil, *Ecl.* 4; Horace, *Carmen Saeculare*.

W. W. Fowler, *Religious Experience of the Roman People* (London 1911) 439ff.; L. R. Taylor
in *OCD*[2] *s.v.* Secular Games; P. Brind' Amour in *ANRW* 2.16.2, 1334–1417; L. Moretti in
Rendiconti della Pontificia Accademia Romana di Archeologia 55–6 (1982–4) 361–79 (new
material).

(Lines 50–7) On the 10th day before the Kalends of June (May 23), in
the voting area [of Julius, present at the writing were: Quintus] |

Aemilius Lepidus, Lucius Cestius, Lucius Petronius Rufus [---.] |

Whereas the consul Gaius Silanus said that the Secular Games would take place [in the present year] after very many [years, conducted by Imperator Caesar] | Augustus and Marcus A[grip]pa, (both) holding the tribunician power, [and that because it is fitting that as many people as possible should see them] | for *religious reasons* and because [nobody will be present a second time] at such a spectacle, [it seemed

55   right to permit] ‖ those not yet married [to be present on the days] of those Games without [detriment to themselves, (and whereas he asked) what the senate wished to be done about this matter, concerning this matter the senate decreed as follows: that, since these Games] | have been instituted for religious reasons [and it is not permitted] any *mortals* more than once [to see these Games,] | which the masters, (i.e.) the quindecimviri of sacred affairs, *will present*, permission to see them will be granted to those who [are bound] by the law concerning marriageable [classes ----.] |[2]

(Lines 90–166) On the next night[3] in the open field by the Tiber [Imperator Caesar Augustus sacrificed to the Fates nine ewe-lambs] | to be burned completely in the Greek ritual, and in the same [ritual (he sacrificed) nine she-goats to be burned completely and he prayed as follows:] |

'Fates! As [it is written] for you in those books[4] – [and because of these things, may something better happen for the Roman People Quirites![5] – to you | shall sacrifice be made of nine] ewe-lambs and nine [proper] she-goats. [I beg of you and pray that the empire and majesty of the Roman People] | Quirites in war and in peace *will be increased by you*, [and that the Latin(s) will always obey us; that safety forever,]

95   ‖ victory, and good health [you will give to the Roman People Quirites, and that you will look with favor upon the Roman People Quirites and upon the legions of the Roman People] | Quirites, [and keep safe] the Republic of the Roman People [Quirites and make it greater, and that you will be] favorable and *propitious* [to the Roman People] | Quirites, to the quindecimviri of sacred affairs, [to me, to my house, and my household; and that] you will be receptive [of this] sacrifice of nine | ewe-lambs and nine [she]-goats, the *proper kind* for sacrificing; because of these things, be honored by this ewe-lamb | to be sacrificed, be [favorable] and propitious to the Roman People Quirites, to the quindecimviri of sacred affairs, to me, to my house, and my household.'

100   ‖ At night, when the sacrifice was finished, plays were performed on a stage to which no theater was attached and no provisions made | for seats.[6] One hundred and ten matrons,[7] to whom notice had been sent by summons of the quindecimviri of sacred affairs, held sellisternia[8] | with two seats set up for Juno and Diana. |

On the Kalends of June (June 1) in the Capitolium Imperator Caesar Augustus sacrificed a proper bull to Jupiter Best and Greatest, and in the same place | Marcus Agrippa (sacrificed) another, and they prayed
105   as follows: ||

'Jupiter Best and Greatest! As it is written for you in those books – and because of these things, may something better happen for the Roman People | Quirites – to you shall sacrifice be made of this beautiful bull. I beg of you and pray . . . ' The rest as above. | At the Atalla[9] were Caesar, Agrippa, Scaevola, Sentius, Lollius, Asinius Gallus, Rebilus. | Then the Latin plays were performed in a wooden theater which had been set up in the open field *along* the Tiber, | and in the same manner the mothers of families held Sellisternia, and those
110   *plays* which had been started at night were not interrupted. ||

(Lines 110–14: the quindecimviri of sacred affairs issued an edict to reduce the period of mourning for matrons.)

(Lines 115–18: Augustus sacrificed special cakes to Ilithyia, Greek goddess of childbirth, and prayed as above.)

(Lines 119–33: on June 2 Augustus sacrificed a cow to Juno, as did Agrippa, and prayed to Juno as above. Agrippa then led the matrons in prayer to Juno. Plays were then presented.)

(Lines 134–8: that same night Augustus sacrificed a pregnant sow and prayed to Mother Earth, as above.)

(Lines 139–46: on June 3 on the Palatine Augustus and Agrippa sacrificed special cakes to Apollo and Diana, and prayed.)

(Lines 147ff.) When the sacrifice was completed, [twenty]-seven boys, to whom notice had been sent and both of whose parents were still living, and the same number of girls | sang a hymn (on the Palatine). The same thing was done on the Capitolium. | Quintus
150   Horatius Flaccus composed the hymn.[10] || Quindecimviri of sacred affairs who were present: Imperator Caesar, Marcus Agrippa, Quintus Lepidus, Potitus Messalla, Gaius Stolo, Gaius Scaevola, Gaius Sosius, | Gaius Norbanus, Marcus Cocceius, [Marcus] Lollius, Gaius Sentius, Marcus Strigo, Lucius Arruntius, Gaius Asinius, Marcus Marcellus, Decimus Laelius, | Quintus Tubero, Gaius Rebilus, Messalla Messallinus.[11] |

When the theatrical plays were finished, [----] next to the place where the sacrifice had been made on the previous nights and | the theater and stage erected, turning-posts were put into place and four-horse chariots were raced, and Potitus Messalla brought out acrobatic
155   riders. || An edict was published as follows: 'The quindecimviri of sacred affairs declare: | We have added honorary games for seven days to the games of the festival, to be started by us on the Nones of June (June 5), the Latin (plays) in the theater | of wood by the Tiber at the

second hour (after daylight), the thymelic[12] Greek plays in the theater
of Pompey at the third hour, and the Greek stage plays in the theater |
in the Circus Flaminius at the *fourth* hour.' |

    There was an interval of a day, which was the day before the Nones
160 of June (June 4) [---.] ‖ On the Nones of June (June 5) the [honorary]
games of seven days were started, [the Latin (plays) in the] | theater of
wood, the *thymelic* Greek plays [in the theater of Pompey, and the Greek
stage plays in the theater in the Circus Flaminius.] |

    On the third day before the Ides of June (June 11) an edict was
published [as follows: 'The quindecimviri of sacred affairs declare:] |
On the day before the Ides of June (June 12) we will give a beast-hunt
[in ---- and begin games of the circus ---'] | On the day before the Ides
a parade was held [and squadrons of older and younger boys presented
165 the Trojan Games.] ‖ Marcus Agrippa [brought out] four-horse
chariots [and a beast-hunt was held in ----.] |

    All these events were produced by the quindecimviri of sacred
affairs: [Imperator Caesar Augustus, (etc. as above, in lines 150–2)].

1 The Secular Games were traditional Roman ceremonies designed to celebrate the
    end of one human age and the beginning of another, at intervals of 100 years or
    slightly more. They had been ordered by the Sibylline Books which outlined the
    program of events: preserved by Zosimus in his *New History* 2.1ff. and reproduced
    by Pighi, *op. cit.* 56–7. Originally Greek, these Games were gradually overlaid with
    Roman practices and traditions.
2 Lines 58–89 contain a second decree of the Roman senate authorizing the inscrib-
    ing of a record of the Games on bronze and marble. This is followed by an edict of
    the quindecimviri of sacred affairs concerned with public participation and the
    ritual of purification.
3 May 31, AD 17.
4 The Sibylline Books are meant. See above, n. 1.
5 'Quirites' is of unknown origin, but the ancient Romans connected it with the old
    Sabine town of Cures. The word appealed to the heart and soul of Roman
    citizenry, evoking feelings of patriotism and national pride.
6 A reflection of conditions before the Greek theater was introduced into Rome.
7 One matron for each of the 110 years since the last celebration of Secular Games.
8 These were feasts for goddesses whose images were placed on chairs, correspond-
    ing to the *lectisternia* for gods.
9 The word is found only here and may be some sort of an earthenware pot or vase
    used in the ceremonies, which were then named after the objects.
10 The *Carmen Saeculare* of Horace has been preserved.
11 Seventeen members of this 'Board of Fifteen of sacred affairs' are listed, not count-
    ing Augustus and Agrippa. They include some of the most prominent senators of
    the age: Quintus Aemilius Lepidus (*PIR*[2] A 376, cos. ord. 21 BC); Potitus Valerius
    Messalla (cos. 29 BC); Gaius Licinius Calvus Stolo (*PIR*[2] L 171); Gaius Mucius
    Scaevola; Gaius Sosius (cos. ord. 32 BC); Gaius Norbanus Flaccus (cos. ord. 38
    BC); Marcus Cocceius Nerva (*PIR*[2] C 1224, cos. ord. 36 BC); Marcus Lollius (*PIR*[2]
    L 310, cos. 21 BC); Gaius Sentius Saturninus (cos. ord. 19 BC); Marcus Fufius
    Strigo (*PIR*[2] F 513); Lucius Arruntius (*PIR*[2] A 1129, cos. ord. 22 BC); Gaius Asinius

Gallus (*PIR²* A 1229, cos. ord. 8 BC); Marcus Claudius Marcellus (*PIR²* C 927, perhaps the cos. of 22 BC); Decimus Laelius Balbus (*PIR²* L 27, cos. ord. 6 BC); Quintus Aelius Tubero (*PIR²* A 274, cos. ord. 11 BC); Gaius Caninius Rebilus (*PIR²* C 391, cos. 12 BC); Marcus Valerius Messalla Messallinus (cos. ord. 3 BC). For the priesthood as a whole and for its individual members see Martha W. Hoffman Lewis, *The Official Priests of Rome under the Julio-Claudians* (Rome 1955) 48–56 and 86–91, who shows that there was some sort of significance to the order in which the above names were listed.

12 In a Greek theater the thymele was the altar of the god Dionysos located in the central dancing floor, around which the chorus sang and danced, while the actors appeared on a raised stage beyond it. 'Thymelic' performances were musical with dancing and declamation, not acting in the usual sense.

12   Greek translation of funeral oration given by Augustus for Agrippa. 12 BC.

Greek papyrus of the first century BC, the Fayûm in Egypt.

L. Koenen in *ZPE* 5 (1970) 226 (+ photograph); **P. Köln* 10; M. Gronewald in *ZPE* 52 (1983) 61–2 (+ photographs). Cf. Dio 54.28.1–5.

Koenen, *op. cit.* 217–83; *idem* in *ZPE* 6 (1970) 239–43; E. W. Gray in *ZPE* 6 (1970) 227–38; M. W. Haslam in *CJ* 75 (1979–80) 193–9; E. Badian in *CJ* 76 (1980–1); R. K. Sherk in *ZPE* 41 (1981) 67–9; J.-M. Roddaz, *Marcus Agrippa* (Paris 1984) 338ff., esp. 343–51.

[---] the tribunician power for fi|ve years in accordance with[1] a decree of the senate | was given to you when the Lent<ul>i[2] were consuls
5   (18 BC); and | again this (power) for another five-year period[3] ‖ was granted when the consuls were Tiberius (Claudius) Nero[4] | and (Publius) Quin<ti>lius Varus (13 BC), your sons-in-law. | And into whatever | provinces the Republic of the Ro|mans should ever summon
10   you, ‖ it had been sanctioned in a law that your power <was to be> not *less* than (that of) any (other magistrate) in th|ose (provinces).[5] However, you were elevated to the *supreme* | height (of power)[6] by our zeal and by your own excellent | qualities through the consent of a|ll men [---][7]

1 Koenen, *op. cit.* 274, believed that the tribunician power had been given to Agrippa 'by' a decree of the senate alone, but the Greek phrase is a translation of the Latin *ex senatus consulto* and means simply 'in accordance with a decree of the senate'. Thus, as Badian (*op. cit.* 99–101) has argued, the further action was taken by some other body than the senate. He believes that further action could only have been the vote of the Roman People.
2 P. Cornelius Lentulus Marcellinus and Cn. Cornelius Lentulus.
3 The Greek translator used the word 'Olympiad', no doubt in an attempt to translate the Latin *lustrum* or *quinquennium*.
4 He is the future emperor Tiberius.

5 Koenen argues that this means *imperium maius*, but Gray thinks of it as *imperium aequum*. *Imperium* was the supreme administrative power in the Republican government in both the military and the judicial field, duly conferred by law upon a Roman magistrate or ex-magistrate and confined to a certain sphere of activity called *provincia*. One magistrate's *imperium* was neither lesser nor greater than that possessed by another magistrate within the same rank and is called *aequum* ('equal') for that reason. Even M. Antonius in 74 BC and Cn. Pompeius in 67 BC possessed *imperium aequum*. In 43 BC, however, a special grant of *imperium maius*, i.e. 'greater' *imperium*, was given by the senate to Brutus and Cassius, and in 23 BC a similar grant was given to Augustus. See H. Last, *JRS* 37 (1947) 157–64, and E. Badian, *op. cit.* 105–6, who rightly follows Gray.

6 The 'supreme height of power' is the tribunician power: cf. Tacitus, *Ann.* 3.56.

7 For this last sentence, recovered after the publication in *P. Köln*, see Gronewald, *loc. cit.*

13   Five edicts of Augustus and a decree of the senate. 7/6 and 4 BC.

Marble stele over two meters high, complete on all sides, in the agora of Cyrene.

SEG IX 8; F. de Visscher, *Les Édits d'Auguste découverts à Cyrène* (Louvain–Paris 1940) 16–26 (+ photograph); *FIRA* I 68; *RDGE* 31 (Edict V and the decree).

De Visscher, *op. cit.* 31–210 (full commentary); *RDGE* pp. 174–82.

Edict I

Imperator Caesar Augustus, pontifex maximus, holding the tribunician | power for the seventeenth time (7/6 BC), imperator for the fourteenth time, | *vv* DECLARES[1] *vv* | Since I find that all the Romans
5 in the province of Cyrene ‖ are two hundred and fifteen of every age *v* | who have a census valuation of twenty-five hundred denarii or more, | from whom the judges are (chosen), and that there are conspiracies among these (Romans) | – so the embassies of the cities from the province have complained – which have oppre|ssed the Greeks in
10 capital cases,[2] the same people taking turns as ac‖cusers and as witnesses for each other, and (since) I myself have found that some in|nocent people in this way have been oppressed and brought to the ulti|mate penalty, until the senate may decide about this | or I myself may find something better, *vv* the fair and appropriate course of action, it seems to me, | would be for those who govern the province of Crete
15 and Cyrene to set up (a list) in the ‖ province of Cyrene of Greek judges of the highest census valuati|on, equal in number to the Roman (judges), none of them younger than twenty-five years, Roman | or Greek, with a census valuation and property, if there is a sufficient number of such m|en, of no less than seventy-five hundred denarii, or, if in this way | the number of judges which ought to be listed cannot be

20   filled, ‖ they shall list those people who have half and no less than half of this census valuation to be judges in │ capital cases of the Greeks. *vv* If a Greek is on tri│al, one day before the accuser begins to speak he shall be given the pow│er (to decide) whether he wishes his judges to be Romans or │ half of them Greeks. If he chooses half Greeks, then, after

25   the balls have been weighed[3] ‖ and the names inscribed on them, from the one ur│n the names of the Romans, and from the other the names of the Greeks shall be drawn by lot, │ until in each group twenty-five have been selected. Of these names │ the accuser, if he wishes, shall reject one from each group, but the defendant (may reject) three of all the names, │ *vv* on condition that he reject neither all Romans nor all

30   Greeks. Then ‖ all the others shall be sent to cast their votes and they shall cast their votes, │ the Romans separately into one basket, the Greeks separately into another. Then, when the counting has been finished sep│arately for the votes in each group, whatever the majority of all shall have │ decided the praetor (i.e. governor) shall declare publicly (as the verdict). And since unjust deaths, for │ the most part, the relatives of victims do not allow to go unavenged, and it is likely

35   that ‖ Greek accusers will not be lacking in procuring justice for the guilty on behalf of their murdered │ relatives or (fellow) citizens, *vv* the correct and appropriate course of action, it seems to me, wou│ld be if the future governors of Crete and Cyrene, │ in the province of Cyrene, would not permit a Roman to be the accuser of a Greek in a case of the murder of a Greek man or woman, │ except that someone who has been honored with Roman citizenship may go to court on behalf of the death

40   of one of his relatives or (fellow) citizens. ‖ *vv*

Edict II

Imperator Caesar Augustus, pon│tifex maximus, holding the tribunician power for the seventeenth time (7/6 BC) *v* DECLARES:[1] *v* Ill-will and blame │ ought not be (directed) to(ward) Publius Sextius Scaeva[4] because he saw to it that Aulus Stlaccius, son of Lu│cius, Maximus and Lucius Stlaccius, son of Lucius, Macedo and Publi│us

45   Lacutanius, freedman of Publius, Phileros, *vv* when they ‖ said they knew and wished to tell something that pertained to my safety and to the Republic, │ were sent in chains to me from the Cyrenaica, │ for in this Sextius acted properly and with vi│gilance. *v* Moreover, since they know nothing of matters that pertain to me and the republic │ and stated and made it clear[5] to me that this, which they said in the

50   province, had been a fa‖brication and a falsehood, I have set them free │ and released them from custody. *vv* But (as for) Aulus Stlaccius │ Maximus, whom envoys of the Cyreneans accuse of removing statues from │ public places, among them being the one beneath which the city

has inscribed my name, until | I have formed an opinion about this
55   matter, I forbid him to leave (Rome) without my order. ‖ *vv*

Edict III

Imperator Caesar Augustus, pontifex macimus, holding the
tribunician power | for the seventeenth time (7/6 BC) *vv* DECLARES:[1]
vv If any people from the Cyrenaican provin|ce have been honored with
(Roman) citizenship, I order them to perform the personal (?)[6]
liturgies, nevertheless, in their role[7] | as Greeks, *vv* with the exception
of those to whom in accordance with a law or decree of the senate | (or)
decree of my father or of myself, immunity from taxation has been
60   granted along with the citizenship. ‖ And it pleases me that these men
to whom immunity has been given *vv* shall have exemption only for that
pro|perty which they had at the time (of the grant). For all newly
acquired property | they shall pay the taxes. *vv*

Edict IV

Imperator Caesar Augustus, ponti|fex maximus, holding the
tribunician power for the seventeenth time (7/6 BC) *vv* declares: *vv*
Whatever | disputes shall arise between Greeks in the Cyrenaican
65   province, ‖ except for those who are liable for capital offenses, in whose
case the one who governs the province | has the duty of conducting the
investigation and rendering judgments himself or establishing a list of
judges, | – for all other matters it pleases me that Greek judges shall be
granted to them, unless some | defendant or accused wishes to have
Roman citizens for judges. For the parties | to whom Greek judges will
be given in consequence of this decree of mine, it pleases me that no
70   judge should be given ‖ from that city from which the plaintiff or
accuser comes, or th|*vv*e defendant or accused. *vv* | *vacat* |

Edict V

Imperator Caesar Augustus, pontifex maximus, | holding the
tribunician power for the *vv* 19th time (5/4 BC) *vv* declares:[1] | A decree
of the senate was passed in the consulship of Gaius Calvisius (Sabinus)
75   and Lucius ‖ Passienus (4 BC). I was present and par|ticipated in its
writing, and since it pertains to the security of the allies of the People |
of the Romans, in order that it might be known | to all those under our
care I have decided to send it to the provinces and | to append it to this,
80   my edict, from which it will be clear to all ‖ inhabitants of the provinces
how much concern | I and the senate have that no one of our sub|jects
may suffer unduly any harm or extortion. *vv* | *vv* DECREE OF THE
85   SENATE *vv* | Whereas Gaius Calvisius Sabinus and Lucius Passie‖nus
Rufus, consuls, spoke about matters which *vv* Imperator Caesar *vv*

Augustus, our Princeps,[8] | after consultation with the Advisory Board
which he had drawn by lot from the senate,[9] | wished to be introduced
to the senate by us because they pertain to | the security of the allies of
90   the People of the Romans, it has been de‖creed by the senate: *vv* Our
ancestors have passed laws for legal action | in the recovery of money[10]
in order that our allies | more easily might be able to begin proceedings
for the wrongs done to them and to recover the money of which they
have been de|prived. But because the form of such court ac|tions some-
times is very burdensome and disagreeable to those very people for
95   whom the law was writ‖ten, poor people and those weak with illness or
old age | being dragged from far-off provinces as witnesses, it plea|ses
the senate: If any of our allies after the passage of this | decree of the
senate either publicly or as individuals have been deprived of money
and wish to reco|ver it, without introducing a capital charge against the
100 extorter,[11] and if they present themselves about ‖ these matters and
declare them to any one of our magistrates who has the power to
con|vene the *senate*, the magistrate shall introduce these people as
quickly as possible into the senate | and give them an advocate who will
speak on their behalf before the senate, any | (advocate) they might ask
for, but no one shall unwillingly serve as advocate to whom in accord-
ance with our laws | an exemption from this public duty has been given.
105 *vv* In order that the (trials) may be heard (?) ‖ for those people who may
bring charges in the senate,[12] whatever magistrate gives them access to
the | senate shall, on the same day in the presence of the senate with no
less | than two hundred being present, draw by lot four of all the
consulars who are either in Rome itself | [or] within twenty miles of the
city; likewise three of all the prae|torians who are in Rome itself or
110 within twenty miles of the ci‖ty; likewise two of the rest of the senators
or of all those who have the right to express their o|pinion before the
senate, who may then be either in Rome or within twenty | miles of the
city. Nobody shall be chosen who is seventy or | more years old or who
holds a magistracy or is in an official position[13] or is a president of a
cou|rt or is in charge of the grain supply or is a person whom illness
115 prevents from performing this public du‖ty and who so swears before
the senate and produces | three members of the senate to swear to it, or
who is a person who is re|lated by kinship or marriage to him (i.e. the
accused) so that by the Julian Judiciary Law[14] he may not be forced to
testify as a witness | against his will in a public court, or is a person who
the accused swears before the senate | is hostile toward him; but he
120 shall not reject on oath more than three. Of the nine men ‖ drawn by lot
in this way the magistrate who does the drawing shall see | to it that
within two days those seeking recovery of money and the person from
whom | they seek it take turns in rejection, until five are left. | Whoever

of these judges may die before the case is decided or if any other reason pre|vents him from deciding and his excuse is approved by five men
125   under oath fr‖om the senate, then the magistrate, in the presence of the judges and those seek|ing recovery of money and the person from whom they are seeking it, shall draw by lot a substitute from (among) those | men who are the same rank and have held the same magistracies as that man happen|ed to hold into whose place they are being assigned by lot as a substitute, on condition that he does not as|sign a man who
130   cannot be assigned against the accused by this decree of the sen‖ate. *v* Those who have been chosen as judges shall only about those matters he|ar and render decisions concerning which someone is accused of having, at the expense of the public or of an individual, ap|propriated (funds), *vv* and whatever sum of money his accusers may sho|w has been taken from them privately or publicly, just so much shall they order to be restored, | on the condition that the judges render their
135   decision within thirty days.[15] Those (judges) who must ‖ decide about these cases and pronounce their decision, until they do decide and pronounce | their decision, shall be relieved of every public liturgy except public wor|ship. *vv* And it pleases the senate that the magistrate who has conducted the drawing by lot | of the judges or, if he is unable, the consul who has priority,[16] | shall preside over this investigation and
140   for the summoning of witnesses who are in Ita‖ly shall grant power, on condition that to a man seeking recovery as a private individual (it shall be) no mo|re than five (witnesses), and to those in a public capacity no more than ten (that) he shall give permission to summon. | Likewise it pleases the senate that the judges who are chosen by lot in accordance with this <decree of the senate> | shall pronounce openly what each of them has decided, *vv* | and whatever the majority pronounces shall stand (as the decision).

1   In extra large letters on the stone. Cf. lines 41 and 56. In line 73 the letters merely have more space between them.
2   I.e., in cases involving the death penalty and not the loss of civil rights.
3   They must all weigh the same to prevent a particular name from being singled out in the selection process.
4   Governor of Crete-Cyrene.
5   Textual observations made by J. H. Oliver in *Memoirs of the American Academy in Rome* 19 (1949) 107–8, are followed here.
6   This is a celebrated crux, and the solution given by A. Wilhelm in *Wiener Anzeiger* 80 (1943) 2–10 and accepted later by many others is followed here. De Visscher has a text which means: 'I order that they, nevertheless, following their turn, should hold the personal liturgies of the Greeks'. Oliver, in *Hesperia* 29 (1960) 324–5, felt an addition was necessary: '<financial and> personal liturgies'. But K. M. T. Atkinson, *Studies Presented to Victor Ehrenberg on his 75th Birthday* (Oxford 1966) 21–36, believes that no emendation of the text or additions to it are necessary, and instead

of 'personal' liturgies she sees a more specific reference to military service. See also
Sherwin-White, *Citizenship*[2] 334–6, for further discussion.

7   A. Wilhelm (above, n. 6) thus interprets this difficult phrase. De Visscher and
others have accepted his view. It is a question of double citizenship: see Sherwin-
White, *Citizenship*[2] 295–306.

8   Augustus speaks of himself as *princeps* three times in his *Res Gestae* (13; 30; 32).

9   The existence of such an imperial Advisory Board to be used by Augustus is known
from Dio (53.21.4) and Suetonius (*Div. Aug.* 35.3). See J. Crook, *Consilium Principis*
(Cambridge 1955) 8ff. See the Glossary *s.v.* Advisory Board.

10 For these earlier laws: de Visscher, *op. cit.* 156–83; A. N. Sherwin-White, *PBSR* 17
(1949) 5–25; P. A. Brunt, *Historia* 10 (1961) 189–99.

11 A controversy exists over this phrase. Was extortion in itself a capital offense in
previous legislation? What if the accuser does wish to introduce a capital charge?
See the works cited above, n. 10.

12 There are textual and grammatical difficulties in this clause, although the general
meaning is clear enough. Oliver, *op. cit.* above, n. 5, 109–13, follows the word order
on the stone: 'In order that <there might be judges> for these (trials) to be heard
for those who bring charges in the senate'. De Visscher and others have inverted
two words of the original.

13 The Greek contains a word that might render the Latin *potestas*, i.e. 'power'. See
de Visscher, *op. cit.* 145–6.

14 It is not known whether the reference is to legislation of Julius Caesar or of
Augustus.

15 This is not an exclusionary clause. The judges are expected to give their decision
within thirty days.

16 Explained by de Visscher as the consul who has the fasces at that particular time:
see Aulus Gellius 2.15.4ff., and de Visscher, *op. cit.* 149, and cf. J.-L. Ferrary in
MÉFR 89 (1977) 647–52.

14   Control over priestly credentials in Egypt. 4 BC.
Papyrus from Busiris in Egypt. [Greek]

BGU IV 1199.

Reinmuth, *Prefect* 30–1.

Copy of a letter. Gaius Turranius[1] [---|----] not enough of them are
described in written form, | [the] priests who take up their functions
year after year | and their functionaries who are not of the priestly order
5   and do not ‖ take upon themselves the liturgies [--|--]. Therefore, I
order a registration of the | priests who take up their functions (year
after year) and their temple functionaries and the | others of all the
10 temples [--] | and their children, and what services they perform ‖ they
shall make clear, so that in this 26th year of Cae[sar] (Augustus, 4 BC,)
I may make an examination of them. Those not of the priestly order
shall be removed from | office without delay.

1 Prefect of Egypt 7–4 BC: Stein, *Präfekten* 19–20.

15 Oath of loyalty sworn in Paphlagonia to Augustus and his descendants. March 6, 3 BC.

Stele of sandstone, Phazimon.

IGRR III 137; *OGIS* 532; *ILS* 8781; Cumont, *Studia Pontica* III No. 66; P. Herrmann, **Der Römische Kaisereid*, Hypomnemata 20 (Göttingen 1968) No. 4, pp. 123–4.

Magie, *RRAM* I 465; Herrmann, *op. cit. passim.*

Of Imperator Caes[ar,] | son of the god, Augustus the twelfth consul-
ship (5–3 BC), | third year (of the province, 3 BC),[1] *on the day before* | the
5   Nones of March (March 6) in Gangra in [camp (?),][2] the *oa*‖*th* completed
by *the inhabitants* of [Pa]|phlagonia [and the] R[omans] *who do business
among* | them; *v* | I swear by Zeus, Earth, Sun, all the gods [and] *god*|*desses*,
and Augus[t]us himself that I will be favorably disposed toward
[Cae]‖sar Augustus and his *children and descendants* | all the time of my
10   [life] in *wo*|*rd* and deed and thought, considering as *friends* | those whom
they may consider (friends) and *holding* as enemies | those whom they
15   may judge to be (enemies), and for things that are of interest *to them* ‖ I
will spare neither my body [nor] | my soul nor my life nor my children,
but in *every* | way for the things that *affect* them | I will undergo every
20   danger; and whatever I might *perceive* | or hear against them being *sa*‖*id*
or plotted or done, | I will report it and *I will be* an enemy to *the* | person
saying or plotting or doing [any of] *the*|*se* things; and whomever they
may judge to be their enemies, *the*|*se*, on land and sea, with arms and
25   ‖ steel will I pursue and ward off. | If I do anything contrary to this
[oath] | or anything not in agreement with what I have *sw*|*orn*, I pray
30   that there may come upon myself, my *bod*|*y* and soul and life, my *chil*‖*dren*
and all my *family* | and whatever is of use to us, destruction, total
destructio|*n* till the end of all *my* line [and] | of all my descendants, and
may neither the [bodies] | of my family or of my descendants by earth
35   or [se‖a] be received, nor may (earth or sea) bear fruit [for them.] | In
the same words was this oath sworn by all the [inhabitants of the land]
| in the *tem*|*ples* of Augustus throughout the districts (of the province)
by the altars [of Augustus.] | And likewise the Phazimonians living in
40   what is [now] called [Neapo]‖lis [swore the oath,] | all of them, in the
temple of Augustus by the [altar of] | Augustus. *v*

Other examples of loyalty oaths from the Greek East are to be found in: Assos in the
Troad (*IGRR* IV 251; *SIG*[3] 797); Samos (*Athen. Mitt.* 75 (1960) 70ff.); Palaipaphos on
Cyprus (*JRS* 50 (1960) 75; *SEG* XVIII 578). All of these can also be examined in
Herrmann, *op. cit.* 123–6.

1 The provincial era of Paphlagonia began when Paphlagonia was attached to the
province of Galatia, in 6/5 BC.
2 Cumont has 'in [camp]', but Dittenberger (in *SIG*[3]) and Dessau (in *ILS*) have 'in the
[Agora]'.

16 Rome and the Far East.

A: Pliny, *Nat. Hist.* 6.84–5. B: D. Meredith in *Chronique d'Égypte* 29 (1954) 283 (+ photograph); Ehrenberg–Jones, *Documents*[2] 360a. Greek inscription roughly cut in the rock face of a cave shelter at Wādi-Menīḥ near the Berenike Road in the eastern desert of Egypt. 2 BC. C: D. Meredith in *JRS* 43 (1953) 38 (+ photograph); Ehrenberg–Jones, *Documents*[2] 360b;; *SEG* XIII 614. Greek and Latin inscription on the same rock face as above (B). AD 6. D: Ptolemaeus, *Geography* 1.11.6. See M. Cary in *Classical Quarterly* 5 (1955) 130–4, and M. Raschke in *ANRW* 9.2.643 with notes.

Cf. Pliny, *Nat. Hist.* 6.101–6 and Strabo 17.798. See Raschke, *op. cit.* 604ff. and 643ff.; L. Casson in *TAPA* 110 (1980) 21–36.

A. Pliny, *Nat. Hist.* 6.84–5

More careful information came to us in the principate of Claudius, when envoys also arrived from that island (of Ceylon). It happened in the following way: Annius Plocamus, who had purchased from the Fiscus (Imperial Treasury) a contract for the collection of the taxes of the Red Sea, had a freedman who was sailing around Arabia and was taken by the north winds beyond Carmania.[1] On the fifteenth day he sailed into the port of Hippuri on Ceylon and, enjoying the king's hospitality, in six months he learned the language and, afterwards, upon being questioned by him, told the king about the Romans and about Caesar. When he had heard about them, the king came to admire in a remarkable way their justice, because the money that was in the possession of the captive – in denarii – was of equal weight, although the different images on them indicated that they had been minted by many (different emperors). Greatly moved by this friendship, he sent four envoys (to Rome), their leader being Rachias.

B. D. Meredith in *Chronique d'Égypte* 29 (1954) 283, Egypt

Gaius Numidius Eros was here | in the 28th year of Caesar (2 BC) on his | return from India. In the month Phamenoth (February–March).

C. D. Meredith in *JRS* 43 (1953) 38, Egypt

(Greek) Lysas, (slave) of Publius Annius Plocamus. | I came here in the 35th year of Caesar (AD 6) on the 8th day of Epeith (July 2).

D. Ptolemaeus, *Geography* 1.11.6

(Marinus of Tyre) says that Maes, also called Titianus, a Macedonian man and a merchant after his father, had a contract for the survey (of a trade route). He did not go himself but sent on some others to the Seres.[2]

1 For the importance of these winds in commerce with the East see G. W. Bowersock, *Roman Arabia* (Cambridge, Mass. 1982) 21, especially n. 33.
2 I.e. the Chinese.

17   Letter of Augustus to his grandson. AD 1.

Aulus Gellius, *Attic Nights* 15.7.3.

The ninth day before the Kalends of October (September 23). Greetings, dear Gaius, my most delightful little donkey, whom I always miss, by all that's holy, whenever you are absent. However, especially on such days as today my eyes search for my Gaius, and I hope that wherever you have been on this day you are safe and sound and have celebrated my sixty-fourth birthday. For, as you see, I have passed the grand climacteric, common to all old men, the sixty-third year. I beg the gods that whatever time I have left I might pass with (all of) us in good health and with the State in the happiest condition, and with (the two of) you[1] behaving like men and succeeding to my post of honor.

1 I.e. Gaius and his brother Lucius Caesar.

18   Gaius Caesar in the Greek East. AD 2.
Stone stele damaged at top and bottom, Messene in Greece.

A. K. Orlandos in *Archaiologikè Ephemerís* 1965, 110ff. (+ photograph); *SEG* XXIII 206; J. E. G. Zetzel in *GRBS* 11 (1970) 259–60. Cf. Velleius Paterculus 2.101ff. and Dio 55.10–10a.

Zetzel, *op. cit.* 261–6.

Secretary of the council-members was Philoxenidas in the magistracy of Theodo[ros.] | *vv* Decree. *vv* | Since Publius Cornelius Scipio, quaestor with pro praetorian power,[1] with un|excelled goodwill toward
5 Augustus and his whole house, ‖ having made a single very great and most honorable vow | to guard him against all harm, as displayed (subsequently) by each of his | actions, has conducted the Games of Caesar and has omitted no expense | or enthusiasm, nor on behalf of the sacrifices for Augustus | (has he spared his) giving of thanks to the gods, and at the same time preparing most of the cities in the province
10 ‖ to do the same thing along with him; and when he learned that Gaius, | the son of Caesar, involved in battle against the barbarians on behalf of all men, | was in good health, had escaped the dangers, and had taken vengeance on the ene|my,[2] with exuberant joy at this best of news he instructed everyone to wear wreaths | and to sacrifice in undisturbed
15 holiday, and he himself sacrificed oxen for ‖ the safety of Gaius and gave a variety of (theatrical) performances, zealous to make them rival | those given in the past on the one hand, and on the other to preserve equally the revered status (of Gaius); | he omitted two days from the days of Augustus and made the beginning of the | sacrifices for Gaius

20

from the day on which for the first time he was designated consul | and
ordered us to celebrate this day each year with ‖ sacrifices and the
wearing of wreaths as graciously as we can, | and the council-members
decreed on the fifteenth day before the Kalends of [----]

1 The precise relationship of this senator to other Cornelii Scipiones of the Augustan
   age is unknown.
2 The young Gaius Caesar had been sent by Augustus, his adoptive father and real
   grandfather, to the East with proconsular authority because of trouble in Armenia.
   While in the East he became consul in AD 1, in which year he waged war successfully
   somewhere beyond the eastern frontiers. In AD 4 he died in Lycia on his return to
   Italy, his death the result of a wound suffered in battle. See F. E. Romer in *TAPA* 109
   (1979) 199–214; G. W. Bowersock, *Roman Arabia* (Cambridge, Mass. 1983) 56.

19 Honors decreed in Pisae for the dead Gaius Caesar. AD 4.
White marble tablet, Pisae in Etruria. [Latin]

CIL XI 1421; *ILS* 140; Ehrenberg–Jones, *Documents*² 69; *I. Ital.* VII 1.7 (+ photograph);
Sherk, *Municipal Decrees* 48; Gordon, *Epigraphy* No. 31 (+ photograph); A. R. Marotta
D'Agata, **Decreta Pisana (CIL* XI 1420–1) (Pisa 1980) 21–5 (+ photograph).

Present (as witnesses to the writing) were Quintus, son of Quintus,
Atilius Tacitus; Publius Rasinius, son of Lucius, Bassus; Lucius
Lappius, | [son of Publius, G]allus; (nine more names follow.)

5

‖ Whereas it was noted that, since in our colony (of Pisae), because of
the campaigning of candida|tes, there were no magistrates (in office)
and since action was taken as written here below: | Since on the *4th day*
before the Nones of April (April 2) a message had been received that
Gaius Caesar, son of Augustus – who is father of his country, | pontifex
maximus, guardian of the Roman Empire and defender of the whole

10

world – and grandson of the deified, after the consulship which ‖ he had
completed while waging successfully a war beyond the farthest frontiers of the Roman People and after his fine administration of the state
and after conquering | or receiving into our *protection* the most warlike
and the most mighty nations, had been wounded in service on behalf of
the | state and, in consequence of this disaster, had been taken away
from the Roman People by the cruelty of fate, at a time when he had
been designa|ted Leader, most just and most like his father in manly
excellence, | and the sole defender of our colony; and (since) not yet

15

had there been any rest from the grief which ‖ our entire colony had
experienced at the death of [Lucius C]aesar, his brother, consul desig-
nate, augur, our patron, and leader | of the youth, this (new disaster)
renewed and multiplied | the *sorrow* of each one of us, for these reasons
all the de|curions and colonists, when at the time of this event in our

colony there were neither duoviri nor prefects | nor anyone in charge of
the administration of justice, have agreed among themselves that,
20 because of ‖ the magnitude of such a great and so unforeseen disaster,
from that day | on which his death had been announced to the day on
which his bones will be brought back and | buried and the last rites
performed for his departed spirit, all of us should change into mourn-
ing clothes, that the temples | of the immortal gods and the public
baths and taverns should all be closed, | that we should abstain from
25 banquets, that married women in our colony should lament, ‖ and that
the day on which Gaius Caesar died, the 9th day before the Kalends of
March (February 21), should, like the day of the Allia,[1] | be made into
a day of grief and so marked down (in the calendar) in the presence of
everyone by their order and wish, | and that precautions be taken that
no public sacrifice or offerings of propitiation | or weddings or public
banquets in the future on that day | or for that day, the 9th day before
30 the Kalends of March, take place or be conceived or be ‖ announced,
and that no performances of the theater or circus take place or be seen
on that day; | and (it was agreed) that on that day annually a festival of
the Family Dead should be performed to his departed spirit by our
magistrates or by those | who are in charge of the administration of
justice at [Pi]sae in the same place and in the same way as | that festival
has been instituted for Lucius C[ae]sar;[2] *vv* | and (it was agreed) that an
arch should be erected in the most celebrated place of our colony and
35 should be deco‖rated with the *spoils* of those nations conquered or
received into our protection by him, and that on its top | should be
placed a statue of him on foot in triumphal dress and that on both sides
of him *vv* should be | two gilded statues, of Gaius and Lucius Caesar on
horseback; | and (it was agreed) that, as soon as in accordance with the
law of our colony we can elect and have duoviri, | the first duoviri to be
elected should refer to the decurions this (whole) matter, which the
40 decurions ‖ and all the colonists have found agreeable, | *and* that after
the public authority of the decurions has been legally obtained, this
(whole matter) should be provided for and by their authorship | should
be entered into the public records; (and that) meanwhile, Titus
Statulenus Iuncus, | priest of Augustus, minor pontifex of the public
rites of the Roman People, should be as|ked, along with envoys, to
45 excuse the present difficulty of our colony[3] and ‖ to make known, by
sending a formal communication, our public sense of respect and wish
of everyone | to Imperator Caesar Augustus, father of his country,
pontifex maximus, holding the tribunician | power for the 26th time
(AD 4);[4] *vv* | and [Titus St]atulenus Iuncus, leader of our colony, priest
of Augustus, | minor pontifex of the public rites of the Roman People,
50 did this and did send a formal communication, as written above, ‖ to

[Imp]erator Caesar Augustus, pontifex maximus, holding the
tribunician power for the 26th time, father | of his country: Therefore,
it is decreed that everything, which, on the 4th day before the Nones of
April (April 2) | when [Sextus] Aelius Catus and Gaius Sentius
Saturninus were consuls (AD 4), had been done, enacted, and deci|ded
by the consensus of all orders, shall be so done, en|acted, and accepted
by Lucius Titius, son of Aulus, and by Titus Allius, son of Titus, Rufus
55   – the (new) duoviri – and by whoever ‖ afterwards will be prefects for
the administration of justice in our colony, | and that everything shall
be done, enacted, accepted, and observed in perpetuity; and that
Lucius Titius, | son of Aulus, [and Titus Al]lius, son of Titus, Rufus –
the (new) duoviri – shall see to it that everything written above in
accordance with our decree | shall be entered, in the presence of the pro
quaestors, at the earliest opportunity | by the public scribe into the
60   public records. ‖ Decreed.

1 On July 18 of 390 (or 387) BC at the Allia River north of Rome the Roman army
   suffered a disastrous defeat by the Gauls.
2 This festival (February 13–21) included days reserved for private celebrations at the
   graves of family dead. See J. M. C. Toynbee, *Death and Burial in the Roman World*
   (Ithaca, NY 1971) 63ff.
3 The difficulty is the fact that Pisae at the moment has no magistrates in office to call
   legally a meeting of its senate in order to pass a valid decree of the senators (the
   decurions) about these honors for the dead Gaius Caesar. It does not wish to give
   the impression of being slow to respond to his death.
4 Augustus held the tribunician power for the 26th time up to the first day of July,
   when his 27th such year began.

20   War against the Gaetulians in Africa. AD 3–6.

A: *CIL* VIII 16456; *ILS 120; Ehrenberg–Jones, *Documents*[2] 127. Stone found near the
Roman colony of Assuras in Africa. **B**: Eustathius, *Paraphrase of Dionysius Periegetes*, in
Geographi Graeci Minores (ed. C. Müller, Paris 1861) II p. 253, lines 8–10. **C**: Justinian,
Institutiones 2.25. **D**: Orosius, *Against the Pagans* 6.21.18. **E**: P. Romanelli in *Epigraphica* 1
(1939) 100 (drawing); Ehrenberg–Jones, *Documents*[2] 43; Reynolds–Perkins, *IRT 301
(photograph). Limestone panel. Probably from Lepcis Magna.

Cf. Dio 55.28; Florus 2.31; Velleius Paterculus 2.116.2.

R. Syme in *CAH* 10.347; *idem* in *Studies in Roman Economic and Social History in Honor of Allan
Chester Johnson* (Princeton 1951) 118–21 (*Roman Papers* I 222–3); J. Desanges in *Hommages
à Marcel Renard* II (Brussels 1968) 197–231; J. Gascou in *MÉFR* 82 (1970) 723–36;
D. Fishwick and B. D. Shaw in *Historia* 25 (1976) 491–4.

A. *ILS* 120. Near Assuras, Africa

Sacred to Juno Livia, (wife) of Augustus. | When Lucius Passienus
Rufus the imperator | was in charge of Africa,[1] Gnaeus Cornelius, son

5   of Gnaeus, (of the tribe) Cornelia, Rufus | and Maria, daughter of
     Gaius, Galla, (wife) of Gnaeus, ‖ having been saved,[2] gladly and with
     good cause discharged their vows.

B. Eustathius, *Paraphrase of Dionysius Periegetes*, **in** *Geographi Graeci Minores* **II p. 253, lines 8–10**

For they (i.e. the Nasamones[3]) treacherously killed Lentulus, a certain
general of the Romans, when he came there. For this reason they were
enslaved by the Romans.

C. Justinian, *Institutiones* 2.25

Before the time of Augustus it is agreed that the right of codicils did not
exist. Lucius Lentulus, from whose person *fideicommissa* began, was the
first to introduce codicils.[4] For when he was dying in Africa, he wrote
codicils that had been confirmed by his testament, by which he
requested Augustus through a *fideicommissum* to perform a certain act.[5]

D. Orosius, *Against the Pagans* 6.21.18

And then in Africa, when the Musolani and the Gaetuli roamed far and
wide, Cossus, general of Caesar,[6] reduced their frontiers, confined
them, and compelled them by fear to keep away from the Roman
fortified borders.

E. Reynolds–Perkins, *IRT* **301**

vv Sacred to Mars Augustus. | Under the auspices of Imperator Caesar
Augustus, | pontifex maximus, father | of his country (and) under the
5   command of Cossus Lentulus, ‖ consul (1 BC), quindecimvir of sacred
     affairs, | (and) proconsul, the province of Africa | was liberated from the
     Gaetulian War. The city of Lepcis (made this dedication).

1 After 23 BC the title of *imperator* was given only rarely to commanders outside the
   imperial family, and even then such men were not considered as fighting under their
   own auspices. Rufus (cos. 4 BC) could have been proconsul in Africa as early as
   AD 1 or even 1 BC. He won the *ornamenta triumphalia*.
2 These two Roman citizens probably made the vow when confronted by the threat of
   raids from the nomadic tribes of the Gaetulians.
3 They were one of the numerous nomadic peoples living on the fringes of Roman
   Africa.
4 A *fideicommissum* was originally a request by a testator to his heir to carry out some
   specific act, usually payment of money or transfer of property to a third party. A
   codicil was a written document by a testator for certain wishes to be implemented
   after his death. For Lucius Lentulus see *PIR*[2] C 1384.
5 Cf. Desanges, *op. cit.* 197–8 for a probable sequence of events. Augustus complied
   with his wishes and set a precedent.
6 This is Cossus Cornelius Lentulus (cos. 1 BC; *PIR*[2] C 1380). Because of his success
   against the Gaetulians his sons added the epithet 'Gaetulicus' to their names.

21　Fabricius Tuscus and a levy of troops at Rome. AD 6.

Stone slab, Tuzla in the Troad. [Latin]

G. E. Bean in J. M. Crook, *The Troad* (Oxford 1973) 412 (No. 50 with photograph); Ehrenberg–Jones, *Documents*[2] (enlarged edition, 1976) 368.

P. A. Brunt in *ZPE* 13 (1974) 162–85; M. Speidel in *TAPA* 106 (1976) 340–1 (*Roman Army Studies* 1.92–3); W. Orth in *ZPE* 28 (1978) 57ff.; R. Syme in *Phoenix* 33 (1979) 317–18 (*Roman Papers* III 1207).

To Gaius Fabricius, son of Gaius, | (of the tribe) Aniensis, Tuscus: duovir, augur, | prefect of the Cohort of Apulians and | of the works
5　which in the colony ‖ have been finished by order of Augustus, military tribune of the Legion Third | Cyrenaica for eight (years), tribune of the levy of free-born men | which was conducted at Rome by Augustus *vv* | and Tiberius Caesar,[1] prefect of the fabri[2] for four (years), prefect of the cavalry | of the Ala of Praetorians for four (years), with Parade Spear
10　and Wreath ‖ of Gold decorated by Germanicus | Caesar the commander in the German War. | By decree *vv* of the decurions.[3]

1　For the date and constitutional problem see Brunt, *loc. cit.*
2　Literally 'prefect of engineers', but the phrase in this age is coming to mean 'aide' to some higher authority: see B. Dobson in *Britain and Rome: Essays Presented to Eric Birley on his Sixtieth Birthday* (Kendal 1966) 61–84.
3　These must be the local senators of the colony Alexandria Troas, the only reasonable site to which the inscription points.

22　Equestrian officer takes the census. AD 6.

Marble stele broken into two parts (upper is lost), provenance unknown but from somewhere in Syria.[1] [Latin]

CIL III 6687; *ILS* 2683; Ehrenberg–Jones, *Documents*[2] 231. Cf. Luke 2.1–5; Josephus, *Ant. Jud.* 17.13.15, 18.1.1–2, 20.5.2; *Bell, Jud.* 2.17.8.1.

L. R. Taylor in *AJP* 54 (1933) 120–33; F. Cumont in *JRS* 24 (1934) 187–90; H. Braunert in *Historia* 6 (1957) 192–214; Levick, *Colonies* 206–12; J. and J. C. Baltry in *ANRW* 2.8.117–20.

Quintus Aemilius, son of Quintus, | (of the tribe) Palatina, Secundus[2]
[in] | the camp of the deified Augustus under | Publius Sulpicius
5　Quirinius, *legate* ‖ of Caesar over Syria:[3] decorated | with honors, prefect | of Cohort One of Augustus, prefect | of Cohort Two Classica. Also, |
10　by order of Quirinius I conducted the census ‖ of the city of Apamea | of 117,000 citizens;[4] | also, I was sent by Quirinius against the | Ityraeans
15　on Mt Lebanon | and I captured their fortress; and, before ‖ service (in my equestrian officer posts), I was prefect of the fabri[5] and | was transferred to the trea|sury; in my colony | I was quaestor, aedile twice,

20   duovir twice, | and pontifex. ‖ Stationed there were Quintus Aemilius,
son of Quintus, (of the tribe) Palatina | and Aemilia Chia, freedwoman.
| This monument will not pass any further in the possession of an heir.

1   The stone came to light in Italy, in Venice, but probably was brought there from
    Syria (Berytus?) as ballast in a ship.
2   See *PIR*[2] AS 406 and Devijver, *Prospographia* 1.A.90.
3   Quirinius was governor of Syria in AD 6.
4   The *civitas* of Apamea included not just the city proper but also all its surrounding
    territory, including towns.
5   See the previous document (n. 2).

23   Centurion killed in the disaster of Varus. AD 9.

Stone cenotaph broken at lower left corner, relief of a centurion in tunic
and cuirass with military decorations and an inscription below. To
right and left are the busts of two freedmen with their names. Castra
Vetera in Germany. [Latin]

CIL XIII 8648; *ILS* 2244; Ehrenberg–Jones, **Documents*[2] 45. Cf. Suetonius, *Augustus* 23;
Dio 56.18–22; Velleius Paterculus 2.117; Florus 2.30.

R. Syme in *CAH* 10.375 and 943; E. Sander in *Rhein. Mus.* 95 (1952) 79–96; E. Bickel, *ibid.*
97–135; Webster, *Army* 133–4 (+ photograph opp. p. 48); D. Timpe, *Arminius-Studien*
(Heidelberg 1970); Maxfield, *Decorations, passim* (+ photograph, Plate 2a); Kienast,
Augustus 305ff.; H. Benario in *Historia* 35 (1986) 114–15.

To Marcus Caelius, son of Titus, (of the Tribe) Lemonia, (from)
Bononia,[1] | [---][2] centurion of the Eighteenth Legion. Fifty-three years
old, | he fell (in battle) in the Varian War. As for the bones | [of his
freedmen (?),] permission will be given to bury them (here).[3] P. Caelius,
5   son of Titus, ‖ (of the tribe) Lemonia, his brother, made (this monument).

1   Bononia is in Cisalpine Gaul.
2   Sander saw part of a single letter here (I, F, or T) followed by an O. He argued that
    this was an abbreviation to indicate a centurion in charge of a veteran unit of a
    legionary cohort. Caelius is a centurion, but the qualifying abbreviation is unclear.
3   The two freedmen of Caelius would have accompanied him on the march to the
    battleground in Germany. They may have perished with him and their bones were
    never recovered, or, if they were still alive at the moment of engraving, legal per-
    mission is given by the surviving brother for them to be buried in the same plot as
    Caelius. Their names are Marcus Caelius Privatus and Marcus Caelius Thiaminus.

24   Rebellion in Athens against Rome. About AD 13.

A: Eusebius, Olympiad 197, fourth year (Schoene II p. 147). B: Eusebius, Armenian
version, Olympiad 198 (tr. Karst p. 212). C: Syncellus, *Chron.*, year 5513 (p. 602, ed.

Bonn). **D**: Orosius, *Against the Pagans* 6.22.2. **E**: *IG* II² 3233 and *Hesperia* 17 (1948) p. 41, No. 30; Ehrenberg–Jones, **Documents²* 81a. Honorary inscription from Athens.

P. Graindor, *Athènes sous Auguste* (Cairo 1927) 41–3; V. Ehrenberg in *Studies Presented to David M. Robinson* (St Louis 1953) 2.938–44; Bowersock, *Augustus* 106–8; D. J. Geagan in *ANRW* 2.7.1.379.

A. Eusebius, Olympiad 197, 4

The Athenians ceased from their arrogant stirring-up of rebellion when the initiators of the sedition were punished.

B. Eusebius, Armenian version, Olympiad 198

The Athenians had dared to revolt, but they stopped after the punishment of the initiators of the sedition.

C. Syncellus, *Chron.*, year 5513

The Athenians began seditious activity, but they stopped after being punished.

D. Orosius, *Against the Pagans* 6.22.1–2

In the year 752 of the city (of Rome, i.e. 2 BC), when all nations from east to west, north to south, and everywhere in the whole circumference of the Ocean, were joined in bonds of peace, Caesar Augustus closed the gates of Janus for the third time. And these gates, from that time, were always shut up tight for almost twelve years in perfect stillness, as indicated by the rust on them. They were not opened until in the extreme old age of Augustus they were beaten upon by the sedition of the Athenians and a commotion of the Dacians.[1]

E. Ehrenberg–Jones, *Documents²* 81a, Athens

[--- leg]ate of Impera[tor Caesar Augustus] and Tiberius Caesa[r ----][2]

1 On this passage see R. Syme in *AJP* 100 (1979) 196ff. (*Roman Papers* III 1186ff.).
2 This unknown official is a legate of the emperor but probably not the governor of the province, for the title here lacks the phrase 'with pro praetorian power'. He may have been sent to Athens on special assignment. To put down the Athenian rebels? Cf. Stein, *Mosien* 18.

25 Minutes of an audience in Rome given by Augustus with his Advisory Board to envoys from Alexandria. First half of AD 13.
Verso of a papyrus of the early first century AD,[1] Oxyrhynchus in Egypt.

*P. Oxy. 2435, lines 29–61 (+ photograph).

E. G. Turner on *P. Oxy.* 2435, pp. 102–12; A. K. Bowman, *JRS* 66 (1976) 154.

30   [Roll no. -,][2] *column* 80. Year 42 of Caesar (AD 13), ‖ (month of) [--] the
      4th (or 24th), the 9th hour. Au[gustus] sat | in the temple of Apollo | [in
      the R]oman Library and *lis|tened* to the envoys of the Alexan|[drians,]
35   and seated with him were Tib[e]rius ‖ [Caesar] and D[r]usus the (son)
      of Caesar,[3] | [and Va]l[e]rius Messalinus Corvinus[4] | [--]us and
      Ti[--]us Den(?) [--]tor, | [--]us Ma[s]o[ni]us, Titus [--]inus | [--]o,[5]
40   Marcus Avidius Org<ol>anius,[6] ‖ [--]sianus (?) T[--.] Alexandros
      gave (him) the | *decrees* and said, | ['--] my city sent me | [--] to present
45   to you | [--] and to deliver the decrees ‖ [--] and of Livia | [--] and [of
50   Tib]erius (?) [Caes]a[r --|--|--] *envoys* between [--‖-] whose *justice* you
      decided, we as|k you [--] victory [--|--'] *v* Augustus (said), 'I have seen
      it.' | (Shouts)[7] 'Good luck! Good luck!' After | [this] Timoxenos the
55   orator (said), 'As much ‖ [--] as you grant to the [--|--,] lord Augustus,
      just so mu|ch also we beg you to grant to *your* A[l]exandrians | today,
      for (although) in a manner of speaking | we are here to make a request
60   of you, the truth is ‖ that with all zeal [our city] is worshipping your
      most sacred | [Fortune] and [--']

1 The recto of this papyrus contains a speech, punctuated by applause, of an unnamed
   'imperator' to the citizens of Alexandria. He is almost certainly Germanicus Caesar,
   adopted son of Tiberius.
2 The present document was merely one of very many others included in a papyrus
   roll, which was itself one of a large collection of such rolls.
3 These two are the future emperor Tiberius and his natural son Drusus.
4 This is the consul of 3 BC, the son of the famous orator M. Valerius Messalla
   Corvinus (consul in 31 BC) who had fought at Philippi on the side of Brutus and
   Cassius but had later joined Octavian. The son, after his consulship, became
   governor of Illyricum and campaigned with Tiberius against King Maroboduus,
   winning the *ornamenta triumphalia* ('triumphal decorations').
5 All names in lines 37–8 are uncertain.
6 The editors decided to treat the papyrus reading 'Organios' as an error for
   'Orgolanios', making him the father or brother of the Urgulania in Tacitus (*Ann.*
   2.34; 4.21–2) who was an intimate of the Imperial family.
7 Perhaps from the envoys or, more likely, from bystanders. These shouts are familiar
   from the later so-called Acts of the pagan martyrs: see H. A. Musurillo, *The Acts of the
   Pagan Martyrs* (Oxford 1954).

26   The 'Res Gestae' of Augustus. Composed AD 12–14.

Engraved on the wall of the temple (of Roma and Augustus?) in Ancyra.
[Latin and Greek][1]

J. Gagé, *Res Gestae Divi Augusti*[3] (Paris 1977), with photographs; H. Volkmann, *Res
Gestae Divi Augusti*[3] (Berlin 1969).

(Heading) The accomplishments of the deified Augustus by which he
subjected the whole world to the empire of the Roman People, | and the

expenses which he incurred for the state and the Roman People, inscribed | on two bronze pillars which have been erected at Rome – a copy of them is given below.

Col. 1   (1.1) When I was nineteen years old, by my own deliberation and at my own expense, I raised an army | by which I brought the Republic, oppressed by the domination of a faction, | into a condition of freedom. (1.2) For that *reason* the senate by honorary decrees | [enrolled][2] me into its order in the consulship of [Gaius Pansa and Aulus Hirti]us (43 BC),

5   ‖ [assigning] me consular position [to express my opinion and] giving me imperium. | (1.3) That the Republic [should suffer no harm it ordered] me as pro praetor, together with | the consuls, to make provisions. (1.4) The People, moreover, in the same year | made me consul, when [both consuls] *had fallen in battle* and also (made me) triumvir for

10   the constitution | of the Republic.[3] ‖
        (2.1) Those who [murdered] my father I drove into exile, by leg|al tribunals having avenged their *crime*, and afterwards when they waged war against the Republic, | I defeated them *twice* in battle.[4]|
        (3.1) Wars on land and sea both *domestic* and foreign throughout the whole world I often [waged] | and as victor I spared all citizens [who

15   sought forgiveness.] (3.2) *Foreign* ‖ nations who could be safely [pardoned] I preferred to save rather than to cut down. | (3.3) Around five hundred thousand Roman citizens were under my military oath. | Of these I sent out to *colonies* or sent back to their own municipalities, when their *discharges had been* | *earned*, somewhat [more] than three hundred thousand, and to all of these [I assigned] lands | or gave them money as [rewards] for military service.[5] (3.4) I captured six hundred

20   ships, [apart from] ‖ those which were smaller than *triremes*.[6]. |
        (4.1) [Twice I celebrated] ovations and three curule triumphs[7] and I was acclaimed twenty-|one times imperator. When the senate [decreed] *more* triumphs for me, [a|ll] *of them* I declined. The [laurel from] my *fasces* I deposited in the Capitolium, the [vows which] | I had made for each war *being thus fulfilled*. (4.2) Because of the things which [I

25   or legates of] ‖ mine, acting under my auspices, accomplished successfully on land and sea, *fifty-fi|ve times* the senate decreed thanksgiving should be offered to the immortal gods. The days | on which in accordance with a decree of the senate there was thanksgiving were 890. (4.3) [In my triumphs] | before my chariot were paraded [nine] kings or children of *kings*. (4.4) [Consul] | thirteen times had I been when [I wrote] these words [and held] for the *thirty-seventh time* ‖ the tribunician

30   power (AD 14). ‖
        (5.1) The *dictatorship*, [offered to me] in my absence and in my presence [by both People] and *senate* | [in the consulship of Marcus Marcel]lus and Lucius Arruntius (22 BC), I did not accept. (5.2) [I did

not] refuse, in the *great* | scarcity *of grain*, the superintendency of the *grain-supply*, which I *administered* in such a way [that within] | a few days
35 [I freed] the *whole* state from fear and immediate danger ‖ at my own [expense and] care. (5.3) The *consulship* also at that time, annual and [perpetual,] | was *offered* [to me. I did not accept it.] |

(6.1) [In the consulship of Marcus Vinicius and Quintus Lucretius (19 BC)] and later in that of Publius Lentulus and Gnaeus L[entulus (18 BC) and a third time | in that of Paullus Fabius Maximus and Quintus Tubero (11 BC) the senate and the Roman People agr|eed] that [I should be made sole guardian of the laws and morals with the
40 highest authority, ‖ but I did not accept any magistracy, though offered, which was contrary to the custom of our ancestors. (6.2) The actions, which then through me | the senate] *wished* [to be taken, I carried out] by virtue of my *tribunician* [power, and in this power] | voluntarily I asked for and received a colleague [five times from the senate.] |

(7.1) *I was triumvir for the constitution of the Republic* [for ten continuous] *years.*[8] | (7.2) [I was the] leading member [of the senate up to] *the day* [on
45 which I wrote these words, ‖ for] forty [years.] (7.3) I was *pontifex* [maximus, augur, quindecimvir of sacred affairs, | septemvir] for *religious banquets,* [Arval Brother, fellow of the society of Titius,] fetial priest.[9] |

Col. 2 (8.1) The number of patricians I increased in my fifth consulship (29 BC) by order of the People and the senate. (8.2) The sen|ate's roll I revised three times. And in my sixth consulship (28 BC) I held a census of the People with my colleague Marcus Agrippa. | I conducted a lustrum after forty-one years. At that lustrum Roman citi|zens were
5 registered to the number of four million and si‖xty-three thousand. (8.3) Then again, with consular imperium, | I conducted a lustrum by myself, in the consulship of Gaius Censorin[us and Gaius] Asinius (8 BC), at which lustrum were registered | four million two hun|dred and thirty-three thousand Roman citizens. (8.4) And a *third time*, with consular imperium, | [I conducted] a lustrum with my colleague Tiberius Cae[sar, my son,] in the consulship of Sextus Pompeius and Sextus
10 Appuleius (AD 14), ‖ at which lustrum were *registered Roman citizens* to the number of four mi|llion nine hundred and thirty-seven thousand.[10] | (8.5) By new laws, carried with me as [sponsor,] many model traditions of our ancestors that were falling out of use | in our [gener-ation] *I restored* and [handed on] as *models* of many things to be imi|tated
15 by posterity. ‖

(9.1) That vows for [my health should be taken] *by the consuls* and priests every fifth | [year was decreed by the senate. In consequence of these] vows [games] were often performed in my life|time, [sometimes by] the four most distinguished priest|hoods, [sometimes by the con-

suls.] (9.2) *Individually* and by whole municipalities all the | [citizens
unanimously and continuously] at all the seats (of the gods) prayed for
20   my ‖ health. |

(10.1) My name *by decree of the senate* was included in the Salian Hymn,
and the fact that I should be sacro|sanct forever and that as long as I
live the tribunician power | should be mine, was [sanctioned by law.]¹¹
(10.2) That I should become pontifex maximus in place of my *collea|gue*
while he still lived, [even though the People] offered me that *priesthood,*
25   which my father ‖ [had held, I refused.] That priesthood, after some
years, at the de|ath of one who had seized it on the occasion of [a civil
disturbance,] and when from all Italy | as great a *multitude* streamed in
[to my elections] as never | [before recorded] at Rome, I accepted in the
consulship of Publius Sulpicius and Gaius Valgius (12 BC). |

(11.1) The alter of [Fortune Who Brings Back,] in front of the temple
30   of Honor and Virtue at the Porta ‖ Cap[ena, for my] *return* was conse-
crated by the senate, on which (altar) the *ponti|fices and Vestal Virgins*
[were ordered] to make an annual sacrifice | [on the day when,] in the
consulship of [Quintus Luc]retius and [Marcus Vi]nicius (19 BC), [I
returned] to the city from | [Syria,] and (the senate) called [that day
Augusta] after my name.¹² |

(12.1) [On the authority of the senate] some [of the praetors and]
35   tribunes ‖ [of the plebs, with the consul Quintus] Lucretius and the
leading men, for the purpose of meeting me | were sent [to Campan]ia,
an honor which [up to] this time to nobody ex|cept me has been
[decreed.] (12.2) When from *Spain and Gaul,* affairs in those provinces
having been success|fully handled, [I returned to] R[ome in the consul-
ship of] Tiberius Nero and Publius Qui[ntilius (13 BC) | the senate
decreed that an] altar of Augustan [Peace] should be consecrated for
40   my return in the Cam‖pus [Martius, on which the] magistrates and
priests and *Vestal Virgins* | [were ordered] to make an *annual sacrifice.*¹³ |

(13.1) [Our ancestors wished that (the temple of) Janus] Quirinius
was to be closed | when throughout the whole [empire] of the Roman
People [on land and sea] peace had been won by vic|tories, and
although before my birth it is recorded that [from the foundation] of
45   the city it had been closed only twice, ‖ the senate ordered it closed
three times with me as princeps.¹⁴

(14.1) My sons, whom as *young men fortune* took from me, Gaius and
Col. 3   Lucius Caesar, | out of honor to me the senate and the Roman People,
in their fifteenth | year, designated them as consuls so that they could
enter that magistracy after a five-|year period. And from the day on
which they made their entrance into public life they were to be involved
in the councils | of state by decree of the senate. (14.2) Moreover, all the

5   Roman Equites ‖ called each of them Leader of the Youth and gave
them silver shields | and spears. |

     (15.1) To the Roman plebs man for man I paid out three hundred
sesterces in accordance with the testament of my father | and in my own
name I gave them each four hundred sesterces from the spoils of war
when I was consul | for the fifth time (29 BC), and again in my tenth

10   consulship (24 BC) from my patrimony ‖ I paid out a largess man for
man of four hundred sesterces each, and while consul | for the eleventh
time (23 BC) I measured out twelve grain distributions apiece with
grain purchased at my own expense, | and while holding the tribunician
power for the twelfth time (12–11 BC) | I gave four hundred sesterces
man for man for the third time. These largesses of mine never reached

15 | less than two hundred and fifty thousand persons. ‖ (15.2) While
holding the tribunician power for the eighteenth time (5 BC) and while
consul for the twelfth time, to three hundred and | twenty thousand city
plebs I gave sixty denarii (240 sesterces) man for man. | (15.3) And to
colonists of my soldiers, while consul for the fifth time (29 BC), from
booty man for man | I gave one thousand sesterces, and this largess, at
my triumph, was received | in colonies by about one hundred and

20   twenty thousand men. (15.4) While consul for the thir‖teenth time I
gave sixty denarii (240 sesterces) each to those plebs who were receiv-
ing public grain, | and they were a little more than two hundred
thousand persons.[15] |

     (16.1) Money for the lands, which in my fourth consulship (30 BC)
and afterwards in the consulship | of Marcus Crassus and Gnaeus
Lentulus Augur (14 BC) I assigned to soldiers, I paid to the munici-
palities. This | [amount] was about six hundred million sesterces which

25   for Italian ‖ estates I paid out, and about two hundred and sixty million
which I paid for land | in the provinces. I was the first and only one of
all those who led out | colonies of soldiers in Italy or in the provinces,
down to the memory of my time, | to have done this. (16.2) And after-
wards, in the consulship of Tiberius Nero and Gnaeus Piso (7 BC) and
likewise of Gaius Antistius | and Decimus Laelius (6 BC) and likewise
of Gaius Calvisius and Lucius Pasienus (4 BC) and likewise of Lucius

30   Lentulus and Marcus Messala (3 BC) ‖ and likewise of Lucius
Caminius and Quintus Fabricius (2 BC), to the soldiers, whom, after
they had ear|ned their discharges, [I led] to their own municipalities, I
granted rewards of money. | For this I spent about four hundred |
million sesterces.[16] |

     (17.1) Four times with my own money I helped the treasury so that

35   ‖ I transferred one hundred and fifty million sesterces to those in charge
of the treasury. (17.2) And when Marcus Lepidus | and Lucius

Arruntius were consuls (AD 6), into the military treasury, which on my advice | was established to give bonuses to soldiers after twenty *years or* | more military service, I transferred one hundred and *seventy* million
40   sesterces | from my patrimony.[17] ||

(18.1) [From the year] when Gnaeus and Publius Lentulus were consuls (18 BC), when there was a lack | of tax-revenue, [sometimes] to a hundred thousand people and sometimes to many more I made gr|ain and money [contributions from] my granary and patrimony.[18]

Col. 4   (19.1) The Curia and the Chalcidicum adjacent to it, the temple of Apollo on | the Palatine with its porticoes, the temple of the deified Iulius; the Lupercal, the portico by the Cir|cus Flaminius, which I permitted to be named Octavia after the name of the one who | had built an earlier one in the same place; the Imperial Box at the Circus
5   Maximus; || (19.2) the temples of Jupiter the Subduer and Jupiter the Thunderer on the Capitolium; the temple of Quirinus, | the temples of Minerva and Juno the Queen and Jupiter Freedom on the Aventine; | the temple of the Lares at the head of the Sacra Via, the temple of the gods Penates on the Velia; | the temple of Youth, the temple of the Great Mother on the Palatine – (all these) I built. |

(20.1) The Capitolium and Pompey's Theater I repaired, both works
10   at great expense || without inscribing my name on them. (20.2) The channels of the aqueducts, in many places | tottering with age, I repaired, and the (capacity of the) aqueduct called Marcia I doubled | by having a new spring brought into its channel. (20.3) The Forum Iulium and the basilica, | which was between the temple of Castor and the temple of Saturn, projects begun and well advanced | by my father,
15   I completed, and when that same basilica was destroyed by fi||re, I enlarged its site and in the name of my sons I sta|rted its foundations, and if I have not completed it in my lifetime, I have ordered it to be completed by [my] heirs. | (20.4) Eighty-two temples in the city in my sixth consulship (28 BC) with the *authority* | of the senate I repaired, passing over none which at that time [ought to have been repaired.] | (20.5) In my seventh consulship (27 BC) [I repaired] the Via Flaminia
20   from the [city] to Ari[minum,] including the bridges, || all of them except the Mulvian and the Minucian.[19] |

(21.1) On private ground the temple of Mars the Avenger and the Forum Augustum [out] of the spoi|ls of war were built by me. The theater by the temple of Apollo, on a site purchased in large measure from *private owners*, | was built by me, which was to be in the name of Marcus Marcellus, my son-in-law. (21.2) Gifts from | the spoils of war on the Capitolium and in the temple of the deified Iulius and in the
25   temple of Apollo and in the tem||ple of Vesta and in the temple of Mars the Avenger were consecrated by me, which cost me | about one

hundred million sesterces. (21.3) Crown gold, weighing thirty-fi|ve thousand pounds, to the municipalities and colonies of Italy – which they were collecting for my triumphs | – I remitted in my fifth consul-ship (28 BC), and afterwards, whenever I was acclaimed imperator, | I did not accept the crown gold, although it was decreed by the munici-

30 palities‖and colonies with the same willingness as they had before.[20] |

(22.1) Three times I gave gladiatorial exhibitions in my name and five times in that of my sons | or grandsons, in which exhibitions men fought | to the number of about ten thousand. On two occasions athletes were summoned from everywhere | to put on spectacles which I *furnished* to the people in *my name* and on a third occasion in my grand-

35 son's na‖me. (22.2) I presented (other) games *in my name* four times and in place of other *magistrates* | twenty-three times. *On behalf of* the quin-decimviri and as master of that (Priestly) Colle|ge and with Marcus Agrippa [I presented] the Secular Games in the consulship of Gaius Furnius and Gaius Silanus (17 BC).[21] | As consul for the thirteenth time (2 BC) *I was the first to present the games of Mars*, which after that time | *in subsequent* years [in accordance with a decree of the senate and a law] *the*

40 *consuls presented.* (22.3) *Beast-hunts*‖ (with animals) from Africa in my name or in that of my sons and grandsons in the cir|cus or in the forum or in the amphitheaters I provided for the people twenty-six times, in which | about thirty-five hundred beasts were killed. |

(23.1) An exhibition of a naval battle to the people I presented across the Tiber where | now is a grove of the Caesars, the ground having been

45 excavated to a length of‖ eighteen hundred feet and a width of *twelve hundred* feet. In it thir|ty beaked ships, triremes or *biremes*, and also even smaller ships engaged in battle. In these fleets there were battles fou|ght by about three thousand men, not counting the rowers. |

(24.1) In the temples of all the cities of the *province* of Asia, as victor

50 ‖I replaced the ornaments which, after the plundering of those temples, that person against whom I was waging war | had taken into his private possession.[22] (24.2) Statues of myself, on foot and on horseback and in | four-horse chariots, were standing in the city, about eighty of them, which I | removed and out of the money (thus saved) I set up gold gifts in the temple of Apollo in my na|me and in that of those who gave me the honor of those statues.[23]‖

Col. 5 (25.1) I pacified the sea, freed it of pirates. In that war the slaves, who had fled from their masters | and had taken up arms against the Repub-lic, I captured about thirty thousand of them | and turned them over to their masters for punishment.[24] (25.2) An oath of allegiance was sworn to me by all | Italy of its own accord and it demanded me as Leader of

5 the war which I won at Actium. The same oa‖th of allegiance was sworn by the provinces of Gaul, Spain, Africa, Sicily, and Sar|dinia.[25] (25.3)

Those who soldiered under [my standards at that time] included more | than 700 senators, among them 83 [who before or] afterward were made consuls, down to the day | on which these words were written, and also about 170 who were made *priests*. |

(26.1) As for all those [provinces of the Roman People] bordered by 10 || tribes not [subject to our Empire,] I increased the frontiers. (26.2) The Gallic and Span|ish provinces [and Germany, an area] enclosed by the Ocean from Gades to the mou|th of the Elbe River, [I pacified. (26.3) The Alps, from the] region which is nearest to the Ad|riatic Sea [as far as the Tuscan Sea, I pacified] without waging unjust war upon any people. | (26.4) *My fleet* sailed through the [Ocean] from the mouth of 15 the Rhine to the eastern re||gion up to the land [of the Cimbri,] which either on land or | on sea no Roman before this time had ever entered, and the Cimbri and Charydes | and Semnones and other Germanic peoples of the territory through their envoys | sought my friendship and that of the Roman People.[26] (26.5) By my order and under my auspices [two] armies were led | at almost the same time into Aethiopia 20 and Ar[a]bia, which is ca|||lled Blessed, and *great forces* of the enemy from both nations | were cut down in battle and *many* towns were captured: in Aethiopia it was as far as the to|wn of Nabata that they advanced, next to which is Meroe.[27] In Arabia it was as far | as the frontier of the Sabaei, to the town of Mariba that the army marched.[28] |

(27.1) I added Egypt to the empire of the [Ro]man People. (27.2) 25 Greater Armenia, at the assassi||nation of its king Artaxes, *when* I could have made it a province, I preferred, | following the example of our ancestors, to hand it over as a kingdom to Tigranes, son of King Artavasdes and grandson | of King Tigranes, acting through T[iberius Ne]ro, who was at that time my stepson.[29] | This same nation when it later revolted and rebelled, but was pacified by Gaius, | my son, I handed over to King Ariobarzanes, son of King Artabazus of the 30 Medes, to be ru|||led (by him) and after his death by his son Artavasdes. When he was assassinated, I sent Tig[ra]nes, | who was sprung from the royal family of the Armenians, into that kingdom.[30] (27.3) The pro|vinces, all those which lie to the east across the Hadriatic Sea, as well as Cyre|ne, with kings possessing them for the most part, and even earlier Sicily and | Sardinia, which had been seized in the Slave War, 35 (all these) I have recovered. ||

(28.1) I established colonies of soldiers in Africa, Sicily, Macedonia, the two Spains, Achaia, Asia, Syria, | Gallia Narbonensis, and Pisidia. (28.2) And Italy has 28 *coloni|es* which have become very much frequented and populous during my lifetime, (all) by my [authority] | established. |

(29.1) Very many military standards, *lost* by other commanders, I

40   *recovered*, after defeating the enemy, ‖ from Spain and [Gaul and the
Dalm]atians. (29.2) I forced the Parthians to *return* three Roman
Armies' | spoils and standards[31] to me and to beg as suppliants for the
friendship of the Roman People. | And these standards I restored to the
inner shrine, which is in | the temple of Mars the Avenger. |
(30.1) The tribes of the Pannonians, whom before me as Leader of

45   the Roman People an army[32] had ne‖ver approached, were conquered
(by me) through Tiberius [Ne]ro, who was at that time my stepson and
legate, | and I added them to the empire of the Roman People and
extended the frontier of Illyricum to the bank of the River |Danube.[33]
(30.2) When an army of [D]a[cians] crossed to this side of that (river),
under my *auspices* it was defeated and utterly destroy|ed, and later *my
army* crossed the Danube and [forced] the Da[cian] | tribes [to submit

50   to] the commands of the R[oman] P[eople.][34] ‖
(31.1) To me [embassies of kings were often sent] from In[dia, not
seen before this] *age* | in the presence of *any* commander of the
R[omans.] (31.2) Our *friendship* was *sought* | through envoys by the
Bastarnians and [Scythians] and by kings of the Sarmatians, who live
[on this side of] the River | Tanais (Don) [and] beyond it, and by the
king of the [Alba]nians and of the Iberians *and* [of the Medes.] |
(32.1) To me kings fled as suppliants: (kings) of the Parthians,

Col. 6   Tiridates and later Phrates, ‖ son of King Phrates; of the Medes,
Ar[tavasdes; of the Adiabenians,] Artaxa|res; of the Britons,
Dumnobellaunus and Tin[commius; of the Sugambr]ians, | Maelo; of
the Marcomanian Suebians, [---rus.] (32.2) To [me the] *king* of the
Parthians, | Phrates son of Orodes, sent all his sons [and] grandsons

5   into Italy, not ‖ (because he was) conquered in war, but because he
sought our friendship through the pledges | of his children.[35] (32.3)
And very many other nations made *trial* of the good faith [of the Roman
People,] under me as their Lea|der, for which earlier [there had existed
no] exchange with the Roman People of embassies | and friendship. |
(33.1) From me the nations of the Parthians and Medes, [through

10   envoys] (composed of) the leading men of their na‖tions, received their
kings when they asked for them: the Par[thians, Vonones] son of [King
Ph]rates, | grandson of King Orodes; the Medes, Arioba[rzanes] son of
King Artavazdes, | grandson of King Ariobarzanes. |
(34.1) In my sixth and seventh consulships (28–27 BC), *after* I had
extinguished the *civil* wars | and by the consent of all had [acquired

15   control] of everything, I transferred the Republic ‖ from my power to
the discretion of the senate and the *Roman* [People.][36] | (34.2) In return
for this service of mine by senatorial [decree] I was *called* Augustus and
with laurel | the door-posts of my house were [decorated] *publicly* and a
civic [crown] was placed above | my door and a *golden shield* in the Curia

Iulia was put | in place, which the senate and the *Roman People* gave to
20 me because of my courage, cle‖mency, justice and piety, as evidenced
by the shield's | own [inscription.][37] (34.3) After that *time* [I excelled all
men] by my authority, | *but* [I had] no more *official power* than other men
[who were] my | colleagues in each *magistracy*.[38] |

(35.1) [When I was] in my thirteenth consulship, the *senate* and the
25 equestrian order ‖ and the Roman People as a whole *called* me *father* of
my country and | voted that this should be inscribed on the porch of my
house and in the Curia [Iulia] and in the Forum Augustum | below the
four-horse chariot which had been set up for me by decree of the senate.
[When] *I wrote* these words, | I was in my seventy-[sixth] year. |[39]

1 When Augustus died on August 19, AD 14, at Nola in Campania at the age of 76, a
meeting of the senate was called by Tiberius, and various papers of Augustus were
read aloud. These included an account of his *Res Gestae* ('Accomplishments'):
Suetonius, *Augustus* 101; Dio 56.33. In these papers Augustus specified that his *Res
Gestae* were to be engraved on bronze tablets and set up before his mausoleum.
These tablets have never been found, but copies of the text have come to light in
the province of Galatia. The fullest was discovered in the sixteenth century at
Ancyra, and it included the Latin along with a translation into Greek. Further
fragments since then have been found at Antioch toward Pisidia (Latin only, very
fragmentary) and at Apollonia in Pisidia (Greek only, very fragmentary). The
translation given here was made from the Latin copy found at Ancyra, which
extended over six columns of text engraved on the inside wall of the pronaos of the
temple (of Roma and Augustus?). The Greek translation was engraved on the
outside of the right temple wall. The best modern commentary with photographs,
notes, and bibliography is the one by Gagé, *op. cit.* Brief but to the point are the
notes in Volkmann's edition and in the book by P. A. Brunt and J. M. Moore, *Res
Gestae Divi Augusti* (Oxford 1967). For a good political analysis see Z. Yavetz in
Caesar Augustus: Seven Aspects, edited by F. Millar and E. Segal (Oxford 1984) 1–36.
2 Restorations throughout this document are different from those in most of the
others, for here we have available a Greek translation to aid us in filling out the
gaps of the Latin. Square brackets, therefore, in this one document represent a
translation from the existing Greek copy, which presents us almost everywhere
with a control on the Latin. In only one passage (end of 32.1) are we unable to
reconstruct the Latin original when it shows a lacuna: the name of a Germanic king
is missing, but even then only the first part of his name.
3 See Suetonius, *Augustus* 8–13; Nikolaos of Damascus, *Life of Augustus* 13 ff.; Dio 45–6;
Appian, *Bell. Civ.*, Bks. 3–5.
4 Brutus and Cassius were defeated in two battles at Philippi in 42 BC: Dio 47.41ff.;
Appian. *Bell. Civ.* 4.110–31.
5 Further details on colonies and land grants are given below, in Ch. 16. See Brunt,
Manpower, Ch. 15 with Appendix 15.
6 The reference is the sea-battles against Sextus Pompeius and against Antonius at
Actium.
7 The triumphs were over Dalmatia, Actium, and Egypt.
8 See Suetonius, *Augustus* 27.1; Dio 48.54.6. The years in question were November of
43 to December of 38 BC and then from late 37 to December of 32 BC. Why

Augustus here says 'continuous' years is unknown. See Kienast, *Augustus* 32–3, 46, 55, and R. Syme, *Roman Revolution* 277–8 n. 6.

9 Cf. Dio 53.17.8. See Millar, *Emperor* 355ff.

10 On his purge of the senate: Dio 52.42.1–4; 54.13.ff.; 54.35.1; Suetonius, *Augustus* 27.5; Dio 52.42.5. On the census figures and their significance: Brunt, *Manpower*, Chs. 9–10. The word 'lustrum' refers to the purificatory ceremony carried out by the censors after they had completed the census proper.

11 On the tribunician sacrosanctity (in 36 BC): Dio 49.15.5–6. On the full tribunician power (in 23 BC): Dio 53.32.5. See H. Last in W. Schmitthenner, *Augustus* (Darmstadt 1969) 241ff. (= *Rendiconti del Ist. Lomb. di Scienze e Lettere* 84 (1951) 93ff.).

12 Augustus had been away from Italy for three and a half years. The altar (Fortuna Redux) at the Porta Capena was set in place on October 12 of 19 BC. Cf. Dio 54.10.3.

13 Augustus had been absent in Spain and Gaul since 16 BC, returning to Rome on July 4 of 13 BC, and on that day the altar (Ara Pacis) was set up to symbolize peace in the two provincial areas. For the procession that took place see E. Strong in *CAH* 10.546–55 and I. S. Ryberg in *Memoirs of the American Academy in Rome* 19 (1949) 79–101.

14 Cf. above, Document No. 8 sect. 11.

15 See Brunt, *Manpower* 382 with references, and Kienast, *Augustus* 166–7.

16 See Dio 51.4.5–8; Pliny, *Nat. Hist.* 18.114.

17 See Dio 55.25.1–6; Suetonius, *Augustus* 49. Full study by M. Corbier, *L'Aerarium Saturni et l'Aerarium militaire* (Rome 1974).

18 On the whole subject see D. van Berchem, *Les Distributions de blé et d'argent à la plèbe romaine sous l'empire* (Geneva 1939).

19 On the building program of Augustus: E. Strong in *CAH* 10.570ff.; Kienast, *Augustus* 336–43.

20 The practice of subjects in the provinces contributing 'crown gold', i.e. gold to be made into crowns as gifts to the emperor, may have been introduced into Rome during the late Republic: Dio 42.50.2.

21 For the Secular Games see above, Document No. 11.

22 Independent evidence has been found illustrating this general measure at Kyme in Asia Minor: Sherk, *RDGE* 61 = Sherk, *TGDR* 4 No. 95 (above, No. 2).

23 See Dio 53.22.3.

24 The reference is to the victory over Sextus Pompeius in 36 BC.

25 For the oath in 32 BC: Suetonius, *Augustus* 17.2. See R. Syme in *Roman Revolution*, Ch. 20. For its general nature we can examine the oaths taken by provincials that have been preserved on stone: see P. Herrmann, *Der Römische Kaisereid* (Göttingen 1968). Cf., in the present volume, Documents Nos. 15 and 41.

26 See J. G. C. Anderson in *CAH* 10, Ch. 9; R. Syme in *CAH* 10, Ch. 12; Kienast, *Augustus* 274–310 for these campaigns.

27 This is the campaign of C. Petronius, while prefect of Egypt, in 24–22 BC: Strabo 17.1.54: Dio 54ff.

28 This is the campaign of Aelius Gallus, prefect in Egypt, in 25–24 BC: Strabo 16.4.22–4; Dio 53.29.3ff.

29 Tacitus, *Ann.* 2.3; Suetonius, *Tiberius* 9; Dio 54.9.4ff.

30 Suetonius, *Augustus* 21; Dio 55.10a.4–8; Tacitus, *Ann.* 2.4.

31 These were lost in 53 BC with the defeat of Crassus, in 40 BC with the defeat of Decidius Saxa, and in 36 BC with the retreat of M. Antonius.

32 Alternative translation: 'no army of the Roman People before me as Leader', but see L. Wickert in *ANRW* 2.1.16–25.

33 The first Pannonian campaign of 12–9 BC which brought the *ornamenta triumphalia* to Tiberius: Velleius Paterculus 2.96.3; Suetonius, *Tiberius* 9.2; Dio 54.31.4; and 55.2.4.

34 Dio 54.36.2; Strabo 7.3.11; Suetonius, *Augustus* 21.1 and *Tiberius* 7; Florus 2.28.19.

35 Suetonius, *Augustus* 21.3; 43.4; Strabo 6.4.2; 16.1.28; Velleius Paterculus 2.94.4; Tacitus, *Ann.* 2.1.

36 Cf. Dio 53.1–20.

37 On his name 'Augustus': Suetonius, *Augustus* 7.2; Dio 53.16.7–8. The laurel and the civic crown refer to bravery in saving fellow citizens: Dio 53.16.4; Valerius Maximus 2.8.7. See A. Alföldi, *Die zwei Lorbeerbäume des Augustus* (Bonn 1973). For the shield: one of marble has been found at Arelate (Arles), dated to 26 BC, published by F. Benoit in *Revue Archéologique* 39 (1952) 48ff., with Fig. 11. It contains an inscription: 'The senate and the Roman People gave to Imperator Caesar, son of the deified, Augustus in his eighth consulship (26 BC) this shield of Courage, Clemency, Justice, and Piety toward gods and country.' See A. Wallace-Hadrill in *Historia* 30 (1981) 298–323.

38 The Greek translator had difficulty rendering the Latin *auctoritas* ('authority', 'prestige'): Dio 55.3.4–5. The word 'each' in the Latin might be a different word spelled the same and meaning 'also'. Thus: '[who were] also my | colleagues in a magistracy'. The Greek translator has not faced the problem.

39 An Appendix follows, not written by Augustus, summarizing the expenses incurred on public projects.

27 Imperial edict concerning violation of sepulchres. Date disputed: Augustus or Tiberius or Claudius.
Stele of white marble, provenance unknown (Nazareth?). [Greek]

F. Cumont in *Revue Historique* 163 (1930) 241–2 (+ photograph); F. E. Brown in *AJP* 52 (1931) 2; L. Robert, *Collection Froehner*, I: *Inscriptions grecques* (Paris 1936) No. 70 (+ photograph); *FIRA* I 69; **SEG* VIII 13; Ehrenberg–Jones, *Documents*[2] 322.

Cumont, *op. cit.* 241–66; Brown, *op. cit.* 1–29; A. Momigliano, *Claudius: The Emperor and his Achievement* (Oxford 1934) 35–6, 100–1; J. H. Oliver in *Classical Philology* 49 (1954) 180–1; F. De Visscher, *Le Droit des tombeaux romains* (Milan 1963).

Edict of Caesar. | It pleases me, in regard to graves and tombs, | whoever has made them for the cult of ancestors | or children or kinsmen,
5 ‖ that these (things) remain undisturbed | forever; and if someone reports that any|one has either destroyed or in any other | way removed
10 the buried dead | or has moved them to other ‖ locations with evil intentions | to the injustice of the | buried dead or if the tombstones or st|ones have been moved, against a person | of this sort I order that a
15 trial ‖ be started, just as in the case of gods, | (just so) for the cults of mortals. | There will be much greater need | to honor the buried dead.
20 | In general, nobody will have permission to mo‖ve them; otherwise, such a person | will be liable to capital punishment on a charge | of violation of sepulchre. This is my wish.

TIBERIUS
(14–37)
TIBERIUS CAESAR AUGUSTUS

Titles: HOLDER OF THE TRIBUNICIAN POWER:
apparently renewed each year on July 1 (less probably on June
26). When Augustus died, Tiberius was holding the tribunician power for the 16th time (thus XVI to XXXVIII)
CONSUL: AD 18 (III), 21 (IV), 31 (V) PONTIFEX
MAXIMUS

Death: March 16, AD 37.

The *consules ordinarii* **under Tiberius**

AD

15	Drusus Caesar	C. Norbanus Flaccus
16	Sisenna Statilius Taurus	L. Scribonius Libo
17	L. Pomponius Flaccus	C. Caelius Rufus (Nepos?)
18	Ti. Caesar Augustus III	Germanicus Caesar II
19	M. Iunius Silanus Torquatus	L. Norbanus Balbus
20	M. Valerius Messalla Messallinus	M. Aurelius Cotta Maximus Messallinus
21	Ti. Caesar IV	Drusus Caesar II
22	D. Haterius Agrippa	C. Sulpicius Galba
23	C. Asinius Pollio	C. Antistius Vetus
24	Ser. Cornelius Cethegus	L. Visellius Varro
25	Cossus Cornelius Lentulus	M. Asinius Agrippa
26	Cn. Cornelius Lentulus Gaetulicus	C. Calvisius Sabinus
27	L. Calpurnius Piso	M. Licinius Crassus Frugi
28	C. Appius Iunius Silanus	P. Silius Nerva
29	F. Fufius Geminus	L. Rubellius Geminus
30	M. Vinicius	L. Cassius Longinus
31	Ti. Caesar V	L. Aelius Seianus
32	Cn. Domitius Ahenobarbus	L. Arruntius (Furius) Camillus Scribonianus
33	L. Livius Ocella Sulpicius Galba	L. Cornelius Sulla Felix
34	Paullus Fabius Persicus	L. Vitellius
35	C. Cestius Gallus	M. Servilius Nonianus
36	Sex. Papinius Allenius	Q. Plautius
37	Cn. Acerronius Proculus	C. Petronius Pontius Nigrinus

28   Calendar entries for Tiberius.
Extracts from local Italian calendars. [Latin]

A: September 13, AD 16. Fasti Amiternini. Ehrenberg–Jones, *Documents*[2] p. 52; **I. Ital.*
XIII 2, p. 193.

Festival in accordance with a decree of the senate, because on this day the impious plans, which Marcus (Scribonius) Libo had started concerning the safety of Tiberius Caesar and his children and ‖ other leaders of the state and concerning the Republic, were exposed.[1]

5

B: May 26, AD 17. Fasti Amiternini. Ehrenberg–Jones, *Documents*[2] p. 49; *I. Ital.* XIII 2 p. 187.

[Festival in accordance with a decree of the senate, because] on this day | [Germanicus C]aesar | was driven [in triumph into the city.][2]

C: October 10, AD 19. Fasti Antiates. Ehrenberg–Jones, *Documents*[2] p. 53; *I. Ital.* XIII 1 p. 329.

Sacrifices in honor of the dead Germanicus.[3]

D: May 28, AD 20. Fasti Amiternini. Ehrenberg–Jones, *Documents*[2] p. 49; *I. Ital.* XIII 2 p. 187.

[Festival in accordance with a decree of the senate, because] on this day | [Drusus Caesar | was driven in triumph into the city.][4]

E: September 14, AD 23. Fasti Viae dei Serpenti (Oppium). Ehrenberg–Jones, *Documents*[2] p. 52; *I. Ital.* XIII 2 p. 215.

Sacrifices in honor of the dead Drusus Caesar.

F: Fasti Ostienses. Ehrenberg–Jones, *Documents*[2] p. 42; *I. Ital.* XIII 1 pp. 187 and 189.

October 18, AD 31: Sejanus *was strangled.*
October 24, AD 31: Strabo, [Sejanus'] | son, was strangled.
October 26, AD 31: [Apicata,] | (wife) of Sejanus, committed suicide
                    [---.] | Decimus Capito Aelia[nus and] | Iunilla,
                    daughter of Sejanus, lay dead [on the Gemonian
                    steps.][5]

G: Fasti Ostienses. Ehrenberg–Jones, *Documents*[2] p. 43; *I. Ital.* XIII 1 p. 191.

March 16, AD 37: Tiberius Caesar at Misenum | died.
March 29, AD 37: His body | was carried in the city by soldiers.
April 3, AD 37:   (His body) was brought forth in public funeral.[6]

1 The whole affair is described fully by Tacitus, *Ann.* 2.27–32. See Syme, *Tacitus* I 399ff.; Garzetti, *Tiberius to Antonines* 46.
2 The Fasti Ostienses add that his triumph was over Germany.
3 See Tacitus, *Ann.* 2.72–3, for his death. His widow reached Rome in the beginning of the next year with his ashes.
4 The Fasti Ostienses add that his triumph was over Illyricum, and Tacitus (*Ann.* 3.11 and 19) speaks of an ovation rather than a triumph.

5 See Tacitus *Ann.* 5.9, and Dio 58.11.5ff. The Gemonian Steps led down from the
  Aventine Hill and had been the place for public exhibition of dead murderers and
  enemies of the state.
6   See Tacitus, *Ann.* 6.50; Suetonius, *Tiberius* 73, 75; Dio 58.28 and 59.3.7.

29   Edict of the governor of Galatia on requisitioning of transport. AD 14–15 (or AD 18–19?).

Stele of marble with pediments and acroteria. Bilingual, the Latin
(translated here) followed by a Greek translation. Found at Burdur in
Pisidia.

S. Mitchell in **JRS* 66 (1976) 106–31 (+ photograph), with textual corrections in *ZPE*
45 (1982) 99–100; *SEG* XXVI 1392.

Sextus Sotidius Strabo Libuscidianus, legate | of Tiberius Caesar
Augustus with pro praetorian power[1] *vv* proclaims: | It is the most
unjustifiable thing of all for me by my edict to confirm something
about which the Augusti – one of them the greatest of the gods, the
other | the greatest of leaders – have most carefully taken precautions
that nobody should use wheeled vehicles free of charge. However, since
5   the immoderate behavior of certain people ‖ demands a prompt exac-
tion of retribution, I have set up a register of those things which I judge
ought *to be made available* in each and every town | and village. It is my
intention to keep those things under observation and, if they are
neglected, to exact punishment not only through my own power but |
also through the majesty of our excellent Leader, from whom I have
received *precisely this* (message) in written directives.[2] *vv* |
   The People of Sagalassos are obligated to provide the service of ten
wagons and the same number of mules for the use – the unavoid|able
use – of transients and to receive, for each wagon and each schoenus (of
distance),[3] from those who use them ten bronze āsses[4] and for each
10   mule ‖ and each schoenus four bronze āsses, but if they prefer donkeys
they should give two of them at the same price as one mule. | Or, if they
choose otherwise, for each mule and each wagon (the money) which
they would have received, if they themselves had furnished them, *vv* |
they may prefer to give to those people of another town or village to
perform this duty, in order that (the users of the service) might make
the same progress. | And they are obligated to furnish wheeled vehicles
as far as Cormasa and Conana.[5] Nevertheless, not to every|one will be
given the right to this arrangement, but to our excellent Leader's
procurator and his son[6] will be given the use of up to ten wagons, or
15   ‖instead of a single wagon three mules, or instead of a single mule two
donkeys each, (and) for these at the ti|me they use them they are to pay

the price established by me. In addition, the (right to this arrangement will be given) to those in military service, both to those who have a diploma[7] | and to those who travel on military duty, in such a way that for a senator of the Roman People no more than | ten wagons, or instead of a single wagon three mules or instead of a single mule two donkeys each, will be provided. (And such senators) will pay what | I have prescribed. For a Roman eques, who is on duty for our excellent Leader,

20   three wagons, or for a single wagon three mules or ‖ for a single mule two donkeys each, will be the obligation to provide under the same condition. If he needs more, he will have to hire them | at the judgment of the person putting them up for hire. For a centurion (there will be an obligation to provide) a wagon, or three mules or six donkeys, under the same condition. For those who | transport grain or anything at all like that, whether for personal profit or use, it is my wish that nothing be provided, and nothing for anyone for | his own baggage train or for those of their freedmen or slaves. In regard to lodging for all those who are on | my staff and for those on military duty from all provinces and

25   for our excellent Leader's freedmen and their baggage train, ‖ there is an obligation to provide it, in such a way that they do not demand further services, unpaid for, from unwilling people.[8] *vv*

1   Sotidius was a praetorian governor of Galatia. For discussion of the date see G. H. R. Horsley, *New Documents Illustrating Early Christianity* (Macquarie University 1981) 40–2.
2   For the reading of this clause I have relied upon P. Frisch in *ZPE* 41 (1981) 100.
3   Note that for the secondary roads within the province the Roman mile is not used. Mitchell believes the schoenus 'was associated in some way with the [Persian] parasang' and was the distance that could be traveled in an hour.
4   The Roman *ās*, smallest of Roman coins. See the Glossary.
5   Thus, Cormasa and Conana were within the territory belonging to Sagalassos.
6   Reference is to the procurator's son: see G. Alföldy in *Chiron* 11 (1981) 201 n. 163.
7   This kind of a diploma was a 'pass' issued by the emperor to each governor, who could then in turn issue them to his assistants and officers for use on the *cursus publicus*, the imperial post service. See Pliny, *Epist.* 10.45–6, 64, 83, 120–1.
8   Despite all these orders about use of the transport system in the provinces, the abuses continued to the end of the Principate. See Mitchell, *op. cit.* 111–12.

30   Charioteer at the Games in honor of Caesar's Victory. AD 15.

Slab of white marble, perhaps intended to be nailed up in the stables or training school of the charioteers. Rome by the Corso di Porta Pinciana.

CIL VI 37836; *ILS* 9349; Ehrenberg–Jones, *Documents*[2] 362; Gordon, **Album* 1.52 (photograph).

When Drusus Caesar *vv* | and Gaius Norbanus Flaccus *vv* were *consuls* (AD 15), | Menander, (slave) of Gaius Cominius Macer *vv* | and Gaius Cornelius Crispus, as driver of a two-horse chariot was victorious *vv*
5 || in the Ludi Martiales (Games of Mars), which were put on by the consuls, with his horses Basiliscus and Rusticus, | and in the Ludi Victoriae Caesaris (Games of Caesar's Victory),[1] which were put on by Publius Cornelius Scipio | and Quintus Pompeius Macer, the praetors, with his horses Hister and Corax.

1   Perhaps celebrated because of the victory of Germanicus in Germany: Tacitus, *Ann.*
    1.55. However, triumphal honors were decreed in that same year to Aulus Caecina,
    Lucius Apronius, and Gaius Silius: Tacitus, *Ann.* 1.72.

31   Letter of Tiberius refusing divine honors. AD 15.
Stone stele, Gytheion in Laconia. [Greek]

S. B. Kougeas in *Helleniká* 1 (1928) 7–44, 152–7 (+ photograph); *SEG* XI 922;
Ehrenberg–Jones, *Documents*[2] 102b. Cf. Tacitus, *Ann.* 4.38; Dio 56.35–42; Suetonius,
Tiberius 26.

M. I. Rostovtzeff in *Revue Historique* 143 (1930) 1–26; L. R. Taylor in *TAPA* 60 (1929)
87–111; *idem*, *Divinity* 239 ff.; A. D. Nock in *CAH* 10.494–5; M. P. Charlesworth in *PBSR*
15 (1939) 1–10; Garzetti, *Tiberius to Antoninus* 570–2; Price, *Rituals* 72.

vv [Letter of Tiber]ius.[1] *vv* | [Tiberius Caesar,] son of the [god Aug]ustus, Augustus, pontifex maximus, holding the tribunician power | [for the sixteenth time (AD 15),] to the Gytheian ephors and the city, greetings. When he was sent by you | [to] me and my mother
5   as an envoy, Decimus Turranius Nikanor || *delivered* your letter to me, to which had been attached the items voted into law | [by] you to show your piety for my father and your esteem for us. | [For] these things I praise you and believe it fitting that in general all me|n and in particular your city should hold in reserve – because of the great size of the | benefits of my father to all the world – the honors that are appropriate
10 || for gods; || I myself am content with more moderate honors, as befit men. My mo|ther will give you her answer, when she learns from you what decision you have made about honors for her.

1   Preceding this heading on the stone are the mutilated remains of what must have
    been a decree of Gytheion.

32   Sacred law for a festival of the imperial cult. About AD 15.
Stone stele, Gytheion in Laconia. [Greek]

S. B. Kougeas in *helleniká* 1 (1928) 16–38 (∥ photograph); *SEG* XI 923; Ehrenberg–Jones, *Documents*[2] 102a.

M. I. Rostovtzeff in *Revue Historique* 143 (1930) 1–26; Price, *Rituals* 210–11; A. Wilhelm, *Griechische Inschriften Rechtlichen Inhalts* (Athens 1951) 87–8 (textual corrections).

[--∥-|-] |[1] (The agoranomos)[2] shall celebrate the first day for god Caesa|r, son of a god, Augustus the Savior and Deliverer, the second day for Imperator [Ti]∥berius Caesar Augustus and father of his
10   country, the third day for Iulia Augusta, ∥ the Fortune of our nation and city, and the fourth day for Germanicus Caesar, (a day) of Vic|tory, and the fifth day for Drusus Caesar, (a day) of Aphrodite, and the sixth day for Titus Quinctius | Flamininus,[3] and he shall see to the good order of the contestants. And he shall render | an account of all the payment for the performers and for the administering of the sacred funds to the city | after the contest at the first meeting of the Assembly. If he is found to
15   have misappropriated funds or to have submitted a false account, ∥ if convicted he shall no longer hold any public office and his possessions shall be confiscated. Whatever of them are confiscated, | these shall be sacred property and from them the archons of the year shall construct additional ornamentation (for the city). | Any citizen of Gytheion who wishes shall have permission to act as public advocate for the sacred funds with impuni|ty. *vv* After the celebration of the days of the gods and the rulers, the agoranomos shall introduce thy|melic games[4] for two more days of performances, one to the memory of Gaius Iulius
20   Eurykles,[5] ∥ benefactor of our nation and city in many ways, and a second for the honor of Ga|ius Iulius Laco,[6] guardian of our nation and our city's security and safety. | He shall celebrate the games of the goddess on whatever days he can, and when from office | he takes his departure, the city shall hand over to the one who happens to be (the next) agoranomos, by public document, all the sacrificial victims for the games, | and the city shall obtain a hand-written receipt from the
25   one who receives them. When the agoranomos ∥ celebrates the thymelic games, he shall conduct a procession from the temple of Asklepios and Health, | including in it all the ephebes and young men and other citizens wearing garlands of bay leaves, | and in white clothing. They shall be accompanied in the procession by the sacred maidens and the women in | their sacred clothing. And when the procession comes to the Caesareion (temple of Caesar), the ephors shall sacrifice a bu|ll on behalf of the safety of our rulers and gods and the eternal continuance
30   of their rule, and ∥ after their sacrificing they shall constrain the common messes and the collective magistracies to sacrifice in the agora. And if they do not con|duct the procession or do not sacrifice or after sacrificing do not constrain the | common messes and collective magis-

tracies to sacrifice in the agora, they shall pay to the gods two thousand sacred drachmas. Permission shall be given to any | citizen of Gytheion who wishes to accuse them. *vv* While Chairon is strategos[7] and priest of go|d Augustus Caesar, the ephors who are colleagues of Terentius

35 Biades shall deliver three painted images[8] of the go‖d Augustus and Iulia Augusta and Tiberius Caesar Augustus, and for the theater (they shall deliver) the | platform for the chorus and four doors for stage performances and footstolls for the orchestra. And they shall erect a ste|le of stone with an inscription on it of this sacred law and they shall deposit in the public archives | a copy of the sacred law, in order that, reposing in a public place and in the open air for everyone to see, this la|w may continuously display the gratitude of the People of Gytheion

40 toward their rulers for all me‖n (to see). And if they do not inscribe this law or do not erect the stele in front of the temple or do not write | up [a copy ----]

1 The first six lines are mutilated. They contain bare references to the imperial family, their images, a table in the theater, sacrifices, and performances on behalf of the Roman rulers.
2 The agoranomos was an official in a Greek city who kept public order in the market, supervised the food supply, and maintained the market buildings. His duties were often broadened to include other civic functions.
3 Quinctius Flamininus (cos. 198 BC), the victor over Philip V in 197 BC, had been deeply involved in the war against King Nabis in the Peloponnese and had freed Gytheion from his domination.
4 Thymelic games: see above, Document No. 11, n. 12.
5 Gaius Iulius Eurykles, dynast of Sparta, had aided Augustus at Actium and had been given control of Sparta. See G. W. Bowersock in *JRS* 51 (1961) 112ff. and in his *Augustus* 59–60.
6 Laco was the son of Iulius Eurykles.
7 A local magistrate.
8 For these cult images see L. Robert, *Opera Minora* 2.832ff.

33 Germanicus at the Olympic Games. AD 17.
Limestone block from a base (for a pedestal?), Olympia. [Greek]

I. Olympia 221; **SIG³* 792.

Germanicus Caesar, son of Imperator | Tiberius Caesar Augustus, | victorious in the Olympic Games with his chariot drawn by four fully-grown horses.[1] | (This monument to him was erected by) Marcus

5 Antonius Peisanus, ‖ to his own patron. To Olympian Zeus.

1 The name of Germanicus, in a corrupted form, appears in the official list of victors under the 199th Olympiad (AD 17).

34   Germanicus in Egypt. AD 18–19.

A: E. G. Turner in *P. Oxy.* 2435 recto (+ photograph). Papyrus from Oxyrhynchus in
Egypt. [Greek]. **B**: U. von Wilamowitz-Moellendorf and F. Zucker in *Sitzungsberichte der
Preussischen Akademie der Wissenschaften* (Berlin 1911) 794ff.; *SB* 3924; Ehrenberg–Jones,
*Documents[2] 320. Papyrus from Egypt, AD 19. [Greek] Cf. Tacitus, *Ann.* 2.59–61.
C: Wilcken, *Chrestomathie* 413. Ostracon from Thebes in Egypt. January 25, AD 19.
[Greek]

C. Cichorius, *Römische Studien* (Stuttgart 1922) 375–88; F. De Visscher in *Muséon* 1946,
259–66; Turner, *op. cit.* 102ff.; Goodyear, *Annals* (II) 372–6 and Appendix 3; D. G.
Weingaertner, *Die Aegyptenreise des Germanicus* (Bonn 1969); D. Hennig in *Chiron* 2 (1972)
349–65.

A. *P. Oxy.* 2435 recto, Oxyrhynchus

[The] exegetēs:[1] 'I have given to the Imperator himself both | decrees.'
vv The Imperator:[2] 'Having been sent | [by my] *father*, men of Alexandria
5   [---]' | [The] crowd shouted: 'Hurrah, lord, good luck! ‖ You will receive
much good luck.' *vv* The Imperator: 'Great importance | have you
placed, men of Alexan[dria,] | on my speech, but wait until I complete
my remarks to each of your questions and then give your | approval. As
10   I said, I have been sent by my father ‖ to set in order the overseas
provinces[3] | – a most difficult command, first of all because of the |
sailing and because of the separation from my father and grandmother
| and mother and sisters and brothers and children and close friends |
15   [----] present *command* [----‖---] the house [---] | and a new sea, first of
all, that I might see you|r city [---]' The crowd shouted: 'Good luck!' |
The Imperator: 'I already thought that it was | a brilliant sight, first of
20   all because of the ‖ hero and founder (of Alexandria), to whom there is
a common *debt* | for those who cling to the same (goals),[4] and then
because of the bene|fits of my grandfather Augustus and my father |
[---] as is just for you toward me, and I keep silent [---]' | [The crowd]
25   shouted | 'Live on, a longer life!' The Imperator: ‖ '[---] about what each
of you knows, and I remembered how I found these (greetings) becom-
ing larger and | larger, stored up as they were in your | *prayers*. For
decrees have been written up to grant honors by a few men in their
assemblies [---|---].'

B. Ehrenberg–Jones, *Documents*[2] 320, papyrus from Egypt

(First edict) [Germanicus Caesar, Augustus' | son, grandson of the
deified Augustus, | proconsul, declares: in anticipation of my | visit I
5   hear now] ‖ that *requisitions* [---- of boats] | and beasts of burden have
been made and | the rights of hospitality appro|priated by force for my
10   lodging, | and private citizens terrorized. ‖ I have thought it necessary
to make it cle|ar that no boat | or beast shall be taken by anyone, and

15   that is my wish, | unless Baebius | my friend and secretary ‖ issues an
order, and the rights of hospitality shall not be appro|priated. For if
there is such a need, Baebius himself | fairly and justly will distribute
20   the lodging. | For the requisitioned | boats or animals ‖ payment will be
given according to | my schedule. Such is my order. | Those who oppose
my order | I wish to be brought before my secretary, | who will himself
25   forbid the in‖jury of private citizens, or he will re|port to me. In the
passage through the city | of beasts of burden I forbid those who happen
| upon them to take them by force. | For that is an act of acknowledged
30   ‖ robbery. |
    (Second edict) Germanicus Caesar, son of Augustus, | grandson of
the deified Augustus, proconsul, | declares: your goodwill, | which you
35   always display whenever you se‖e me, I accept, but odious | to me are
your shouts (appropriate only to) the godlike, | and I decline them in
every way. | They are fitting for the true savior only | and the benefactor
40   of the entire ‖ race of men, my | father and his mother (who is) my |
grandmother. Whatever merits I have are the consequences of their
45   divinity (alone), so that | if you do not obey me, you force me ‖ not to
appear before you very often.

C. Wilcken, *Chrestomathie* 413, Thebes in Egypt

Payment has been made into the *bank* at Great Diospolis by Phatres, |
son of Psenthotes, for the price of the wheat from the granary [---|---]
for the visit of Germanicus | Caesar [---,] debased drachmas [---]. Year
5   5 of Tiberius ‖ Caesar Augustus. Tybe 30 (January 25). Menedoros.[5]

1   The exact nature of this document is not clear, for it is neither an official document
    of the government nor a strictly private record. 'A kind of pamphlet literature which
    passed from hand to hand' (Turner) was common in Alexandria and the present
    document may be one aspect of it. The exegetēs figures regularly as an Alexandrian
    spokesman in such texts.
2   He is Germanicus, the elder son of Drusus and Antonia, and adopted by Tiberius.
3   Cf. Tacitus, *Ann.* 2.43 for the *maius imperium* granted to Germanicus by senatorial
    decree. He thought such authority included Egypt.
4   The reference is to the feats of Alexander the Great.
5   Phatres was ordered to provide wheat for Germanicus and company. When he could
    not provide it, he had to pay a money penalty into the local bank. The money was
    used to purchase wheat from the public granary. Our ostracon is the receipt given to
    him by Menedoros.

35   Roman upper classes forbidden to participate in public performances. AD 19.

Bronze tablet, cut down to be used for a tablet of patronage on the other
side, Larinum in Italy.

M. Malavolta in *Studi pubblicati del Istituto Italiano per la Storia Antica* 27 (Rome 1978) 347ff.; B. Levick in **JRS* 73 (1983) 98. Cf. Dio 48.43.2ff.; 54.2.5; 56.25.7ff.

Levick, *op. cit.* 99–115.

Decree of the senate. *vv* | [---] on the Palatine in the portico which is by the (temple) of Apollo. Present at the writing were: Gaius Ateius, son of Lucius, (of the tribe) Aniensis, Capito; Sextus Pomp[eius, son of Sextus, (of the tribe) ---;|--] Octavius, son of Gaius, (of the tribe) Stellatina, Fronto; Marcus Asinius, son of Curtius, (of the tribe) Arnensis, Mamilianus; Gaius Gavius, son of Gaius, (of the tribe) Poplilia, Macer, quaestor; Aulus Did[ius ----] Gallus, quaestor. |

    [Whereas Marcus Silan]us (and) Norbanus Balbus, the consuls (AD 19), said that they had composed a memorandum, just as they had

5   been commissioned to do, [----] ‖ pertaining to [---][1] or to those who, contrary to the dignity of their social order, had [appeared] on the stage or in the games [or had agreed | to enter the arena,] punishable by decrees of the senate which had been passed in that regard in earlier years,[2] and thus had committed an offense by which [they had diminished] the majesty of the senate, [concerning the pleasure of the senate about what action should be taken in this matter, concerning this matter the senate has decided as follows:] | *it is the senate's pleasure* that no senator's son, daughter, grandson, granddaughter, great-grandson, great-granddaughter, or that no man [whose father or grand-father,] | whether paternal or maternal, or whose brother, or that no woman whose husband or father, whether paternal or [maternal, or whose brother] | ever had the [right] of watching the games in seats reserved for equestrians, should be brought on the stage by anyone or

10   that they should be [requested] for a fee [to fight ‖ in the arena] or to remove the plumes (from the helmets) of gladiators or to take the foil (from a gladiator) or in any other way to furnish a service of similar (servile) nature;[3] [and that nobody] | should hire him, if any (of the above persons) offered [himself;] no one of those persons should hire himself out, and it is for that reason that diligent care must be exercised in preventing that (from happening), [because there have been some (?)] | who, having the right to sit in seats reserved for equestrians, had, for the purpose of evading the authority of that social order, | seen to it either that they did incur [public disgrace] or that they were con-demned in a notorious court case and then, after they had [voluntarily withdrawn from] | their equestrian seats, had agreed to enter the arena or to appear on stage; and no one of those persons [mentioned above,

15   if he (or she) acted contrary to the dignity of their social or‖der (?),] should have proper burial, unless any of them had already appeared on the stage or [had hired out their] services [for the arena] or | were born

from – whether male or female – an actor or gladiator or gladiatorial manager or a procurer. | [And in regard to what was] written or [provided for (?) in the senatorial] decree which was passed on the motion of Manius Lepidus and Titus Statilius Taurus, the consuls (AD 11), [that no free-born female who | was less than] twenty years old or that no free-born male who was less than twenty-five years old should be permitted to enter the arena or to hire out his services [for the arena or stage (?) |---,] except for any of them who by the deified Augustus or by
20   Tiberius Caesar Aug[ustus ---||---]⁴

1 Perhaps: '[concerning things] pertaining to [the lust for women]' or '[concerning things] pertaining to [the deception of women]'. Cf. Suetonius, *Tiberius* 35.2 and Tacitus, *Ann.* 2.85.1ff. See Levick, *op. cit.* 110–14.
2 For earlier decrees and evidence on the same subject see Levick, *op. cit.* 105–8, who cites Dio 48.43.2; 54.2.5; 56.25.7ff.
3 Such actions were considered demeaning and on a par with actually acting like a gladiator.
4 Several long clauses are extant from the last lines (20–1), but the key phrases that make them intelligible are missing.

36   Honors for the dead Germanicus. AD 19–20.

A: Tabula Siarensis: two fragments of bronze found at Siarum near modern Seville, in Baetica. [Latin] J. González in *ZPE* 55 (1984) 55–100. **B**: Tabula Hebana: bronze tablet badly damaged and in three parts, margin missing on right side, found at Heba in Etruria. [Latin] P. Raveggi, A. Minto, and U. Coli in *Notizie degli Scavi* 72 (1947) 49–68 (+ photograph); U. Coli in *La Parola del Passato* 21 (1951) 433–8 (two new fragments); J. H. Oliver and R. E. A. Palmer in *AJP* 75 (1954) 225–48 (+ photograph); Ehrenberg–Jones, *Documents*² 94a; Gordon, *Epigraphy* No. 36 (+ photograph); F. J. Lomas in *Habis* 9 (1978) 323–54. See G. Tibiletti, *Principe e magistrati repubblicani* (Rome 1963) *passim*; Oliver–Palmer, *loc. cit.*; A. H. M. Jones in *JRS* 45 (1955) 9–21 (*Studies* 27–50); R. Syme, *Tacitus* II 756–60; P. A. Brunt in *JRS* 51 (1961) 71ff.; E. S. Staveley, *Greek and Roman Voting and Elections* (Ithaca, NY 1972) 218–20; J. Béranger, *Principatus* (Geneva 1973) 209–42; Lomas, *op. cit.*

For both documents see Tacitus, *Ann.* 2.73, 2.82–3, 3.1–6; *CIL* VI 911 (31199).

A.   Tabula Siarensis, Siarum in Baetica

(Fragment I)
[--- for the purpose of preserving the memory of Germanicus Caes]|ar, who ought never to die away, [--- the senate has decided that a decree of the senate shall be passed concerning | the honors] owed to Germanicus Caesar [---, and therefore it has pleased (the senate) that there shall be a discussion | about] this matter together with the advice
5   of Tiberius Caesar Augustus, [our] *Leader*, [and that a document] || shall be prepared for him with the total amount of (senatorial) opinions (about such honors), and that he (the emperor), with his customary

[indulgence,] shall select [from all the] | honors, which the senate decided should be granted, [those which Tiberius Caesar Augustus and] | Augusta his mother and Drusus Caesar and the mother of Germanicus Ca[esar and Agrippina his wife,] | invited by them also (to take part) in the deliberation, will have judged appropriate enough to be granted (to Germanicus). [Concerning this matter it has been decided as follows:] |

It has pleased (the senate) that a marble archway shall be con-
10   structed in the Circus Flaminius at [public expense, set up] ‖ in the place where statues [have already been dedicated] to the deified Augustus and to the Augustan House | by Gaius Norbanus Flaccus,[1] together with *gilded* reliefs of the defeated nations [and with an inscription] | on the front of the archway (stating) that the senate and Roman People had *dedicated* this [marble] monument | to the memory of Germanicus Caesar after he had defeated the Germans in war [and then] | had cleared them out of Gaul, recovered our military standards,[2]
15   avenged the perfidious [defeat] ‖ of the army of the Roman People, established the status of the Gauls, and had been sent as proconsul to the overseas *provinces* [of Asia] |[3] to give shape to them and to the king-doms of the same area in accordance with the orders of Tiberius Caesar Au[gustus, and had placed] a ki|ng on (the throne of) Armenia, not sparing his labor until by decree of the senate [an ovation was granted to him] | and he had died for the sake of the Republic; (it has also pleased the senate) that above this archway a statue of Ger[manicus Caesar] | shall be erected, (with him) in a triumphal chariot and at his
20   sides shall be statues of D[rusus Germanicus his father,] ‖ the natural brother of Tiberius Caesar Augustus, and of Antonia his mother, [and of Agrippina his wife, and of Li]|via his sister, and of Tiberius Germanicus his brother, and of his sons and *daughters*. |

(It has also pleased the senate that) a second archway shall be con-structed in the grove of mount Amanus which is in [the province of Syria, or in any other place which | may seem] more suitable to Tiberius Caesar Augustus, our Leader, [in the regions which | had come under] the care and protection of Germanicus Caesar in accordance with the
25   authority [of Tiberius Caesar Augustus;] ‖ likewise, his statue shall be erected (there) and an inscription engraved on it that is consistent [with the accomplishments of Germanicus Caesar;] | a third archway or [monument shall be constructed at the bank of the Rhine round about the tomb] | which [the army of the Roman People had speedily raised up] for Drusus the brother of Tiberius Caesar Augustus, [our Leader,] | and then later had been *finished* with the permission of the deified Augustus, [and, likewise, an honorary tomb of Germanicus Cae]|sar shall be raised up (which will show him) receiving [suppli-

30   cations from Germans and especially from the Gau]‖ls and the
Germans who [live] on this side of the Rhine [and whose states had
been ordered by the deified] | Augustus to [perform] a divine ceremony
at the tomb [of Drusus;[4] and (likewise) they shall give to his memory a
solemn and ritual] | sacrifice, performing the rites at his tomb [each
year on the day when Germanicus Caesar passed away;] | and since
35   there was in the region [----] | of Germanicus Caesar [-----] ‖

Likewise, it has pleased the senate that a [marble sepulchre shall be
erected to the memory of Germanicus Caesar at Antioch] | in the forum
[where the body of Germanicus Caesar had been cremated ---,] | and
that [at Epidaphna, where Germanicus Caesar had breathed his last, a
platform shall be constructed ----,][5] *vacat*

(Fragment II)
(Col. a) [--- (And it has pleased the senate) that on the sixth day before
the Ides of October (October 10) each year in front of the altar,] which
is | [in front of the tomb of Germanicus Caesar,] ceremonies to his
spirit shall be performed [publicly to his memory | by the masters of the
sodales] Augustales[6] clothed in the [dark] togas of mourning, whose |
[legal and divine right it is to wear] the toga of that color on that day,
5   with the same ritual of sacrifice as ‖ [is performed publicly in the
ceremonies] to the spirits of Gaius and Lucius Caesar; and that a
bronze tombstone next to the | [tomb of Germanicus Caesar] likewise
shall be engraved, so that these decrees of the senate may be inscribed
on it which | [pertain to his honors,] and that on that day no permission
to conduct publicly any serious business | [shall be given to the magis-
trates in charge of the administration of justice in a] municipality or a
colony of Roman or Latin citizens, | [and that on that day no public
banquets hereafter] or weddings of Roman citizens or betrothals shall
10   take place, ‖ [and that nobody] shall take [from anyone money that is
owed (to him)] or shall give it to anyone, and that no public games shall
be presented or | [looked at, and that nothing at all connected with the
games] shall be done. *vv* And (it has pleased the senate) that the Scenic
Games of Augustus,[7] | [which] customarily [take place on the fourth
day before the Ides of October (October 12) in memory of the deified
Augus]tus, shall be presented on the fifth day before the Kalends of
November (October 28) with a | [postponement of two nundinae,[8]
beginning with] that day on which Germanicus Caesar died, | [in order
that his funerary ceremonies may not be marred] by a day of scenic
games. *vv*
(Col. b) [-----|-- Tiberius Caesar Augustus, our] Leader, | [-----] day
5 | [----] and an address ‖ [----] to approve | [----] urban tribes and | [----]
promised; therefore it has pleased | [the senate that the urban plebs

shall erect at public expense statues of Germa]nicus Caesar with
triumphal cloak | [in those temples and in] those public places in which
10   the deified Augus‖[tus and Augusta] had erected (statues) [for Drusus
Germanicus, his (i.e. Germanicus Caesar's) father,] together with an
inscription of the urban plebs' | [thirty-five tribes; and that likewise]
the verse,[9] which Tiberius Caesar Augustus set forth before this
(senatorial) order on the 17th day before the Kalends of January
(December 16) | [to praise the dead Germanicus,] shall be engraved on
bronze and set up in whatever public place | might please [his father;][10]
and the senate thought it would be even more just, because | the most
intimate [document of Tiberius] Caesar Augustus and of Germanicus
15   Caesar, his son, contained not so much a prai‖se as a methodical order-
ing of his whole life and a true testimony of his excellence, | that it
should be passed on to eternal memory, and (because) he himself had
testified in that same document that he did not wish to dissimulate |
and (because) he judged that it would be useful for the youth of our
children and descendants. |

Likewise, in order that the piety of Drusus Caesar might be even
better attested, it has pleased (the senate) that the document which he
| had read aloud at the last meeting of the senate shall be inscribed on
bronze and fixed in position in whatever place might be pleasing to his
20   father and himself. ‖

And, likewise, (it has pleased the senate) that this decree of the
senate shall be inscribed on bronze together with that decree of the
senate which was passed on the 17th day before the Kalends of January
(December 16) and that the bronze (tablet) shall be fixed in position on
the Palatine in | the portico which is next to the temple of Apollo, where
the senate held its meeting. Likewise, the senate wished | and decided
it was just, in order that the piety of all the orders toward the Augustan
House and the con|sent of all citizens for honoring the memory of
Germanicus Caesar might appear more easily, that the consuls | shall
publish this decree of the senate with an edict of their own and shall
25   order the magistrates and legates of municipalities and colonies ‖ to
send out a copy of it to the municipalities and colonies of Italy and to
those colonies which are in | the provinces, and that also those men
who are in charge in the provinces would act rightly and in proper form
if they would see to it that this decree of the senate | is fixed in position
in the most frequented place. And (it has pleased the senate) that
Marcus Messalla (and) Marcus Aurelius | Cotta Maximus, consuls
designate (for AD 20), as soon as they enter the magistracy and when
by the | auspices it is permitted them, without delay of two or three
30   nundinae, shall see to the passage of a law before the People ‖ about
honors for Germanicus Caesar.[11] Decreed. In the senate 285 (senators)

were present. This decree of the senate, by a second session, | was made into one (with the decree of December 16).

(Col. c)[12] And (it has pleased the senate) that on the Palatine [in the portico by the temple of Apollo, in which the senate] | is accustomed to meet, [amid the images of men of illustrious character shall be placed

15   those of Germanicus Caesar] ‖ and Drusus Ger[manicus, his natural father and brother of Tiberius Caesar Augustus,] | who was also himself (i.e. Drusus Germanicus) [of creative ability, (the images to be placed) on the capitals] | of the columns [of that pediment by which the statue of Apollo is protected.] | And (it has pleased the senate) that the Salii[13] [shall place] in their *hymns* [the name of Germanicus Caesar to honor] | his memory, [which honor was also granted to Gaius and Lucius Caesar, brothers of Tiberius] ‖ Caesar Augu[stus, and that to the ten centuries of the Caesars, which | are accustomed to cast their vote for the destinatio[14]] of consuls and praetors, [there shall be added | five centuries.][15]

B. Tabula Hebana, Heba in Etruria

[----] And (it has pleased the senate)[16] that on the Palatine in the portico by the temple of Apollo, in which the senate is accustomed to meet, [amid the ima|ges] of men of illustrious character shall be placed those of Germanicus Caesar and Drusus Germanicus, his natural father and brother | of Tiberius Caesar Augustus, who was himself (i.e. Drusus Germanicus) of creative ability, (the images to be placed) on the capitals of the columns of *that pe|diment* by which the statue of Apollo is protected. *vv*

5   And (it has pleased the senate) that the Salii[17] shall place in their hymns the name of Germanicus Caesar to ‖ honor his memory, which honor was also granted to Gaius and Lucius Caesar, brothers of Tiberius Caesar Augustus. *vv*

[And (it has pleased the senate) that to the ten] | centuries of the Caesars, which are accustomed to cast their vote for the destinatio[18] of consuls and praetors, there shall be added five centuries. [And since] | the first ten will be named for Gaius and Lucius Caesar, the following (five new centuries will be named) for Germanicus Caesar, and in all these [centuries] | the senators and equites of all the jury-panels, which have been or will be constituted for public trials, shall | cast their votes; and whatever magistrate, for the purpose of making the destinatio, will send out the call to the senators and to those permitted

10   to express their opinions in the senate ‖ and also to the equites for them to assemble in the voting area – in accordance with the law which L. Valerius Messalla Volesus and Gnaeus Cornelius Cin[na Magnus,] | the consuls (AD 5), passed – (to assemble) for the purpose of casting

their votes, that (magistrate) [shall take care] that the senators and
also the equites of all jury-panels, which │ have been or will be consti-
tuted for the sake of *public* [trials,] shall cast their votes, as far as this
[can be done, in │ fifteen centuries;] in regard to whatever casting of lots
in accordance with that law among the so-called 900 (voting) guards[19]
for ten centuries [has been pro│vided or prescribed] to be carried out,
that person who in accordance with that law or this bill will be required

15   to cast those lots among the so-called 900 guards ‖ shall do so for fifteen
centuries, just as if in that law he were required to make or hold │ a
casting of lots among the 900 guards for fifteen centuries. *vv*

And (it has pleased the senate) that on the day on which, in accordance with the law which L. Valerius M[essalla Vole]│sus and Gnaeus
Cornelius Cinna Magnus, the consuls, passed, or in accordance with
this bill, the senators and equites [will be required] to be present for
the purpose of casting their votes, the person (in charge) │ shall, in the
presence of the praetors and tribunes of the plebs, order fifteen large
wicker baskets to be placed before his tribunal, into which the *tablets for
vo│ting* shall be deposited; and likewise he shall order the waxed tablets

20   to be placed behind the baskets, as many as [will be needed] ‖ in his
estimation; and likewise he shall see to it that whitened tablets, on
which the names of the candidates have been written, shall be located
in a place where they can be most *easily* [read.] │ Then, in sight of all the
magistrates and those who are [about to cast] their votes, │ while they
are sitting on the benches, just as they were accustomed to sit when the
votes were cast for the ten centuries of the Caesars, [the person (in
charge)] │ shall order the voting-balls, as nearly equal in weight as
possible, of the thirty-three tribes, (the tribes) of Succusana and
Esquilina being excepted,[20] to be thrown into a revolving urn, and he
shall order the *cas│ting of lots* to be proclaimed. This casting of lots shall
determine which senators and equites will cast their votes into what

25   basket. Although for the first [centuries] ‖ which are named for Gaius
and Lucius Caesar the casting of lots shall be made in such a way that
two tribes each shall be allotted to the first, second, third, and fourth
baskets, │ three (tribes each) to the fifth basket, two (tribes) each to the
sixth, seventh, eighth, and ninth (baskets), and three (tribes each) to
the tenth, for the centuries which are named for Germanicus Caesar
the *casting of lots* [shall be made in such a way] │ that two tribes each shall
be allotted to the eleventh, twelfth, thirteenth, and fourteenth baskets,
and three tribes to the fifteenth (basket); with the result that, when he
calls out one tribe to vote, *whichever one* [the lot] has de│termined, [he
shall call out ---][21] the senators and those permitted to express their
opinions in the senate – (all of) whom will be from that (one) tribe – │
and he shall order them to step up to the first basket and cast their

votes; then, when *they have cast their votes* in that way and returned to

30   their [benches,] ‖ from that same tribe he shall call out the equites
[and] order them to cast their votes [into] the same basket; *then* [the
next and] | the next tribe (and so forth) shall cast their votes and *in such
a way* [shall he call out] the senators and then the equites of each [of all
the tribes that] they cast their votes [into that basket wherein] | they
ought to cast them; [then provision will be made] concerning votes of
any (senators or equites) [from the tribes of Succusana] | or Esquilina,
and likewise (will he act) if in any tribe there will be no senator or no
eques, (or) [if] there will be [less than five] senators [and equites;] |
(and) likewise in regard to the sealing of the baskets when the votes
have been cast and in regard to the [transporting (of the baskets)] to
the praetors who are or will be in charge of the Aerarium, (the person

35   in charge will see to it) [that with the votes] ‖ of the destinatio (procedure) they will be carried into the Saepta;[22] and the verification of the
seals and the sorting of the votes, [all the things which have been
written or included] for the purpose of [---|--] in that law which the
consuls Cinna and Volesus passed concerning the ten centuries of the
Caesars, [(the person in charge) will watch | over,] and he shall see to
it that he does and brings about all the same things for the fif<teen>
centuries that must be done and brought about as he ought to do and
bring about in accordance with that law *which* [Cinna and Volesus, the
consuls,] | *passed* [for the ten] *centuries of the Caesars*, and whatever will
have been thus done will be legal [and valid. Then, when the so|rting]
of the votes [on the destinatio of consuls and praetors] from the fifteen
centuries of Gaius and Lucius Caesar and Germanicus Caesar [has
been completed, and when the tablet (of the result of the voting) of the

40   century has been brought forward ‖ – whatever one that may be] – the
person who will have this destinatio [will read out] (the result) of that
tablet [in the same way as that person who, in accordance with the law
| which L. Valerius Messall]a Volesus and Gnaeus Cornelius Cinna
Magnus, the consuls, passed for the ten centuries [of the Caesars,] was
obliged to read [that tablet which | had been drawn by lot from those
(ten) centuries,] provided that care be taken that whatever tablet of
[each] century of Gaius [and Lucius Caesar comes out by lot, | that
(same) tablet under the name] of Gaius and Lucius Caesar must be
read aloud, and that whatever candidates have been destinated by that
century each one of them | (by name) must be read aloud under the
names of those (two Caesars), (and provided that care be taken) that
whatever tablet of those centuries, named for Germanicus Cae[sar in

45   accordance with this bill, comes out by lot, ‖ that (same) tablet] under
the name of Germanicus Caesar must be read aloud, and that whatever
candidates [have been destinated] by that century [each one of them

(by name) | likewise] must be pronounced aloud. And that group of centuries which has been added by this bill to the *group* [of centuries of Gaius and Lucius Caesar] |[23] shall function (as voting units) just as it was *specifically* and comprehensively provided in the law which Cinna and [Volesus, the consuls, have passed,] | for said group of ten centuries to function; and that person who [will hold the assembly] for the election of consuls and praetors shall, *after* the destinatio [is performed,][24] see to it that | their count shall be taken and that the vote shall thus be cast. Other details which *have not been* expressly *mentioned*
50   in this bill, all of them, || shall be done and brought about and protected just as (one will find them) in accordance with the law passed by Cinna and Volesus, the consuls.

And (it has pleased the senate) that at the Games of Augu[stus, when the benches of the sodales (priests)] | are placed in the theaters, the curule chairs of Germanicus Caesar shall be placed among them with [oak crowns in memory] | of his priesthood. When the temple of the deified Augustus will be completed, those chairs shall be [carried] from that temple, but they shall be placed [meanwhile in the temple] | of Mars the Avenger and carried from there. And whoever will conduct the Games described above shall see to it that from the temple described above | the (chairs) will be placed in the theaters and, when they are to be removed, they will be replaced in that temple.

And (it has pleased the senate) that [on the day when provision has
55   been made that the bones of Germanicus] || Caesar are to be brought to the tomb, the temples of the gods shall be closed and the men of [each] order (senatorial and equestrian) shall go to the procession; and those who have the broad-stri|ped (toga) and wish to do their duty and [are not impeded] by health or [death] in the family, [and including those without the broad]|-striped (toga) who possess the public horse (and wear the narrow-striped) trabea[25] – all of them shall come to the Campus Martius.

And (it has pleased the senate) that for the [memory of Germanicus Caesar on the day on which he di]|ed the temples of the immortal gods which [are or ever will be] in the city of Rome or closer than [one mile] to the city [of Rome] | shall be closed each year on that day. And those who have or [will have] contracts for supervision of those temples [shall make provisions] that this may be done. [And for his memory,
60   the masters] || of the sodales Augustales, whoever they will be in each year, shall see to it that sacrifices to the dead will be performed before his tomb [on that same day to the spirit of Germanicus Cae]|sar, or, if the masters, one or more, [should not be able to be present] for the sacrifice, those who during the nex|t year will be obligated to perform

the office of master [shall perform them] in place of those who [were not able to perform] this duty. [----]

1 He was consul ordinarius with Drusus Caesar in AD 15.
2 These were the standards lost under Varus in AD 9: see Tacitus, *Ann.* 2.41; Dio 57.18.
3 Cf. Tacitus, *Ann.* 2.43.
4 Cf. Dio 55.2.3; Suetonius, *Claudius* 1.3; Eutropius 7.13.1.
5 Cf. Tacitus, *Ann.* 2.83.
6 The *sodales Augustales* formed a brotherhood of priests devoted to the worship of the deified Augustus. See also the Glossary.
7 These annual games were established by the senate (cf. Dio 54.34) and lasted for eight (later ten) days in October. Cf. Tacitus, *Ann.* 1.15 and Dio 56.46.
8 Nundina was a market-day occurring at regular intervals of eight days, i.e. every ninth day (Roman count). See below, No. 198, n. 1.
9 Most likely an *elogium*, an old Republican form of enumerating in brief manner the achievements of great Romans and affixed to the sacrophagus, tomb, or pedestal of the statue of the deceased.
10 Germanicus Caesar was the son of the elder Germanicus, who was the brother of Tiberius the emperor. After the death of the elder Germanicus in 9 BC Tiberius adopted the young Germanicus as his son.
11 See n. 16.
12 Lines 1–12 are badly damaged and most of the lines are missing. Isolated phrases can be made out, e.g.: 'Games of the Victory of Caesar', '[temple] of Concord', 'equestrian statues'.
13 These are priests, especially of Mars, whose stylized songs and dances were connected with the beginning and ending of the annual military campaigning season, spring to autumn.
14 The *destinatio*, i.e. the 'marking-out' or selection of certain candidates for the consulship and praetorship in order to guarantee their later election in the Assembly of the People.
15 This whole section of the *tabula Siarensis* (lines 13–22) is identical with the opening section of the *tabula Hebana*.
16 Only one bronze tablet of the *tabula Hebana* survives, but it was the second in a series of (probably) three. The contents of the first can be seen in the remains of the *tabula Siarensis*. This document from Heba is a *rogatio* ('bill') initiated in the senate and intended to be ratified later by the Assembly of the People, but it was engraved before ratification into *lex* (law') took place. Cf. the *tabula Siarensis*, Fragment II col. b, lines 29–30. Although the purpose of the document was to honor the memory of Germanicus Caesar, the incidental discussion of how to add five voting groups (centuries) of equites and senators to the already existing ten centuries named for Gaius and Lucius Caesar has created a controversy among modern scholars about the whole electoral process under Augustus and Tiberius, revolving around the notice by Tacitus (*Ann.* 1.15) that in AD 14 'for the first time the elections were removed from the Campus [Martius] to the patres [i.e. the senate]'. The present document appears to make it necessary to modify that statement in some way: see Jones, *op. cit.* 46ff. Restorations, therefore, in the sections devoted to the operation of these centuries are highly controversial and not to be accepted uncritically.
17 See n. 13.
18 See n. 14.

19 See Pliny, *Nat. Hist.* 33.7.31.
20 Not only these two but all four urban tribes were filled with the city mob, including only a few equites and senators.
21 About ten letters are missing, restoration uncertain.
22 The Saepta was a series of fenced-in areas in the huge Campus Martius in Rome to accommodate the voters in an organized fashion.
23 Tibiletti: 'the *group* [of the rest of the centuries]'. For him the *destinatio* process was performed in the Assembly of all the citizens, whereas Oliver thought that the ten centuries seemed to act as a special kind of Electoral Board whose purpose was the *destinatio*. Tibiletti felt that no such Electoral Board existed.
24 Tibiletti, in keeping with his views about *destinatio*, restores differently: 'and that person who [will hold] the destinatio for the election of consuls and praetors shall see to it that the count [of this group (of centuries) in the assembly] shall be held and that the vote shall thus be cast'. For Tibiletti the *destinatio* process within the Assembly of the People acted like the *centuriae praerogativae* of the Republic, which announced the results of their votes to the remaining voters in advance, with the result that the remaining voters then knew how those centuries had voted and thus were influenced in their voting.
25 Senators wore a broad-striped toga, while equites wore a trabea which had two narrow purple stripes.

37   The new equestrian order. AD 23.

Pliny, *Nat. Hist.* 33.29–33.

A. Stein, *Der Römische Ritterstand* (Munich 1927) 54ff.; G. H. Stevenson in *CAH* 10.185ff.; T. P. Wiseman in *Historia* 19 (1970) 67–83; F. Kolb in *Chiron* 7 (1977) 346ff. (on status symbols).

However, rings[1] plainly introduced a third order between the plebeian and the senatorial, and the name ('eques') formerly granted by (the possession of) military horses is now assigned by the indications of money. And this was done not long ago in the past. (30) When the deified Augustus was regulating the panels (of jurymen) the majority of jurymen were among those wearing the iron ring, and they were not called equites but jurymen. The title eques was held by those in the squadrons of public horses. Of the jurymen also there were at first only four panels, and there were hardly a thousand of them in each panel, since the provinces had not as yet been admitted to that duty. This condition has been preserved to the present day, that no one of the new citizens may be a juryman on them. (31) The panels themselves were differentiated by many names, (e.g.) Treasury Tribunes, Select Members, Jurymen. Besides these there were also the so-called Nine Hundred, chosen from all (citizens) to watch over the baskets of votes at the elections. And this order was also divided by the haughty use of names, since one man called himself one of the Nine Hundred, another one of the Select Members, and another a Tribune. (32) At last, in the ninth year of the principate of Tiberius, the Equestrian Order achieved unity, and a regulation for the right of ownership of rings was established in the consulship of Gaius Asinius Pollio and Gaius Antistius Vetus (AD 23), in the 775th year of the founding of our city. The reason for this, something for us to wonder at, was the almost trifling fact that Gaius Sulpicius Galba, on the look-out for gaining youthful favor with the emperor (Tiberius) by penalizing eating-establishments, complained in the senate that shopkeepers defended themselves against a charge by means of their rings. For this reason it was ordained (by the emperor?) that nobody was to have this right except a free-born person whose father and father's father had been free-born and who had a census evaluation of 400,000 sesterces and who in accordance with the Julian Law concerning the theater had a seat in the first fourteen rows.[2] (33) Afterwards, great masses of men began to seek this kind of status. Because of the disputes involved in this, our Leader Gaius added a fifth panel, and so much arrogance has been the result that these panels, which could not be filled out under the deified Augustus, cannot now contain that order. Everywhere, even freedmen make the jump over to these ornaments of status, something that never happened before, since equites and jurymen were differentiated from others by the iron ring.

1 Pliny had been discussing gems and rings, especially signet-rings from early times.
2 'But aspirants to the proud title of *eques Romanus* had long made it unofficial usage', so Wiseman, *op. cit.* 76.

38   The imperial cult in Galatia. Reign of Tiberius.
Inscription on the left anta of a temple in Ancyra.[1] [Greek]

OGIS 533; L. Robert, *Les Gladiateurs dans l'Orient grec* (Paris 1940) 135–7; Ehrenberg–Jones, *Documents*[2] 109; Bosch, **Quellen* 35–49, No. 51; R. K. Sherk in *ANRW* 2.7.972–5; K. Tuchelt and F. Preisshofen in *Archäologischer Anzeiger* 1985, 317–22 (+ photographs).

Of the [Ga]latians: those | who were priests | of the god Augustus | and of the goddess Roma.[2]

5
10
15
20
25

‖ [*vv* In the governorship of -----. *vv* ----,][3] son of King Brigatos, gave a public banquet, ‖ distributed olive-oil for four months, presented spectacles, gave a show of thirty pairs of gladiators and a hunt ‖ of bulls and wild animals. Rufus gave a public banquet and spectacles and a hunt. *vv* In the governorship of Metilius. *vv* ‖ Pylaimenes, son of King Amyntas, twice gave a public banquet, twice presented spectacles, gave a gymnastic competition, a chariot race and a horse race, ‖ and

also a bull-fight and animal-hunt. He distributed oil to the city, he
presented (the city with) property where the Sebasteion is located and
30 where the festival and horse-racing take place.[4] ‖ Albiorix, (son) of
Ateporix, gave a public banquet and set up statues of Caesar and Iulia
35 Augusta.[5] Amyntas, (son) of Gaizatodiastos, ‖ twice gave a public
banquet, sacrificed a hekatomb,[6] presented spectacles, gave a distribution of grain at five modii each.[7] [------,] (son) of Diognetos (was
priest). [Al]biorix, (son) of Ateporix, (was priest) for a second time.
40 ‖ He gave a public banquet. *vv* In the governorship of Fronto. *vv*
Metrodoros, (son) of Menemachos, natural (son) of [Do]rylaos, gave a
45 public banquet, distributed [olive-oil] for four months. ‖ Mousanos,
(son) of Artiknos, gave a public banquet. [----,] (son) of Seleukos, gave
a public banquet and distributed oil for four months. Pylaimenes, son
50 of *King* Amyntas, gave a *public banquet* to the three ‖ tribes[8] and
[sacrificed] a hekatomb in Ancyra, presented spectacles and a parade,
and also a bull-fight and bull-fighters and 50 pairs of gladiators, and he
55 distributed oil during the whole ‖ year to the three tribes, and he gave
an animal-hunt. *vv* [In the governorship] of Silvanus. *vv* [Ga(?)]llios
gave a public banquet in Pessinus, 25 pairs of gladiators (in Ancyra)
60 ‖ and 10 (pairs) in Pessinus. He distributed oil to two tribes for the
whole year and set up a statue in Pessinus. [Se]leukos, (son) of
Philodamos, twice gave public banquets to the two cities, distributed
65 oil ‖ to two tribes for the whole year, and presented *spectacles*. Iulius
Pontikos gave a public banquet, sacrificed a hekatomb, and distributed
70 oil for the whole year. ‖ Aristokles, (son) of Al[biorix,] gave [a public
banquet,] and distributed oil for the whole year.[9]

1 The *Res Gestae* of Augustus are inscribed on the same temple.
2 Because of the very short length of the lines 5–70 only every fifth line is indicated for
   this document.
3 For the identities of each of the governors of Galatia mentioned in this document see
   Sherk, *loc. cit.* The names that appear after each governorship are those of the high
   priests of the imperial cult, most of them Celtic in origin. Each priest served for one
   year in that capacity, thus giving us an indication of how long each governor was in
   office.
4 It has been suggested that this means that the Sebasteion here mentioned is not
   identical with the temple on which the inscription was found, i.e. that it is a case of
   two separate structures: for a discussion see Tuchelt–Preisshofen, *op. cit.* If this is
   true, then the identity of the temple on which the inscription was found assumes
   even greater importance. Tuchelt–Priesshofen believe it was a temple of Magna
   Mater, the 'Great Mother', and that the inscribing of the *Res Gestae* of Augustus on
   its walls was a symbolic joining of an eastern cult with Roman political reality. The
   word 'Sebasteion' need not always mean a temple of Augustus, for it could indicate
   an altar used in the imperial cult.
5 Iulia Augusta was the wife of Augustus.
6 A hekatomb was a sacrifice of 100 oxen.

7 A modius was about 8.5 kilograms.
8 These were the three original Celtic tribes which entered Galatia: Tolistobogii, Tectosages, and Trocmi.
9 The list and the record continue on into the reign of Gaius.

39   Pontius Pilatus, prefect of Judaea. AD 26–36.

A: A. Frova in *Rendiconti del Istituto Lombardo, Accademia di Scienze e Lettere, Classe di Lettere* 95 (1961) 419–34; B. Lifshitz in *ANRW* 2.8.501 (+ photograph); J.-P. Lémonon, **Pilate et le gouvernement de la Judée* (Paris 1981) 23–32 (+ photograph); Gordon, *Epigraphy* 38, pp. 113–14 (+ photograph). Limestone block from the Roman theater at Caesarea. [Latin] Cf. Tacitus, *Ann.* 15.44. B: The Suda *s.v.* Korbanas.

A. Lémonon, *Pilate et le gouvernement de la Judée*, p. 29, Caesarea

[----][1] (this) temple of Tiberius | [---- by Po]ntius Pilatus, | *prefect*[2] of Iuda[ea, | has been built.]

B. The Suda *s.v.* Korbanas

Among the Jews (the Korbanas is) the holy treasury. Pilatus spent the holy treasury on an aqueduct and stirred up a riot. It brought in (water) from a distance of 400 stades.[3] Bringing in his soldiers he killed many (Jews).

1 There may have been a date here. See E. Weber in *Bonner Jahrbücher* 171 (1971) 194–200; '[On the Kalends of July]' (?).
2 Literary sources call him 'procurator' because such was the title of Judaea's governor at a later date.
3 This incident is mentioned by Josephus, *Bell. Jud.* 2.175–7 and *Ant. Jud.* 18.60–2. See Lémonon, *op. cit.* 159–71.

40   The fall of Sejanus, later recollection. AD 31–2.

A: *CIL* VI 10213; *ILS* 6044; Ehrenberg–Jones, **Documents*[2] 53; Sir Ronald Syme in *Hermes* 84 (1956) 258 (= *Roman Papers* I 306). Large marble slab with cornice, broken at top, bottom and on left side, but with right margin intact, Rome. [Latin] B: *ILS* 158; Ehrenberg–Jones, *Documents*[2] 52; **I. Cret.* IV 272. Stone tablet, Gortyn on Crete. [Latin] C: *CIL* XI 4170; **ILS* 157; Ehrenberg–Jones, *Documents*[2] 51. Marble tablet, inscribed with three clearly separated dedications (a–c), the first two side by side, the third beneath them, Interamna in Italy. AD 32. [Latin] D: Valerius Maximus 9.11.4 (ext.) E: Scholia on Juvenal, *Satires* 10.63 *s.v.* Seianus.

Syme, *op. cit.* 257–66 (= *Roman Papers* I 305ff; D. Hennig, *L. Aelius Seianus* (Munich 1975) Ch. 11.

A. Ehrenberg–Jones, *Documents*[2] 53, Rome

[---] | now since [---] | 60 years, *wicked* Sejanus' |*importunate demands*[1] and
5   the improper elections || which were (held) on the Aventine, when |

[Se]janus was made consul[2] and I | a feeble, useless companion of the
walking-stick, | to be made into a suppliant. Now | I beg of you, good
10   fellow-tribes‖men,[3] if at any time I appeared | to you to be a good and
useful tribes|man, if never of [my] *duty* | have I been [unmindful] and
not of [----]

B. *I. Cret.* **IV 272, Gortyn**

To the *divine majesty* and foresight | [of Tiberius Ca]esar Augustus and
of the senate, | (foresight)[4] of that day which was the fifteenth before
the Kalends of November (October 18).[5] | [Publius] Viriasius Naso,
5   proconsul for a third term,[6] with his own funds ‖ consecrated (this
monument).

C. *ILS* **157, Interamna**

(a) To the perpetual safety of Augusta | and to the public liberty | of the
Roman People.

   (b) To the protecting deity of our municipality in the year after | the
founding of Interamna (year) 704 up to (the time of) Gnaeus Domitius
| Ahenobarbus, consul with [[Lucius Arruntius Camillus
Scribonianus.]][7]

   (c) To the foresight of Tiberius Caesar Augustus, born for the
eternity | of the Roman name, now that the most deadly enemy of the
Roman People has been removed.[8] | Faustus Titius Liberalis, Sevir of
Augustus for the second time, | saw to the erection (of this monument)
with his own funds.

D. **Valerius Maximus 9.11.4 (ext.)**

However, why do I pursue those examples or linger with these, when I
see the entire range of wicked deeds exceeded by the contemplation of
a single assassination? Therefore, I am forced by every impulse of my
mind, by all the force of my indignation to lash out at it with righteous
rather than intense emotional reaction: for, now that confidence in
friendship is extinct, who could find sufficiently effective words to
consign to the deepest depths of a well-earned curse an attempt to bury
the human race in blood and darkness? Would you, plainly more cruel
than monstrous and unbridled barbarism, would you have been able to
seize the reins of the Roman Empire, which our Leader and parent
holds in his wholesome right hand? Or, in your mad state of mind,
would the world have remained in its upright position? It was your
intention, in the frantic objectives of your crazed mind, to revive and
outdo the capture of our city by the Gauls, the River Cremera defiled
by the slaughter of three hundred men of a famous clan, the day at the
Allia, the Scipios crushed in Spain, Lake Trasimene, Cannae, and the

fury of the civil wars dripping with domestic blood.[9] However, the eyes of the gods were wide awake, the stars kept their strength; the couches (holding the images of the gods) and the temples with their ever-present divine majesty were well protected. Nothing which was supposed to watch over the head of Augustus and our country was allowed to relax its guard, and above all else the author and protector of our safety took precautions by his divine wisdom that his superlative achievements would not be buried in the ruin of the whole world. Thus, peace stands firm, the laws are in force, the true course of private and public duty is preserved. And he who tried to overturn all these by violating the bonds of friendship, along with his entire family, has been smashed by the might of the Roman People and is suffering well-deserved punishment in the underworld, if it has admitted him.[10]

E. Scholia on Juvenal, *Satires* 10.63 *s.v.* Seianus

Seianus was such a dear friend to Tiberius that whatever he sought from Tiberius was given to him, and so <ungrateful was he that> he even contemplated his death so that, when his associates in the conspiracy had been placed in position and Tiberius had been killed, he might rule. When Tiberius learned this, he sent a letter over his name to the senate, and Seianus was thus condemned by the consuls with all his family, to the point that the senate ordered his daughter to be defiled by the executioner and put to death so that it would appear she had been killed with legal sanction.

1   Syme suggested '*wicked importunate demands* of Sejanus'.
2   In the past elections had regularly been held in the Campus Martius, hence the word 'improper'. For the significance of the Aventine Hill in these elections see Syme, *loc. cit.* Tiberius and Sejanus were consuls in AD 31 until May 8. Five months later Sejanus was put to death (see above, No. 28 F).
3   Line 9 is in very large letters. The identity of the speaker is unknown. Tiberius himself? In a letter? For his state of mind at this time see B. M. Levick in *Historia* 27 (1978) 95–101.
4   Mommsen had supplied here: 'in memory'. However, nothing seems to have been inscribed at the beginning of the line.
5   This is the day on which Sejanus had been put to death.
6   From Dio (58.23.5) we learn that proconsuls held their provinces for as long as three years, under Tiberius.
7   They were consuls in AD 32. Thus, Interamna was founded in the year 673 BC. The name of Lucius Arruntius Camillus Scribonianus was erased because after a civil war in Dalmatia he was declared an enemy of the State (Dio 60.15; Suetonius, *Claudius* 13).
8   I.e. Sejanus.
9   These were among the greatest disasters to befall the Roman people in the previous 450 years.
10   Valerius Maximus does not mention the name of this person, but there is no doubt at all about his identity: Sejanus. See E. Koestermann in *Hermes* 83 (1955) 354 and Hennig, *op. cit.* 146.

GAIUS (CALIGULA)
(37–41)
GAIUS CAESAR AUGUSTUS GERMANICUS

Titles: PONTIFEX MAXIMUS
FATHER OF HIS COUNTRY (38)
HOLDER OF THE TRIBUNICIAN POWER: first
time in AD 37, then annually on March 18
CONSUL: AD 37 (I), 39 (II), 40 (III), 41 (IV)

Death: January 24, AD 41.

Memory condemned.

The *consules ordinarii* **under Gaius**

AD		
38	M. Aquila Iulianus	P. Nonius Asprenas
39	C. Caesar Augustus Germanicus II	L. Apronius Caesianus
40	C. Caesar III	C. Laecanius Bassus
41	C. Caesar IV	Cn. Sentius Saturninus

41   Oath of allegiance to Gaius. AD 37
Bronze tablet, incomplete at bottom, Aritium in Lusitania. [Latin]

CIL II 172; *ILS* 190; Bruns[7] 101; Smallwood, *Documents Gaius* 32; P. Herrmann, **Der römische Kaisereid* (Göttingen 1968) p. 122.

Herrmann, *op. cit.* 50–2 and 105–7.

To Gaius Ummidius Durmius Quadratus, | legate of Gaius Caesar
Germanicus Imperator | with pro praetorian *vv* power. | *vv* Oath of the
5   Aritiensians. *vv* ‖ It is in accordance with my inner conviction that I will
be an enemy to those | who I come to learn are enemies to Gaius Caesar
Germanicus, | and if danger to him or to his welfare | is brought or will
be brought by anyone, with armed might and war of extermination | on
10   land and sea I will never cease to pursue him until ‖ he pays the penalty
to (Gaius Caesar). Neither myself nor my children | will I consider
dearer than his welfare, and those who | will have hostile intentions
toward him will be considered hostile toward me; | if knowingly I swear
15   or will swear falsely, then | may Jupiter Best and Greatest and ‖ the
deified Augustus and all the other immortal | gods deprive me and my
children of our motherland, our safety, and all our fortunes. | *vv* (Sworn)
on the fifth [day before] the Ides of May (May 11) in the | old town of
Aritium when Gnaeus Acerronius | Proculus and Gaius Petronius

20   Pontius Nigrinus were consuls (AD 37), ‖ *vv* when the (local) magis-
trates *vv* | were Vegetus son of Tallicus and [----]

42   Client states and kings.

A: *IOSPE* II 36 (+ drawing); *IGRR* I 879; E. H. Minns, *Scythians and Greeks* (Cambridge 1913) p. 653, No. 42; Ehrenberg–Jones, *Documents*[2] 172; *CIRB* 40. Age of Augustus, Tiberius, and Gaius. Base of white marble, Panticapaeum in the Bosporan Kingdom. [Greek] Cf. Strabo 7.4.1–8. **B**: *IGRR* IV 145; *SIG*[3] 798; Smallwood, *Documents Gaius* 401. AD 37. Inscription from Cyzicus. [Greek] Cf. Tacitus, *Ann*. 2.64–7. See Charlesworth in *CAH* 10.645–6 and 806; Magie, *RRAM* I 512–14; Price, *Rituals* 244. **C**: *IGRR* I 829; Smallwood, *Documents Gaius* 201b. Inscription from Maroneia in Thrace. [Greek] Cf. Dio 59.12.2. **D**: *BMC Galatia* p. 106, No. 1 (+ photograph, Pl. XIV 9); Smallwood, *Documents Gaius* 205. Bronze coin of Antiochus IV, Commagene. Cf. Tacitus, *Ann*. 12.55.3; 13.7.1; 14.26.3; Suetonius, *Gaius* 16.3; Dio 59.8.2 and 24.1. **E**: *BMC Palestine* p. 230, No. 10; Smallwood, *Documents Gaius* 208. Bronze coin, Ad 39/40. Cf. Josephus, *Bell. Jud*. 2.181–3; *Ant. Jud*. 18.109–24 and 240–55. **F**: *IG* II[2] 3449; Smallwood, *Documents Gaius* 212a. Large marble base, Athens. Cf. Josephus, *Bell. Jud*. 2.220; *Ant. Jud*. 18.132.

A.   *CIRB* 40, Panticapaeum

Great King Aspourgos,[1] friend of the Romans, (son) of King
Asandrochos,[2] | friend of Caesar and friend of the Romans, king of all
the Bosporos: (king) of Theodosia, | the Sindoi, the Maitai, the
Tarpeites, the Toretai, the Psesoi, and the Tanaeitai.[3] | He subjugated
the Scythians and the Tauroi. Menestratos II, in charge of the island,[4]
(dedicated this statue) to his savior and benefactor.

B.   *SIG*[3] 798, Cyzicus

In the hipparchy[5] of Gaius Caesar, on the ninth day of the month
Thargelion. | Decreed by the People, the motion introduced by all the
archons, the secretary of the Boule Aiolos, son of Aiolos, (of the tribe)
Oinops, speaking for them at the mid-session in the | (prytany presi-
dency (?)) of Menophon: Since the New Sun Gaius Caesar Augustus
Germanicus wished to illuminate with his own rays of light even | the
bodyguard[6] kings of his rule, in order that the greatness of his immor-
5   tality even in that regard might be more worthy of respect ‖ – and the
kings put a great amount of thought into discovering appropriate
recompense to show their good feeling for the gracious act of such a
great god, but failed to dis|cover one – (and since) the sons of Kotys,[7]
i.e. Rhoimetalkes and Polemon and Kotys, had been his foster-brothers
and had become his companions | and had been established by him (i.e.
Gaius Caesar) in the kingdoms rightfully owed to them from their
fathers and ancestors; and the sons, | reaping the abundance of his
immortal favor, in this regard became greater than those before them

because, although they held (the royal power) from their fathers, they | became kings in the joint rule of such great gods as a consequence of
10 the favor of Gaius Caesar, and the favors of gods differ ‖ from human successions (of power) as sunlight from night and as the immortal from mortal nature; having become greater than the great | and more wonderful than the brilliant, Rhoimetalkes and Polemon have now come to our city to join in the sacri|fices and festivals with their mother who is celebrating the games of the goddess New Aphrodite, Drusilla,[8] not only as | to a friendly but also as to a legitimate home-city, because Tryphaina,[9] the daughter of kings and the mother of kings, is their mother | who considers this to be her home-city and has made this
15 place the hearth of her home and the luck of her life, con‖tent in her children's kingdoms that have not incurred the anger of the gods; (and since) the People, considering most pleasant their lodging here, with all | enthusiasm have instructed the archons to introduce a decree of welcome for them, by means of which they will express their gratitude | to their mother Tryphaina for having wished to benefit our city and will make clear the Peo|ple's good disposition toward them, let it be decreed by the People to praise the kings Rhoimetalkes and Polemon and Kotys and their mother Tryphaina (etc.)[10]

C. *IGRR* I 829,. Maroneia in Thrace

The *People* | (dedicate this monument to) Rhoimetalkes, *king* of the Thracians, | son of [K]otys,[11] benefactor of the [Bist]onians.

D. *BMC Galatia* p. 106, No. 1

(Obverse: bust of Antiochus IV,   GREAT KING ANTIOCHOS
beardless, with diadem)   EPIPHANES

(Reverse: a scorpion in a laurel   OF THE COMMAGENIANS[12]
wreath)

E. *BMC Palestine* p. 230, No. 10

(Obverse: palm-branch, and date   [HERO]DES, TETRARCH[13]
showing across the field:
'Year 43' = AD 39/40)

(Reverse: within a wreath, tied at   TO GAIUS CAESAR
the bottom)   GERMANICUS

F. *IG* II[2] 3449, Athens

The Boule of the Areiopagus and | the Boule of the 600 and the People (dedicate this monument to) Iu|lia Berenike, great queen, | King
5 Iulius Agrippa's ‖ daughter[14] and descendant of great kings who were

benefactors of the ci|ty, because of her fore|sight. Epimelete of the city is Tiberius Claudius Theogenes | (of the deme) Paiania.

1   Under Augustus the ruler of the Bosporan Kingdom was Asandros. At his death the rule fell to Queen Dynamis, who married Polemon, a Greek of Asia Minor, at the command of Augustus. When she quarreled with her husband, she was forced to flee to the East. In the Kuban she married Aspourgos, a Sarmatian or Maetaian tribal king. With his help she overcame Polemon and regained the rule over Bosporos. Rome recognized her as a vassal queen. After her death Aspourgos ruled until he died (probably about AD 38–9). He left two sons, Mithridates and Kotys. See M. I. Rostovtzeff, *Iranians and Greeks in South Russia* (New York 1922) 151–3, and V. F. Gajdukevič, *Das Bosporanische Reich*[2] (Berlin 1971) 323ff.
2   Evidently Asandrochos is not to be identified with Asandros.
3   Theodosia, the Scythians, and the Tauroi were located to the southwest of the Sea of Azov in the Crimea. The Sindoi, Maitai, Tarpeites, Toreitai, Psesoi, and the Taneitai lived in the Kuban, i.e. the area east of the Sea of Azov and as far north as the Tanais (Don) river.
4   In antiquity the area on the Asiatic side called today the Taman Peninsula was actually an island: Strabo 11.2.9. This was the heart of the kingdom of the Bosporos.
5   The hipparch was the eponymous magistrate of Cyzicus and for the present occasion the emperor is accorded that honor.
6   This is the literal meaning. The word can also mean 'satellite', making it the same as 'client-king'.
7   Kotys was king of Thrace. See Bowersock, *Augustus* 152ff. and R. D. Sullivan in *ANRW* 2.7.1.200ff.
8   Sister of Gaius Caesar.
9   Tryphaina was almost certainly a relative of the triumvir Marcus Antonius. See R. D. Sullivan in *ANRW* 2.7.2.920ff.
10   The inscription continues for five more lines detailing the welcome to be given to the three sons.
11   This is Rhoimetalkes III, granted sovereignty over Thrace by Gaius in AD 38 and sanctioned by the senate.
12   His full name is Gaius Iulius Antiochus (IV) Epiphanes: see *PIR*[2] I 149. He was made king of Commagene by Gaius in AD 38. On the Roman citizenship of such kings see D. C. Braund, *Rome and the Friendly King* (New York 1984) p. 41.
13   He is Herodes Antipas, one of the sons of Herod the Great.
14   Marcus Iulius Agrippa (*PIR*[2] I 131) was a grandson of Herod the Great.

43   Cult of Gaius and the administrative districts of Asia. AD 40–1.
Base of white marble found in the ruins of a temple of Gaius at Didyma in Asia. [Greek]

L. Robert in *Hellenica* 7 (1949) 206–7; *I. Didyma* 148; Smallwood, *Documents Gaius* 127 (incomplete). Cf. Dio 59.28.

Robert, *op. cit.* 206–38; Magie, *RRAM* II 1366–7; Chr. Habicht in *JRS* 65 (1975) 63–91; G. P. Burton, *Ibid.* 92–106.

[Imperator Gaius Ca]esar Germanicus, | son [of Germanicus,] god
Augustus. | Those who were his first neopoioi,[1] | when Gnaeus
5 Vergilius Capito was high-priest ‖ of the temple of Gaius Caesar in
Miletus for the fi|rst time and of Asia for the third time, when Tiberius
Iulius, | son of Demetrios the nomothetes,[2] Menogenes was high-priest
| for the second time and neokoros[3] of the temple in Miletus, and when
10 | Protomachos, son of Glycon, of Iulia was the archineopoi‖os and
sebastoneos and sebastologos[4] – they, out of their own ⌈ funds *vv* dedi-
cated (his statue): *vv* |

Protomachos, son of Glycon, of Iulia; Neon, son of Artemon, | Gaius-
loving Milesian; Theopompos, son of Theopom|pos, Asklepiogenes
15 the Pergamene; Sochares, son of Sochares, ‖ of Antioch; Peithias, son
of Pytheas, of Cyzicus; Diokles, | son of Moitas, of Apamea; Glycon,
son of Euarchos, of Laodicea; Hierokles, | son of Artemidoros, of
Caesarea; Daimenes, son of Antigonos, of Adramy|ttion; Pylades,
son of Pantaleon, of Philomelion; Aspa|sios, son of Aristokles, of
20 Halicarnassos; Olympianos, ‖ son of Poplios, Hieronymos of Smyrna;
Hermippos, son of Her|mippos, of Sardis. These are the Augustus-
loving (neopoioi) | whose names are written here (in an order deter-
mined) by lot.[5]

1 Literally 'Temple-builders', these temple officials performed a variety of temple
   functions during their tenure. Here they enjoy special honor, since they are the first
   for the cult of Gaius.
2 Literally 'Lawgiver', the nomothetes was a relatively rare official in Asia Minor.
3 The neokoros was a kind of temple-warden or sexton, even cities receiving this title
   when they became the seat of an imperial cult.
4 The archineopoios was 'chief neopoios'; the significance of sebastoneos (new word)
   is unknown, but some kind of temple official connected with the imperial cult;
   sebastologos was the official who pronounced prose eulogies of the emperor at cult
   ceremonies.
5 Robert has demonstrated that these neopoioi are representatives from every district
   of the province of Asia and that each is a delegate of the *conventus*, i.e. the assize or
   judicial administrative district of the province. The cities mentioned are the district
   centers where the provincial governor would conduct court hearings. For details see
   Habicht and Burton.

CLAUDIUS
(AD 41–54)
TIBERIUS CLAUDIUS CAESAR AUGUSTUS
GERMANICUS

Titles: PONTIFEX MAXIMUS (AD 41)
FATHER OF HIS COUNTRY (AD 41)
BRITANNICUS (AD 43)
CENSOR (AD 47 and 48)
HOLDER OF THE TRIBUNICIAN POWER: first
time in AD 41, then annually on January 25 (?)
CONSUL; AD 37 (I), 42 (II), 43 (III), 47 (IV), 51 (V)
Death: October 13, AD 54.

The *consules ordinarii* **under Claudius**

For the suffect consuls see P. A. Gallivan in *Classical Quarterly* 28 (1978) 407–26).

AD

42	Ti. Claudius Caesar Augustus Germanicus II	C. Caecina Largus
43	Ti. Claudius III	L. Vitellius II
44	T. Statilius Taurus	C. (Sallustius) Passienus Crispus II
45	M. Vinicius II	T. Statilius Taurus Corvinus
46	D. Valerius Asiaticus II	M. Iunius Silanus
47	Ti. Claudius IV	L. Vitellius III
48	A. Vitellius	L. Vipstanus Publicola Messalla
49	Q. Veranius	C. Pompeius Longinus Gallus
50	C. Antistius Vetus II	M. Suillius Nerullinus
51	Ti. Claudius V	Ser. Cornelius (Scipio) Salvidienus Orfitus
52	Faustus Cornelius Sulla Felix	L. Salvius Otho Titianus
53	D. Iunius Silanus Torquatus	Q. Haterus Antoninus
54	M'. Acilus Aviola	M. Asinius Marcellus

44   Letter of Claudius to the Alexandrians. AD 41.
Papyrus found at Philadelphia in the Fayûm, Egypt. [Greek][1]

P. London 1912; H. I. Bell, *Jews and Christians in Egypt* (London 1924) 1–37 (+ photograph); Tcherikover–Fuks, *CPJ* II 153; Smallwood, *Documents Gaius* 370.

Bell, *loc. cit.*; V. M. Scramuzza, *The Emperor Claudius* (Cambridge, Mass. 1940) 64–79; Tcherikover–Fuks, *op. cit.* pp. 36–60; E. Mary Smallwood, *The Jews under Roman Rule* (Leiden 1976) Ch. 10; E. Huzar in *ANRW* 2.32.2.641–4.

(Col. 1) Lucius Aemilius Rectus[2] declares: | Since at the reading of the

most holy | and the most beneficent letter to our city | the whole city
5   could not be present ‖ because of its large population, | I thought it
necessary to publish | the letter in order that, man for man, | as you read
it, the greatness |of our god Caesar might be an object of wonder to you
10 ‖ and that for his {--}³ goodwill toward our city | you might be grateful.
Year 2 of Tiberius Claudius | Caesar Augustus Germanicus Imperator,
in the month Neos | Sebastos the fourteenth (= November 10, AD 41). |
   (Col. 2) Tiberius Claudius Caesar Augustus Germanicus Imperator,
15 pontifex ‖ maximus, holding the tribunician power, consul designate,
to the city of Alexandria, | greetings. Tiberius Claudius Barbillus,
Apollonius son of Artemidoros, | Chairemon son of Leonidas, Marcus
Iulius Asklepiades, Gaius Iulius Dionysios, | Tiberius Claudius
Phanias, Pasion son of Potamon, Dionysios son of Sabbion, | Tiberius
Claudius <Archibios>, Apollonius son of Ariston, Gaius Iulius
20 Apollonius, Hermaiskos ‖ son of Apollonius, your envoys,⁴ gave me
your decree and | spoke at length concerning your city, directing me
clearly to your | goodwill toward us, which from long ago – you may be
sure – your city has found stored up in my memory. | By nature you are
pious toward the Augusti, as | known to me from many things, and
25 especially ‖ have you shown interest in my house, an interest recipro-
cated by us, – to mention the la|st and to pass over the others, the
greatest witness of this is my brother | Germanicus Caesar who
addressed you in very sincere terms.⁵ | Thus, I was happy to accept the
honors given by you to me, | although I am not inclined toward such
30 things. First of all, as an Augustan (Day) ‖ I permit you to treat my
birthday⁶ in the manner you have reques|ted and also for you to erect
in various locations statues | of me and my family. I grant such per-
mission because I see | that memorials everywhere of your piety toward
my house | you have been interested in founding. Of the two golden
35 statues ‖ the one of the Pax Augusta Claudiana, as suggested ⌐ and
entreated by my most esteemed Barbillus, even when I wished to reject
| the idea for fear of *seeming to be* quite arrogant, shall be erected at
Rome,⁷ | (Col. 3) and the other shall be carried in the manner you
requested in processions on my name-days | among you, and a throne
40 shall be carried with it {with it}, ‖ adorned with whatever decoration
you wish. Perhaps it would be foolish for me, after | receiving such
honors, to refuse your creation of a Claudian tribe and | the existence
of planted groves after the custom of Egypt, and therefore these things
| I also grant to you. If you wish, | you may erect equestrian statues of
45 Vitrasius Pollio, my procurator.⁸ For the ‖ erection of four-horse
chariots, which <at the en>trances to your country you wish to be set
up for me, | you have my permission: one to be erected at the place
called Taposiris in Libya, | a second at Pharos in Alexandria, and a

third at Pelusium | in Egypt. But a priest for me and erection of temples
50 | I reject, not wishing to be offensive to the men of my time ‖ and judging
that temples and such things to the gods alone | should be reserved and
granted by every age. |
   Concerning the requests which you have been interested in obtaining
from me, | here is my decision. To all those who have become ephebes[9]
55   up to | my rule I con{con}firm and guarantee Alexandrian ‖ citizenship
with all privileges and benefits, | except for those who deceived you by
| becoming ephebes though born of slaves, and the other benefits I wish
to be | secure – all such benefits – which were so graciously given to you
by the emperors before me | and by kings and prefects, just as the god
60   Augustus also secured them. ‖ The overseers in Alexandria of the
temple of the god | Augustus I wish to be chosen by lot in the same way
as those in Kanopos | of the same god Augustus are chosen. And con-
cerning your polit|ical offices, it seems to me that you have been well-
advised that they should be for three-year periods, | since your magis-
65   trates, out of fear of giving an account of bad ‖ government, will act
more moderately in their | terms of office. However, concerning the
Boule (Council), about what was your custom | under the old kings I
have nothing to say, but under the | Augusti before my time you know
very well that it did not exist. Since this is a new | proposal for the
present time placed before me, and since it is uncertain whether it will
70   be of ‖ use to your city and to my affairs, I have written to Aemilius
Rectus | to investigate it and to reveal to me whether it is necessary for
the institution to be established, | and, if it ought to be established, in
what manner this should be done.[10] | As for the disturbance and riot
against Jews – rather, if the truth be told, | the war – and what people
75   were responsible for it, although ‖ in the confrontation (with their
opponents) your envoys | were most vigorous, especially Dionysios son
of Theon, nevertheless | I did not wish to make a strict investigation,
storing up within myself | unrepentant anger at those who started it up
again. | I simply tell you that unless there is an end to this des‖tructive
80   and remorseless anger of yours against each other, I will be forced | to
show what kind of a person a benevolent Leader can be when he has
been turned to justifiable anger. | Therefore, even now I earnestly ask
of you that the Alexandrians | conduct themselves more gently and
kindly toward the Jews who | have lived in the same city for a long time,
85   ‖ and that they do not inflict indignities upon any of their customs in
the worship | of their god, but that they allow them to keep their own
practices | just as in the time of the god Augustus, which practices I too
| have confirmed, after hearing both sides. As for the Jews, | on the
other hand, I order that they do not seek more than they previously
90   ‖ have had, that they do not, as if having homes in two cities, | send two

embassies[11] in the future, | a thing not done in the past. I also order that
they do not intrude (?) | into the games held by the gymnasiarchs or the
kosmetai,[12] | since they enjoy their own affairs and have the benefit of
95 || an abundance of many good things, | and that they do not introduce
or invite Jews who sail in from Syria or Egypt, | in consequence of which
act I will be compelled | to form even greater suspicions. If they do not
100   obey, in every | way I will move against them just as if || they were raising
up some common plague for the inhabited world.[13] If | both of you stop
these actions and with gentleness | and kindliness wish to live together,
| I too will exercise the highest forethought for your city, | as (a city)
105   that has been one of our own from olden times. || You have my word
about Barbillus, my friend, that he has always taken thought for you in
my court and that now also with all ze|al he has conducted your case
before me, and likewise about Tiberius Claudius Archibios, my friend.
| Farewell.

1   There are numerous minor errors in the copying of this text, and occasionally even
   the meaning has been obscured by slips of the pen. Some stylistic defects may be
   due to the fact that the original letter was composed in Latin and then put into
   Greek.
2   He is attested as prefect of Egypt in AD 41–2.
3   A word here has been partially chiseled out. It resembles the word for 'goodwill'.
4   Most of these envoys belonged to the learned circles of Alexandria and especially
   men of the Museum. Six of them were Roman citizens. There were no Jews:
   'Sabbion' seems a Syrian name. Barbillus was the leader of the embassy and he may
   be identical with the later prefect of Egypt.
5   Germanicus visited Egypt in AD 19: see above, Document No. 34.
6   His birthday was on August 1.
7   The hesitancy of the emperor seems to have resulted from the thought of linking
   himself with the deified Augustus.
8   Gaius Vitrasius Pollio had been prefect of Egypt immediately before Aemilius
   Rectus.
9   Ephebes are those young men who have been entitled to enter the Greek gymnasium and to receive the benefits of its educational program. Many Jews had long
   coveted such a status in Alexandria because of the Roman citizenship to which it
   led. Greeks steadfastly resisted their entrance.
10   It is still a matter of controversy among modern scholars whether the city of
   Alexandria had such a Boule under the Ptolemaic kings. See P. M. Fraser, *Ptolemaic
   Alexandria* (Oxford 1972) I pp. 94–5 with the notes.
11   For a discussion of what embassies Claudius may have had in mind see
   Tcherikover–Fuks, *op. cit.* 50–3.
12   The gymnasiarch was the official in charge of the gymnasium, while the kosmetai
   were officials of lower rank.
13   Some scholars maintain that the phrase 'some common plague for the inhabited
   world' is a reference to the Christian movement: cf. Tacitus, *Ann.* 15.44.

45   Trial of Isidorus and Lampon before Claudius.[1] AD 41 or 53.

A series of many fragments of Greek papyri in three recensions: Berlin–
Cairo (A), London (B), Berlin (C). Egypt.

H. A. Musurillo, *The Acts of the Pagan Martyrs* (Oxford 1954) IV pp. 18–26; Tcherikover–
Fuks, *CPJ* II No. 156; H. A. Musurillo, **Acta Alexandrinorum* (Leipzig 1961) IV pp. 11–17;
Smallwood, *Documents Gaius* 436. Cf. Philo, *Flaccus* 15–17.

Musurillo (1954) commentary pp. 117–40; Tcherikover–Fuks, *op. cit.* pp. 66–81;
D. Hennig in *Chiron* 5 (1975) 324ff. (argues against date of AD 41).

(Recension A, col. 1, 16–20). Summons to appear were sent | to [the
Alexandrian] *envoys* and an adjournment was made by | [the emperor]
for their hearing [on the next] day. | [Thirteenth (?) year of Claudius
20   Caesar] Augustus ‖ [----] Fifth day of Pachon. |
    (Col. 2.) *Second* day. [Sixth day of] Pachon. | Claudius Caesar hears
the case [of Isidorus,] | gymnasiarch[2] of the city of A[lexandria,] |
25   against Agrippa the king,[3] [in the ----] ‖ Gardens. *Seated with him* | were
twenty senators and, [in addition to them] | sixteen consulars; also
present | were women [--- of] | Isidorus. Isidorus was among the first [to
30   speak:] ‖ 'My lord Caesar, by your knees [I beg you] | to hear from me
the distress [of our city.'] | The emperor: 'I will assign you [this] | day.'
35   In agreement were [all the | senators] seated with him, ‖ knowing what
kind of a [man Isidorus was.] Claudius Caesar: ['Do not say anything]
| against my [friend. For | you have already destroyed] two of my
40   friends, | Theon the exegetēs [and Naevius the prefect[4] | ----] ‖
    (Col. 3) [----] envoy [----] city. | Lampon to Isidorus: 'I have already
seen | the death [-----].' Clau]dius Caesar: | 'Isidorus, you have killed
many of my friends.' | [Isi]dorus: 'I was then obeying the king who
45   ‖ gave me orders. And you, name anyone you wish. | I'll accuse him.'
Claudius Caesar: 'Really, | Isidorus, are you (the son) of a music-girl?'
Isidorus: | 'I am not a slave and not a music-girl's | son, but a
50   gymnasiarch of the outstanding city of Alexan‖dria. You, however, are
the Jewess Salome's | abandoned son! Therefore, [---|-----].' La[mp]on
said | to Isidorus: 'What else is there for us, except | to give an oppor-
55   tunity to a crazy king?' ‖ Claudius Caesar: 'Those to whom I gave orders
| for the death of Isidorus and Lampon | [----].'

(Recension B, col. 1) [--- in the ---] *Gardens* and [seated with | him] were
twenty senators [and sixteen] consulars, | with women also
5   present at the meeting | [----] of Isidorus. ‖ [Isidorus] began the first
speech, say|ing: ['My lord Caesar,] by your knees I beg you | [to hear]
the distress of our ci|ty.' [Claudius] Caesar: 'I assign you this | [day.' In
10   agreement were ‖ all the senators] seated with him, knowing what kind
of a man was | [Isidorus. Claudi]us Caesar: 'Do not say anything

[-----|-- against my] friend. For | you have destroyed [two of my]

15 *friends*: Theon | [the exegetēs and Na]evius the prefect of Egypt ‖ and
commander in Rome of the | [(Praetorian) Guard. (These) you have
already] destroyed. This | [is the man you are now prosecuting.'
Isid]orus: 'My lord Caesar, what | [do you care about Agrip]pa, a cheap

20 little Jew[5] | [----]?' Claudius Caesar: 'What ‖ [are you saying?] You're
the [surliest] of all creatures | [in] that [----] to have spoken.' | [Isidorus:

25 '---- I will not] deny | [---] quiet | [--- struck ‖ ---] Olympian Cae|[sar
--|--|--].

30   (Col. 2) [----|-- ‖ (several lines missing)--] I am brought here, the
gymnasiarch [of Alexandria ---]' (etc.)[6]

(Recension C, col. 2)[7] [----] Isidorus: | 'Lord Augustus, B[albillus][8]

20 speaks well ‖ [about] your affairs. [In reply,] | Agrippa, to what | you
brought up [about Jews,] I will put up a counterpoint. *I charge* | [that
they wish] the whole world | [to be in turmoil.] It is necessary by each

25 [one of them (?) ‖ to judge] the whole pack of them. They are different
from the Al[exandrians] | in feelings, but in the manner of the
Egyptians [----] | are they not like those who pay the poll-tax?' | *vv*

30 Agrippa: *vv* | 'Their rulers have put taxes on *Egyptians* ‖ [---,] but nobody
(has put them) on the (Jews) (?)1 | *vv* Balbillus: *vv* | 'Look at *how much*
brazenness either [his] god or | [----].'

1 Apparently Isidorus brought forward a charge against King Agrippa of stirring up
   trouble, perhaps seditious in nature, in Alexandria. Isidorus and Lampon eventually
   were heard in Rome by the emperor, whose sympathy was turned against them and
   they were condemned to death. This reversal probably occurred as a result of new
   evidence produced by someone.
2 The gymnasiarch was the supervisor of the gymnasium. See the Glossary.
3 There were two Jewish kings called Agrippa in this period: one (Agrippa I) was in
   Rome in AD 41 (Josephus, *Ant. Jud.* 19.274ff.), the other, his son (Agrippa II) was in
   Rome in AD 52–3 (Josephus, *Ant. Jud.* 20.135).
4 Theon is otherwise unknown. Naevius is Naevius Sertorius Macro, who had been
   selected to become prefect of Egypt in AD 38 but was then forced by the emperor
   Gaius to commit suicide before he could take up his office: Dio 59.10.6. He had been
   prefect of the Praetorian Guard. Exactly how Isidorus was involved in his downfall
   we do not know.
5 Literally he calls Agrippa a 'three-obol' person.
6 No connected sense can be made out of the extant phrases of lines 35–51.
7 Column 1 consists of only one or two words for each line of text.
8 He is Titus Claudius Balbillus (Barbillus), known to have been an envoy from
   Alexandria to Rome: cf. the letter of Claudius to the Alexandrians, above, Document
   No. 44, line 14. He may be the prefect of Egypt under Nero: Stein *Präfekten* 33–4.

46   Edict of the prefect of Egypt on illegal requisitions. AD 42.
Greek papyrus from Egypt.

P. *London* III 1171 verso; Wilcken, **Chrestomathie* 439; Abbott–Johnson, *Municipal Administration* 162; Smallwood, *Documents Gaius* 381. Cf. above, Document No. 29.

Lucius Aemilius Rectus[1] declares: | Nobody is permitted to press into service the people in the countryside | or to demand provisions for travel or any other gift without | my diploma,[2] and each of those people ‖ having my diploma may take sufficient necessities | and pay the price of them. If there is any | report of any of the soldiers or men under arms | or any of the attendants in public | service having acted contrary to my order or having used ‖ force against any of those from the countryside or having levied money, | against such a person I will administer the highest penalty. | Year 2 of Tiberius Claudius Caesar Augustus Imperator, | Germanicus the fourth.[3]

5

10

1 Prefect of Egypt AD 41–2: Stein, *Präfekten* 29–30.
2 Cf. above, Document No. 29, n. 7.
3 Apparently an Egyptian month had been renamed 'Germanicus'. Wilcken equates it with Pachon (April–May).

47   Slaves and freedmen in the household of Claudius.

A: O. Marucchi in *Dissertazioni della Pontificia Accademia Romana di Archeologia*, Series 2, 15 (1921) 285ff. (+ photograph); Gordon, **Album* 1.122 (+ photograph); Smallwood, *Documents Gaius* 188. Small marble slab, Rome. [Latin]. B: *CIL* XIV 163; **ILS* 1533; Smallwood, *Documents Gaius* 173. Round bronze plaque, Ostia (?). [Latin]. See R. Meiggs, *Ostia*[2] (Oxford 1973) 298–9. C: *CIL* XI 3885; **ILS* 1643; Smallwood, *Documents Gaius* 177. Marble tombstone, Capena in Etruria. [Latin]. D: *CIL* VI 32775; **ILS* 2816; Smallwood, *Documents Gaius* 182. Marble tombstone, Rome. [Latin]. E: *CIL* VI 8636; **ILS* 1682; Smallwood, *Documents Gaius* 183. Marble tombstone, figure of a pitcher to left of text, another of a dish to the right. Rome. [Latin]. F: *CIL* VI 8443; **ILS* 1546; Smallwood, *Documents Gaius* 172. Marble tombstone, Rome. [Latin].

A. Gordon, *Album* 1.122, Rome

To Claudia Phthonge, | nurse of Britannicus.[1] | Aphnius, Caesar Augustus' | secretary,[2] to his (slave) wife | deserving the very best.

B. *ILS* 1533, Ostia (?)

Of Claudius | Optatus, | freedman of Augustus, | procurator of the port

5   ‖ of Ostia.[3]

C. *ILS* 1643, Capena in Etruria

To the departed spirit | of Tiberius Claudius, freedman of Augustus, | Daus, | financial accountant ‖ of the patrimony | of the Caesars, | 59 years old. | Servilia Aphro | to her dearest husband.

5

D. *ILS* 2816, Rome

To Tiberius Iulius, freedman of Augustus, | Xanthus, manager | for
5 Tiberius Caesar and | the deified Claudius, || and sub-prefect of the
fleet | at Alexandria:[4] | Atellia Prisca his wife | and Lamyrus his freed-
man, his heirs. | He was 90 years old.

E. *ILS* 1682, Rome

Tiberius Claudius | Lemnius, freedman of the deified Claudius |
Augustus, director of library studies.

F. *ILS* 1546, Rome

To the departed spirit | of Tiberius Claudius, | freedman of Augustus,
5 | Saturninus, || procurator of the Five Percent Tax on Inheritances | in
the province | of Achaia. Saturnina his wife erected (this monument).

1 Son of the emperor Claudius by Messalina.
2 Subordinate to the Chief Secretary: Weaver, *Familia Caesaris* 259ff.
3 For his duties see Meiggs, *op. cit.* 298–9.
4 The post itself may have been only temporary: C. G. Starr, *The Roman Imperial Navy*[2]
   (London 1960) 110–11.

48 Governor's decree on altering documents. AD 43–8.
Limestone stele, Myra in Lycia. [Greek]

G. E. Bean in *Anzeiger der Österreichischen Akademie der Wissenschaften, Phil.-hist. Klasse* (1962)
pp. 4–9, No. 2; M. Wörrle in J. Borchhardt (ed.), *Myra, eine lykische Metropole in antiker
und byzantinischer Zeit* (Berlin 1975) pp. 255–6 (+ photograph).

Bean, *loc. cit.*; Wörrle, *op. cit.* 254–86.

vv Decree *vv* | of Q[uintus Ve]ranius, legate | of T[ibe]r[ius Cl]audius
5 Caesar Augustus, | with pro praetorian power.[1] *vv* || T[ry]phon, *public
slave* of the city of Tlos, | has [not] learned his lesson either from my
edicts or | threats or from the punishment of slaves | who have com-
10 mitted errors of a similar nature, | that it is not permitted to receive (for
registration in the city archives) documents of the administration | that
have interpolations and erasures. | I have introduced him to the [realiz-
ation] of my displeasure in such matters | by having him lashed with
15 the whip, | and I have demonstrated to him by such a method that || [if]
he is again careless of my orders concerning registration | of docu-
ments, not only by beatings | but also by the supreme punishment | will
I force the rest of the *public slaves* to forget their form|er indifference.
20 Trypho||n's exposer, Apollonius, son of Diopeithes, from Pata|ra shall
receive from the city of Tlos, | through the incumbent treasurers, three

hundred drachmas, | for such is the courtesy amount (of money) I have
set for those who ex|pose public slaves.
25   In order that those who expedite ‖ administrative documents – on
whose behalf it has been my concern in this matter | to order investi-
gations – (that they) should stop acting contrary to their own | security,
I make it clear that every administrative document of any | type will be
invalid from today onward if it is | written [on] a palimpsest or has
30   interpolations or erasures, ‖ whether it is a contract or a handwritten
note or a | regulation or a clarification or a set of specific instructions |
or an account rendered or a legal challenge or | a disclosure about a
legal situation or a | decision of arbitrators or *judges*. And if, through
35   some su‖ch *document*, a fixed period of time is required (for something
to be done), and in such a way that | the fixed period is to be filled in
later, the one who does not *follow* my orders | will disrupt the adminis-
tration. For, in regard to those (documents) which in their delivery (to
the archives) | are open to suspicion, | after being *subject to forgetfulness*
after the passage of much time, [how] can they not appear unreliable
40   ‖ when the reason why the interpolations and the *erasures* were made |
can no longer be clear to those who intend to review the documents? |
In no less a manner will also those | public slaves who accept such
documents be punished. | Throughout the whole *province* which is
45   entrusted to me the local officials ‖ shall publish this decree in the *month*
of Artemision.

1 For the career of Quintus Veranius see A. E. Gordon, *Quintus Veranius Consul A.D. 49*
(Berkeley 1952). He was the first governor of Lycia-Pamphylia. Cf. R. Syme in
Classical Quarterly NS 7 (1957) 123–5 (*Roman Papers* I 333–5) for his family.

49   Officers and men in the conquest of Britain. AD 43 or later.

A: *CIL* V 7003; **ILS* 2701; Smallwood, *Documents Gaius* 282. Stone found at Colonia Iulia
Augusta Taurinorum (modern Turin). [Latin] **B**: M. Dubois in *BCH* 5 (1881) 473–4 (+
drawing); *IGRR* IV 1086; *SIG*³ 804; Smallwood, **Documents Gaius* 262. Stone base broken
at top, Khiragomas near Pili on Cos. Cf. Tacitus, *Ann.* 12.61 and 67; Pliny, *Nat. Hist.*
29.7. See R. Herzog in *Historische Zeitschrift* 125 (1922) 216–47; Pflaum, *Carrières* 1,
No. 16; Millar, *Emperor* 85–6. **C**: *CIL* III 6809; **ILS* 2696; Smallwood, *Documents Gaius*
281. Tombstone, first three lines in very large letters, Antioch towards Pisidia. **D**: **RIB*
201; Smallwood, *Documents Gaius* 284a. Tombstone, sculptured relief at top in niche of
a cavalryman in scale-armor, oval shield on left arm, riding on a horse beneath which
is a naked barbarian; above the niche is a winged sphinx flanked by two lions; the
inscription is in a smoothed area below the niche: photograph in *RIB*, Pl. V, and a
close-up of the cavalryman in D. R. Dudley and G. Webster, *The Roman Conquest of Britain*
(London 1965) opp. p. 23. Found at Camulodunum (Colchester). **E**: **RIB* 200;
Smallwood, *Documents Gaius* 284b. Tombstone, sculptured relief at top in a niche of a

standing centurion in full uniform, the inscription at bottom. Photograph in *RIB*, Pl. V,
and Dudley and Webster, *op. cit.* opp. p. 20. Found at Camulodonum (Colchester).
F: *CIL* VII 156; **RIB* 293 (+ drawing). Tombstone, at top of which is a pine cone flanked
by two lions, Viroconium (Wroxeter). Photograph in Dudley and Webster, *op. cit.* opp.
p. 189, and in G. Webster, *Rome Against Caratacus* (London 1981) Pl. XV. **G**: *CIL* VII 155;
*RIB 294 (+ drawing). Tombstone, broken horizontally through the middle,
Viroconium (Wroxeter). Photograph in Dudley and Webster, *op. cit.* opp. p. 189, and in
Webster, *loc. cit.*

A. *ILS* 2701, Colonia Iulia Augusta Taurinorum

(Dedicated) to Gaius Gavius, son of Lucius, | (of the tribe) Stellatina,
Silvanus, | primipilaris of the Eighth Legion Augusta, | tribune of the
5   Second Cohort of Vigiles, ‖ tribune of the Thirteenth Urban Cohort, |
tribune of the Twelfth Praetorian Cohort,[1] | decorated by the deified
Claudius | in the Britannic War | with Collars, Armbands, Discs,
10 ‖ (and) a Golden Wreath,[2] | patron of our colony, | by decree of the
decuriones.[3]

B. Smallwood, *Documents Gaius* 262, Cos

[--- Gaius Stertinius,][4] son of Herakleitos, (of the tribe) Corne|[l]ia,
Xenophon, the | chief physician of the gods Au|gusti[5] and in charge of
5   Gre‖ek Responses,[6] tri|bune of soldiers and prefect | of fabri[7] | and
10 decorated in the | triumph [over] the Britons with a Crown ‖ of gold and
a Parade-Spear, *son* of the people, | [[Nero-loving,]] Caesar-loving,
Augustus-|loving, Roman-loving, | fatherland-loving, benefactor of his
15 father|land, chief priest of the gods and priest *throughout* ‖ *his life* of the
Augusti and of Asklepios | <and> of Health and of Epione.[8] Temple-
treasur|er Marcus Septicius (?), Marcus' | *son*, Rufus, and Ariston son
of | Philokles, both of them Caesar-loving.

C. *ILS* 2696, Antioch toward Pisidia

To Publius Anicius, | son of Publius, (of the tribe) Sergia, Maxi|mus,
5   prefect | of Gnaeus Domitius Ahenobar‖bus,[9] primipilaris of the Legion
Twelfth Fulminata, commandant | of the camp of the Legion Second
Augusta in | Britain, prefect of the army which is in Egypt, | decorated
10 by the emperor with | military decorations because of the expedi‖tion,
honored | with a Mural Crown and a | Parade-Spear because of the war
15 | in Britain. The city | of Alexandria which is ‖ in Egypt, to honor him.

D. *RIB* 201, Camulodunum

Longinus, Sdapeze|matygus' son, double-pay (cavalryman) | in the Ala
I of the Thracians, from the district | of Serdica, 40 years old, 15 years
5   in service. ‖ His heirs in accordance with his will *had this set up.* | He is
buried here.

E. *RIB* 200, Camulodunum

Marcus Favonius, son of Marcus, (of the tribe) Pollia, Faci|lis, centurion of the Legion Twentieth (Valeria Victrix). Verecund|us and Novicius, his freedmen, set | this up. He is buried here.

F. *RIB* 293, Viroconium

Gaius Mannius, | son of Gaius, (of the tribe) Pollia, Secu|ndus from
5 Pollentia, | soldier of the Legion Twentieth (Valeria Victrix), || 52 years old, | 31 years in service, | beneficiarius (i.e. aide) to the legate with pro praetorian power. | He is buried here.

G. *RIB* 294, Viroconium

Marcus Petronius, | son of Lucius, (of the tribe) Menenia, | from
5 Vicetia, age | 38 years, || soldier of the Legion | Fourteenth Gemina, served for | 18 years, was standard-bearer. | He is buried here.

1 His promotions are given in ascending order. As tribune of the Twelfth praetorian Cohort he figured in the Conspiracy of Piso against Nero in AD 65 and, although acquitted, committed suicide: Tacitus, *Ann.* 15.50; 60–1; 71.
2 For military decorations see Maxfield, *Military Decorations.*
3 These decuriones were the senators of the colony.
4 Easily restored, since Gaius Stertinius Xenophon is known from many other inscriptions: Pflaum, *loc. cit.*
5 I.e. Augustus and Tiberius.
6 Cf. Josephus, *Ant. Jud.* 14.210. He gave the emperor's answers to requests by Greek envoys to the court.
7 See above, Document No. 21 n. 2.
8 In Greek mythology Epione was the wife of Asklepios, god of healing, while the personified Health was one of his daughters.
9 He was consul ordinarius in AD 32 and father of Nero: *PIR*[2] D 127.

50   Favors granted the city of Volubilis by Claudius.[1]
Stone found on the steps of a temple, Volubilis in Mauretania. [Latin]

L. Chatelain in *CRAI* 1915, 396; *ILAfr* 634; Abbott–Johnson, *Municipal Administration* 53; *FIRA* I 70; Smallwood, **Documents Gaius* 407b.

Chatelain, *op. cit.* 394–7; Abbott–Johnson, *op. cit.* 357–8; M. P. Charlesworth in *CAH* 10.675; Millar, *Emperor* 404; Sherwin-White, *Citizenship*[2] 241–3 and 341–3; U. Schillinger-Häfele in *Chiron* 4 (1974) 443ff.

Marcus Valerius, Bostar's | son, (of the tribe) Galeria, Severus, | aedile,
5 sufes,[2] duovir, | first flamen || in his municipality, | prefect of soldiers against Aedemo|n (who was) crushed in the war,[3] | – to him (this has been dedicated by) the municipal senate of Volubilis because of his
10 meri|torious actions on behalf of the city and the emba||ssy so well

conducted by him, through which he obtained for his (countrymen)
from the deified | Claudius Roman citizenship | and legal marriage
rights with for|eign women, immunity (from imperial taxes) | for ten
15   years, (new) settlers, and the property of citizens ‖ killed in the war
whose he|irs were no longer alive.[4] *vv* | *vv* | Fabia Bira, daughter of
Izelta, as wife on behalf of her most consider|ate husband, who showed
20   her every respect, ‖ has here remitted the expense | and from her own
funds has given and dedicated (this monument).

1   The present monument was erected after the death of Claudius, but the actions of
    the deceased M. Valerius Severus, took place back in AD 44, as we know from
    another inscription found in the same city (Smallwood, *Documents Gaius* 407a).
2   The 'sufes' was a local magistrate found in Punic cities. After Volubilis became a
    municipality on the Roman model M. Valerius Severus became its Roman-style
    magistrate, the duovir. He was of Punic origin, as shown by his father's name.
3   Toward the end of the reign of Gaius a revolt began in Mauretania under a leader
    called Aedemon (Pliny, *Nat. Hist.* 5.1.11). This is probably the war mentioned here.
    Severus helped to suppress it and Claudius gave the people of Volubilis the Roman
    citizenship and the other favors.
4   Such property ordinarily would have reverted to the Roman treasury rather than to
    the city: see Cuq in *Journal des Savants* 15 (1917) 481ff.

51   Vow for victory in Britain. AD 45–6.
White marble, six-sided block, damaged at the top, Rusellae in Etruria.
[Latin]

V. Saladino in *ZPE* 39 (1980) 229, No. 24 (+ photograph)

Having undertaken the discharge of a vow | for the safety and return
5   and | victory in Britain | of Tiberius Claudius Caesa‖r Augustus
Germanicus, | pontifex maximus, holding the tribunician power for the
fifth time (AD 45–6), imperator | for the tenth time, father of his
country, consul designate for the fourth time, | Aulus Vicirius Proculus,
10 | priest of Augustus and tribune of the soldiers, ‖ for the victory in
Britain | has fulfilled his vow.

52   Edict of Claudius granting Roman citizenship. AD 46.
Bronze tablet found near Tridentum in the Italian Alps. [Latin]

CIL V 5050; ILS 206; Bruns[7] 79; Abbott–Johnson, *Municipal Administration* 26; *FIRA* I 71;
Smallwood, *Documents Gaius 368. Photograph: Bruns, *Fontes Iurus Romani Antiqui* II,
Simulacra (Tübingen 1912) XV, No. 17.

Abbott–Johnson, *op. cit.* 348–51; Charlesworth in *CAH* 10.684–5; Sherwin-White,
Citizenship[2] 231 and 374–5.

In the consulship of Marcus Iunius Silanus and Quintus Sulpicius
Camerinus (AD 46), | on the Ides of March (March 15) at Baiae in the
imperial quarters, an edict | of Tiberius Claudius Caesar Augustus
5   Germanicus was published, | which is recorded below. ‖ Tiberius
Claudius Caesar Augustus Germanicus, pontifex | maximus, holding
the tribunician power for the sixth time (AD 46), imperator for the
eleventh time, father of his country, consul designate for the fourth
time, declares: |
     Since, because of old and long pending controversies, even in the |
time of my uncle Tiberius Caesar, (when) he had sent Pinarius
10   Apollinaris to settle them | – these controversies were only, ‖ if I
remember correctly, between Comum and the Bergalei – | (since) he
(i.e. Pinarius Apollinaris), at first because of the persistent absence of
my uncle | and then in the rule of Gaius because it was not demanded
of him, | had neglected to send in a report, not because of foolishness I
may add, and (since) later | Camurius Statutus had informed me that
15   several fields ‖ and forest-pasturelands were within my jurisdiction, I
dealt with this immediate situation by sending | Iulius Planta, my
friend and companion. | Since he has conferred with my procurators
who were either in other | areas or in the immediate vicinity and since
he has with the greatest care inves|tigated the matter and has held a
hearing, in regard to these various matters, as they have been brought
20   to my atten‖tion by the written report made by him, I grant him per-
mission to decide them and to de|liver verdicts. *vv* |
     Concerning the status of the Anauni and Tulliassi and Sinduni,[1] |
some of whom, an informant is said to have proved, are attributed to
25   the Triden|tini, while others are not attributed,[2] ‖ although I under-
stand that this class of people do not have a very strong case | for Roman
citizenship, nevertheless, since by long | usage it is said they are in
possession of it and are so associ|ated with the Tridentini that they
cannot be withdrawn from them without serious injury to that splendid
municipality, | I permit them to remain in that legal status in which
30   they believed they were. ‖ I do this as a favor to them, indeed I do it all
the more freely because | many of this class of people are said to be even
soldiers in my Praetorian Guard, | some actually line commanders, |
and some few enrolled in panels at Rome to judge cases at law. |
     I do them this favor so that in regard to whatever things they have
35   done as if‖ they were Roman citizens, or whatever measures they have
taken either among themselves or with | the Tridentini or with anyone
else, I may now order those things or measures to be legally binding.
And the names, | which they had before acting as if they were Roman
citizens, I now permit them to retain.

1 Two separate issues are involved in this edict: one is a controversy between Comum and the tribe of the Bergalei, the other a matter of citizenship. The final report of Statutus may have shown a connection between them or at least made it reasonable for Claudius to combine them in a single edict.

2 Small towns or settlements were regularly 'attributed' to the nearest city government for administrative purposes. Thus, surrounding tribes might easily assume that their own legal status was that of the city government to which they were connected. The citizens of Tridentum possessed Roman citizenship.

53   Claudius repairs the road from the Po to the Danube. AD 47 (?)
Milestone found near Feltria in northern Italy. [Latin]

*CIL V 8003; *ILS* 208.

G. Walser in *Historia* 29 (1980) 438–62.

Tiberius Claudius, son of Drusus, | Caesar Augustus Germa|nicus,
5   pontifex maxi|mus, holding the tribunician pow‖er for the sixth time
(AD 46–January 25, 47), consul for the fourth time (AD 47), imperator
for the eleventh time, father of his country, | censor, repaired the Via
Claudia | Augusta. Drusus, | his father, when the Alps had been opened
10   up by war,[1] | constructed this (road), from ‖ Altinum to the river |
Danube 350 miles.[2]

1 This refers to the victory over the Raeti in 15 BC, which resulted in the formation of the province Raetia.
2 Altinum is near the sea-coast some distance north of the delta of the Po River. A similar milestone (*CIL* V 8003) of the same time was found near Meran, north of Verona, in the Athesis River valley, more than eighty miles due west of Altinum. In place of 'from Altinum' it reads 'from the Po River'.

54   Letter of Claudius about Dionysiac performers. AD 48–9.
Marble block, perhaps part of a base (?), Miletus. [Greek]

*Milet III (1914) 156 (+ photograph of squeeze); Smallwood, *Documents Gaius* 373b.

Magie, *RRAM* I 543; M. Amelotti in *Studia et Documenta Historiae et Iuris* 21 (1955) 137ff.

[Ti]berius Claudius Caesar Augustus Germ[ani|c]us, holding the
tribunician power for the eighth time (AD 48–9), consul for the [fourth
time,] | imperator for the fifteenth time, father of his country, censor, |
5   to the Dionysiac sacred victors and per‖formers,[1] greetings. The fact
that you made mention of the things which I gr|anted to you, when I
confirmed the rights given to you by the Au|gusti before me and by the
senate, | I approve and will try to increase them, since you are so
10   pi|ously disposed toward my hou‖se. This was brought to me by Marcus

Vale|rius Iunianus, member of my household, a man whom I also pr|aised as one so disposed toward you. | [Farewell (?)]

1 See the Glossary *s.v.* Dionysiac Artists.

55   Speech of Claudius to the senate. AD 48.

Bronze tablet, upper part missing, inscribed in two columns, Lugdunum in Gaul [Latin]

CIL XIII 1668; *ILS* 212; Bruns[7] 52; Ph. Fabia, *La Table Claudienne de Lyon* (Lyon 1929) (+ photograph); *FIRA* I 43; Smallwood, **Documents Gaius* 369; Gordon, *Epigraphy* 42 (+ photograph). Cf. Tacitus, *Ann.* 11.23–4 (paraphrase of the speech).

Fabia, *loc. cit.*; A. Momigliano, *Claudius the Emperor and his Achievement* (New York 1961) 10–16; V. M. Scramuzza, *The Emperor Claudius* (Cambridge, Mass. 1940) 99–110; K. Wellesley in *Greece and Rome* (1954) 13–35; Syme, *Tacitus* 1.317–19 and 2.703–8; J. Carcopino, *Les Étapes de l'impérialisme romain* (Paris 1961) 174-208; Sherwin-White, *Citizenship*[2] 237ff.; E. Huzar in *ANRW* 2.32.2.627–32; M. Griffin in *Classical Quarterly* 32 (1982) 404–18.

(Col. 2)[1] Of course, | breaking with the past, the deified Aug[ustus,] *my great uncle*, and my uncle Tiberius | Caesar wished the whole flower of the colonies and the municipalities everywhere, | that is, the men of
5   worth and wealth, to be in this senate house. ‖ But what then? Is not an Italian senator to be preferred to a provincial? | When I begin to obtain approval for this part of my censorship, what | I feel about this matter I will reveal to you. But not even provincials, | provided they can be an ornament to the senate house, do I think ought to be rejected. |
      Look at the most flourishing and powerful city of Vienna.[2] For how
10   ‖ long a time has it been sending senators to this senate house? From that co|lony comes the jewel of the equestrian order – one of a few – Lucius Vestinus,[3] | whom I esteem most highly and retain today in the conduct of my affairs. His childr|en, I pray, will enjoy the first level of priestly offices and, later with | the years, I pray, they will reach higher
15   offices of their rank. The fearful name of the ban‖dit I would not even mention – I hate that wrestling-school prodigy – a man who brought into his hou|se the consulship even before his colony (of Vienna) had acquired the solid benefit of Roman citizenship.[4] | I can say the same about his brother – | a miserable and most shameful affair it was – that
20   he could not be useful to you | as a senator. *vv* ‖ Now it is time, Tiberius Caesar Germanicus,[5] to reveal yourself to the conscript fathers,[6] | (explaining) in what direction your address is heading, for already (in it) you have come to the farthest borders of Gallia Nar|bonensis. *vv* | Just look! As many young men as I see here cause us no more regret | (that they are) senators than it causes regret to Persicus, a most noble

25   man, a fri‖end of mine, to read among the images of his ancestors the
      na|me 'Allobrogicus'.[7] If you agree that this is so, what more do you
      de|sire than that I point out to you the fact that the land beyond the
      borders | of the province of Narbonensis is already sending senators to
      you, since | we do not regret having such men from Lugdunum within
30   our order? ‖ Indeed with hesitation, conscript fathers, have I gone
      beyond your customary and familiar pro|vincial boundaries, but even
      haltingly the case for Gallia Comata ⌐ must be made. In this matter, if
      anyone looks at the fact that in war for te|n years they fought against
      the deified Iulius, let him set against that fact the one hundred years |
35   of quiet loyalty and obedience which by many critical sit‖uations of
      ours were more than merely tested. When my father Drusus | was
      subjugating Germany, they provided for him quietly with a safe and
      secure peace in his rear, | indeed even when he had been called away to
      that war from the census, which was at that time a new procedure to
      which the Gauls were un|accustomed. How ar|duous for us even now is
40   the census, although nothing more than ‖ recording our resources is
      required, | we know from all too vivid experience. *vv*

1 The first column of 40 lines is here omitted. It contains a brief survey of early Roman
   history by Claudius.
2 The modern Vienne.
3 Lucius Iulius Vestinus (*PIR*[2] I 622) later rose to become prefect of Egypt. Cf. Tacitus,
   Hist. 4.53.
4 Claudius refers to Valerius Asiaticus: see Tacitus, *Ann.* 11.1–3. He was a provincial
   who rose to a second consulship (AD 46), was (falsely) accused of a plan to start a
   revolt against Rome, and, after a spirited defence in the presence of Claudius and
   Messalina, was allowed to commit suicide. Tacitus glorifies him.
5 Claudius here addresses himself.
6 The usual form of address to members of the senate.
7 Paullus Fabius Persicus (*PIR*[2] F 51) was governor of Asia under Claudius (AD 48).
   His edict, concerning the administration of funds of the temple of Artemis at
   Ephesus, has survived (*SEG* IV 516). Some Gauls, among the Allobroges, in the past
   had become *clientes* of the Fabian clan and, thus, after acquiring Roman citizenship,
   had used 'Fabius' as their nomen, while, on the other hand, some of the Fabii had
   adopted the epithet 'Allobrogicus' and added it to their names. Cf. Seneca. *De Benef.*
   4.30.2.

56   Cogidubnus, client-king in Roman Britain.
Marble slab in four pieces, left side missing, Noviomagus in Britain
(Chichester). [Latin]

*RIB 91 (+ drawing); Smallwood, *Documents Gaius* 197.

P. Salway, *Roman Britain* (Oxford 1981) 90–2, 659, 748–52; G. Webster, *Rome Against
Caratacus* (London 1981) 124–30 (by A. Barrett).

To Neptune and Minerva | this temple | for the safety of the divine
5 house | by the authority of [Tiberius] Claudius || [Co]gidubnus, *great
king*[1] of Britain, | has been given by the *guild* of smiths and its members
| out of their own resources. The site has been donated by | [---]ens, son
of Pudentius.

1 The reading of the stone at this point was formerly thought to be 'king (and) *legate of
Augustus* in Britain', but J. E. Bogaers (in *Britannia* 10 (1979) 244–5) has shown that
such a reading is incorrect. His suggestion is followed here. See Barrett in Webster,
loc. cit. Tacitus (*Agricola* 14) says that Cogidumnus (= Cogidubnus) was given certain
native states or areas in Britain to rule over as king. Claudius apparently was the
emperor who conferred the title on him.

57 Sextus Afranius Burrus, praetorian prefect (AD 51–62).
Three fragments of a base, Vasio in Gallia Narbonensis. [Latin]

CIL XII 5842; *ILS 1321; Smallwood, *Documents Gaius* 259. Cf. Tacitus, *Ann.* 12.42 and
14.51; Suetonius, *Nero* 35.5.

Griffin, *Nero* 67–9 and *passim.*

The Vocontii of Vasio[1] (dedicated this monument to) | their patron, |
Sextus Afranius, son of Sextus, | (of the tribe) Voltinia, Burrus,
5 || tribune of the soldiers, procurator of Augus|ta (Livia), procurator of
Tiberius Caesar, | procurator of the deified Claudius, | prefect of the
Praetorian Guard, with the orna|ments of consular rank.

1 Burrus seems to have been a native son of Vasio, the site of modern Vaison. For his
career see *PIR*[2] A 441 and Pflaum, *Carrières* No. 13. The Vocontii were Celtic in origin.

58 Discharge diploma for a sailor at Misenum. AD 52.
Two small bronze tablets, inscribed on both sides, with small holes to
tie them together, Stabiae in Italy. [Latin]

ILS 1986; *CIL XVI 1; Smallwood, *Documents Gaius* 295.

C. G. Starr, *The Roman Imperial Navy* (London 1960) 88–96; J. C. Mann in *Epigraphische
Studien* 9 (1972) 233–41; S. Dušanić in *Arheološki Vestnik* 33 (1982) 201; *idem* in *ZPE* 47
(1982) 149ff.

(Exterior of first tablet)[1] Tiberius Claudius Caesar Augustus
Germanicus, | pontifex maximus, holding the tribunician power for the
twelfth time (AD 52), imperator for the twenty-seventh time, | father of
his country, censor, consul for the fifth time: | to the trierarchs[2] and
5 rowers who have ser||ved in the fleet which is at Misenum under the
command of Ti|berius Iulius, freedman of Augustus, Optatus and who

have been discharged | honorably, whose names have been written below,[3] | to them, their children, and their descendants | he has given
10   citizenship and legal marriage ‖ with the wives which they had at the time | when citizenship was given to them, or, if any | were unmarried, with those women whom afterwards | they married, provided only one to each. | *vv* On the third day before the Ides of December (December
15   11), *vv* ‖ when Faustus Cornelius Sulla Felix *vv* | (and) Lucius Salvidienus Rufus Salvianus were consuls (AD 52). | *vv* To ordinary sailor *vv* | Sparticus, son of Diuzenus, Dipscurtus, of the Bessi.[4] | Copied
20   and certified from the tablet of bronze ‖ which is attached on the Capitolium in Rome to the temple | of Loyalty of the Roman People, on its right side.

1   This is the earliest known discharge diploma and, like the hundreds of others of later
    date, it consists of two small (about 17 × 14 cm) bronze tablets firmly tied together,
    so that only the exterior sides of both tablets can be read without untying them. The
    exterior reproduces the text of the interior, but includes the names of witnesses to
    the authenticity of the document. None of the original tablets fixed on the
    Capitolium has survived, only the separately engraved diplomas like the present
    one. They provide an invaluable source of information about Roman military units
    and their strengths throughout the Roman world.
2   These were naval captains, regularly Greeks.
3   The original bronze tablet (see above, n. 1) contained all the names of soldiers
    discharged from a particular province at a particular time – hence the plural 'names'.
4   The Bessi were Thracians.

59   Claudius and the aqueducts. AD 52–3.
Inscription on the Aqua Claudia, Rome at the Porta Praenestina.
[Latin]

CIL VI 1256; *ILS 218; Smallwood, *Documents Gaius* 309; Gordon, *Album* 44 (+ photo-graph). Cf. Frontinus, *On the Aqueducts* 1.13–15; Tacitus, *Ann.* 11.13; Suetonius, *Claudius* 20.1.

E. B. Van Deman, *The Building of the Aqueducts* (Washington 1934) 13–14, 187–270, 271–330.

Tiberius Claudius, son of Drusus, Caesar Augustus Germanicus, pontifex maximus, | holding the tribunician power for the twelfth time (AD 52–3), consul for the fifth time, imperator for the twenty-seventh time, father of his country, | saw to it that the Aqua Claudia was brought into the city from the springs which are called Caeruleus and Curtius from the 45th milestone, | and also the Anio Novus from the 62nd milestone, at his own expense.[1]

1 On the same aqueduct are other inscriptions which show that repairs were needed
  in AD 71 and 81.

60   Ofonius Tigellinus, rags to riches. Claudius–Nero.

Scholia on Juvenal, *Satires* 1.155, *s.v.* 'Picture Tigellinus!' Cf. Dio 59.23.9, 60.4.1;
Tacitus, *Ann.* 14.51.2.

Ophonius Tigellinus, whose father from Agrigentum was banished to
Scyllaceum, was poor as a young man but quite handsome, intimately
associated with Marcus Vinicius and Lucius (? = Gnaeus)[1] Domitius,
husbands of Agrippina and Fulvia (? = Iulia),[2] sisters of Caesar
(Caligula), and he was equally suspect in the case of both wives. For
this reason he was banished from Rome and lived as a fisherman in
Achaia until, after inheriting a fortune, he was recalled on the condition
that he remain out of sight of Claudius. Therefore, he bought pasture
lands in Apulia and Calabria, bred horses for the chariot-games,
obtained the friendship of Nero, and was the first to instill in him the
passion for the circus games.

1 'Lucius' is a mistake. Agrippina was the wife of Gnaeus Domitius Ahenobarbus,
  consul AD 32 (*PIR* D 127).
2 'Fulvia' is a corruption of 'Iulia', i.e. Iulia Livilla.

NERO
(AD 54–68)
NERO CLAUDIUS CAESAR AUGUSTUS
GERMANICUS

Titles: PONTIFEX MAXIMUS (AD 54)
FATHER OF HIS COUNTRY (AD 56)
HOLDER OF THE TRIBUNICIAN POWER: first in
AD 54, then annually on December 4 (?)
CONSUL: AD 55 (I), 57 (II), 58 (III), 60 (IV), 68 (V)

Death: June 9, AD 68.

Memory condemned.

The *consules ordinarii* **under Nero**

(For the suffect consuls see J. Ginsburg in *AJAH* 6 (1981) 60ff.)

AD		
55	Nero Claudius Caesar Augustus Germanicus	L. Antistius Vetus
56	Q. Volusius Saturninus	P. Cornelius (Lentulus?) Scipio
57	Nero II	L. Calpurnius Piso
58	Nero III	M. Valerius Messalla Corvinus
59	C. Vipstanus Apronianus	C. Fonteius Capito
60	Nero IV	Cossus Cornelius Lentulus
61	P. Petronius Turpilianus	L. Caesennius Paetus
62	P. Marius Celsus	L. Asinius Gallus
63	C. Memmius Regulus	L. Verginius Rufus
64	C. Laecanius Bassus	M. Licinius Crassus Frugi
65	A. Licinius Nerva Silianus Firmus Pasidienus	M. (Iulius) Vestinus Atticus
66	C. Luccius Telesinus	C. Suetonius Paullinus II?
67	L. Iulius Rufus	Fonteius Capito
68	Ti. Catius Asconius Silius Italicus	P. Galerius Trachalus

61   Draft of a proclamation of Nero as emperor. AD 54.
Papyrus from Oxyrhynchus in Egypt. [Greek]

P. Oxy. 1021; Wilcken, *Chrestomathie* 1.2.113; Smallwood, **Documents Gaius* 47; Hengstl, *Griechische Papyri* 10.

A. S. Hunt, commentary on *P. Oxy.* 1021; Hengstl, *op. cit.* 49–50.

Fulfilling the debt | to his ancestors, the ma|nifest god Caesar | has
5 departed to them, ‖ and the expected and hoped | for imperator | of the
world has been pro|claimed: the good | spirit of the ‖ world, the *origin* |

of [[the greatest of]] all | good things, Nero | has been proclaimed
10   Caesar. | For this reason, all of us ought ‖ to wear wreaths | and sacrifice
oxen, | to show to all the gods | our gratitude. Year 1 of Nero | Claudius
15   Caesar Augustus Germanicus, ‖ on the twenty-first of the month New
Augustus.[1]

> 1 Claudius died on October 13, AD 54. Considering the delays in transportation by
> sea and the bureaucratic work necessary in Rome and Alexandria to disseminate the
> information, 35 days is not an excessive period of time from the day of Claudius'
> death to the present date of November 17. Here at Oxyrhynchus the strategos would
> have communicated the proclamation to the local inhabitants and he seems to have
> prepared his own text, for the style and the corrections in the text before us show
> that it is a draft.

62   Nero refuses divine honors. AD 55 (?).
Greek papyrus from the Arsinoite nome, Egypt.

P. Med. inv. 70.01 verso; O. Montevecchi and G. Geraci in *Akten des XII Internationalen
Papyrologenkongresses* (1971) (Munich 1974) 293 (+ photograph); Q. Montevecchi in
*Aegyptus 50 (1970) 6–7 (+ photograph).

Montevecchi, *op. cit.* 5–33, and in *La Parola del Passato* 30 (1975) 48–58.

(Col. 1) [----] of the remaining | two (honors) your temple I de|cline
5   because to gods alone | is this honor ‖ to be granted rightly by men, |
and the gold crow|n I released to be sent | back to you, not wishing at
10   the be|ginning of my principate to bur‖den you. Whatever (privileges)
| the six thousand fo|ur [hundred] and seventy-|[five] of you[1] have |
15   received from the *emperors*[2] before me ‖ [I wish to be securely yours,] |
(Col. 2) for all of you in common and | each according to his share to
guard, | yourselves to be free from insult and to be unmolested, | just as
20   the god my father ‖ wished. You have given testimony | for everything
which he has granted both to the | city and to the six thousand four |
hundred and seventy-five of you, | and I approve and *take you under my*
25   *care*. The en‖voys were [Ai]akidas son of Ptolemaios, | Antenor [----
]ethos, Nibitas | son of Nibitas, Po[lykra]tes son of Didymos, | [----]

> 1 The same phrase occurs in other documents from Egypt, including a dedication to
> Nero of AD 60/61 (*OGIS* 668 = *IGRR* I 1124), for all of which see Montevecchi, *op. cit.*
> 20–4. The numbers refer to Greek *katoikoi*, i.e. military colonists of the Arsinoite
> nome.
> 2 The writer of this letter cannot be Augustus or Tiberius, for the plural 'emperors
> before me' would be inappropriate. Claudius could not speak of Gaius as 'my father'
> (line 19), and therefore Nero or Titus or Domitian come into consideration.
> Montevecchi has shown that the envoy Nibitas (lines 26–7) can be dated to Nero's
> reign by other evidence.

63   Prefect of Egypt honored at Bousiris. Between AD 55 and 59.

Stone stele damaged at upper right corner, Memphis in Egypt near the pyramid of Chephren. [Greek]

OGIS 666; *IGRR* I 1110; *SB* 8303; Smallwood, *Documents Gaius* 418.

With good luck. | Since [[Nero]] Claudius Caesar Augustus |
Germanicus Imperator, the good spirit of the | inhabited world, along
5   with all the good deeds of his benefactions ‖ to Egypt has shown the
most manifest foresight | in sending to us Tiberius Claudi|us Balbillus
as governor,[1] and because of this man's fa|vors and benefactions Egypt
10   is full of all good things, | sees the gifts of the Nile growing ‖ greater year
by year, and | now enjoys even more the well-balanced rising of the god
(i.e. the Nile), it has been decided | by the people from the village of
Bouseiris of the Letopoli|te (nome) who live near the pyramids[2] and |
15   by the district secretaries and villa‖ge secretaries who dwell in (the
nome) to pass a decree and to erect | a stone stele near [the greatest
god,] the Sun | Harmachis, from the good deeds engraved on it | [show-
ing] his benefactions | and letting [everyone] know his noble character
20   and conduct toward all of ‖ Egypt. For it is [fitting] that his god-like
favors, recor|ded by sacred writings, forever be re|membered. He came
| into our nome and performed an act of adoration of the Sun
25   ‖ Harmachis, overseer and savior, having fully enjoyed the pyra|mids'
greatness and magnificence. And when he had seen the great size of the
sand (and) because of the length | of time [----]

1 He was prefect of Egypt AD 55–9: Stein, *Präfekten* 33–4.
2 Cf. Pliny, *Nat. Hist.* 36–76.

64   Governor of Moesia, and the barbarians. About AD 57–67.

Marble tablet damaged on left edge and upper right corner, found in front of the tomb of the Plautii near Tibur. [Latin]

CIL XIV 3608; *ILS* 986; *I. Ital.* IV 1².125; McCrum–Woodhead, *Documents* 261;
Smallwood, *Documents Gaius* 228; Gordon, *Epigraphy* 49 (+ photograph).

L. Halkin in *Ant. Class.* 3 (1934) 121–61; A. Stein, *Die Legaten von Moesien* (Budapest 1940)
29–31; L. R. Taylor in *Memoirs of the American Academy in Rome* 24 (1956) 9–30;
E. Condurachi in *Epigraphica* 19 (1957) 49–65; Garzetti, *Tiberius to Antonines* 180 and 620;
A. Mócsy, *Pannonia* 41; P. Conole and R. D. Milns in *Historia* 32 (1983) 183–200.

(Dedicated) to Tiberius Plautius, son of Marcus, (of the tribe)
[Aniensis,] | Silvanus Aelianus, | pontifex, fellow of the priesthood of
the deified Augustus, | triumvir in charge of the mint, quaestor of

5   Tiberius Caesar, ‖ legate of the Fifth Legion in Germany, | urban
praetor, legate and companion of Claudius | Caesar in Britain, consul
(AD 45), | proconsul of Asia, legate with pro praetorian power of
Moesia,[1] | in which (command) he led across (the Danube) more than
10 100,000 ‖ of the multitude of the Transdanubian peoples[2] | to make
them pay tribute, along with their wives | and children, their leaders or
their kings. | A growing movement of the Sarmatians[3] | he suppressed,
15 although a large part of his army ‖ had been sent by him to Armenia. |
Kings previously unknown or hostile to the Roman People | he led to
the bank (of the Danube), which he was guarding, to make them honor
the military standards of the Romans; | he restored to the kings of the
Bastarnians[4] and | Rhoxolanians their sons, (to the king) of the Dacians
20 his brothers ‖ who had been captured or rescued from their enemy, and
from | some of them (i.e. barbarian kings) he received hostages. By this
(policy of his) he | strengthened and advanced the peace of the
province, | also removing the king of the Scythians from his siege of the
Chersonesus | which is beyond the Borysthenes (Dnieper River).[5]
25 ‖ With a huge amount of wheat from his province (of Moesia) he was
the first | to alleviate the grain supply (problem) of the Roman People.
When he was legate | to Spain, he was recalled to become City Prefect
(in Rome), | and the senate during his prefecture | honored him with
30 triumphal decorations, initiated by Imperator ‖ Caesar Augustus
Vespasianus, whose very words from | his speech are given here: | 'He
governed Moesia in such a way that there ought to have been | no
waiting for me to grant him the honor of his triumphal | decorations,
35 except that the greater ‖ rank of City Prefect came to him because of the
delay.' | In his prefecture of the city Imperator Caesar | Augustus
Vespasianus made him consul for the second time (AD 74).

1 He was governor of Moesia from about AD 57 to 67, the first year of his governorship
   perhaps as early as 57 (so D. M. Pippidi in *Studi si cercetari di istorie veche* 6 (1955) 355ff.)
   as against the year 60 proposed by Stein, *loc. cit.*
2 The pressure of barbarians north of the Danube had been felt even earlier than this
   period, for Strabo (7.303) reports that a certain Aelius Catus – probably the consul
   of AD 4 – had transported 50,000 Getae across the Danube and settled them in
   Thrace.
3 The Sarmatians were nomadic people who, beginning in the second century BC, had
   gradually replaced the earlier nomads called Scythians north of the Black Sea. As
   they moved farther westward they formed a confederacy in a band from the
   Carpathian Mountains to the shores of the Caspian Sea. The Rhoxolanians (line 19)
   were part of that confederacy.
4 Bastarnians were Germanic in origin and they first appeared on the lower Danube
   in the early second century BC.
5 The city called Chersonesus, originally a Greek colony, was located in the southern

Crimea. Nero granted the whole area the protection of a Roman garrison: see Josephus, *Bell. Jud.* 2.16.4, and cf. V. F. Gajdukevič, *Das Bosporanische Reich* (Berlin–Amsterdam 1971) 335ff. It was, however, under the control of the Bosporan king (Strabo 7.4.3).

65 Domitius Corbulo, commander on the eastern front. AD 60–6.

A: *ILS* 9108; F. K. Dörner in *Wiener Jahreshefte* 32 (1940) 128–9, No. 9 (+ photograph); Smallwood, *Documents Gaius* 51a; E. Schwertheim, **I. Kyzikos* II 26 (+ photograph). Marble plaque broken on left side and bottom, Miletopolis near Cyzicus. [Latin and Greek] B: *CIL* III 6741; **ILS* 232; Smallwood, *Documents Gaius* 51b. Stone base, Charput in Armenia Minor.

Cf. Tacitus, *Ann.* 15.

J. G. C. Anderson in *CAH* 10.758–73; Magie, *RRAM* I 554–61; R. Syme in *JRS* 60 (1970) 27–39 (*Roman Papers* II 805–24); R. K. Sherk in *ANRW* 2.7.2.982–8.

A. *I. Kyzikos* **II 26, Miletopolis**

(Latin) [The Sixth Legion F]errata, which | [wintered over] in Armenia [Maior] under Gnaeus Domitius | [Corbulo,] the *legate* [[of Nero]]

5 || [Caesar] Augustus with pro praetorian power, (dedicated this monument) | to [----,] son of Publius, (of the tribe) Scaptia, Asper | [----,][1] to honor him.

B. *ILS* **232, Charput**

Nero Claudius | Caesar Augustus Germanicus | Imperator, pontifex maximus, holding the tribunician power for the eleventh time (AD 64), | consul for the fourth time, imperator for the ninth time, father of his

5 country, || Gnaeus Domitius Corbulo | being the legate of Augustus with pro praetorian power, | and Titus Aurelius Fulvus[2] being the legate of Augustus | of the Third Legion Gallica.

1 There is no certainty about the identity of the person honored by the legion. A Greek translation follows the Latin text, but it is extremely fragmentary.
2 Aurelius Fulvus (*PIR*[2] A 1510) was the grandfather of the future emperor Antoninus Pius (SHA, *Pius* 1). Cf. Tacitus, *Ann.* 15.26 and *Hist.* 1.79. See R. Syme in *JRS* 43 (1953) 154 (*Roman Papers* I 242–3 and 257–8).

66 Accommodations on the highways of Thrace. AD 61–2.
Marble plaque found near the foot of the Haemus Mountains, 36 km from Philippopolis, Thrace. [Latin]

CIL III 6123; *ILS* 231 with addenda; H.-G. Pflaum, *Essai sur le cursus publicus* (Paris 1940) 222; Smallwood, **Documents Gaius* 351.

[[Nero]] *Claudius,* – | son of the deified Claudius, | grandson of
5 Germanicus Caesar, | Tiberius Caesar Augustus' || great-grandson,
great-great-grandson of the deified Augustus, | – Caesar Augustus
Germanicus, | pontifex maximus, holding the tribunician power | for
the eighth time (AD 61–2), imperator for the eighth time, | consul for
10 the fourth time, || father of his country, ordered inns and rest-houses |
along the military highways | to be constructed through | Tiberius
Iulius Ustus,[1] procurator | of the province of Thrace.

1 *PIR*[2] I 632 and Pflaum, *Carrières* 31.

67   Roman veterans meet with the prefect of Egypt. AD 63.
Two papyri records of the same event. [Greek]

A: The official report: *P. Fouad* I 21 (+ photograph); *FIRA* III 171a; Smallwood, **Documents Gaius* 297a. Papyrus, complete on top and bottom, but damaged on the left side, provenance unknown but from somewhere in Egypt. **B**: The soldiers' report: *P. Yale* 1528 (ed. by C. B. Welles in *JRS* 28 (1938) 41–2 with photograph); *FIRA* III 171b; Smallwood, **Documents Gaius* 297b. Papyrus, complete, in two columns, with irregularities of syntax and spelling, purchased in Paris from an Egyptian dealer. Both **A** and **B** date from September of AD 63.

Welles, *op. cit.* 42–9; W. L. Westermann in *Classical Philology* 36 (1941) 21–9; U. Wilcken in *Archiv für Papyrusforschung* 14 (1941) 174–5; Stein, *Präfekten* 36; E. Balogh and H.-G. Pflaum in *Revue historique de droit français et étranger* (1952) 123 (Iulius Lysimachus may be related to Philo).

A. Smallwood, *Documents Gaius* **297a**

vv Copy of Official Record. *vv* | Year 10 of Nero Claudius Caesar
Augustus | Germanicus Imperator, in the month Sebastos 7
(September 4), | in the Great Hall at the tribunal.[1] Present on his
5 Advisory || Board were: Norbanus Ptolemaios the Iuridicus and | the
Idiologos,[2] Avilius Quadratus and Tennius Vetus, | [----] Atticus,
Papirius Pastor and Baebius Iuncinus | the *corps commanders* (?), Iulius
Lysimachus, Claudius Herakleides the dioiketēs,[3] | [Clau]dius
10 Euktemon, Claudius Secundus. *vv* || [In] the matter of the discharged
soldiers, on the subject of (Roman) citizenship. *vv* | [Tuscus:][4] 'I told
you previously that neither similar nor identical | is the basis of com-
plaint for [each] of you, for some of you are *veterans* of the legions, |
others of the alae, others of the cohorts, and still others of the oarsmen,
| [with the result that] the legal right of all of you is *not* the same. I will
15 take care of th||is matter, and I have written to the strategoi nome by
nome in order that the (imperial) goodwill in its entirety | might be
observed for [each] of you according to each one's legal right.' *vv* | (In a
different handwriting) I [----][5] have written (this).

B. Smallwood, *Documents Gaius* **297b**

(Col. 1) Copy of an audience. *vv* | The legionaries made their approach, on the road of the | camp by the temple of Isis. *vv* | Tuscus the prefect
5 (of Egypt) answered *us*: 'Do not speak || impious *rebellion*.[6] Nobody oppresses | you. Write on tablets where each one | of you is staying and I will write to the strategoi (of the nomes) | so that nobody will cause you trouble.' On the 4th of the month Sebastos (September 1) | we gave
10 him the tablets || in the camp headquarters and he said to us: | 'Did you give them separately, each for himself?' And they said to hi|m, they the legionaries, 'We gave them separately.' | On the 5th of the *same month* (September 2) we greeted him near | the Paliourus[7] and he answered
15 our greeting, and on the || [6th] of the same month (September 3) we greeted him in the Hall, | as he sat upon the tribunal. | Tuscus said to us: 'I told you in the camp | and now I tell you the same thing. There is
20 a procedure for | legionaries, another for men of the cohorts, || (Col. 2) still another for oarsmen. Go, | each of you, back to your own (places) and do not be | idle.' *vv*

1 Located in Alexandria. The prefect of Egypt presided.
2 The Iuridicus was an official with judicial power in Egypt who was a Roman equestrian and received his post directly from the emperor. The Idiologos (or Idios Logos) was also a Roman equestrian who was responsible for all irregular or occasional sources of revenue. Both of these men were subordinate to the prefect. Norbanus Ptolemaios held both posts.
3 The *dioikētēs* was a finance officer under the prefect.
4 His name has been supplied from B. He is Gaius Caecina Tuscus (*PIR*[2] C 109), prefect of Egypt from AD 63 probably to as late as 66. Stein, *Präfekten* 35–7.
5 Here would have appeared the signature of the scribe responsible for having the copy made from the official record.
6 Only a few letters remain here: 'rebellion' according to Westermann, 'thing' according to Welles, who conflates with the preceding word to 'impiety'.
7 Location unknown.

68   Nero addresses the Praetorian Guard. AD 64–6.
Sestertius minted at Rome.

Mattingly, **BMC* 1, No. 122 (+ photograph); Smallwood, *Documents Gaius* 292.

M. P. Speidel in *Germania* 62 (1984) 31–45.

(Obverse: NERO CLAUDIUS CAESAR AUGUSTUS
laureate head   PONTIFEX MAXIMUS, HOLDER OF THE
of Nero)   TRIBUNICIAN POWER, IMPERATOR,
                       FATHER OF HIS COUNTRY.

(Reverse: Nero,   ADDRESS TO A COHORT.[1]
Praetorian   IN ACCORDANCE WITH A DECREE
Prefect behind   OF THE SENATE.[2]
him, harangues
three prae-
torians with
standards)

1 Some scholars have thought the soldiers being addressed were members of Nero's
  German bodyguard, but Speidel has shown that is incorrect.
2 This authorizes the minting of the coin.

69   Betrayal of the plot to assassinate Nero. AD 65

Plutarch, *Moralia* 505C–D (*On Talkativeness*). Cf. Tacitus, *Ann.* 15.54ff.

On the Pisonian Conspiracy: A. Momigliano in *CAH* 10.726–34; Garzetti, *Tiberius to
Antonines* 166–8; Griffin, *Nero* 168–70; R. A. Bauman, *Impietas in Principem* (Munich 1974)
146ff.

The talkativeness of a single person prevented the city of Rome from
becoming free after deliverance from Nero. For it was just one night
before the tyrant was to die and everything had been readied, and the
man who was to kill him was going to the theater and happened to see
a certain one of the prisoners at the gates (of the Palatine?) about to be
brought before Nero and bitterly lamenting his fate. He went up close
to him and in a whisper said, 'Good sir, pray that today above all others
will pass by and that tomorrow you will thank me.' The prisoner
grasped the obscure remark and, I guess, thinking that

> A fool is one who leaves what is within his reach and pursues / what
> is not (Hesiod, Frag. 61 Merkelbach–West)

chose the more lasting form of safety instead of the more just. For he
betrayed to Nero the man's message, and that man was immediately
arrested, tortured by fire and whipped, but denied, in his reply to force,
what he had revealed without it.[1]

1 The account in Tacitus (*Ann.* 15.54–5) differs from this one in a number of ways.

70   Religious acts celebrating the safety of Nero. AD 65 or later.

A: *Anthologia Palatina* 9.352; D. L. Page, **Further Greek Epigrams* (Cambridge 1981)
p. 533, No. 29 (Leonides of Alexandria). Greek elegiac couplets. B: *CIL* XI 1331; **ILS*
233; Smallwood, *Documents Gaius* 149 (slightly different arrangement). Marble tablet
with two inscriptions, Luna in Etrurua. [Latin]

A. Page, *Further Greek Epigrams* No. 29

The Nile[1] celebrates with a festival beside the holy water of the Tiber, / having vowed to make sacrifice for the preservation of Caesar; / one hundred ox-felling axes stained the willing necks of the bulls / with blood on the altars of heavenly Zeus.[2]

B. *ILS* 233, Luna in Etruria

(First inscription) (Dedicated) to Imperator Nero Claudius – son of the deified Claudius, grandson of Germanicus | Caesar, great-grandson of Tiberius Caesar Augustus, great-great-grandson of the deified Augustus – Caesar Augustus Germanicus, pontifex maximus, holding the tribunician power for the thirteenth time (AD 66–7), imperator for the eleventh time, consul for the fourth time, | by Lucius Titinius, son of Lucius, (of the tribe) Galeria, Glaucus Lucretianus, priest of Roma and Augustus, duovir four times, ‖ patron of the colony, sevir of a squadron of Roman Knights, curial priest, prefect of fabri to a consul,[3] tribune of the soldiers of Legion Twenty-Second Primigenia, prefect with power of a legate | of the Baliaric Islands, tribune of the soldiers of Legion Sixth Victrix, in fulfillment of a vow undertaken for the safety of Imperator | Nero, which he had vowed for the Baliarians in the year in which Aulus Licinius Nerva had been consul (AD 65),[4] the duoviri (of Luna) being Lucius Saufeius | Vegetus and Quintus Aburius Nepos when he wished it to be erected, (and) having been granted his prayer, he erected it to Jupiter, Juno, | Minerva, Happiness of Rome, the deified Augustus.

(Second inscription) (Dedicated) to the deified Poppaea Augusta, | (wife) of Imperator Caesar Augustus, (etc., as given above, line 4 to end).

1 This is a poetic expression for all the people of Egypt as well as Egyptians who happen to live in Rome.
2 The phrase 'heavenly Zeus' refers to Nero. The MS states that the poem is addressed 'to Nero Caesar'. The sacrifice of 100 oxen indicates an event of great magnitude, almost certainly the uncovering of the plot of Piso against Nero in AD 65: cf. Tacitus, *Ann.* 15.71–4.
3 See above, Document No. 21 n. 2.
4 The colleague in the consulship of Licinius Nerva was Marcus Vestinus Atticus, not mentioned here because of Nero's hatred for him. Although no charges of implication in Piso's plot had been made against him, Nero ordered his death and he committed suicide: Tacitus, *Ann.* 15.68–9.

71   Nero liberates the province of Greece. AD 67.

Marble stele, damaged at top and on right side, containing a speech of Nero and a decree of Akraiphia in Boeotia, where it was found. [Greek]

71 Nero liberates the province of Greece

M. Holleaux in *BCH* 12 (1888) 510–28; *idem, Discours prononcé par Néron à Corinthe en rendant aux Grecs la liberté* (Lyon 1889) (+ photograph); *IG* VII 2713; *SIG*³ 814; *ILS* 8794; Abbott–Johnson, *Municipal Administration* 56; Smallwood, **Documents Gaius* 64. Cf. Suetonius, *Nero* 24.2; Plutarch, *Titus Flamininus* 12.13; Pliny, *Nat. Hist.* 4.22; Dio 63.11.1; Pausanias 7.17.2.

A. Momigliano in *CAH* 10.735–6; Garzetti, *Tiberius to Antonines* 183–4; J. H. Oliver in *GRBS* 12 (1971) 221–37; P. A. Gallivan in *Hermes* 101 (1973) 230–14 (for the date); S. R. F. Price in *JHS* 104 (1984) 82–3; Griffin, *Nero* 208ff.

Imperator Caesar declares: For its good|will and piety toward me I wish to give something in exchange to noble-mind|ed Greece, and thus
5 I order as many people as possible | from this province to assemble || at Corinth on the fourth day before the Kalends of De|cember (November 28). *vv* |
   When the crowd had gathered in assembly, he sp|oke the following words: *vv* |
10 For you, men of Greece, it is an unexpected gift which, || even though nothing from my generous nature is | unhoped-for, I grant to you, as great a gift as you would be un|able to request. All Greeks inhabiting Achaia and what is | now known as the Peloponnesus,[1] | receive freedom with no taxation! A thing which none of you ever possessed in your
15 most for||tunate of times, | for you were subject to others or to your-selves. | Would that Greece were still at its peak as I gra|nt you this gift, in order that more people might en|joy this favor of mine. For this
20 reason I blame the times || for exhausting prematurely the size of my favor. | At present it is not out of pity for you but out of goodwill that I bestow this bene|faction, and I give it in exchange to your gods whose forethought on | land and sea for me I have always experi|enced, because they granted me the opportunity of conferring such benefits.
25 || Other leaders have liberated cities, | [[only Nero]] a province. *vv* |

(Decree of Akraiphia)
The high-priest of the Augusti for life and of Nero | Claudius Caesar Augustus, Epameinondas | (son) of Epameinondas, made the motion:
30 he moved that a preliminary decree || be forwarded to the Boule and the People: | Since the lord of the whole world, Nero, Imper|ator supreme, holding the tribunician power for the thir|teenth time (AD 67) desig-nate (?),[2] father of his country, | New Sun shining upon the Greeks, has
35 || chosen to be a benefactor of Greece, requiting | and reverencing our gods who stood by him | at all times for care and deliverance; what was from | most ancient times our native and indigenous free|dom, formerly
40 taken away from Greeks, has been given back to us by the one || and only supreme Imperator of those in the past, | Greece-loving [[Nero]] Zeus the Deliverer, | (and since) he has done us this favor, has restored the

111

pris|tine state of our autonomy and freedom, and has added to this |
45   great and unexpected gift also freedom from ‖ taxation, which none of
the former Augusti has quite completely given us, | – for all these
reasons it has been decreed by the ar|chons and fellow councillors and
the People to dedicate at the | present time an altar by (the statue) of
Zeus Savior, with an inscription | on it 'To Zeus the Deliverer, Nero
50   forever', and statu‖es in the temple of Apollo Ptoos[3] to be dedicated |
together with our ancestral gods of [[Nero]] Zeus | the Deliverer and of
the goddess Augusta [[Messalina,]] in order that, | when these have
been completed in that manner, our city | might seem to have fulfilled
55   every honor and act of piety ‖ toward the house of our lord Augustus
[[Nero]]. | This decree shall be engraved on a stele in the (temple) of
Zeus Sa|vior in the agora and in the temple of Apollo | Ptoos. *vv*

1   The impression is felt that the 'Peloponnesus' is about to be given a new name. Nero
may have hoped that out of gratitude the Greeks might rename it 'Neronesus'
('Nero's Island'): see Suetonius, *Nero* 55. This freedom of Greece was short-lived, for
Vespasian withdrew it: Suetonius, *Vespasian* 8.4; Pausanias 7.17.4.
2   The inclusion of this word seems to be an error.
3   Mt Ptoon was in Boeotia.

72   Nero's canal across the Corinthian Isthmus. AD 67.

Philostratus, *Life of Apollonius of Tyana* 4.24. Cf. Dio 62.16; Suetonius, *Nero* 19.2

He (i.e. Nero) left the palace and went to Greece to subject himself to
the herald's announcements in the Olympic and Pythian Games, and
he also was victorious at the Isthmian Games. His victories were in
singing to the accompaniment of the cithara and in (the contest of) the
heralds. And he won also (in the contest of) tragedians at Olympia.
Then it was, it is said, that he seized on the idea of cutting the Isthmus
to work out a way for sailing through it and to unite the Aegean with
the Adriatic Sea, so that every ship would not sail around Malea and
most of them could make the journey through the canal by this short-
cut of the long sail around. But how did the prediction of Apollonius
turn out? The canal was begun at Lechaion and had progressed perhaps
four continuous stades of digging when Nero is said to have stopped
the excavation. Some say Egyptian scientists told him about the seas
and that the sea above Lechaion would flood and destroy Aegina,
others that he feared a revolution over his rule. Such was the prediction
of Apollonius that the Isthmus would be and would not be cut.

73   The Panachaian League and the freedom of Greece. About AD 67.

Marble base, Epidauros. [Greek]

*SIG*³ 796A; *IG* IV² 1, 80–1; Smallwood, *Documents Gaius* 65.

A Momigliano in *JRS* 34 (1944) 115–16; J. A. O. Larsen, *Representative Government in Greek and Roman History* (Berkeley 1955) 112–13.

Achaians and Boiotians and | Phokians and Euboians and | Lokrians and Dorians (dedicated this statue to) Titus | Statilius Timokrates,
5 ‖ having been their secretary, | because of his excellence. | Since Titus Statilius Timokrates, a remarkable man | of the first rank who in every way has lived his life in a manner worthy of respect | and admiration and has [administered] the government most honorably, [and, having
10 been chosen] ‖ secretary after the grant of freedom to us, [in] | times of the most burdensome and perilous difficulties has *magnanimously* [undertaken] tasks and *services* | greater than (should be asked) of one man and *too many* (tasks) for one year, and since by these actions he has many times | administered our affairs well and placed on a firm basis our still shaky conditions of freedom, for | all these reasons it has been decreed by the Panachaian Council to praise this man and to erect
15 ‖ bronze statues of him at the locations of the Pa[nachaian] festivals [and in Amarios' | precinct] and in Epidaurus in the temple of Asklepios, inscribed [as follows: Achaians and Boiotians | and Pho]kians and Euboians and Lokrians and Dorians (dedicated this statue to) Titus Statilius Timokrates, | [having been their secretary,] because of his excellence.

74   The so-called 'five good years' of Nero's reign.

Aurelius Victor, *Liber de Caesaribus* 5.2–4.

M. K. Thornton in *Historia* 22 (1973) 570–82; Griffin, *Nero* 37–8 and 84ff.

Although for a long time the young man had exercised absolute rule, for as many years as his stepfather, nevertheless he (i.e. Nero) was of such importance, especially in increasing the city, that Trajan justifiably said quite often that all emperors were far behind Nero's quinquennium ('five-year period'). In that period he also reduced Pontus to the legal rule of a province with the permission of Polemon, after whom it is called Pontus Polemoniacus, and likewise the Cottian Alps at the death of King Cottius.[1] (3) Therefore, it is sufficiently established that age is no impediment to excellence, (but) excellence is easily changed when the character is corrupted by permissiveness, and that the lack of

rules governing the conduct of young persons has a later and more
disastrous effect. (4) For he spent the rest of his life so shamelessly that
one is displeased and ashamed that there had ever been such a person,
much less a ruler of nations.

1   Pontus Polemoniacus was made part of Galatia in AD 64, while the Cottian Alps was
    placed under an equestrian governor about the same time (AD 65?). This would
    seem to place Nero's 'five good years' at the end of his reign rather than at the
    beginning.

75   Nero's agents confiscate statues in Greece.

Dio Chrysostom 31 (*To the Rhodians*) 148–9. Cf. Tacitus, *Ann.* 15.45; 16.23.

Nero had such a great desire and enthusiasm for this activity (i.e.
plundering of statues) that he could not even keep away from those of
Olympia or Delphi, even though he honored their temples most of all.
What is more, he carried away the majority of (statues) from the
Acropolis at Athens and many of them from Pergamum, whose very
precinct even belonged to him. Why bother to mention those of other
places? However, he left your statues alone and displayed such a great
goodwill and respect toward you (Rhodians) that he judged your whole
city more sacred than the most prestigious sanctuaries. For you know
that fellow Acratus, who traveled around almost the whole world for
this purpose and omitted not a single village[1] – you know how he came
here, and, when you began to groan, as is natural, how he said he was
here for sight-seeing and that he had no power to seize any of the things
here.

1   Tacitus (*Ann.* 15.45) mentions Acratus, a freedman of Nero, and a certain Secundus
    Carrinas. See J. Day, *An Economic History of Athens under Roman Domination* (New York
    1942) 179–80.

76   Tombstone of a member of Nero's German bodyguard.
Yellowish-brown tombstone, Rome. [Latin]

Gordon *Album* 1.120 (+ photograph); Smallwood, *Documents Gaius* 293; H. Bellen, *Die
germanische Leibwache der römischen Kaiser des julisch-claudischen Hauses* (Wiesbaden 1981)
p. 111, No. 15 (+ photograph).

5   Indus, | Nero Claudius | Caesar Augustus' | bodyguard, ‖ in the squad
    of Secundus, | by nationality a Batavian, | lived 36 years (and) is buried
10 here. | Erected by | Eumenes, his brother ‖ and heir, from the fraternity
    of Germans.[1]

1 The *Germani* or *corporis custodes* formed the personal bodyguard of the Julian-Claudian emperors. Galba finally dismissed them. Despite their military duties they were Imperial slaves or freedmen: Weaver, *Familia Caesaris* 83. For details see Bellen, *loc. cit.*, and M. P. Speidel in *Germania* 62 (1984) 31–45.

77   Nero breaks up private estates in Africa.

Pliny, *Nat. Hist.* 18.7.35.

To tell the truth, large estates have ruined Italy and now the provinces too: six owners were in possession of half of Africa, when our Leader Nero put them to death.[1]

1 Henceforth provincial land was the property of the Roman People or the emperors. See V. Weber in K. P. Johne and V. Weber, *Die Kolonen in Italien und den westlichen Provinzen des römischen Reiches* (Berlin 1983) 280–1, with reference to the basic article by T. Frank in *JRS* 17 (1927) 141–61. Cf. J. Bleicken in *Chiron* 4 (1974) 359–419.

78   Nero honored at Athens.

A: *IG* II² 3277; K. K. Carroll, **The Parthenon Inscription* (Greek, Roman and Byzantine Monograph 9) (Durham, NC 1982) 16 (+ photographs and drawings). On the architrave of the Parthenon in Athens are small cuttings below the triglyphs. The cuttings had once been used to attach bronze letters to the structure. From careful study of the relative placement of the cuttings it has been possible to establish what bronze letters, now lost, originally were placed there. Carroll has reconstructed the text. Date of inscription: AD 61. **B**: **IG* II² 3278; Smallwood, *Documents Gaius* 145. Small marble base, Athens. Cf. Suetonius, *Nero* 53; Dio 62.20.5.

A. Carroll, *The Parthenon Inscription* 16, Athens

The Boule of the Areiopagos and the Boule of the Six Hundred and the People of Athens (have honored) the greatest Imperator Nero Caesar Claudius Augustus | G[erm]anicus, son of god, when the Hoplite General for the eighth time, epimeletēs, and nomothetēs | was Tiberius [Cl]audius Novius, son of Philinos,[1] and when the priestess (of Athena) was Paullina, daughter of Kapito.

B. *IG* II² 3278, Athens

To Imperator [[Nero]] | Caesar Augustus, | the new Apollo.[2]

Tiberius Claudius Novius was a very important figure in Athens at this time, having been Hoplite General at least eight times and, as such, the most important magistrate in the city. The *epimeletēs* of the city is known as an official from the reign of Nero to that of Hadrian, but his function is unknown. As *nomothetēs*, he was involved with the making of law, perhaps even a revision of the Athenian constitution. See Carroll, *op. cit.* 43–58.
2 Nero was hailed as 'Apollo' by the Greeks when he appeared in their athletic games.

GALBA
(June 9 to January 15, AD 69)
SERVIUS GALBA IMPERATOR CAESAR AUGUSTUS

OTHO
(January 15 to April 17)
IMPERATOR MARCUS OTHO CAESAR AUGUSTUS

VITELLIUS
(January 2 to December 20)
IMPERATOR AULUS VITELLIUS CAESAR

VESPASIAN
(69–79)
IMPERATOR CAESAR VESPASIANUS AUGUSTUS

Titles: PONTIFEX MAXIMUS
FATHER OF HIS COUNTRY (AD 69)
CENSOR (73)
HOLDER OF THE TRIBUNICIAN POWER: first
time in AD 69, then annually after July 1
CONSUL: AD 70 (II), 71 (III), 72 (IV), 74 (V), 75 (VI),
76 (VII), 77 (VIII), 79 (IX)

Death: June 23, AD 79.

The *consules ordinarii* **under Vitellius and Vespasian**

(For the suffect consuls from Vespasian to Hadrian see P. A. Gallivan in *Classical Quarterly* 31 (1981) 186–220.)

AD

69	Ser. Sulpicius Galba Imperator Caesar Augustus II	T. Vinius (Rufinus?)
70	Imp. Caesar Vespasianus Augustus II	Titus Caesar Vespasianus
71	Imp. Vespasianus III	M. Cocceius Nerva
72	Imp. Vespasianus IV	Titus Caesar II
73	Caesar Domitianus II	L. Valerius Catullus Messallinus
74	Imp. Vespasianus V	Titus Caesar III
75	Imp. Vespasianus VI	Titus Caesar IV
76	Imp. Vespasianus VII	Titus Caesar V
77	Imp. Vespasianus VIII	Titus Caesar VI
78	D. Iunius Novius Priscus (Rufus?)	L. Ceionius Commodus
79	Imp. Vespasianus IX	Titus Caesar VII

79   The year of the four emperors. AD 68–9.

A: *CIL* V 5702; *ILS 982; McCrum–Woodhead, *Documents* 23. Stone found near Milan.
[Latin] **B**: Mattingly, *BMC 1, p. 293; McCrum–Woodhead, *Documents* 26. Denarius,
Spanish mint, AD 68. **C**: Mattingly, *BMC 1, No. 63; McCrum–Woodhead, *Documents*
28. Sestertius, Spanish mint type, AD 68–9. **D**: Mattingly, *BMC 1, No. 1, p. 364;
McCrum–Woodhead, *Documents* 32. Aureus, mint of Rome, AD 69. **E**: Mattingly, *BMC
1, No. 99, p. 388; McCrum–Woodhead, *Documents* 36. An *ās*, Spanish mint, AD 69.
F: *CIL* VI 929; *ILS 242; McCrum–Woodhead, *Documents* 81. Marble base, Rome
[Latin] **G**: *CIL* VI 1402; *ILS 983; McCrum–Woodhead, *Documents* 40. Stone lost,
preserved in copy, Rome (?). [Latin] Cf. Tacitus, *Hist.* 4.24–59. **H**: *CIL* XI 1196; *ILS
2284; McCrum–Woodhead, *Documents* 386. Tombstone from Veleia in Italy. [Latin]

A. *ILS* 982, near Milan

To Jupiter Best and Greatest | in return for the safety | and victory of
5   Lucius | Verginius Rufus.[1] | Pylades, his steward, ‖ discharges his vow.

B. Mattingly, *BMC* 1, p. 293, denarius, Spanish mint

(Obverse: busts of Spain and Gaul facing each other, figure of Victory between them facing a globe	HARMONY OF SPANIARDS AND GAULS.
(Reverse: draped Victory standing in a chariot with bow in one hand and reins in the other)	VICTORY OF THE ROMAN PEOPLE

C. Mattingly, *BMC* 1, No. 63, p. 318, sestertius of Spanish mint

(Obverse: head of Galba, laureate)	SERVIUS GALBA IMPERATOR CAESAR AUGUSTUS, HOLDER OF TRIBUNICIAN POWER.
(Reverse: legend within oak-wreath)	BY SENATORIAL DECREE. BECAUSE OF CITIZENS SAVED.

D. Mattingly, *BMC* 1, No. 1, p. 364, aureus of Roman mint

(Obverse: head of Otho, bare)	IMPERATOR OTHO CAESAR AUGUSTUS, HOLDER OF TRIBUNICIAN POWER.
(Reverse: draped figure of Peace standing and holding a branch and caduceus)	PEACE OF THE WHOLE WORLD.

E. Mattingly, *BMC* 1, No. 99, p. 388, *as* of Spanish mint

(Obverse: head of
Vitellius, laureate, globe
below his neck)

AULUS VITELLIUS
IMPERATOR GERMANICUS.

(Reverse: helmeted Mars
with spear in one hand, an
eagle and military flag in the
other)

CONSENT OF THE ARMIES.
BY DECREE OF THE SENATE.

F. *ILS* 242, Rome

Aulus Vitellius, son of Lucius, | imperator, | perpetual consul.[2]

G. *ILS* 983, Rome (?)

To Gaius Dillius, son of Aulus, (of the tribe) Sergia, Vocula,[3] tribune of
the soldiers of the First Legion, quattuorvir for road repair, quaestor of
the province of Pontus-Bithynia, tribune of the plebs, praetor, commander in Germany of the Legion Twenty-Second Primigenia. Helvia,
daughter of Titus, Procula, his wife, made this (monument).

H. *ILS* 2284, Veleia in Italy

[To ----, soldier of the Legion] | Fourth Macedonica, | twenty-five years
5   old, | two years in the service. ‖ The standard-bearers | of three legions
– | Legion Fourth Macedonica, | Legion Twenty-First Rapax, | Legion
Twenty-Second Primigenia – | erected (this monument) out of their
own funds.[4]

1 See Pliny, *Letters* 2.1. In AD 68, at the death of Vindex, it was thought that Verginius
  Rufus would become emperor.
2 See Suetonius, *Vitellius* 11.
3 See Tacitus, *Hist.* 4.24–7 and *passim* for his role in the uprising on the Rhine in AD 69.
4 The dead soldier of line 1 was almost certainly killed in the Battle of Placentia in
  AD 69. All three legions were part of the Rhine armies.

80   Edict of Tiberius Iulius Alexander. July 6, AD 68.

Inscription on the façade of the north gateway to the temple of Hibis,
in the oasis of El-Khargeh, Egypt. [Greek]

OGIS 669; *IGRR* I 1263; Abbott–Johnson, *Municipal Administration* 165; H. G. Evelyn-
White and J. H. Oliver, *The Temple of Hibis in the El-Khargeh Oasis*, Part II *Greek Inscriptions*
(New York 1938) 23–45; McCrum–Woodhead, *Documents* 328; G. Chalon, **L'Édit de
Tiberius Iulius Alexander* (Lausanne 1964) 27–34 (+ photographs).

Abbott–Johnson, *loc. cit.*; Reinmuth, *Prefect* 47ff.; Evelyn-White and Oliver, *loc. cit.*;
N. Lewis in *Journal of Juristic Papyrology* 9–10 (1955–6) 117ff.; Chalon, *op. cit. passim.*

Iulius Demetrius, strategos of the T[hebai]d Oasis. Of the edict sent to
me by our lord prefect, | Tiberius Iulius Alexander, I have appended a
copy to you, in order that you may learn of it and enjoy his benefactions.
Year 2 of Lucius Livius Augustus Sulpicius | Galba,[1] Imperator,
Phaophi 1 (September 28, AD 68), Iulia Augusta's Day.[2]

Tiberius Iulius Alexander[3] declares: I have been taking every pre-
caution that the city (of Alexandria) remains in its proper con|dition of
enjoying the benefactions which it has from the Augusti and that Egypt
continues to be stable and cheerfully helps (Rome) with its supply of

5   grain and with its very ‖ great prosperity at the present, not oppressed
by new and unjust exactions. However, almost from the time when I
entered the city I have been shouted at by men appealing to me – in
small numbers and also in | great throngs, composed of both respect-
able people here and of those who farm the countryside – complaining
about abuses committed against them, and I have not ceased exercising
all my power in the correction of these urgent | matters. And in order
that you may more cheerfully hope for everything from the one who, for
us, has illuminated the way to the salvation of the whole human race,
our benefactor Augustus Imperator Galba, – everything for your
salvation | and for your enjoyment – and in order that you may know
that I have taken thought for the things that pertain to your assistance,
I have of necessity given public notice about each of the requests,
whatever of them it is possible for me to ju|dge and take action about.
As for the larger issues that need the authority and majesty of the
emperor, I will reveal them to him with all truthfulness, for the gods

10   have reserved for this ‖ very sacred moment the security of the
inhabited world.

First of all, I acknowledge your most reasonable request about men
who are unwilling to enter tax-farming or o|ther leases pertaining to
(imperial) estates being forced to do so, contrary to the general custom
of the provinces. (I know) that no little harm has been done by these
actions when many men, lacking experience in su|ch business, are
burdened with the necessity of tax-collecting thrust upon them. Therefore, I have not forced anyone into tax-farming or leases and I will not
force anyone, since I know that it | is advantageous to the imperial
accounts also to have willing and capable men doing this work with
zeal. I have been persuaded that in the future nobody (will recruit by)
force unwilling tax-farmers | or tenants holding leases but will assign
leases to those willing to come forward voluntarily, preserving the
constant practice of earlier prefects rather than imitating the
occasional injustice of some.

15   ‖ Since some (officials), using the pretext of the interest of the State,

have assigned to themselves other peoples' debts and have put some
(of them) into debtors' prison and into other restraints, which for this
very reason | I have come to know have been suppressed in order that
the recovery of debts may be made out of the property and not out of
the persons involved, I therefore follow the will of the god Augustus
and order that nobody, using the interest of the State as a pre|text, shall
have debts transferred from others to himself which he had not
incurred himself from the beginning, and that in no way shall any free
man be held in any kind of confinement, unless he is a criminal, or in
the debtors' pri|son, except those in debt to the imperial account.

In order that the interest of the State in no way may burden the
contracts between (private) individuals and that the public credit may
not be hindered by | those who use the right of first payment for
unnecessary reasons, concerning this matter I have also been forced to
give public notice. For it has been revealed to me frequently that
already some (officials) have tried to cancel mortgages that have been
20   legally ‖ made, to demand back by force from the debtors loans already
granted, and to rescind sales by withdrawing the property from those
who bought it, under the pretext that | (the buyers) had made contracts
with those who collected delayed payments from the fiscus,[4] either
with strategoi or tax-officials or others of the men who had obligations
to the public account. Therefore, I order that whatever | procurator of
the emperor or whatever official is suspicious of anyone in the public
domain, he shall register his name or give public notice in order that
nobody may enter into a contract with such a person, | or part of his
property will be sequestrated in the public record office against his
debt. And if anyone has made a loan, with a mortgage legally acquired,
to a person whose name has not been so registered and whose property
has not been seques|trated or who demands payment of the loan before
the due date or who buys something from one whose name is not so
registered or whose property is not sequestrated, that person will not
have any trouble. ‖
25   Dowries belonging to others and which are not the property of the
husbands who received them the god Augustus has ordered – as also
the prefects – that they shall be paid from the fiscus to the women
whose right of prior lien must be kept secure.

(Lines 26–9 reaffirmation of former grants of immunity and tax-
exemption.)
30   (Lines 29–32: concerning rentals on estates sold by the State.)

(Lines 32–4: no native-born citizen of Alexandria shall be forced to
perform the liturgies while residing in the country districts for business
reasons.)
35   (Lines 34ff.) It will also be a concern of ‖ mine, after holding the

assizes, of entrusting the functions of strategoi for three-year terms to those who have been nominated. In general I order that a prefect, concerning a case brought before him, when he has alrea|dy decided to dismiss it, may not bring the case into court again for trial. And if two prefects have already expressed similar conclusions, the accountant should be punished who brings up the same question for the assizes, | and he accomplishes nothing except to leave for himself and the other officials a pretext for extortion. Indeed, as an alternative, many have decided to abandon their own property, | on the grounds that they had already spent more than it was worth, because at each assize the same questions were brought to trial.

I also set down the same principle concerning questions brought before the Idiologos,[5] that | if anything has been judged and dismissed, or will be dismissed by the one appointed (to hear the case) before the Idiologos, it shall no longer be possible for an accuser to bring a charge on this matter or to bring it to trial, otherwise the person who does so

40   will be unmer||cifully punished. For there will be no limit to malicious accusations, if questions that have been dismissed are constantly brought up, until someone condemns them. Now, since the city has become almost uninhabitable because of the | number of informers and because every household is disrupted, of necessity I order that, if any of the prosecutors in the office of the Idiologos introduces a complaint as advocate for someone else, he will be accompanied by | the one who lodged the complaint, so that he too may not escape jeopardy. And if he introduces three complaints in his own name and does not establish his case, he will no longer be permitted to prosecute, but half of his | estate shall be confiscated, for it is most unjust that the one who brings many people into jeopardy of losing their property and being fined should himself be completely free from liability. And in general | I will order that the Code of Regulations of the Idiologos [remain in force,][6] since I have corrected the innovations (practiced) contrary to the concessions of the Augusti. And I will give public notice [in clear language

45   how] || I have punished informers, deservedly, who have already been *convicted.*

I am not unaware of the fact that you are very concerned that Egypt *continue* to be prosperous, from which [----] |[7] abundance which you have, I have corrected as much as I could. For often the cultivators of the land as a whole have met with me and revealed that they have had imposed upon them, without precedent, [---|---] assessments of grain and money, although it ought to be impossible, for anyone wishing to do so, to make recklessly any new procedure of a general nature. These and similar adverse judgments have spread not only into the Thebaid and the Heptanomia[8] | and the far-off nomes of the Lower Nile but also into the suburbs of the city, the so-called land of the Alexandrians, and the Mareotic [nome. Therefore, I order | the] strategoi of the nomes that, if any unprecedented assessments in the last five years not

50   previously imposed upon all or most of the nomes or toparchies[9] ‖ have been made against farmers, they shall restore these to the previous arrangement and stop their demands. If such cases are brought to my court at the assizes [---|---].

Also previously I have restricted the unlimited power of the accountants because everybody accused them of making very many assessments by | [analogy (with those elsewhere),] from which it happened that they grew wealthy while Egypt was ruined. And now I order them to make no assessments by analogy | nor anything else in general without a decision from the prefect. And I order the strategoi to receive nothing from the accountants without written | permission from the prefect. And the other officials, if they are found to have made any false or improper assessments, shall give back to the private individuals as

55   much as they have exacted and shall pay a fine ‖ of equal amount to the public treasury. The same kind of fraudulent practice is the so-called collection (of taxes) by averaging and not by the real rising | [of the Nile,] but by a comparison of certain other earlier risings, [although] nothing seems to be more just than the truth itself. I [wish] men to be confi|dent and to farm with enthusiasm, [knowing] that in accordance with the true state of the real rising and of the ir|rigated land the collection (of taxes) will be made, and not made in accordance with the dishonest practices and assessments based on averaging. If anyone is convicted of falsifying [---|---] he will be fined triple. As for those who have been fearful after hearing about a survey of the ancient land in the

60   [territory] of the Alexandrians [and ‖ in the] Menelaite (nome), land which has never been subjected to the measuring-line, let them not worry. For nobody has [ever yet] dared [to ma|ke] a survey (of this land), nor *will anyone*. Its ancient rights ought to remain in place. I establish the same principle [also] concerning additions ma|de to it, so that no changes will be made concerning it.

Concerning your older arrears of taxes and your insistence [---|---] they accomplished *nothing* more than the enrichment of the officials and the *ruin* of the [people,] I will write [to Cae|sar A]ugustus Imperator along with the other matters *which* I will report to him, who is alone

65   capable of eliminating such practices *completely*, [and whose] ‖ *constant* beneficence and foresight [are causes] for the salvation of us all.

First year of [Luc]ius Livius | [Gal]ba Caesar Augustus Imperator, Epeiph 12 (July 6, AD 68).

1 The new emperor's name was Servius Sulpicius Galba, but earlier in his life he had

started to use the name Lucius Livius Sulpicius Galba after his father was married a second time, to a woman called Livia Ocellina. Upon becoming emperor he reverted to his original name, but apparently the authorities in Egypt had not yet been notified of the change. As for the date, the Egyptian year began on August 29, and, therefore, September 28 of AD 68 was in Galba's second year in Egyptian terms.

2 Certain days of importance to the imperial family were set aside for commemorative purposes and named after the person.

3 On Tiberius Iulius Alexander see *PIR*[2] I 139; Stein, *Präfekten* 37–8; E. G. Turner in *JRS* 44 (1954) 54ff.; V. Burr, *Tiberius Iulius Alexander* (Bonn 1955). For his Jewish ancestry see now R. D. Sullivan in *ANRW* 2.8.300–5.

4 The *fiscus* was a Roman treasury as distinct from the great central treasury at Rome called the *aerarium*. Provinces had *fisci* for the local administrative affairs, and the emperor had another of his own into which poured the revenues from his personal estates. In line 13 it is called the 'imperial accounts' and in line 21 'fiscus' and 'public account' signify the same thing. See also the Glossary.

5 On the Idiologos see above, Document No. 67, n. 2, and also the Glossary.

6 Alternative restoration: '[be made public]' as suggested by C. B. Welles in P. R. Swarney in *Proceedings of the Twelfth International Congress of Papyrology* (Toronto 1970) 458. The 'Code of Regulations' is the *Gnomon* in the office of the Idiologos.

7 No restoration appears satisfactory.

8 These are divisions of Egypt, the Heptanomia ('Land of the Seven Nomes') being located on the south of the Nile Delta.

9 Nomes were divided into smaller districts called toparchies.

81 Acclamation of Vespasian in Alexandria. AD 69.

Small, mutilated papyrus, Egypt. [Greek]

P. Fouad 8; P. Jouguet in *Mélanges à Alfred Ernout* (Paris 1940) 201–10; H. Musurillo, *The Acts of the Pagan Martyrs. Acta Alexandrinorum* (Oxford 1954) 30–1; R. Merkelbach, **Archiv für Papyrusforschung* 16 (1956) 111–12 (best text); Tcherikover–Fuks, *CPJ* II 418a; McCrum–Woodhead, *Documents* 41.

Jouguet, *loc. cit.*; Stein, *Präfekten* 38; E. G. Turner in *Gnomon* 27 (1955) 461ff.; V. Burr, *Tiberius Iulius Alexander* (Bonn 1955) 60–1 (+ photograph); Tcherikover–Fuks, *op. cit.* 190–1; L. Koenen in *Gnomon* 40 (1968) 256; A. Henrichs in *ZPE* 3 (1968) 59.

5   [---|--- Tibe]rius Alexa[nder[1] --|---|---||---|---] | *vacat* | [---] the emperor
10 [---|--into] the city *vv* the crowds [coming out to meet ‖ him] *throughout* the entire Hippodrome [---|--,][2] 'In good health, lord Caesar, [may you come! (?)] | Vespasian, the one savior and [benefactor!] | Son of [Amm]o[n] rising up [---|--][3] Keep him for us [in good health (?).
15 ‖ Lord] Augustus. *vv* [--] Sar[apis (?) --|--][4] Son of Ammon *and in a word* [the one god (?) | ---] We thank Tiberius [Alexander | --.]' Tiberius
20 [said (?) ---|--] god Caesar. *vv* [--] in good health! ‖ [--] god Caesar Vespasian! [--|---] lord Augustus! *vv* [---|---]

1 On July 1, AD 69, Tiberius Iulius Alexander, prefect of Egypt, along with his legions hailed Vespasian as emperor (Suetonius, *Vespasian* 6.3), and Vespasian called that

day his *dies imperii* (Tacitus, *Hist.* 2.79) rather than December 21, when the senate finally ratified the act. A month or so later Vespasian himself came to Egypt (Dio 64.9) and was greeted by the Alexandrians as he entered the Hippodrome by the Canopic Gate. The present document is an account, perhaps a 'worked-up literary account', of this moment, the crowd shouting his name and linking it with imperial titles. For a discussion of these imperial acclamations in imperial history see C. Roueché in *JRS* 74 (1984) 181ff.

2 Perhaps '[gave a loud | shout:]', Jouguet. See J. Colin, *Les Villes libres de l'Orient gréco-romain et l'envoi au supplice par acclamations populaires* (Brussels 1965) Ch. 4.

3 The 'son of Ammon' (cf. line 16) is a reference to Alexander the Great in his capacity as pharaoh of Egypt. The title applied to Vespasian, 'rising up [forever (or to the gods)]' (various editors), is equivalent to the recognition of Vespasian as ruler.

4 Perhaps '[the new] *Sar*[apis]' as proposed by A. D. Nock in *JRS* 47 (1957) 118 n. 28 (*Arthur Darby Nock. Essays on Religion and the Ancient World* (ed. Z. Stewart), Vol. II (Harvard 1972) 838 n. 28).

82 Law on the imperial powers of Vespasian. AD 69–70.

Bronze tablet, probably the second in a series of two, complete on all sides, Rome. [Latin]

CIL VI 930; *ILS* 244; Bruns[7] 56; *FIRA* I 15; McCrum–Woodhead, **Documents* 1; Gordon, *Epigraphy* 46 (+ photograph).

H. Last in *CAH* 11.404–6; P. A. Brunt in *JRS* 67 (1977) 95–116.

[--- and that][1] he (Vespasian) shall be permitted to make a [---] or a treaty with whom he wishes, just as permission was given to the deified Augustus, | to Tiberius Iulius Caesar Augustus, and to Tiberius Claudius Caesar Augustus Germanicus,[2] | and that he shall be permitted to hold a meeting of the senate, to make and refer a matter to it, | and to make senatorial decrees by referring a matter to it and by
5 division (of members) for the vote, || just as permission was given to the deified Augustus, to Tiberius Iulius Caesar Augustus, and to Tiberius Claudius Caesar | Augustus Germanicus; *vv* |
  And that, when in accordance with his wish or authority or order or command | or in his presence a meeting of the senate is held, the right of all transactions | shall be held to be and be considered just as if the senate meeting had been called and held in accordance with a law;
10 || and that whatever magistrates seeking power, military and civil authority, or superintendencies | of anything he recommends to the senate and Roman People, | and to whomever he gives or promises his vote, at their | elections consideration shall be given to each of them out of the regular order;[3] *vv* |
  And that he shall be permitted to extend and move forward the

boundaries of the *pomerium*[4] whenever he decides it will be in accord-
15 ance with the best interest of the Republic, ‖ just as permission was
given to Tiberius Claudius Caesar Augustus │ Germanicus; │ *vv* and that
whatever he decides will be in accordance with the advantage of the
Republic and with the majesty of things divine, │ human, public, and
private, │ he shall have the right and the power so to act and do, just as
20 (such right and power) were possessed by the deified Augustus ‖ and
Tiberius Iulius Caesar Augustus and Tiberius Claudius Caesar │
Augustus Germanicus; *vv* │

And that by whatever laws and plebiscites it has been written that
neither the deified Augustus │ nor Tiberius Iulius Caesar Augustus nor
Tiberius Claudius Caesar Augustus │ Germanicus shall be restricted,
25 from such laws and plebiscites Imperator Caesar ‖ Vespasianus shall
be exempted; and whatever things in consequence of each law or bill │
it was necessary for the deified Augustus or Tiberius Iulius Caesar
Augustus or Tiberius │ Claudius Caesar Augustus Germanicus to do, │
it shall be permitted Imperator Caesar Vespasianus Augustus to do all
these things; │ and that whatever things before the passage of this law
30 have been done, accomplished, ‖ decreed, or ordered by Imperator
Caesar Vespasianus Augustus │ or by his order or mandate by anyone,
such things shall be approved and legally binding just │ as if they had
been done by order of the People or Plebs. *vv* │ SANCTION │

If anyone because of this law (but) contrary to laws, bills, plebiscites,
35 ‖ or decrees of the senate has acted or will act, or if there is anything
that because of this law, bill, │ plebiscite, or decree of the senate he
ought to do and has not done because of this law, this shall not be an
offense for him, nor shall he be liable to pay any fine on this account to
the People, │ nor shall anyone have the right of legal action or judicial
inquiry about this matter, nor shall anyone │ permit proceedings about
this matter in his court.

1 The investiture of a Roman emperor with imperial authority and power was conducted in two stages: a decree of the senate followed by a law passed in the Assembly
of the People. The present text of the law apparently followed the phraseology of the
senatorial decree, for the first tablet of this law, now lost, would have contained a
phrase such as 'It has pleased the senate that . . . ', which would have served to
introduce all the clauses that followed in both tablets. On the imperial investiture
see B. Parisi, *Désignation et investiture de l'empereur romain* (Paris 1953).
2 Note that Gaius, Nero, Galba, Otho, and Vitellius are not mentioned and that
Claudius is not called 'deified'.
3 For the pre-election support of candidates by the emperor see above, Document No.
36, the 'Tabula Hebana'.
4 This was the earliest boundary of Rome, marked out, it was said, by Romulus. It was
the line beyond which the auspices could not be taken. Cf. Tacitus, *Ann.* 12.23.4.

83 The Jewish War under Vespasian and Titus.

A: *IGRR* III 1015; *OGIS* 586; McCrum–Woodhead, *Documents* 330; **IGLS* VII 4011.
AD 70–80. Base of a statue (?), Aradus (modern Rouad, an island off the coast of Syria).
[Greek] **B**: Sulpicius Severus, *Chron.* 2.30.6–7. **C**: *CIL* VI 944; **ILS* 264; McCrum–
Woodhead, *Documents* 53. AD 80–1. Inscription on an arch no longer extant, originally
in the Circus Maximus, now preserved only in a copy, Rome. [Latin] **D**: *ILS* 9200;
Pflaum, *Carrières* 50; McCrum–Woodhead, *Documents* 372; **IGLS* VI 2796 (+ photo-
graph). Statue base, Heliopolis in Syria. [Latin] **E**: Mattingly, **BMC* 2, 604, p. 131.
Roman *ās*, dated AD 71. **F**: *CIL* VI 8604; **ILS* 1519; McCrum–Woodhead, *Documents*
203. Marble tombstone, Rome. [Latin] **G**: *P. Edfou* I, ostracon No. 120; Tcherikover–
Fuks, *CPJ* II 165; Hengstl, **Griechische Papyri* No. 18. Ostracon from Apollinopolis
Magna in Egypt, June 2, AD 72.

A. *IGLS* VII 4011, Aradus in Syria

[---] the Boule [and People | to ---]inius Secun[dus ----] |[1] prefect of the
First Cohort of Thra[cians,] | prefect of [---‖---,] sub-procurator of
[Tibe|rius] Iulius Alex[ander] the *prefect* of the Iudaean [army,][2] *sub-
procurator* of Syr[ia ---|--] of the Legion [----].

B. Sulpicius Severus,[3] *Chron.* 2.30.6–7

It is said that Titus, before doing anything, called together his Advisory
Board and deliberated whether he should destroy a temple of such
great workmanship. For it seemed to some people that a consecrated
temple, wonderful beyond all mortal works, should not be destroyed. If
it were preserved, it would be proof of Rome's restraint, but if it were
demolished, it would be an eternal mark of her cruelty. Others, including Titus himself in opposition believed that the destruction of the
temple was of prime importance in order to abolish more fully the
religion of the Jews and Christians, saying that these religions,
although opposed to each other, nevertheless began from the same
sources, that the Christians had come out of the Jews and that with the
root destroyed the stem would easily die.

C. *ILS* 264, Rome

The senate and the Roman People (dedicated this arch) to Imperator
Titus Caesar, son of the deified Vespasianus, Vespasianus Augustus,
pontifex maximus, holding the tribunician power for the tenth time
(AD 80–1), imperator for the seventeenth time, consul for the eighth
time (AD 80), father of his country, Leader, (dedicated) because,
following the directions and plans and under the auspices of his father,
he tamed the race of the Jews and destroyed the city of Jerusalem, a
thing either sought in vain by all commanders, kings, and races before
him or never even attempted.

D. *IGLS* **VI 2796, Heliopolis in Syria**

(For a translation see below, Document No. 109.)

E. Mattingly, *BMC* **2, 604, p. 131, Roman** *ās*

(Obverse: head of   IMPERATOR CAESAR VESPASIANUS
Vespasian, laureate)   AUGUSTUS, CONSUL III

(Reverse, a Jewess   IUDAEA CAPTURED
seated at foot of a
palm tree)

F. *ILS* **1519, Rome**

5

10

Tiberius Flavius, freedman of Augustus, | Euschemon | who was chief
secretary | and also procurator ‖ for the collection of the poll-tax of the
| Jews.[4] | (This monument) was made | by Flavia Aphrodisia | to her
patron and husband ‖ who deserves it well.

G. Hengstl, *Griechische Papyri* **No. 18, Apollinopolis Magna**

Josepos, son of Jason, | equivalence of two denarii | of the Jewish tax of
the fourth year: eight <drachmas> two obols. | Year 4 of Vespasian,
Payni | 8 (June 2, AD 72).

1 Mommsen (*Hermes* 19 (1884) 644–9) restored here the name of Gaius Plinius
  Secundus, the Roman author known to have entered on an equestrian career as a
  young man. That identification should now be rejected: Syme in *HSCP* 73 (1969)
  205ff. (*Roman Papers* II 745ff.)
2 Tiberius Iulius Alexander (*PIR*[2] I 139) as prefect of Egypt had supported Vespasian
  for emperor. Josephus (*Bell. Jud.* 5.45–6) mentions his command in the war against
  the Jews, calling him 'prefect of the armies'. See E. G. Turner in *Hibeh Papyri* II
  (London 1955) No. 215, pp. 135–7, and in *JRS* 44 (1954) 64.
3 Sulpicius Severus was a Christian writer of the fourth century AD. His source was
  probably Tacitus: see T. D. Barnes in *Classical Philology* 72 (1977) 224–31.
4 This Greek imperial freedman may have been in charge of the so-called *fiscus Iudaicus*,
  the 'Jewish Treasury' in Rome, to which the tax levied on all Jews everywhere was
  sent after the destruction of the temple in Jerusalem. Cf. Josephus, *Bell. Jud.* 7.6.6,
  and Suetonius, *Domitian* 12. See Smallwood, *Jews* 371–6.

84 Edict of Vespasian on teachers and physicians. AD 74.
Marble stone, broken at top and on left side, Pergamum. [Greek]

R. Herzog in *Sitzungsberichte der Preussischen Akademie der Wissenschaften, Phil.-hist. Klasse* 32
(1935) 967–72; *FIRA* I 73; McCrum–Woodhead, **Documents* 458 (lines 1–20). Cf. *Digest*
27.1.6.8 and 50.4.18.30; Suetonius, *Vespasian* 17–18.

Herzog, *op. cit.* 967–1019; M. S. Woodside in *TAPA* 73 (1942) 123–9; C. A. Forbes in
TAPA 86 (1955) 348–53.

[Imperator Caesar Vespasianus Augustus, pontifex maximus, holding the tribunician power for the sixth time (AD 74), imperator for the fourteenth time, father of his country, consul for the fifth time, designated for the sixth time, censor, declares: -----][1] of physicians and medical practitioners,[2] si|nce [to the sons of Asklepios] alone has the body's *ca|re* [been assigned and they are addressed] as holy and equal
5   to the go|ds, (therefore) I order that no billeting be made ‖ [against them and no] *taxes* be demanded of them in any way. | [And if anyone under] my rule [dares] to injure or to compel them to put up se|curity [or to take (forcibly to court?) any] of the physicians or teachers or medical practitioners, | those guilty of such insolence shall pay a fine to Jupiter Ca|[pitolinus of -- drachmas,] and he who doesn't have the
10   money shall (have his property) sold and to that ‖ god shall the fine [be consecrated] without delay, the fine which | the officer in charge [of such action may impose;] likewise, | [if they find him in hiding,] they may bring him wherever they choose (i.e. to any court) | [and they shall not be obstructed] by anyone. And they (the physicians and teachers) are permitted | [to assemble in their associations] in precincts (of
15   temples) and in shrines and ‖ [in temples] wherever they choose with right of sanctuary; whoever | [drives them out by force] shall be subject to legal action by the Roman People | [on a charge of sacrilege to] the house of the Augusti. I, Imperator | [Caesar Vespa]sianus, have signed this and have ordered it | [to be published on a] whitened board. Pub-
20   lished in the 6th year, in the month ‖ [Loos, 10th day (December 27, AD 75), on the Capitolium] on the sixth day before the Kalends of January (December 27).

1   The entire beginning of this document is missing, but the imperial titles can be restored, since the last two lines give us the date. The original editor, however, attempted to restore the general sense of the missing portion after those titles, basing his restoration on the known goodwill of Vespasian toward physicians and such men. That has been omitted here.
2   The Greek word means a surgeon who practices by anointing his patients with ointments and the like. In the next phrase the 'sons of Asclepios' is another way of saying 'physicians', since the Greek god Asclepios was their patron saint.

85   The Roman presence in the Caucasus. AD 85.

Stone stele with molding, broken at top and damaged at bottom center, Harmozica in Iberia on the route from Tiflis to Mtskhetha. [Greek]

IGRR III 133; *OGIS* 379; *ILS* 8795; *CIL* III 6052; G. V. Tserešeli in *Vestnik Drevnei Istorii* 72 (1960) 123–33 (+ photograph); McCrum–Woodhead, *Documents* 237; **SEG* XX 112.

F. Grosso in *Epigraphica* 16 (1954) 117–79; A. I. Boltounova in *Klio* 53 (1971) 213–22; T. B. Mitford in *ANRW* 2.7.2.1192–4.

[Imperator Ca]esa[r] Ve[s|pasianus Aug]ustus, po|ntifex [maximus,] holding the tribunician *power* | for the [seventh time,] imperator for the
5 || fourteenth time, consul for the sixth time (AD 75) and designa|ted for the seventh, father of his country, *cen|sor*, and Imperator Titus Ca[esar] | son of Augustus, holding the tribunician | power for the fifth time
10   (AD 75), consul for the fourth time and des||ignated for the fifth, cens|or, and Domitianus Caesar, A[ugu]|stus' son, consul for the third time and des|ignated for the fourth – for the king | of the Iberians,
15   Mithridates, son of King Ph||arasmanes and Iamazaspuhi,[1] | friend of Caesar and of the Romans, and for his people they (the emperors) fortified the walls.[2]

1 Iamazaspuhi was the mother of Mithridates: see Terešeli.
2 For the eastern policy of the Flavians see the works of Grosso, Boltounova, and Mitford.

85a   A milestone and the legions in Syria. AD 75.
Cylindrical milestone, two meters high, found on the left bank of the Orontes River in the area of the ancient hippodrome. [Latin]

D. van Berchem in *Museum Helveticum* 40 (1983) 186 (+ photograph) and in **Bonner Jahrbücher* 185 (1985) 85.

Imperator | Vespasianus Caesar | Augustus, pontifex maximus, | holding the tribunician power for the sixth time (AD 75), imperator for the
5   twelfth time, father of his country, consul for the sixth time || (and) designated for the seventh, censor; | Imperator Titus Caesar, son of Augustus, | pontifex maximus, holding the tribunician power for the fourth time, | [consul] for the *fourth* time (and) designated for the fifth,
10   censor; | [[Domitianus]] Caesar, || son of Augustus, consul for the third time. | When Marcus Ulpius Traianus was legate | of Augustus with pro praetorian power,[1] | attention was given to the [construction] of a channel for the river of the Dipotamia[2] | three miles long, with bridges,
15 || by the soldiers of four legions | – the [Third] *Gallica*, the Fourth Scythica, the Sixth Ferrata, the Sixteenth Flavia[3] | – *and also* (by the soldiers) of twenty (auxiliary cohorts) | [and also (?)] (by the militiamen?) of Antioch. | Mile 1.

1 He was the father of the later emperor Trajan.
2 'Dipotamia' means 'land of two rivers', apparently the area beginning where the Orontes and the Karasou join, north of Antioch. For other canal works see below, No. 174.
3 Before this inscription was known, Syria under the Flavians was thought to have only three legions, Sixteenth Flavia being elsewhere.

86   Letter of Vespasian to Sabora in Spain. AD 77.
Bronze tablet (now lost) found at Cañete in Baetica. [Latin]

CIL II 1423; *ILS* 6092; Bruns[7] 81; Abbott–Johnson, *Municipal Administration* 61; *FIRA* I 74;
A. D'Ors, *Epigrafía Jurídica de la España Romana* (Madrid 1953) p. 61, No. 4; McCrum–
Woodhead, **Documents* 461.

Imperator Caesar Vespasianus Augustus, pon|tifex maximus, holding
the tribunician | power for the ninth time (AD 77), imperator for the
eighteenth time, consul | for the eighth time, father of his country,
5   sends greetings to the quattuorviri and ‖ decuriones of Sabora. | Since
you indicate that you in your weakened | condition are hard-pressed by
many difficulties, I give you permission | to build a town under my
10   name, as | you wish, in the plain.[1] The re‖venues, which you say you
received from the deified Augustus, | will be under my control, (and) if
you wish to add any new (revenues), | you will have to approach the
proconsul (of Baetica) about them, for I | can make no decision when
15   there is no official reply.[2] | Your decree ‖ I received on the eighth day
before the Kalends of August (July 25). Your envoys I dis|missed on the
fourth day before the same Kalends (July 29). Farewell. | The duoviri
Gaius Cornelius Severus and Marcus Septimi|us Severus incised (this
document) in bronze at public expense.

1 Vespasian had given the *ius Latii* (Latin Rights) to the Spanish cities. Sabora was a
    municipium.
2 The proconsul should be approached first, and he would contact the emperor.

87   Rescript of Vespasian concerning a land dispute. AD 77 (?).
Bronze tablet found in northern Corsica. [Latin]

CIL X 8038; Bruns[7] 80; Abbott–Johnson, *Municipal Administration* 59; *FIRA* I 72;
McCrum–Woodhead, **Documents* 460.

Imperator Caesar Vespasianus Augustus | to the magistrates and
senators | of the Vanacini, greetings: | I am happy that Otacilius
5   Sagitta, my friend and procu‖rator, exercised his control over you in
such a way | that he has earned a good word | from you. | Concerning
10   the boundary dispute which you ha|ve with the Mariani[1] over ‖ the
lands which you bought from my procurator | Publilius Memoralis, | I
have written to Claudius Clemens, my procu|rator, to fix the bound-
15   aries, and I have sent | him a surveyor. ‖ The privileges assigned to you
by the deified | Augustus after his seventh consul|ship, which to the
time of Galba you have re|tained, I confirm. | Your envoys who handled
20   this matter were ‖ Lasemo, son of Leucanus and priest of Augustus, and

Eunus, son of Tomasus and priest of Augustus. | When Gaius Arruntius Catellius Celer and Marcus | Arruntius Aquila were consuls (AD 77 ?), on the fourth day before the Ides of October (October 12).

1   These were the citizens of a *colonia Mariana*: see Abbott in *Classical Philology* 10 (1915) 374.

88   Career of the Roman conqueror of Masada. Vespasian–Titus.
Two monumental inscriptions (identical) from the ruins of the amphitheater at Urbs Salvia (Urbisaglia) in Italy. [Latin]

AÉ 1969/70, 183a–b; Eck, *Senatoren* 97–8.

Eck, *op. cit.* 93–111; Smallwood, *Jews* 546–7; W. C. McDermott in *Classical World* 66 (1973) 335–51.

[Lucius Flavius, son of ---, (of the tribe) V]elina, Silvia Nonius Bassus, consul (AD 81), pontifex, | [legate of Augustus with pro praetorian power] of the province of Judaea, admitted to patrician status | [by the deified Vespasian and the] deified Titus, censors, admitted to praetorian rank by the same (emperors), legate of the Legion Twenty-First Rapax, | [tribune of the plebs, quaestor, tribune of the soldiers] of the Legion Fourth Scythica, triumvir in criminal cases, praetor quinquennalis[1] twice, patron of his colony, in his own name and (in that)
5   ‖ [of Ann---(?) -----tt]a, his mother, and also | [of ---]milla, his wife, at his own expense and [on his own land] | has seen to the [building of this amphitheater and has dedicated it with] *forty* [regular] *pairs* (of gladiators).[2]

1   As praetor he was the local executive in his home town, the term 'quinquennalis' being added to such a praetor's title every fifth year only.
2   The great expense involved in doing all these things almost certainly means Flavius Silvia came from Urbs Salvia. Eck believes he ruled Judaea after April of AD 73 and that the siege as Masada did not end until the next year.

89   Settlement of tribes around Cirta.
Stone found in region of Aïn-Abid in Numidia. [Latin]

A. Berthier in *Bulletin d'Archéologie algérienne* 3 (1968) 293ff. (+ photograph); *AÉ* 1969/70, 696.

In accordance with the authority | of Imperator Vespasianus | Caesar Augustus, the public lands | of Cirta have been assigned to the Sub‖urbures Regiani and | the Nicibes through | Tullius Pom|ponianus | Capito, legate of Augustus.[1]

1 This same text has also been found at Aïn-el-Bordj (Tigisis): *AÉ* 1957, 175. Nothing else is known of the two native tribes.

90   Vespasian and a dissident senator.

Epictetus, *Discourses* 1.19–21.

These are the things seen by Helvidius Priscus[1] and, having seen them, he did (this). When Vespasian sent a message to him not to come into the senate, he replied, 'It is in your power not to let me be a senator, but as long as I am one I must come to the meetings.' (20) 'All right, but when you come, keep quiet.' 'Don't ask me my opinion and I'll keep quiet.' 'But I must ask your opinion.' 'And I must say what appears just.' (21) 'But if you speak, I'll put you to death.' 'Did I ever say to you that I was immortal? You do yours, I'll do mine. It's yours to kill, mine to die without trembling. It's yours to send into exile, mine to leave without grieving.'

1 Gaius Helvidius Priscus (*PIR*[2] H 59) was praetor in AD 70 and became an outspoken critic of Vespasian (Tacitus, *Hist.* 4.5–8, 43). He was finally exiled and then executed under Vespasian. See Syme, *Tacitus* 1.187 and 212; 2.559.

91   Restoration of public lands. Under Vespasian.
Square stone marker, outside a city-gate at Pompeii. [Latin]

CIL X 1018; *ILS 5924; *FIRA* III 78c; McCrum–Woodhead, *Documents* 339.

By authority | of Imperator Caesar | Vespasianus Augustus: | In regard
5 to public lands which private persons ‖ had in their possession, Titus Suedius Clemens, | tribune,[1] heard arguments in court, had surveys conducted, | and restored them to the re|public of Pompeii.

1 Cf. Tacitus, *Hist.* 1.87 and 2.12. Perhaps he was tribune of a praetorian cohort.

TITUS
(AD 79–81)
IMPERATOR TITUS CAESAR VESPASIANUS AUGUSTUS

Titles: PONTIFEX MAXIMUS
CENSOR (72)
HOLDER OF THE TRIBUNICIAN POWER: first
time in AD 71, ninth time in AD 79 on July 1, then annually on
that day
CONSUL: AD 80 (VIII)

Death: September 13, AD 81.

DOMITIAN
(AD 81–96)
IMPERATOR DOMITIANUS CAESAR AUGUSTUS

Titles: PONTIFEX MAXIMUS
FATHER OF HIS COUNTRY (81)
GERMANICUS (end of 83 and beginning of 84)
CENSOR (85)
HOLDER OF THE TRIBUNICIAN POWER: first
time in AD 81, on September 14 (?), and annually
CONSUL: AD 82 (VIII) to 88 (XIV), 90 (XV), 92 (XVI),
95 (XVII)

Death: September 18, AD 96.

The *consules ordinarii* **under Titus and Domitian**

AD		
80	Imp. Titus Caesar Vespasianus Augustus VIII	Caesar Domitianus VII
81	L. Flavius Silva Nonius Bassus	L.? Asinius Pollio Verrucosus
82	Imp. Domitianus VIII	T. Flavius Sabinus
83	Imp. Domitianus IX	Q. Petillius Rufus II
84	Imp. Domitianus X	C. Oppius Sabinus
85	Imp. Domitianus XI	Cf. Syme, *JRS* 43 (1953) 155; Degrassi, *Athenaeum* 33 (1955) 112–16
86	Imp. Domitianus XII	Ser. Cornelius Dolabella Petronianus
87	Imp. Domitianus XIII	L. Volusius Saturninus
88	Imp. Domitianus XIV	L. Minucius Rufus
89	T. Aurelius Fulvus	M. Asinius Atratinus
90	Imp. Domitianus XV	M. Cocceius Nerva II
91	M'. Acilius Glabrio	M. Ulpius Traianus

92 Imp. Domitianus XVI	Q. Volusius Saturninus
93 Sex. Pompeius Collega	Q. Peducaeus Priscinus
94 L. Nonius Calpurnius Asprenas	T. Sextius Magius Lateranus
Torquatus	
95 Imp. Domitianus XVII	T. Flavius Clemens
96 C. Manlius Valens	C. Antistius Vetus

92   Titus writes to the city of Munigua in Spain. AD 79.

Rectangular bronze tablet with holes in the four corners, beautifully engraved, Munigua in Baetica. [Latin]

H. Nesselhauf in *Madrider Mitteilungen* 1 (1960) 148–9 (+ photograph).

Nesselhauf, *op. cit.* 148–54; A. D'Ors in *Emerita* 29 (1961) 208–18 (+ photograph).

Imperator Titus Caesar Vespasianus Augustus, pontifex maximus, |
holder of the tribunician power for the eighth time (AD 79), imperator
for the fourteenth time, consul for the seventh time, father of his
country, | sends greetings *vv* to the quattuorviri and decurions of
Munigua. | Since you have made an appeal not to pay the money which
5   you owe to Servilius ‖ Pollio in accordance with the decision of
Sempronius Fuscus,[1] a penalty for an unjustified | appeal ought to be
exacted from you.[2] However, I have preferred to speak in accordance
with | my generosity rather than with your impetuosity, and | fifty-
thousand sesterces – because of the public poverty | which you put
forward as pretext – I have remitted. Moreover, I have written to
10   Gallicanus, my friend ‖ and proconsul,[3] that the money which was
assigned to Pollio should have been paid | by you, (but) that from the
day the decision was made he is to free you from the interest | that has
accumulated. *vv* | As for the profits (from the collection) of your own
revenues, which you indicate had been farmed out on contract to
Pol|lio, it is right for these to be entered into the account, so that
15   nothing ‖ in this regard is a loss to your city. *vv* Farewell. | Done on the
seventh day before the Ides of September (September 7).

1   Servilius Pollio apparently lived south of Munigua in Carmo (modern Carmona),
    where the family name occurs. His connection with Munigua was one of business:
    he contracted with the city to collect its revenues, the source of the present legal
    impasse. Sempronius Fuscus was the governor of Baetica to whose jurisdiction the
    case was brought.
2   For the 'appeal procedure' see R. Orestano, *L'appello civile in diritto romano* (Turin
    1953) and J. M. Kelly, *Princeps Iudex* (Weimar 1957) 70ff.
3   He succeeded Sempronius Fuscus as governor of Baetica. His full name was Gaius
    Cornelius Gallicanus (cos. suff. AD 84): *PIR*[2] C 1367. On both of them see G. Alföldy,
    Fasti Hispanienses (Wiesbaden 1969) 159–60.

93   Earthquake damage repaired at Naples. AD 80–1.

Large stone, left side broken off, damaged in upper right corner, very large letters in first line, Naples. [Greek and Latin]

CIL X 1481; *IG* XIV 729; *IGRR* I 435; McCrum–Woodhead, *Documents* 54. Cf. Pliny, *Epist.* 6.20; Dio 66.24.

(Greek) [Imperator] Titus Caesa[r, | son of god Vespasianus, V]espasianus Augustus, | [pontifex maximus,] *holding the tribunician* power for the tenth time (AD 80–1), | [imperator for the fifteenth time,
5   father of his country,] consul for the eighth time, censor, ‖ [in Naples having been the demarchos,] agonothetēs for the third time, and gymnasiarch, | [----, when by earthquakes] they had collapsed, he restored them.[1] |

(A Latin translation follows.)

1   The reference is to the eruption of Mt Vesuvius in AD 79, which was accompanied by great earthquakes.

94   Pay record of a Roman legionary. AD 81.
Papyrus, probably from Egypt. [Latin]

J. Nicole and Ch. Morel, *Archives militaires du 1er siècle. Texte inédit du Papyrus latin de Genève No. 1* (Geneva 1900); Cavenaile, *CPL* 106; R. O. Fink, *Roman Military Records on Papyrus* (Philological Monographs of the American Philological Association, No. 26) (Case Western Reserve University, Cleveland, Ohio 1971) No. 68, Col. 3.

A. von Premerstein in *Klio* 3 (1903) 1–46; G. R. Watson in *Historia* 5 (1956) 332–40; Fink, *op. cit.* 243–9.

(Col. 3) Gaius Valerius Germanus from Tyre: | received first pay of the third year of Domitian (AD 81): 247½ drachmas.[1] | *vv* From this (is
5   deducted) *vv* | hay – 10 drachmas; ‖ for food – 80 drachmas; | boots, leggings – 12 drachmas; | for the Saturnalia in camp – 20 drachmas; | for clothing – 100 drachmas. | *vv* (All these) expenses = 222 drachmas.
10   ‖ Remainder deposited: 25½ drachmas. | And he already had: 21 drachmas. | Total: 46½ drachmas. | (Second hand) He received second pay of the same year: 247½ drachmas. | *vv* From this (is deducted) *vv*
15   ‖ hay – 10 drachmas; | for food – 80 drachmas; | boots, leggings – 12 drachmas; | for the military standards[2] – 4 drachmas. | *vv* (All these)
20   expenses = 106 drachmas. ‖ Remainder deposited: 141½ drachmas. | And he had from prior (account): 46½ drachmas. | Total: 188 drachmas. | (Third hand) He received third pay of the same year: 247½
25   drachmas. | *vv* From this (is deducted) *vv* ‖ hay – 10 drachmas; | for food

– 80 drachmas; | boots, leggings – 12 drachmas; | for clothing – 145½
drachmas. | He has on deposit: 188 drachmas.

1 Legionaries in this period were paid 75 denarii in each pay period of three per year.
  Each denarius was worth four drachmas, which works out to 300 drachmas each
  payment. No modern account of the discrepancy has been universally accepted.
  Fink cautions that the present text 'may well belong to men who had been in service
  only a year or two. Consequently they may not be wholly typical.'
2 Fink notes that this may be a contribution to a burial fund (Vegetius 2.20) or for the
  cult of the *signa* (the military standards).

95 Instructions from Domitian to a procurator. Reign of Domitian.
Stone stele damaged along the right side and bottom, irregular letters
poorly spaced, Epiphaneia in Syria. [Greek]

R. Mouterde and C. Mondésert in *Syria* 34 (1957) 278ff. (+ photograph); *IGLS* V 1998;
SEG XVII 755; McCrum–Woodhead, *Documents* 466; N. Lewis in **RIDA* 15 (1968) 135.

Mouterde–Mondésert, *op. cit.* 278–84; H. W. Pleket in *Mnemosyne* 14 (1961) 304–5;
Lewis, *op. cit.* 135ff.; Millar, *Emperor* 315; B. Lifshitz in *ANRW* 2.8.8–9.

   vv From instructions of Impera|tor [[Dom]]itianus Cae|sar, son of
5 Augustus, Augustus. | To Claudius Athenodorus, || procurator: Among
items of special importance | that required great atten|tion by my
father, the god Ves|pasianus, I know that he gave great care | to the
10 citi|es' privileges. With his mind fixed on them he ordered | that neither
by the renting of beasts of burden nor by | the distress of lodging should
the provinces be burdened, | but, nevertheless, by conscious decision
or not, deliberate neglect | has set in and this order has not been
15 observed, for there remains || up to the present an old and vigorous
custom | which, little by little, will progress into law if it is not |
obstructed by force from gaining strength.[1] I instruct you to see to it |
that nobody commandeers a beast of burden unless | he has a permit
20 from me. For it is most unjust || that, either by the favor or prestige of
certain people, requisitions should take place which no|body but
myself can grant. Therefore, let there be nothing | which will break my
instructions and | spoil my intent, which is most advantageous to the
25 cities, for to help | the weakened provinces is just, || provinces which
with difficulty have enough for the necessities of life. Let no | force be
used against them contrary to my wi|sh, and let nobody commandeer a
guide unless | he has a permit from me, for, when farmers are torn from
30 their homes, | the fields will remain without their attention. || You,
either using your own *beasts* | *of burden* or renting them, will act best [----]

1 The meaning here is that customary actions will inevitably lead to the establishment of a legal precedent.

96 Letter of Domitian about a land controversy. AD 82 or 83.
Bronze tablet, Falerio in Italy. [Latin]

CIL IX 5420; Bruns[7] 82; Abbott–Johnson, *Municipal Administration* 63; *FIRA* I 75; McCrum–Woodhead, **Documents* 462.

Imperator Caesar, son of the deified Vespasian, | [[Domitianus]] Augustus, | pontifex maximus, holding the tribunician power, imperator for the second time, | consul for the eighth time (and) desig-
5 nated for the ninth, father of his country, sends greetings ‖ to the quattuorviri and decurions of the Falerians from Picenum. | What I decided about the unsurveyed parcels of land, when I heard the case | between you and the Firmanians,[1] to acquaint you with it | I have ordered it to be appended to this letter. |
10 In the consulship of Publius Valerius Patruinus and [----] ‖ On the fourteenth day before the Kalends of August (July 19). | I, Imperator Caesar, son of the deified Vespasian, [[Domitianus]] | Augustus, have called in for consultation distinguished men of both orders | and, after the case had been heard between the Fale|rnians and Firmanians, I
15 gave my pronouncement, which | is appended. |
The great age of the controversy, which after so many years | has been reopened by the Firmanians against the | Falernians, moves me very much, | since for the security of those who occupy (the land) a
20 much les‖ser number of years could have sufficed.[2] | And (I am moved also by) the letter of the deified Augustus, a most diligent and gra|cious Leader toward his Fourth Legionaries, | in which he advises | them to
25 assemble all their unsurveyed parcels of land ‖ and sell them. Such beneficial | advice I am sure they obeyed, | and for those reasons I confirm the right of those in occupation (of the land). | Farewell.
Given on the eleventh day before the Kalends of August (July 22) in
30 the Alban (Villa) | under the care of Titus Bovius Verus. ‖ Envoys were Publius Bovius Sabinus | and Publius Petronius Achilles. (Erected) at public (expense) by decree of the decurions (of Falerio).

1 Falerio seems to have been a colony of veterans of the Fourth Legion founded by Augustus. When the original survey of land was made, certain irregular parcels lay outside that survey for the colony and the Firmanians moved onto it. The colonists later claimed that those parcels belonged to them. The Firmanians objected and remained in occupation through the years.
2 As early as the time of the Twelve Tables (mid-fourth century BC) continuous occupation of land for two years gave ownership to the occupiers (Twelve Tables 6.30).

97   The municipal charter of Salpensa.[1] AD 82–4.
Bronze tablet found near Malaga in Baetica. [Latin]

CIL II 1963; Bruns[7] 30a; *ILS* 6088; Abbott–Johnson, *Municipal Administration* 64; *FIRA* I
23; A. D'Ors, *Epigrafía Jurídica de la España Romana* (Madrid 1953) pp. 281–309;
McCrum–Woodhead, **Documents* 453.

Abbott-Johnson, *op. cit.* 56–68 and 372–4; H. Last in *CAH* 11.456–66; D'Ors, *loc. cit.*

[Rubric: That magistrates shall receive Roman citizenship.] [XXI.[2]
Whoever becomes duovir, aedile or quaestor in consequence of this law
shall be Roman citizens when at the end of the year their magistracies]
| have ended, together with their parents, their wives, and their children
who have been born from legal marriages and | subject to the parents'
power, and likewise grandsons and granddaughters | born from a son
and subject to the parents' power, provided that the Roman citizens
will be no more | than the magistrates to be elected in consequence of
this law. ‖

5   Rubric: That those who receive Roman citizenship shall remain in
the legal possession, control, or | power of the same persons. | XXII.
Any man or woman who in consequence of this law or of an edict of
Imperator Caesar Augustus Vespasianus or Imperator Titus | Caesar
Augustus or Imperator Caesar Augustus Domitianus, father of his
country, has or will acquire Roman citizenship, | he or she shall be in
the legal possession, control, or power of that person who has been

10   made a Roman citizen by this law, ‖ in whose (legal possession, control,
or power) he or she ought to be if he or she had not been changed by a
change of Roman citizenship, | and he or she shall have the same right
of choosing a guardian which | he or she would have had if he or she had
been born a Roman citizen and had not been changed by a | change in
citizenship.
      Rubric: That they who acquire Roman citizenship shall retain their
rights over their freedmen. |
      XXIII. Any man or woman who in consequence of this law or edict
of Imperator Caesar Vespasianus Augustus or Imperator Titus Caesar

15   Vespasianus Augustus ‖ or Imperator Caesar Domitianus Augustus
has or will acquire Roman citizenship, in | regard to freedmen or freed-
women – their own or their fathers' – who have not | come into Roman
citizenship and in regard to their goods and duties imposed on them
for the sake of (eventual) freedom, | the same rights and conditions
shall exist as would have existed if he or she had not been changed by
a | change in citizenship.
      Rubric: Concerning the prefect of Imperator Caesar Domitianus
Augustus. ‖

20   XXIIII. (Lines 20–5)[3]

Rubric: Concerning the rights of a prefect left in charge by a duovir. |
XXV. If one of the (two) duoviri who are in charge of the judicial
system in this municipality leaves the municipality after (the other has
left) | and thinks he will not return to the municipality on the day (when
the other will return), whatever | prefect over the municipality – not
less than thirty-five years old and one of the | decuriones or other
senators – he wishes to leave (in his place), he shall make him swear by
30 ‖ Jupiter and the deified Augustus and the deified Claudius and the
deified Vespasianus Augustus and the deified | Titus Augustus and the
tutelary deity of Imperator Caesar Domitianus Augustus and the
Penates gods: | that, whatever a duovir in charge of the judicial system
ought to do in consequence of this law, he also will do, as long as he will
be prefect, provided that those things at that | time can be done and
that he will not act contrary to those things knowingly | in bad faith;
and when he has sworn that oath, he shall leave him as prefect over the
35 municipality. He ‖ who is thus left in charge as prefect, until one or the
other of the duoviri | will return, shall have the rights and powers in all
matters, except in the matter of leaving (another) prefect in charge and
| of acquiring Roman citizenship, which rights and powers by this law
| have been given to the duoviri in charge of the judicial system. While
he is prefect and as of|ten as he leaves the municipality, he shall not be
40 away more than one day. ‖
Rubric: Concerning the oath of duoviri and aediles and quaestors. |
XXVI. The duoviri in charge of the judicial system in this munici-
pality, likewise the aediles in this municipality, and likewise | the
quaestors in this municipality, each of them within five days | following
the passage of this law, and whatever duoviri, aediles, or quaestors
afterwards in consequence of this law | will be created, each of them
45 within five days of when he began to be a duovir, ‖ aedile, or quaestor,
and before the decuriones or the other senators | have held a meeting,
shall swear the oath before a public assembly by Jupiter and the deified
Augustus and the deified Claudi|us and the deified Vespasianus
Augustus and the deified Titus Augustus and the tutelary deity of
Domitianus | Augustus and the Penates gods: that he, whatever he
thinks is in accordance with this law and with the common interest of
the citizens of the municipality Flavia | Salpensa, will do (those things)
50 and nothing against this law or the comm‖on good of the citizens of this
municipality will he do knowingly in bad faith, and that whomever he
can pre|vent from so doing he will prevent; and that he will hold no
meeting of the senate and neither give nor express any opinion other
than | what he judges is in keeping with the common good | of the
citizens of this municipality. The one who does not swear this oath
shall pay a fine of 10,000 sesterces | to the citizens of this municipality,

55 and concerning this money anyone of the ci‖tizens who wishes and who
is permitted to do so by this law shall be permitted the right to take
legal action, to sue, and to pro|secute.

Rubric: Concerning the veto power of the duoviri, aediles, and
questors. |

XXVII. The duoviri, aediles, or quaestors of this municipality – the
duoviri among | themselves and when somebody appeals to either or
both of them (to act) against an aedile or aediles | or against a quaestor
or quaestors, and likewise the aediles among themselves, <and
likewise the quaestors among themselves> – shall have the right and
power of ve‖to within three days after the appeal is made, | and the right
and the power of the veto will be possible in cases where nothing is
done contrary to this law and provided that no more than once | to each
of the magistrates an appeal is made on the same matter, and nobody |
shall do anything against these actions when a veto has been declared. |

Rubric: Concerning the freeing of slaves before the duovir.

60 ‖ XXVIII. (Lines 65–74)[4]

Rubric: Concerning the appointment of guardians.

65 ‖ XXVIIII. (Lines 75–88, end)[5]

1 The chief local magistrate in western municipalities, to which Rome granted
charters, were usually called duoviri, i.e. 'two men', who were the elected executive
heads of the city. Under them were aediles and quaestors with various duties. A
controlled system of granting Roman citizenship was included in such charters, the
so-called 'Latin rights'.
2 Since this tablet begins with section XXI, the earlier sections appeared on the first
two tablets (now lost).
3 In this section we learn that if the chief magistracy is offered to the emperor and if
he accepts, the emperor would select someone to act in his place as prefect.
4 Whenever a slave is freed by a citizen of Salpensa, such a freed person will receive
Latin rights (see n. 1).
5 When asked, and when specific guardians are named, the duoviri will assign
guardians for citizens having no legal guardians, but their colleagues in office must
express their views. If no colleagues are available, the duovir or duoviri must obtain
the approval by decree of two-thirds of the senators.

98 Domitian appoints a new praetorian prefect. AD 83–4.
Papyrus of unknown origin, but probably Egypt. [Latin]

H. Kortenbeutel in *Abhandlungen der Preussischen Akademie der Wissenschaften* (Jahrgang
1939) *Phil.-hist. Klasse* 13 (Berlin 1940) (+ photograph; = *P. Berlin* 8334); A. Piganiol in
CRAI 1947, 376–87; Cavenaile, *CPL 238.

R. Syme, *Tacitus* 2, App. 7; *idem* in *JRS* 70 (1980) 66 (*Roman Papers* III 1279–80).

vv Copy of Codicils *vv* | [Because of your excellent character] and piety,

my dear Maximus,[1] [---] which [have become known | from many
sources] to me, you have always received rewards through me. | [Never-
theless,] I have not been content to crown your distinguished career by
5   reference to the || governorship [of Egypt,] but [when] I transferred
Iulius [Ursus] | into the most honorable order,[2] [when he made use of
his own[3] entreaties] and had long | been desirous (of the transfer), I
immediately reflected upon [your] most devoted *loyalty* and | *diligent
activity* and I have (now) made you the colleague [and partner | of Cor-
nelius F]uscus,[4] with whom I hope there will [soon be not only a most
10 || diligent] but also a most devoted and equal sharing of duty [between
| the two of you.] I do not doubt, [my dear Maximus,] that you will rush
here [with favorable] seas as soon as you can [---] | and will be most
desirous (of coming) [to Rome] to my side. [Given at Rome on ---]

1 He is Lucius Laberius Maximus, known to have been in Egypt as prefect in AD 83:
   Stein, *Präfekten* 41–2.
2 Lucius Iulius Ursus (*PIR*[2] I 630) was moved from equestrian to senatorial rank and,
   thus, could be made consul. He became consul ('the most honorable order') in
   AD 84.
3 The phrase 'his own' should replace 'your' suggested by all others. E. Birley
   suggested 'his own': Syme, *loc. cit.*
4 Cornelius Fuscus (*PIR*[2] C 1365) was praetorian prefect under Domitian. Kortenbeutel had supplied here the name of [Pedianus F]uscus, since he believed that
   'Maximus' had been made consul with that man. Piganiol, however, has shown that
   Maximus was elevated to the post of praetorian prefect and he has, accordingly,
   restored the name of the known prefect Cornelius Fuscus in our text. Followed also
   by Syme.

99   Area destroyed by fire under Nero. Age of Domitian.
Stone pillar found on the Quirinal, Rome. [Latin]

CIL VI 826 (30837 b); *ILS* 4914; Bruns[7] 109; *FIRA* III 75; McCrum–Woodhead, *Documents* 442. Cf. Tacitus, *Ann.* 15.38–44.

This area, within this | boundary of pillars | enclosed by stakes and an
5   altar which | is below, has been dedicated by || Imperator Caesar
Domitianus Augustus | Germanicus in consequence of a vow under-
taken, | but for a long time neglected and not | fulfilled, | to stop the
10   fires || when the city for nine days | burned in the time of Nero. | It was
dedicated by this law so that nobody | would be permitted within these
15   borders | to erect a building, to loiter, || to conduct business, to plant a
tree | or to sow any other thing, | and that the praetor to whom this
region | falls by the lot,[1] | or some other magistrate, shall make a
20   sacrifice || at the Volcanalia on the tenth day before the Kalends of
September (August 23),[2] | every year, | of a red bull-calf | and a red

25   boar-pig, with prayers. | Written below. Shrine [--- before the] Kalends
     of September ‖ [----] give [----] | which Imperator Caesar Domitianus |
     Augustus Germanicus, pontifex maximus, | has decided [----] | to be
     done.

1 Dio (55.8) and Suetonius (*Augustus* 30) report that Augustus divided Rome into 14
   regions.
2 The festival of Vulcan, god of fire, was particularly appropriate.

100   Entrapment of citizens. Time of Domitian.

Epictetus, *Discourses* 4.13.5.

Thus, in Rome reckless persons are entrapped by soldiers. A soldier in
civilian dress sits down next to you and begins by speaking ill of Caesar,
and then, as if you haad received a pledge from him of trust – the fact
that he began the reproaches – you also say what you're thinking. Then
come the chains and the march to prison.

101   Boundary markers of a Roman colony on Crete. AD 84.
Limestone block, Archanes in territory of Knossos on Crete. [Latin]

P. Ducrey in *BCH 93 (1969) 846 (+ photograph); *AÉ* 1969/70, 635. Cf. Appian, *Bell.
Civ.* 4.3; Dio 49.14.5; Velleius Paterculus 2.81.1; Strabo 10.478.

Ducrey, *op. cit.* 846–52; K. J. Rigsby in *TAPA* 106 (1976) 313–30; L. Keppie in *PBSR* 52
(1984) 96–7.

When Imperator Domitianus | Caesar Augustus Germanicus was
consul for the tenth time (AD 84), | between the colony Flavia Augusta
5   Felix | Capua[1] and Plotius Plebeius,[2] ‖ [in accordance with] the decision
     of Titus Imperator Augustus and | according to the decree of the colony
     Capua, | with the agreement of both | *parties*, boundary markers were
     put in place | under the direction of Publius Messius Campanus,
10   ‖ procurator of Caesar.

1 Campanian land in the territory of Knossos is known to us from several sources.
   Relations between Capua and Crete extend back to the fourth century BC (*I. Cret.*
   IV 314).
2 Plotius is known to us as a duovir from the coinage of Knossos, for whose interest he
   acts in the boundary action.

102 Domitian's war against the Dacians. AD 85–6, 88–9.

A: Jordanes, *Getica* 12.74. B: Jordanes, *Getica* 13.76–8. C: Orosius, *Against the Pagans* 7.10.4. D: *ILS* 9200; Pflaum, *Carrières* 50; McCrum–Woodhead, *Documents* 372; *IGLS* VI 2796. Career of a Roman equestrian, translated below, No. 109. [Latin] E:Eutropius 7.23.4. F: Aurelius Victor, *De Caesaribus* 11.4. G: *CIL* III 14214; *ILS* 9107. [Latin] A large, rectangular altar or cenotaph (12 m long) near the Rumanian village of Adamklissi, about 40 miles west of Constanta, in Moesia Inferior. At top of one side is a heading in very large letters originally containing the name of the emperor and the brief words of his dedication to the honored war-dead listed below in column after column. His name is missing. In smaller letters follow the names of the soldiers from the ranks along with their commanding general, whose name is missing. See C. Cichorius, *Die römischen Denkmäler in der Dobrudscha* (Berlin 1904); C. Patsch in *Sitzungsberichte der Akademie der Wissenschaften in Wien, Phil.-hist. Klasse*, 217.1 (1937) 13ff.; E. Dorutiu in *Dacia* 5 (1961) 345–63; I. Berciu in *Apulum* 5 (1964) 259–70; I. A. Richmond in *PBSR* 35 (1967) 29–39; E. Condurachi in *Quaderni Catanesi di storia class. e mediev.* 2.3 (1980) 101–24.

Cf. Dio 67.6–7 and 10; 68.9.3; Tacitus, *Agricola* 41, and *Hist.* 1.2; Suetonius, *Domitian* 6; Martial, *Epigrams* 5.3 and 5.19.3 and 6.10.7ff.; Statius, *Silvae* 3.3.117ff.

R. Syme in *CAH* 11.168–78; Patsch, *op. cit.* 3–52; Garzetti, *Tiberius to Antonines* 287–91, 656–8; Mócsy, *Pannonia* 82–4.

A. Jordanes, *Getica* 12.74

This country (Dacia), located across the Danube within sight of Moesia, is enclosed by a crown of mountains, having only two entrances, one though Boutae and another through Tapae.[1]

B. Jordanes, *Getica* 13.76–8

After a long interval of time, in the reign of Imperator Domitian, the Goths (i.e. Dacians), fearing his greed, broke the truce which they formerly had made with the other emperors. They devastated the bank of the Danube, long possessed by the Roman empire, killing the soldiers along with their generals. Oppius Sabinus was at the head of the province (Moesia) at that time, after Agrippa, and Dorpaneus was the leader of the (Dacians)[2] when the (Dacians) went to war, defeated the Romans, cut off the head of Oppius Sabinus, and invaded and plundered openly many fortresses and cities of the emperor. (77) In this crisis of his people Domitian hurried with all his strength to Illyricum, his troops coming from almost the whole empire. Fuscus was sent on ahead as leader with his elite soldiers, and he tied his boats together like a bridge and forced his men to cross the Danube River beyond the camp of Dorpaneus. (78) Then the (Dacians), full of energy, got out their weapons and soon, at the first encounter, defeated the Romans. They killed Fuscus, the leader, and plundered the military camp of its treasury.[3]

C. Orosius, *Against the Pagans* **7.10.4**

The great battles of Diurpaneus, king of the Dacians, with the commander Fuscus and the great disaster of the Romans I would have
narrated at length, except that Cornelius Tacitus, who has composed
this history most carefully, said that both Sallustius Crispus and very
many other writers had ordained silence about numbers of the slain
and that he himself had adopted the very same principle.[4] Nevertheless, Domitian, puffed up with the most perverse ostentation, held a
triumph in the name of a defeated enemy over his annihilated legions.

D. *IGLS* **VI 2796: see below, Document No. 109**

E. Eutropius 7.23.4

Over the Dacians and Chatti he (Domitian) held a double triumph and
appropriated a single laurel crown (for victory) over the Sarmatians,
but he suffered many disasters in these very wars, for in Sarmatia his
legion along with its commander was killed, and the consular Oppius
Sabinus and Cornelius Fuscus, the praetorian prefect, with their great
armies were killed by the Dacians.

F. Aurelius Victor, *De Caesaribus* **11.4**

When the Dacians and a band of Chatti had been defeated, he called
the month of September 'Germanicus' and October 'Domitianus' after
himself.[5]

G. *ILS* **9107, Adamklissi**

(On the east side of the altar) [----|----|--][6] holding the tribunician
power for the [----|---] to the memory of the very brave [men‖who] lay
here in death on behalf of the State. | [----][7] (from the) colony of
Pompeii, his home at Naples in Italy, prefect [of the camp (?) of the
praetorians (?).] |[8]

1 Boutae was probably located at the 'Red Gate Pass' on the Alt River which controlled
   the approach to Sarmizegetusa from the southeast. Tapae was the site at the 'Iron
   Gate Pass', guarding the approach to Sarmizegetusa from the west, not to be confused with the 'Iron Gate' itself on the Danube at Turn-Severin.
2 Gaius Oppius Sabinus (consul ordinarius AD 84) was the last governor of undivided
   Moesia in AD 85–6. Gaius Fonteius Agrippa was governor of Moesia in AD 69–70
   and was succeeded by three governors before the arrival of Oppius. Dorpaneus may
   be identical with the Douras of Dio (Exc. Val. 67.6.1).
3 Cornelius Fuscus (*PIR*[2] C 1365) was in command of the praetorian guard and
   entrusted by Domitian with overall command against the Dacians: Syme, *Tacitus*
   2.623 and 683ff.
4 This is a reference to a lost passage in the *Histories* of Tacitus. The full text of that
   work probably ended with the death of Domitian. Gaius Sallustius Crispus, the old

Republican historian, had been one of the authors of the past who had influenced
  Tacitus in many ways.
5 Similarly Suetonius, *Domitian* 13.3. Cf. Stein, *Moesien* 36–8.
6 The name of Domitian must have stood here.
7 It has generally been assumed that the name of Cornelius Fuscus originally stood
  here, agreeing with the beginning of his title (prefect of the praetorian guard) toward
  the end of the line. Syme (in *AJP* 58 (1937) 14–18 (*Danubian Papers* 1.79–83) And
  Domaszewski (in *Rheinisches Museum* 60 (1905) 158ff.), however, see a difficulty in
  this, for Pompeii was apparently not his colony. On the other hand, J. Colin (in
  Latomus 15 (1956) 63–71) believes that Pompeii was indeed his colony. Syme believes
  that the monument was erected to the memory of all the soldiers who fell in battle
  under both Oppius and Fuscus, but that the unknown officer named in the lacuna of
  line 6 was a prefect of the camp.
8 Beneath this last line there followed the names of more than 3,000 war-dead from
  various branches of the Roman army, arranged in narrow columns on all four sides.

103   Edict of Domitian on the immunity of veterans. AD 87–8.
One wooden tablet of a diptychon, inscribed on the exterior and
interior faces, similar to the bronze diplomas of military discharges,
Philadelphia in Egypt. [Latin]

Wilcken, *Chrestomathie* 463; *ILS* 9059; *CIL* XVI, p. 146; *FIRA* I 76; Cavenaile, **CPL* 104.

J. Lesquier, *L'Armée romaine d'Égypte d'Auguste à Dioclétien* (Cairo 1918) 297ff. and 333ff.;
F. Schehl in *Aegyptus* 13 (1933) 137–44; H. Wolff in *Chiron* 4 (1974) 496–510.

(Exterior face, a list of nine Romans, all veterans, in Col. 1)
    (Exterior face, Col. 2) When Lucius Nonius Calpurnius Torquatus
Asprenas and Titus Sextius Magius | Lateranus were consuls (AD 94),
on the sixth day before the Nones of July (July 2) in the thirteenth year
of Imperator Caesar Domitianus | Augustus Germanicus, month of
Epip, the eighth day, at Alexandria in Egypt: | Marcus Valerius, son of
Marcus, (of the tribe) Pollia, Quadratus, veteran honorably discharged
5 ‖ from the Legion Tenth Fretensis, testified that he had a copy made |
and certified from the bronze tablet which is fixed | to the Great Temple
of the Caesars,[1] as one climbs the second flight of steps | beneath the
right portico, beside the shrine of Venus in | Marble, on the wall, on
which is written that which follows.
10   ‖ Imperator Caesar, son of the deified Vespasian, Domitianus
Augustus Germanicus, | pontifex maximus, holding the tribunician
power for the seventh time (AD 87–8), imperator for the thirteenth
time, perpetual censor, | father of his country, declares: I have decided
to indicate by edict that | veteran soldiers of your entire population[2] |
ought to be free and immune from all public taxes and harbor fees,
15 ‖ that they, their wives who married them, their children, and their

parents | shall be Roman citizens with all the rights thereof, | that they shall be free unconditionally with every immunity, and that, in regard to every immun|ity, those mentioned above – their parents and their children – shall have the same rights | and the same status; and that 20 their estates, houses, and shops || [----]³

(Interior face, Col. 3)⁴ [----] of veterans with their wives and children mentioned above, (whose names) | have been engraved on bronze, or, if they are unmarried, with those women whom they marry afterwards, | provided only one to each (of the veterans) who soldiered at Jerusalem | in the Legion Tenth Fretensis⁵ and were honorably discharged, after 5 serving out || their time, by Sextus Hermetidius Campanus, legate of Augustus with pro praetorian power, | on the fifth day before the Kalends of January (December 28) in the consulship of Sextus Pompeius Collega and Quintus Peducaeus Priscinus (AD 93). Their military service | began in the consulship of Publius Galerius Trachalus and Tiberius Catius (AD 68) and (in the consulship of) Titus Flavius and Gnaeus Arulenus (AD 69). |

With the authorization (to make a copy granted) by Marcus Iunius Rufus, prefect of Egypt, when Lucius Nonius Calpurnius | Torquatus Asprenas and Titus Sextius Magius Lateranus were consuls (AD 94), 10 on the Kalends of July (July 1), year || thirteen of Imperator Caesar Domitianus Augustus Germanicus, in the month Epip, the seventh day. |

At that place (i.e. in front of the bronze original) Marcus Valerius, son of Marcus, (of the tribe) Pollia, Quadratus, before and in the presence of those | who were to sign (as witnesses),⁶ testified and swore by Jupiter Best and Greatest and by the Genius | of the most sacred Imperator Caesar Domitianus Augustus Germanicus that while he was in military service | Lucius Valerius Valens and Valeria Heraclus and 15 Valeria || Artemis – above-mentioned children – were all three of them born to him and that (their names) had been engraved on the bronze tablet and that they | had received Roman citizenship through the beneficence of the same excellent Leader.

1 Located in the city of Alexandria.
2 Here is followed the reading of the text by Nesselhauf in *CIL*.
3 Schehl restores: '[they shall possess] in an undisturbed condition with no loss or damage, veterans as they are [who testified that they have been honorably discharged.]'.
4 Here apparently begins another edict.
5 This legion had been under the command of Corbulo until his recall in AD 66. It then marched to Jerusalem, took part in the Jewish War, and subsequently became the permanent occupying legion of Judaea with its camp in Jerusalem.
6 Their names, nine in all, appeared on the exterior face in Col. 1.

104 'Nero is still alive.' Reign of Domitian.

Dio Chrysostom 21 (*On Beauty*) 9–10.

Nero in no way was sparing of money, either in giving or taking. Because of his wantonness toward his eunuch he lost his life. For in his anger he revealed Nero's plans to his followers, and thus they revolted from him and forced him to kill himself in whatever way he could.[1] Not even now has this story come to light, since, as far as the rest of the people are concerned, nothing prevented him from ruling forever. Even now everyone desires him to be alive, and the majority of people think he really is, even though in some way he died not once but often, along with those who have been convinced that he is still alive.[2]

1 The reference seems to be to the eunuch Sporus. Griffin (*Nero* 186 with n. 6) thinks he revealed Nero's hiding-place at the end. Cf. Suetonius, *Nero* 49.
2 Dio Chrysostom refers here to the three false Neros who appeared in the Roman world between AD 68 and 88: Tacitus, *Histories* 2.8–9; Dio 64.9; Zonaras, *Chron.* 11.18, printed in texts of Dio 66.19; Suetonius, *Nero* 57. See R. MacMullen, *Enemies of the Roman Order* (Cambridge, Mass. 1967) 143–6; Griffin, *Nero* 214–15.

105 Edict of the prefect of Egypt on public records. AD 89.
Papyrus from Oxyrhynchus, Egypt. [Greek]

P. Oxy. 237, Col. 8, lines 27–43; Mitteis, *Chrestomathie* 192; *FIRA* I 60.

Grenfell and Hunt in *P. Oxy.*, pp. 176–80; Reinmuth, *Prefect* 75–7; R. Taubenschlag, *The Law of Greco-Roman Egypt in the Light of the Papyri* (Warsaw 1955) 222ff.; W. E. H. Cockle in *JEA* 70 (1984) 113–15.

Marcus Metti|us Rufus, prefect of Egypt, declares: Claudius Arius, strategos of the Oxyrhynchite (nome), has made it clear to me that neither private nor public | affairs are being organized properly, because for a long time the necessary procedure has not been followed
30 in administering the | official abstracts in the record-office of real property, even though frequently a decision has been made by prefects before my time that these (abstracts) should receive the necessary re|vision.[1] This is impossible to do well, unless copies are made from the beginning. Thus, I order all owners within six months to re|gister their property in the record-office of real property, money-lenders to register whatever mortgages they may have, and others | to register whatever legal claims they may have. They shall make clear from what source each of them acquired | the property. Women also shall add to the title deeds of their husbands, if, according to some native law, they
35 have a claim to the pro||perty, and likewise children (shall make an

addition) to the title deeds of their parents to whom the enjoyment (of the property) has been obtained by public contracts, but the poss|ession of which after death has been secured for the children, in order that those who make agreements with them may not be deceived by ignorance (of the legal situation). And I order the recor|ders of contracts and the registrars not [to complete any (document) without an order from the record-office; they shall know that] such a thing is [useless,] and, not only that, but | also that those who do it contrary to orders shall suffer fitting punishment. If in the record office there are copies from for|mer times, they shall be guarded with all care, and likewise their abstracts, in order that, if there should be any investi-

40   gation at a ‖ later date concerning persons making false returns, they may be convicted on the evidence (of those returns). [Therefore, in order that] the use of the abstracts may remain *secure* for all time, | to render further registration unnecessary I order the keepers of the record-offices every five years to revise | the abstracts by transferring the last title deed of each person to the new (abstracts), arranged by villages and types. Year 9 of Domitian, fourth day of the month Domitianus (October 1, AD 89).

1   There was a record-office of real property in each of the nome capitals of Egypt. For details see Taubenschlag, *op. cit.* 223–4.

106   Koptos and Red Sea commerce. AD 90.

A: *Periplus of the Red Sea* 19 (ed. Frisk). **B**: Stone stele with gable, Koptos on the Nile. [Greek] *IGRR* I 1183; McCrum–Woodhead, **Documents* 459. Photograph in J. G. Milne, *A History of Egypt Under Roman Rule*[2] (London 1924) 163, Fig. 63.

J. G. C. Anderson in *CAH* 10.245–46; S. L. Wallace, *Taxation in Egypt* (Princeton 1938) 273–5; M. G. Raschke in *ANRW* 2.9.2.648–50 and n. 1350, p. 982.

A. *Periplus of the Red Sea* **19**

On the left of Berenike, as one sails along the adjacent coast for two or three days toward the east from Myos Hormos, there is another port and stronghold called Leuke Kome, through which is <a passage> to Petra (and) to Malichas the king of the Nabataeans. It also has a kind of market and a garrison for the small boats that are equipped and dispatched to it from Arabia. For that reason a customs collector for 25% of the imported merchandise is sent there, as well as a centurion with an army unit for protection.[1]

B. McCrum–Woodhead, *Documents* **459, Koptos**

In accordance with the order [[of Mettius Rufus, | prefect of Egypt.]]
Whatever (toll fees) it is necessary for the publi|cans of the escort-tax,
5   which is under the | control of the customs-director in Koptos, to ex‖act
according to regulations, | these have been inscribed on this stele by
Lucius | Antistius [[Asiaticus, prefect | of Mt]] Berenike:[2] | skipper of a
10 Red Sea (boat), ‖ eight drachmas; [----, | six drachmas;] officer of the
bow, ten drachmas; | *guard*, ten drachmas; | sailor, five drachmas; |
15 shipbuilder attendant, five drachmas; ‖ craftsman, eight drachmas; |
courte|sans, one hundred and eight drachmas; | women who come by
20 boat, | twenty drachmas; women of sold‖iers, twenty drachmas; | permit
for camels, one obol; | seal on a permit, two obols; | for exit passage,
25 each permit | for a man going up ‖ country, one drachma; women | of all
kinds at four drachmas each; | a donkey, two obols; a wagon ha|ving[3]
square sides (i.e. with a covering), four drachmas; | a ship's mast,
30 twenty drachmas; a ship's yardarm, ‖ four drachmas; a funeral go|ing
and coming back, one drachma, | four obols. In the 9th year of
Imperator Caesar | [[Domitianus]] Augustus [[Germanicus,]] Pachon
15.

1 On this whole passage see G. W. Bowersock, *Roman Arabia* (Cambridge, Mass. 1983)
70–1. He shows that the Roman title 'centurion' had been taken over by the
Nabataeans. Thus, the port was administered by Nabataeans.
2 The equestrian prefect of Mt Berenike was in charge of the area between Koptos and
the Red Sea.
3 The words 'women of all kinds at' in the previous line and 'having' are inscribed in
erased areas on the stone. See Raschke, *op. cit.* 893, n. 961 for these women.

107   A Roman governor and a famine in Antioch. AD 91–3.
Large, rectangular stone block with inscription in three columns,
Antioch toward Pisidia. [Latin]

W. M. Ramsay in *JRS* 14 (1924) 179ff., No. 6 (*AÉ* 1925, 126); Abbott–Johnson, *Municipal
Administration* 65a; McCrum–Woodhead, **Documents* 464.

Ramsay, *op. cit.* 179–84; G. A. Harrer in *AJA* 29 (1925) 429–33; Abbott–Johnson, *op. cit.*
382–3; Levick, *Colonies* 84–5, 96–7; R. Syme in *Historia* 32 (1983) 359–74.

(Col. 2)[1] Lucius Antistius Rusticus, legate | of Imperator Caesar
Domitianus | Augustus Germanicus with pro praetorian power,
5 declares: | Since the duoviri and decurions ‖ of the most splendid colony
of Antioch | have written to me that because of | the harsh winter the
market | price of grain has shot | up, and (since) they have requested
10 that ‖ the people have the means of buying it, | – with Good Luck on our

side – all those who are either citizens of the colony of Antioch | or are
inhabitants of it | shall state openly before the duoviri of the colony | of
15   Antioch, within thir‖ty days of the time when | this edict of mine has
been pos|ted, how much | grain each person has and in what place, | and
20   how much ‖ for seed or for | the annual allowance of his family | he
deducts, and the rest | of the grain, the whole supply, | he shall make
25   available to the buyers of the colony of Antioch. ‖ Moreover, for the
selling | time I establish the next Kalends of August (August 1). | But if
anyone does not obey, | he shall know that what|ever (amount) contrary
30   to my edict ‖ has been withheld | I will claim for confiscation, | the
35   informers' rewar|d being one-eighth of the a|mount. Since, ‖ further-
more, it has been confirmed for me that, before | the persistent harsh-
ness of the winter, | eight or | nine āsses was the price of a modius
40   (about ¼ bushel) of gra|in in the colony, ‖ and since it is most unjust |
for the source of anyone's profit to be the hunger of his citizens, |
exceeding one | denarius (16 āsses) for one modius as the price | of
grain (is a practice) I forbid.

1   The first column on the block contains the career record of Antistius Rusticus to his
consulship in AD 90 and his present governorship of Galatia-Cappadocia (AD
91–3); see R. K. Sherk in *ANRW* 2.7.2, 1012–14; Syme, *loc. cit.* The third column on
the block consists of a single, mutilated line mentioning a procurator of Augustus
and the phrase 'Tiberia Platea'.

108   Domitian on teachers and physicians.[1] AD 93–4 (?).
Marble stone, broken at top and on left side, Pergamum. [Latin]

R. Herzog in *Sitzungsberichte der Preussischen Akademie der Wissenschaften, Phil.-hist. Klasse* 32
(1935) 967–72; *FIRA* I 73; McCrum–Woodhead, **Documents* 458 (lines 21–30). Cf. *Digest*
27.1.6.8 and 50.4.18.30.

See above, Document No. 84 of AD 74.

[Imperator Caesar Domitia]nus, holding the tribunician power for the
thirteenth time (AD 93–4), | [imperator for the twenty-second time,
censor perpetual, father of his country,] to Aulus Licinius Mucianus
and Gavius Priscus:[2] | [The greed of physicians and] teachers, whose
profession | [ought to be handed on] to certain [free-born] *young men*
25   (but) is being sold to many ‖ slave [chamberlains] who are being
released most shamelessly [for the practice (of medicine) not] | out of
[humanitarian motives but to increase] their income | – (this greed) I
have decided [must be restricted most tightly. | Therefore, whoever
from the act of teaching slaves derives] income, | [from him shall be
30   taken away the immunity granted by my deified father,] just as if ‖ [he
were practising his art in a foreign city.]

1 On the same stone (lines 1–20) is an edict of Vespasian in Greek on the same topic: above, Document No. 84.
2 These men cannot be identified. Stein (in *PIR*[2] G 107) thinks the author of this document is Trajan, not Domitian.

109 Career of an equestrian under the Flavian emperors.
Base of a statue, Heliopolis (modern Baalbek), Syria. [Latin]

ILS 9200; Pflaum, *Carrières* 50; McCrum–Woodhead, *Documents* 372; **IGLS* VI 2796 (+ photograph).

Gaius Velius, Sal|vius' son, Rufus, primipilus[1] of the Legion Twelfth |
Fulminata, prefect of detach|ed units from nine legions, the First
5 Adiutrix, Second Adiutrix, ‖ Second Augusta, Eighth Augusta, Ninth
Hispana, Fourteenth Ge|mina, Twentieth Victrix, and Twenty-First
Rapax;[2] tribune of Co|hort Urban Thirteenth, leader of the army of
Africa and | Mauretania for the suppression of nations | in Mauretania;[3]
10 de‖corated by Imperator Vespasianus and Imperator | Titus in the
Jewish War with the Rampart-Storming Crown, | Collars, Discs,
Armbands, and also | decorated with the Mural Crown, | two Parade
15 Spears, two Unit Flags, and in the wa‖r against the Marcomanni,
Quadi, and | Sarmatians – against whom an ex|pedition was made by
him through the kingdom of Decebalus, | king of the Dacians[4] – (he was
decorated) with the Mural Crown, two Parade Spears, | and two Unit
20 Flags; procurator of Imperator Cae‖sar Augustus Germanicus of the
province of Pannon|ia and Dalmatia,[5] likewise procurator of the
province | of Raetia with right of sword.[6] He was sent into Parthia and
brought back Epipha|nes and Callinicus, sons of King Antiochus,[7] to
25 Imperator Vespasianus | along with a great mass of people liable ‖ to
the tribute. Marcus Alfius, son of Marcus, (of the tribe) Fabia,
Olympiacus, veteran of the Legion Fifteenth Apollinaris, (dedicated
this statue to him).

1 The primipilus was the highest-ranking centurion in each legion, serving on the staff of the legionary commander. See B. Dobson in *ANRW* 2.1.392–434.
2 Only eight legions are listed here. Either 'nine' is wrong in line 4 or a legion has been omitted by the engraver. These legions were employed in the war against the Germans at the end of the reign of Vespasian or during the reign of Domitian: R. Syme in *CAH* 11.158–64; Garzetti, *Tiberius to Antonines* 255–6 and 286–7.
3 The Mauretanian rebellion took place under Domitian.
4 Syme (*CAH* 11.176–7) puts this event just before or just after the conclusion of Domitian's Dacian war.
5 He was a financial procurator over the area, collecting taxes.
6 Here he was the equestrian governor of Raetia.
7 This feat was performed when he was primipilus of the Legion Twelfth Fulminata, which was stationed at Melitene on the Euphrates frontier. The two sons of King Antiochus of Commagene had fled to Parthia: Josephus, *Bell. Jud.* 7.7.1–3.

NERVA
(96–98)
IMPERATOR NERVA AUGUSTUS CAESAR

Titles: PONTIFEX MAXIMUS
FATHER OF HIS COUNTRY
GERMANICUS
HOLDER OF THE TRIBUNICIAN POWER: first
time in Autumn of AD 96, then each year
CONSUL: AD 97 (III), 98 (IV)

Death: January 25, AD 98.

TRAJAN
(98–117)
IMPERATOR CAESAR NERVA TRAIANUS
AUGUSTUS

Titles: GERMANICUS (Autumn 97)
PONTIFEX MAXIMUS (98)
FATHER OF HIS COUNTRY (98)
DACICUS (December 102)
OPTIMUS (August 10 / September 1, 114)
PARTHICUS (February 20 or 21, 116)
HOLDER OF THE TRIBUNICIAN POWER: first
time in AD 97 on October 27, second time in same year on
December 10, then annually
CONSUL: AD 98 (II), 100 (III), 101 (IV), 103 (V), 112 (VI)

Death: August 9, AD 117

The *consules ordinarii* **under Nerva and Trajan**

AD		
97	Imp. Nerva Caesar Augustus III	L. Verginius Rufus III
98	Imp. Nerva Caesar Augustus IV	Imp. Caesar Nerva Traianus Augustus II
99	A. Cornelius Palma Frontonianus	Q. Sosius Senecio
100	Imp. Traianus III	Sex. Iulius Frontinus III
101	Imp. Traianus IV	Q. Articuleius Paetus
102	L. Iulius Ursus Servianus II	L. Licinius Sura II
103	Imp. Traianus V	M'. Laberius Maximus II
104	Sex. Attius Suburanus Aemilianus II	M. Asinius Marcellus
105	Ti. Iulius Candidus Marius Celsus II	C. Antius A. Iulius Quadratus II
106	L. Ceionius Commodus	Sex. Vettulenus Civica Cerialis

107	L. Licinius Sura III	Q. Sosius Senecio II
108	Ap. Annius Trebonius Gallus	M. Atilius Metilius Bradua
109	A. Cornelius Palma Frontonianus II	P. Calvisius Tullus Ruso
110	M. Peducaeus Priscinus	Ser. (Cornelius) Scipio Salvidienus
111	C. Calpurnius Piso	M. Vettius Bolanus
112	Imp. Traianus VI	T. Sextius Africanus
113	L. Publilius Celsus II	C. Clodius Crispinus
114	Q. Ninnius Hasta	P. Manilius Vopiscus Vicinillianus
115	L. Vipstanus Messalla	M. Pedo Vergilianus
116	L. Fundanius Lamia Aelianus	Sex. Carminius Vetus
117	Q. Aquilius Niger	M. Rebilus Apronianus

110   Nerva and a new beginning. AD 96.

A: Fasti Ostienses (*I. Ital.* XIII 1, p. 195 under AD 96). **B**: *CIL* VI 472; *ILS 274; McCrum–Woodhead, *Documents* 66. Stone long lost, preserved in copy only. Rome. [Latin] Cf. Pliny, *Epist.* 9.13.4; Tacitus, *Agricola* 3; Suetonius, *Domitian* 17. **C**: Mattingly, *BMC* 3, No. 16, Aureus.

A.   *I. Ital.* **XIII 1, p. 195 (AD 96)**

On the 14th day before the Kalends of October (September 18) Domitian *was killed*. │ On the same day Marcus Cocceius N[erva] │ was called Imperator.

B.   *ILS* **274, Rome**

To the Freedom restored by Imperator Nerva Ca<es>ar Augustus in the 848th year of the founding of the city (AD 96), on the 14th day before the [Kalends] of October (September 18), the senate and the People of Rome (dedicated this monument).

C.   Mattingly, *BMC* **3, No. 16**

(Obverse: head of Nerva laureate) IMPERATOR NERVA CAESAR AUGUSTUS, PONTIFEX MAXIMUS, HOLDING THE TRIBUNICIAN POWER, CONSUL FOR THE SECOND TIME, FATHER OF HIS COUNTRY.

(Reverse: personification of Liberty holding a hat and a sceptre) PUBLIC LIBERTY

111   Discharge diploma for auxiliary soldier. AD 98.
Two small bronze tablets inscribed on both sides, with small holes to tie them together,[1] found in a small village in Pannonia. [Latin]

CIL XVI 42.

(Exterior of first tablet) Imperator Caesar, son of the deified Nerva, Nerva Traia|nus Augustus Germanicus, pontifex maximus, | holding the tribunician power, *vv* consul *vv* for the second time: *vv* | to the
5   cavalrymen and infantrymen who served in ‖ two alae and five cohorts, namely, the Ala Si|liana of Roman Citizens[2] and the Ala I Augusta of Ituraeans, the Cohort I of Mon|tanians of Roman Citizens, the Cohort I miliaria[3] of Batavians Reverent and Loyal, the Cohort I | of Lusitanians, the Cohort I Augusta of Ituraeans, and the Cohort II | miliaria of Batavians, and are (stationed) in Pannonia[4] under the com-
10   mand of Gnaeus ‖ Pinarius Aemilius Cicatricula Pompeius | Longinus,[5] and have been given honorable | discharges, and have completed twenty-five or more years of service – their names | are written below[6] – to them, their children, and their descendants | he has given (Roman) citizenship and legal marriage ‖ with the wives which they had at the
15   time when | citizenship was given to them, or, if they were unmarried, | with those women whom afterwards they married, provided only one | to each. On the tenth day before the Kalends of March (February 20), | when Imperator Caesar Traianus Augustus Germanicus for the
20   second time ‖ and Sextus *vv* Iulius *vv* Frontius *vv* for the second time were consuls (AD 98). |

    From the Cohort I Augusta of Ituraeans, whose commander is |Lucius Callidius, son of Lucius, (of the tribe) Stellatina, Camidienus,
25 | and having been honorably discharged | *vv* from infantryman *vv* ‖ (Roman citizenship is given) to Publius Insteius, son of Agrippa, of Cyrrhus. | Copied and certified from the tablet of bro|nze which is attached at Rome to the wall behind | the temple of the deified Augustus to Minerva.[7]

1   Many photographs of diplomas are at the end of *CIL* XVI. See also above, Document No. 58, n. 1.
2   The phrase 'of Roman Citizens' added to a unit's title does not mean that all the men in the ranks have Roman citizenship. It means that in the past for some particular act of bravery in battle or for some other significant action either the whole unit or a group of men in it had been awarded a block grant of Roman citizenship. That award was made only once, but the unit could then add the phrase 'of Roman Citizens' as a unit citation to its other titles.
3   Auxiliary units were either *quingenaria* (500 men strong) or *miliaria* (1,000 men strong), even though the actual strength was regularly much less than those numbers.

4 Pannonia has not yet been divided into two provinces. That was done by Trajan at the beginning of his First Dacian War.

5 He is the consular governor of Pannonia. Consul suffectus in AD 90, he was appointed governor of Moesia Superior and then to his present command in Pannonia.

6 The original bronze tablet, of great size, was to be found only in Rome – see the last three lines – and on it appeared the names of all the soldiers receiving their discharge and their citizenship at that time. All the originals have long been lost. The small bronze tablets, issued to each soldier, like the present one, contained only his own name.

7 Following this notice, appearing on the exterior side of the second tablet – both tablets being tied together – are the name of seven citizen witnesses to the authenticity of the document. For all these military diplomas, their texts, and commentaries see the edition (after T. Mommsen) by H. Nesselhauf in *CIL* XVI, with a supplementary volume (1955). For later editions see Roxan, *Diplomas*.

112   Preparations at the Iron Gate for the Dacian War. AD 100–1.

A: *CIL* III 1699 (8267); *ILS* 5863; Smallwood, *Documents Nerva* 413. Inscription cut into the face of the cliff on the south side of the Danube, upstream from the gorge of the Iron Gate in Moesia Superior. AD 100. [Latin] **B**: M. Gabričević in *Arheološki Vestnik* 23 (1972) 408 (+ photograph); *AÉ* 1973, 473. Votive inscription on a rock in a cave below the Roman road near the Iron Gate. [Latin] **C**: P. Petrović in *Saopštenja* (Belgrade) 8 (1969), 51ff. (+ photograph); *AÉ* 1973, 475; J. Šašel in *JRS* 63 (1973) 80–1 (+ photograph). Marble slab, good lettering on prepared surface, found about 5 km downstream from the Iron Gate. AD 101. [Latin]

Šašel, *op. cit.* 80–4; L. Rossi, *Trajan's Column and the Dacian Wars* (Ithaca, NY 1971) 29–35 (+ photographs of the cliff-road almost at the water's edge) and 182–3 (+ photographs of the scenes from Trajan's column illustrating the road); Strobel, *Untersuchungen* 160–1.

A. *ILS* 5863, near the Iron Gate

Imperator Caesar, son of the deified Nerva, | Nerva Traianus Augustus Germanicus, | pontifex maximus, holding the tribunician power for the fourth time (AD 100), | father of his country, consul for the third time,
5   ‖ cut down mountains, erected the projecting | arms,[1] and constructed this road.

B. *AÉ* 1973, 473, near the Iron Gate

Sacred to Hercules. | The stone-cutters, who were | engaged in making
5   the projecting stone arms, | of the Legion Fourth [Flavia] ‖ and the Legion Seventh C[laudia Respectful and Loyal] | *fulfilled their vow.*

C. *JRS* 63 (1973) 80–1, near the Iron Gate

Imperator Caesar, son of the deified Nerva, | Nerva Traianus Augustus Germanicus, | pontifex maximus, holding the tribunician power for the fifth time (AD 101), father of his country, consul for the fourth time, |

5   because of the danger of the cataracts ‖ drew off the stream and made the Da|nube's navigation safe.[2]

1   The road was built into the face of the cliff along the south bank of the Danube and part of the road had to project out over the water: see the photographs in Rossi, *op. cit.* 24–5.
2   A road was constructed (A, B) to connect the two main military bases on the Danube at Pontes and Lederata, and for navigation around the dangerous gorge of the Iron Gate a canal was built, part of which has been identified: Šašel, *loc. cit.* Cf. Pliny, *Epist.* 10.41–2 and Procopius, *De Aedificiis* 4.6.8.

113   Roman surveyor of the Dacian limes. AD 101–2 or 105–6.

Die Schriften der römischen Feldmesser (ed. Blume, Lachmann, Rudorff), Vol. I (Berlin 1848, repr. Hildesheim 1967) p. 92, lines 7ff.

O. A. W. Dilke, *The Roman Land Surveyors* (Newton Abbot 1971) 42; R. K. Sherk in *ANRW* 2.1.541–2; A. Piganiol, *Scripta Varia* III (Brussels 1973) 131–4.

There intervened the famous expedition of our most sacred emperor, which led me astray from the prompt writing of my book.[1] For, while I occupied myself more with attention to arms, I discontinued this whole business (of writing), as if forgetful of it, and I contemplated nothing else than the glory of war. After we took the first step on hostile territory, immediately, Celsus,[2] the earthworks of our Caesar began to demand of me the calculations of measurements. When a pre-arranged length of marching had been completed, two parallel straight lines had to be produced (on the terrain) at (along?) which a huge defensive structure of palisaded earthworks would rise up, for the protection of communications.[3] By your invention, when a part of the earthworks was cut back to the line of sight, the use of the surveying instrument extended these lines. In regard to a survey of bridges, we were able to state the width of rivers from the bank close at hand, even if the enemy wished to harass us. Then it was that Calculation, worthy of a god's respect, showed us how to know the heights of mountains that had to be captured. It was Calculation that I began to revere more fervently, as if he were worshiped in all the temples, after experiencing and taking part in these great enterprises. And I hurried to complete this book, as if fulfilling vows to a god. Therefore, after our supreme emperor most recently opened up Dacia for us by his victory, the moment that he permitted me to leave the north country in annual rotation, I returned to my studies, to leisure as it were.

1   The writer here is a certain Balbus, otherwise unknown, who wrote a technical treatise on measurements in the form of a letter to Celsus, also otherwise unknown.

The present passage is found near the beginning of that treatise, which is the 'book'
he refers to. Such treatises on surveying have come down to us in a body of literature
known as the *Corpus Agrimensorum.*

2 This Celsus was a surveyor of great renown and much respected by Balbus: see
Blume–Lachmann–Rudorff, *op. cit.* p. 94.1–2. Nothing else of his 'invention' is
known.

3 Piganiol saw that the reference was to a military road protected by earthworks, i.e.
the Roman limes. Mommsen had, however, anticipated him in this observation, in
his essay 'Die Libri Coloniarum' printed in Blume–Lachmann–Rudorff II, pp.
147–8. For this limes as a protected military frontier see E. N. Luttwak, *The Grand
Strategy of the Roman Empire* (Baltimore, MD 1976) 19.

114   Prefect of Egypt issues an edict on the census. AD 104.
Papyrus from Alexandria. [Greek]

P. London 904, Col. 2, lines 18ff.; Wilcken, **Chrestomathie* 1.2.202; Abbott–Johnson,
Municipal Administration 168; Smallwood, *Documents Nerva* 459.

Wilcken, *op. cit.* 235–6; H. I. Bell in *CAH* 10.304–6; S. L. Wallace, *Taxation in Egypt*
(Princeton 1938) 96–115.

20   G[aius Vi]biu[s Maximus,] *prefect* | of Egypt,[1] [declares:] ‖ Since the
house-by-house [census] has begun, | it is necessary [for all those who]
for any | *reason* [are absent from their] | nomes to be *called to re|turn* to
25   their hearths, that the customary ‖ transaction of the *cen|sus* might be
completed and that to their pro|per work of farming they might devote
themselves.[2] | Since I know that some of those [from] ⋮ the country are
30   needed by our city, ‖ I wish all those who think they have a good reason
| for remaining here | to register their reason with Vul[----] | Festus,
prefect of the ala, whom for *this purpose* | I have appointed, and those
35   who have sho‖wn their presence to be necessary | (in the city) shall
receive permits *in accordance with* this edict, | up to [the thirtieth of the]
present mo|nth E[peiph ----][3]

1 On Vibius Maximus, prefect from AD 103 to 107, see R. Syme in *Historia* 6 (1957)
480–7.

2 For the kind of information taken in the census see the *Digest* 50.15.4, 8.5.7. A
complete census return has been found in Egypt at Arsinoe: Wilcken, *Chrestomathie*
1.2.203 of AD 189. It includes the name of the property-owner, the description of the
property, the owner's occupation, the tax liability, his age, his children with their
names and ages, his wife's name and the names of all others living in the same house
with him, with their ages and occupations and then the signature and the date. See
A. C. Johnson, *An Economic Survey of Ancient Rome* (edited by T. Frank), Vol. II: *Roman
Egypt* (Baltimore 1936) 240ff.

3 W. Schubart in *Aegyptus* 31 (1951) 153 has attempted to restore the mutilated remains
here as follows: '*present* mo|nth E[peiph, and the others] will return to their homes
within [-- days. And if anyone] *is found* [without] a permit [-----] very greatly [will he
be punished, for well] do I know [----.]'

115   Cornelius Palma builds an aqueduct. AD 104–5 (?).

Basalt stele from Suweidā' in southern Syria, near the Arabian border.
[Greek]

M. Dunand in *Syria* 11 (1930) 275 (+ drawing); **SEG* VII 969.

5 On behalf of the safe|ty of Imper|ator Ne|rva Traianus ‖ Caesar
 Au|gustus Germanicus Dacicus | this aqueduct of the wa|ter that flows
10 | into Kana‖ta[1] (was built) by the planning of C|ornelius Pal|ma, legate
 | of Augustus with pro | praetorian power.[2]

1 The modern Qanawāt.
2 Aulus Cornelius Palma (*PIR*² C 1412) was *consul ordinarius* in AD 99 and governor of
 Syria in AD 104–5. Then he annexed Nabataea and formed it into the new province
 of Arabia in 106: see G. W. Bowersock in *ZPE* 5 (1970) 37–47 and see his *Roman Arabia*
 (Cambridge, Mass. 1983) Ch. 6.

116   Roman equestrian honored by his native city. AD 105.

Statue base, inscribed on front and side, from Aquileia in Italy. [Latin]

CIL V 875; *ILS* 1374; McCrum–Woodhead, **Documents* 336.

(On the front) Gaius Minicius, son of Gaius, | (of the tribe) Velina,
Italus, quattuorvir for the administration of justice, | prefect of Cohort
V of Mounted Gauls, | prefect of Cohort I of Mounted Roman Citizen
5 Breucians, ‖ prefect of Cohort II of Mounted Varcianians, tribune of
the soldiers of Legion Sixth Victrix, | prefect of cavalry of Ala I Roman
Citizens (Special Services), decorated by the deified | Vespasian with
the Golden Crown and the Parade Spear; | procurator of the Helles-
pontine province, procurator of the province of Asia – which | he gov-
erned by order of our Leader in place of the deceased proconsul[1] –
10 procurator ‖ of the provinces of Lugdunensis and Aquitania and
Lactora;[2] | prefect of the grain supply (for Rome), prefect of Egypt;[3]
priest of the deified Claudius. (This statue erected) by decree of the
decurions (of Aquileia).
 (On the side) Publius Tullius Max[imus (?), -------]amula, the
quattuorviri for the administration of justice, on the third day before
the Kalends of June (May 30), | consulted the senate (of Aquileia).
Present at the writing (of the decree) were: [----] Proculus, Gaius
Appuleius Celer, | Aulus Iunius G[----,] Sextus Cossutius Secundus. |
Whereas they (i.e. the quattuorviri) spoke to the honor [of Gaius
5 Minicius Italus,] (saying that) ‖ whatever popularity or [power through
the highest offices] of equestrian rank could come to that most *splendid*
person, | he turned all of it to the *increase* [and ornamentation] of his

[native city,] | and [he believed that] in no other [official position] was
he happier [than the one in which he] worked for the good of his city, –
what it pleased (the senators) to be done about this matter, concerning
it they decreed as follows: | Since Gaius Minic[ius Italus ----] of his
10 exceptional qualities | an *end* [-----] he enlarged‖ and above and beyond
the other matters [this was known to everyone,] that our most sacred
Leader, | Traianus A[ugustus, upon his request, decreed] that the
resident aliens usually included in our cen|sus [should perform] the
civic burdens [along with us,] and (since it is known) that through him
it *came about* that we receive a very abundant amount of kindness | from
our greatest emperor, it pleases this senate and seems in accordance
with our republic that a statue | of bronze with a [marble base be erected
15 for him] and that our [decree] he inscribed on the base, ‖ in order that
it might be very well attested that there is no other way for us to repay
such a great man [in return for his services and benefactions than] | for
us to glorify him [publicly.] Decreed. | In the consulship of Tiberius
Iulius [Candidus for the second time and Gaius Ant]ius Quadratus for
the second time (AD 105).

1 This proconsul is almost certainly Gaius Vettulenus Civica Cerealis, who was put to
   death in Asia about AD 89 on the order of Domitian. Cf. Tacitus, *Agricola* 42, and
   Suetonius, *Domitian* 10.2.
2 These are all financial procuratorships with competence over various districts,
   provinces, or parts of provinces.
3 He was prefect of Egypt in AD 101–3 (Stein, *Präfekten* 49–50).

117   Roman soldier captures the king of the Dacians. AD 106.
Stele of marble almost nine feet high, the lower end broken off. At the
top are two reliefs: upper shows a Roman cavalryman with spear and
sword riding toward a bearded Dacian who is already dying; lower is a
representation of military decorations. Found near Philippi in
Macedonia. [Latin]

M. Speidel in **JRS* 60 (1970) 142 (+ photograph) (= *Roman Army Studies* 1.173–87); *AÉ*
1970, 583. Cf. Dio 68.14.3.

Speidel, *op. cit.* 142–53; L. Rossi, *Trajan's Column and the Dacian Wars* (Ithaca, NY 1971)
Appendix D (+ photograph); Strobel, *Untersuchungen* 217.

Tiberius Claudius | Maximus, a veteran, | saw to the construction of
(this monument) while still living. He soldiered | as a cavalryman in the
5 Legion Seventh Claudia Respectful and Loyal, pro‖moted to finance
clerk of the cavalry, | guard of the commander of the same le|gion,
standard-bearer | of the cavalry, and | in the Dacian war decorated for

10   bra‖very by Im|perator Domitianus. He was promoted to double-pay
grade | by the deified Traianus in the Ala II | of the Pannonians, and the
same emperor also pro|moted him to scout in his war against the
15   Da‖cians and for bravery he twice | decorated him in his Dacian | and
Parthian wars, and the same emperor promoted him | to cavalry officer
20   in the same ala because | he had captured Decebalus and ‖ brought his
head back to him at Ranissto|rum.[1] He was discharged after extended
service, discharged | honorably by Terent[ius Scau]|rianus, consular
commander of the *ar*|*my* of the *new* (?) province of [----.][2]

1 The upper relief on the monument illustrates this feat of arms. The appearance of
King Decebalus is similar to those shown on Trajan's column and the capture itself
is portrayed on that column (the scene is reproduced by Speidel, *op. cit.*, Pl. XIV).
The king's head was sent back to Rome for display and then thrown down the
Gemonian Steps: *I. Ital* XII 1.5, p. 199, XX. The location of Ranisstorum in Dacia is
unknown.
2 Decimus Terentius Scaurianus was the first governor of the newly created province
of Dacia: see Syme in his *Tacitus* 2.646, No. 15, and 648, No. 36, and Strobel, *op. cit.*
217. Cf. below, Document No. 122. Since Claudius Maximus, however, served in
Trajan's Parthian war, he could not have been discharged while Scaurianus was
governor of Dacia. By 'new' (if the reading is correct) may be meant Mesopotamia
or Armenia or Assyria.

118   Rewards and consequences of the conquest of Dacia.

A: Joannes Lydus, *De magistratibus* 2.28 (Kriton, **FGrHist* 200 F 1); I. I. Russu in *Studii
Clasice* 14 (1972) 17, No. 1. Cf. Dio 68.14.4–5. **B**: Eutropius 8.6.2.

R. Longdon in *CAH* 11.214–17) J. Carcopino, *Les Étapes de l'impérialisme romain* (Paris
1961) 112–17; Strobel, *Untersuchungen* 20 n. 6 and 221–5; J. Scarborough in *The Craft of
the Ancient Historian: Essays in Honor of Chester G. Starr*, edited by J. W. Eadie and J. Ober
(New York 1985) 387–406.

A. *FGrHist* 200 F 1

Trajan was the first to capture it (i.e. Scythia = Dacia) along with
Decebalus, the leader of the Dacians, and he brought to the Romans
[500,000][1] pounds of gold and [1,000,000] pounds of silver, not counting drinking goblets and various objects that go beyond value, herds of
horses, weapons, and fighting men beyond [50,000] along with their
weapons, as Kriton confidently affirmed, and he was present in the
war.[2]

B. Eutropius 8.6.2

Hadrian in envy of the glory of Trajan immediately gave up the three
provinces which Trajan had added, recalled the armies from Assyria,
Mesopotamia, and Armenia, and desired the Euphrates to be the

boundary of empire. When he attempted to do the same to Dacia, his friends held him back, lest many Roman citizens be handed over to the barbarians, because after the conquest of Dacia Trajan had transferred from the whole Roman world an endless number of men to that land for the purpose of cultivating the fields and inhabiting cities. For Dacia had been drained of men because of the long-lasting war of Decebalus.[3]

1   The figures given by Joannes Lydus are too fantastic as they stand: 'five hundred times ten thousand pounds of gold, double that amount of silver' and then 'fifty times ten thousand fighting men'. Thus: 5,000,000 pounds of gold and 10,000,000 of silver, and 5,000,000 prisoners. The original numbers have been corrupted in the transmission of the text, and, by a simple paleographic explanation Carcopino has shown what the real numbers could have been before they were written in long hand. Cf. Strobel, *op. cit.* 221–2 with further references. Dio (68.14.4–5) mentions the discovery of the Dacian treasure, and its presentation to Trajan is represented on his column: see C. Cichorius, *Die Reliefs der Traiansäule*[2] (Berlin 1927) scene no. CXXXVIII.
2   Titus Statilius Kriton was the friend and personal physician of Trajan and accompanied him to Dacia. He even wrote a history of the Dacians (*FGrHist* 200 F 1–8, and Russu, *loc. cit.*).
3   For the Romanization of Dacia see Strobel, *op. cit.* 222–5, with further references.

119   Survey of land for a colony in Pannonia. Reign of Trajan.

Hyginus, *De condicionibus agrorum*, in *Die Schriften der römischen Landmesser* (ed. Blume, Lachmann, Rudorff), Vol. I (Berlin 1848, repr. Hildesheim 1967) p. 121, 7–16.

Recently a certain ex-soldier of Augustus, but recalled to active duty, a man of proven military discipline, and most capable in our profession (of surveying), when he was assigning land in Pannonia to veterans in accordance with the wish and liberality of Imperator Traianus Augustus Germanicus, not only added in writing or made a notation on the bronze maps of the size of the land he was assigning, but he also provided for the amount at the end of each (survey) line for each one (of the veterans): as the measurement of the assigned land was given, he also inscribed its length and width. By this method no quarrels or disputes between the veterans could arise from these lands.[1]

1   For military surveyors see R. K. Sherk in *ANRW* 2.1.534–62.

120   Trajan celebrates his Dacian victory. AD 107–9.
Excerpts from the Fasti Ostienses. [Latin]

I. Ital. XIII 1.5, pp. 199–201 (AD 107–9); Smallwood, *Documents Nerva* 21–2.

R. Longden in *CAH* 214–17; Strobel, *Untersuchungen* 220–1.

A. *I. Ital.* **XIII 1.5 p. 199, AD 107, lines 1–6**

[----] on the seventh day before the Kalends of J[une (or July, May 26 or June 25) Imperator | Traianus ----] gave a public largess of [---denarii,[1] | ---- the] first [preliminary games] | of the [second[2] Gladiatorial Exhibition] he began [to present, ---- days in length] with 332 and a half gladiatorial pairs.[3] ‖ [The second preliminary games] he began [to present,] twelve days in length [with ---- gladiatorial pairs ----] *vv*

B. *I. Ital.* **XIII 1.5 p. 199, AD 108, lines 1–4**

[The third (?) preliminary games of the] second [Gladiatorial Exhibition] | he began to present, which he completed on the third day before the Kalends of April (March 30), | thirteen days in length with 340 gladiatorial pairs. On the day before the Nones of June (June 4) Traianus | began to present the second Gladiatorial Exhibition. *vv*

C. *I. Ital.* **XIII 1.5 pp. 200–1, AD 109, lines 9–16**

On the tenth day before the Kalends of July (June 22) Imperator Nerva Traianus Augustus Germanicus ‖ Dacicus dedicated and opened to the public his Baths. | On the eighth day before the Kalends of July (June 24) in his own name for the entire city he dedicated his Aqueduct. On the Kalends of November (November 1) Imperator Traianus | completed his (second) Gladiatorial Exhibition, 117 days in length,[4] | with 4,941 and a half gladiatorial pairs. On the third day before the Ides of November (November 11) ‖ Imperator Traianus dedicated his (artificial lake? for showing a) sea-battle,[5] | in which for six days 127 and a half pairs (fought). He completed (this contest) on the eighth day before the Kalends of December (November 24).[6]

1 This may have amounted to 500 denarii per head. See Hanslik in *RE* Suppl. X *s.v.* M. Ulpius Traianus, Col. 1083, whose figure is accepted by Strobel, *Untersuchungen* 221. The source of the funds was the enormous treasure captured from the Dacians.
2 At the conclusion of the Second Dacian War in AD 106 Trajan remained in Dacia, while Hadrian returned from there to Rome and was elected praetor. From Trajan he had received two million sesterces to present games to the people: SHA, *Hadrian* 3.8. Thus, it was Hadrian who presented the first Gladiatorial Exhibition before Trajan had returned from the East.
3 When a gladiator was killed or seriously wounded, another took his place. Thus, the final number of gladiators who fought in an exhibition did not always result in an even number of pairs.
4 Dio (68.15) says Trajan gave gladiatorial shows on 123 days, but the Greek text probably experienced a mistake in the copying of the Roman numeral or in the transmission of its Greek equivalent. Dio adds that 11,000 animals were slain and that 10,000 gladiators fought.

5 A special structure may have been erected for these mock sea-battles.
6 Clearly there were many interruptions in the games that started on November 11 and were not finished until November 24. Such was also the case with his second Gladiatorial Exhibition which began on June 4 of AD 108 and was completed on November 1 of AD 109, but which lasted 117 days. Between those dates 516 days were available.

121   Trajan's trophy at Adamklissi. AD 108–9.

Gigantic circular monument, 100 feet in diameter, standing on a round platform of seven steps, the interior of the monument of concrete and stone, at the top of which was a trophy. The dedication was inscribed on the hexagonal pedestal on which the trophy stood.[1] [Latin]

CIL III 12467; G. C. Picard, *Les Trophées romains* (Paris 1957) 394; F. B. Florescu, *Monumental de la Adamklissi*[2] (Bucharest 1960) 63–8; Smallwood, *Documents Nerva* 303; N. Gostar in *Latomus 28 (1969) 120 and 123–4.

C. Cichorius, *Die römischen Denkmäler in der Dobrudscha* (Berlin 1904); C. Patsch in *SBAW* 217.1 (1937) 13, 16ff., 21ff. (+ photographs of a few metopes); Picard *op. cit.* 391–406; Florescu, *op. cit.*, *passim*; I. A. Richmond in *PBSR* 35 (1967) 29–39 (+ photograph of a reconstruction of the monument and arrangement of the metopes around it); Gostar, *op. cit.* 120–5; L. Rossi, *Trajan's Column and the Dacian Wars* (Ithaca, NY 1971) 55–65 (+ photographs of a few metopes); Strobel, *Untersuchungen* 34–40 and *passim*.

(Dedicated) to Mars the Avenger[2] | by Imperator [Cae]sar, deified |
5 Nerva's [son, Ne]rva | [Tr]aianus [Augustus Germanicus] ‖ Dac]i[c]us, *pontifex maximus*, | *holding the tribunician power* for the thirteenth time (December 10, AD 108–December 9, AD 109), | [Imperator for the sixth time, consul for the] fifth time, father of his country, | [the Dacian]
10 army | [of King Decebalus] having been de‖feated (?) [-----][3]

1 For a clear description of the entire complex of war monuments at the site see Richmond, *loc. cit.*, and for the nature of the trophy at the top see Picard, *loc. cit.*, with numerous photographs of Roman trophies known elsewhere. Of particular interest is the series of 54 metopes, each of great size, running around the entire upper part of the circular base and illustrating Dacian warriors.
2 The dedication to 'Mars the Avenger' sets the tone for the whole monument, i.e. vengeance for the defeat of Roman arms earlier under Oppius Sabinus and Cornelius Fuscus and for the numerous Dacian inroads on Roman territory.
3 A new fragment, discovered by P. Nicorescu and reproduced by Gostar shows parts of the words 'consul', 'army', 'Dacian', and perhaps the 'D' of 'Decebalus'. Gostar thinks that there were two versions of the dedication, each containing the same information.

122   Roman colony at Sarmizegetusa in Dacia. AD 110.

Stone lost, text preserved in copy only. From Sarmizegetusa in Dacia. [Latin]

CIL III 1443; Smallwood, *Documents Nerva* 479.

N. Gostar in *Apulum* 9 (1971) 305–21 (dates document to AD 108); H. Wolff in *Acta Musei Napocensis* 13 (1976) 99–118 (opts for date of AD 110); C. Daicoviciu in *RE* Suppl. XIV (1974) Cols. 610–55, *s.v.* Sarmizegetusa; Strobel, *Untersuchungen* 75–7.

[By] *authority* [of Imperator Cae]|sar, the deified Nerv[a's son,] |
5   Traianus Augustus | the Dacian Colony ‖ was founded | through |
[Decimus Terenti]us Scaurianus,[1] | his [legate] with pro praetorian power.

1 The copies of the stone at this point are not clear. The text adopted by Smallwood, *loc. cit.*: 'was founded through the Fifth [Legion] M(acedonia). Scaurianus, his [legate] with pro praetorian power [gave this monument as a gift.]' This Terentius Scaurianus was the first governor of Dacia: on him see N. Gostar in *Epigraphica* 1977, 82–98 and Strobel, *loc. cit.* The official title of the new colony was Colonia Ulpia Traiana Augusta Dacica Sarmizegetusa.

123   Trajan and road repair in Italy.

Galen 10.633 (ed. Kühn).

Of course, with all the roads in Italy in such a (bad) condition, Trajan began their restoration. Those areas that were wet and muddy he paved with beds of stones or elevated the road on high embankments, clearing away the rough and thorny ground and erecting bridges over rivers difficult to cross. Where the road was unsuitably long, he cut out a different one that was shorter. And if it was a difficult road because of the height of some ridge, he changed its direction and made it go through land easier to traverse. If a road was full of wild animals or went through deserted land, he removed it from that area and relocated it in a populated area, smoothing over the rough spots.

124   The Trajanic highway from Syria to the Red Sea. AD 111.

Milestone found 54 miles north of Petra. [Latin]

CIL III 14149.21–2 and 14149.19 and 30; *ILS* 5834; Smallwood, *Documents Nerva* 420.

P. Thomsen, *Zeitschrift des Deutschen Palästina-Vereins* 40 (1917) 1ff.; G. W. Bowersock, *Roman Arabia* (Cambridge, Mass. 1983) 83–5.

Imperator Caesar, | son of the deified Nerva, Nerva | Traianus

5   Augustus Germanicus | Dacicus, pontifex maximus, ‖ holding the
tribunician power for the fifteenth time (AD 111), imperator for the
sixth time, consul for the fifth time, | father of his country, having
reduced Arabia to the form | of a province, the Via | Nova[1] from the
10   border of Syria | to the Red Sea ‖ he opened up and paved through |
Gaius Severus,[2] legate of Au[gustus with pro praetorian power. Mile]
54.

1   This 'New Road' from the Gulf of 'Aqaba northward to Buṣra, where connections
were made to the system up to Damascus, was started almost immediately after the
annexation of Arabia in 106.
2   Gaius Claudius Severus (*PIR*[2] C 1023) was the governor of Arabia for almost all of
the construction period, remaining as governor to at least 115. Trajan's motive in
extending the highway system may have had more than local significance: Eutropius
(8.3.2) says that 'He set up a fleet on the Red Sea in order to lay waste the borders of
India with it.' The present milestone is only one of very many found along the
highway.

125   Career of Hadrian before he became emperor. AD 112.
Marble base found in the theater of Dionysos, Athens. [Latin]

CIL III 550; *ILS 308; *IG* II[2] 3286; Smallwood, *Documents Nerva* 109; Gordon, *Epigraphy*
56, pp. 137–8 (+ photograph). Cf. SHA, *Hadrian*.

R. Syme in *JRS* 54 (1964) 142–9 (*Roman Papers* II 617–28), and in *Arheološki Vestnik* 19
(1968) 101ff. (*Danubian Papers* 204–12); H. W. Benario, *A Commentary on the Vita Hadriani
in the Historia Augusta* (Ann Arbor 1980) *passim*.

Publius Aelius, son of Publius, (of the tribe) Sergia, Hadrianus, | consul
(AD 108), septemvir for religious banquets, fellow of the priesthood of
the deified Augustus, legate with pro praetorian power of Imperator
Nerva Traianus | Caesar Augustus Germanicus Dacicus of Pannonia
Inferior, praetor and at the same time | commander of the Legion First
Minervia Respectful and Loyal in the Dacian War, likewise tribune of
5   the plebs, quaestor of Imperator ‖ Traianus and companion in his
Dacian expedition, decorated with military decorations by him twice,
tribune of the Legion Second | Adiutrix Respectful and Loyal, likewise
(tribune) of the Legion Fifth Macedonica, likewise (tribune) of the
Legion Twenty-Second Primigenia Respectful and Loyal, commander
| of a squadron of Roman Knights,[1] prefect of the Latin Festival,
decemvir concerning civic status.[2]

1   Each year in Imperial Rome there was a parade of all the Knights 'with public horse'
arranged in six squadrons, each of them with its own *sevir* ('commander'). See
A. Stein, *Der Römische Ritterstand* (Munich 1927) 62ff.
2   This 'board of ten men' judged disputes concerning free or servile status. Immedi-

ately following this Latin section there is a short notice in Greek: 'The Boule of the Areopagus and of the Six Hundred and the | People of Athens (dedicate this statue to) their archon ‖ Hadrianus.' Hadrian became archon of Athens in AD 112, the date when the statue with its inscription was erected.

The main posts of P. Aelius Hadrianus (*PIR*² A 184) before his elevation to the throne can be dated fairly accurately. In ascending order they begin with his service in the vigintivirate (see the Glossary) as decemvir concerning civic status in his late teens, then prefect of the Latin Festival, and commander of a squadron of Roman Knights. Then he held three military tribunates, a most unusual number since only one was normal. He served in the Legion Second Adiutrix, almost certainly in Moesia Superior, probably in AD 95 just before his twentieth birthday; in the Legion Fifth Macedonica in Moesia Inferior the next year; and in the Legion Twenty-Second Primigenia in Germania Superior in 97, when he was adopted by Trajan. He became quaestor in 101, tribune of the plebs in 105, praetor in 106 and commander of the Legion First Minervia in Dacia, governor of Pannonia Inferior in 107, consul in 108, and then his two religious priesthoods at some time before 112.

126   The 'curator rei publicae' in Italy. AD 113–14.

Marble tablet, broken into three parts but complete, Caere.

CIL XI 3614; *ILS* 5918a; *FIRA* III 113; Smallwood, *Documents Nerva* 475; Sherk, **Municipal Decrees* 51 (+ photograph on p. 16).

Sherk, *op. cit.* 65–6; W. Eck, *Die staatliche Organisation Italiens in der hohen Kaiserzeit* (Munich 1979) 207 and 209–10.

Vesbinus, freedman of Augustus, made a gift of a phetrium[1] for the Augustales[2] | of the municipality of Caere when he received a place for it from the city. | He decorated it at his own expense. | Copied and
5   certified in the portico of the temple of Mars ‖ from the record-book which Cuperius Hostilianus ordered to be produced by Titus Rustius Lysiponus, | the scribe, in which was recorded that which is given below.[3] *vv* |

In the consulship of Lucius Publilius Celsus for the second time and Gaius Clodius Crispinus (AD 113), on the Ides of April (April 13), | when Marcus Pontius Celsus was dictator and Gaius Suetonius Claudianus was aedile of justice (and) prefect of the treasury.[4] Daily record-book of the municipality | *vv* of Caere, from page 27, section 6:
10   *vv* ‖ Marcus Pontius Celsus the dictator and Gaius Suetonius Claudianus summoned the decurions (i.e. the local senators) to a meeting in the temple of the deified emperors, when Vesbinus, freedman of Augustus, requested | that a place be given to him in the name of the city close up to the portico of the Basilica Sulpiciana, in order that he might build a phetrium on the place, and in accordance with | the consensus of opinion of the decurions the place was given to him

which he had desired, and it was the pleasure of the entire body that, in this matter, the curator Curiatius Cosanus[5] | should be sent a letter. Present at the senate meeting were: Pontius Celsus the dictator, Suetonius Claudianus the aedile of justice, Marcus Lepidus Nepos | the aedile of food, Pollius Blandus, Pescennius Flavianus, Pescennius
15   Natalis, Pollius Callimus, Petronius Innocens, Sergius Proculus. ‖

From the next page, section 1: (The letter) The magistrates and decurions to Curiatius Cosanus, greetings. The Ides of August (August 15). When we were asked | by Ulpius Vesbinus for a meeting of the decurions, we called a meeting, and he asked that a place in the name of the city be given to him in a secluded sector of the portico of the Basilica, because for the Augustales | he promised that he would decorate a phetrium in the name of the city and in keeping with the dignity of our municipality. Thanks were expressed to him by the whole body. Nevertheless, it was their pleasure that you | be sent a letter to see whether you too would agree. The place in the city is not being used and there is no possibility of any revenue from it.

From page 8, section 1: | Curiatius Cosanus to the magistrates and decurions of Caere, greetings. Not only ought I to agree with your desire but also to congratulate you for having someone to beautify our
20   city.‖ I accede therefore to your view, not so much as curator but, as it were, one of your order, since such honorable conduct | ought to be brought out in the open by a beautification that will bring honor to you. Posted on the day before the Ides of September (September 12) at Ameria. *vv* |

Done on the Ides of June (June 13) when Quintus Ninnius Hasta and Publius Manilius Vopiscus were consuls (AD 114). | *vv* Dedicated on the Kalends of August (August 1) when the same men were consuls.

1 The Greek building called 'phratrion' was a temple of the tutelary deities of the Greek *phratriai* ('brotherhoods'). Thus, the Latin *phetrium* is used, apparently, to designate a shrine for the *sodales* (brotherhood) of the Augustales, and could serve as the center for the municipal cult of Augustus.
2 See the Glossary.
3 On the municipal archives see Sherk, *loc. cit.* When the series of events mentioned in this document were completed, the entries in the record-books of Caere were consulted in the archives and the appropriate passages copied out for inscribing on the marble tablet for public display.
4 These two men were the highest local magistrates of Caere.
5 As curator of the municipality of Caere he was in charge of that city's finances. His appointment came from the emperor and the broad power that he possessed made him the most powerful figure in the local government. Thus, one sees here the deference with which he is treated. See G. P. Burton in *Chiron* 9 (1979) 465–87 for the post.

127   Trajan dedicates Dacian spoils. AD 113–14.

Anthologia Palatina 6.332; D. L. Page, **Further Greek Epigrams* (Cambridge 1981) 562
No. 1 (written by Hadrian, then a high officer in Trajan's army). [Greek, elegiac
couplets]

To Zeus Kasios[1] has Trajan, son of Aeneas, dedicated this gift, / the
ruler of men to the ruler of the immortals: / two artistically wrought
cups and from an aurochs[2] / the horn adorned with all-gleaming gold,
5 // chosen from his former spoils when, unyielding, he has wasted the
Getae[3] with his spear. / But you, lord of the dark clouds, grant him the
power / gloriously to complete this Achaimenian conflict,[4] / so that your
10 heart may be twice warmed by the sight // of two spoils, those of the
Getae and those of the Arsacidians.[5]

1 Mt Kasios was at the mouth of the Orontes River in Syria, the whole area being
   Trajan's springboard for his war against Parthia. Cf. Dio 68.18.
2 A species of bison, now extinct.
3 I.e. the Dacians.
4 The Achaemenid dynasty had been the ruling dynasty of the Persian Empire, but
   here it is a poetic word for 'Parthian', referring to Trajan's Parthian expedition.
5 Another way of saying 'Parthians'.

128   Roman troops on the march to Parthia. AD 113–15.
Stone block, Ancyra. [Greek]

IGRR III 173; *OGIS* 544; Smallwood, **Documents Nerva* 215; Bosch, *Quellen* 105. Cf. Dio
69.14.4.

Lepper, *Parthian War* 178–80; Magie, *RRAM* I 626 with n. 54; Bosch, *Quellen* 199–203;
R. D. Sullivan in *Studien zur Religion und Kultus Kleinasiens II (Festschrift für Karl Dörner)*
(Leiden 1978) 931–6.

[Gaius Iul]ius Severus,[1] | [descendant] of King | [D]eiotaros and of
5 Amyntas, | son of Brigatos and Amyntas (the) ‖ son of Dyr(?)ialos,
tetrarchs, | and of King Attalus of Asia, | cousin of the consulars Iulius
10 | Quadratus and King | Alexandros and Iulius A‖quila and Claudius
Severus, and | relative of consulars | in great numbers, brother of Iu|lius
15 Amyntianus.[2] First | of the Greeks, he was a high priest ‖ who surpassed
with contributions | and other acts of munificence those | who had ever
shown their ambition, and | in the same year (as his priesthood) he also
provided olive-oil | continuously during the passage of great crowds
20 (through the city).[3] ‖ He was sebastophantēs (i.e. priest of Augustus),
and he alone was | also the first within memory who as sebastophan|tēs
cheerfully gave money to the city for public works | and did not use |

25   this income for the oil, ‖ as all others before him (had done). He was
     also archon | [and] agonothetēs and agorano|mos;[4] his wife he
     establi|shed as high priestess, who also distinguished herself | with
30   contributions; he received ‖ armies that wintered over | in our city, and
     he conducted them | on their way to the Par|thian War.[5] He lived a ju|st
35   life and maintained equality of privilege. The tribe of Paraka[--]‖line,
     the seventh tribe, has here honored its own benefactor. Tri|bal leader
     was Varus Logios.

1 Gaius Iulius Severus (*PIR*[2] I 573; Halfmann, *Senatoren* No. 62) was later admitted to
   the rank of tribune of the plebs by Hadrian and he rose to become consul in AD 138
   or 139. For that part of his career see below, Document 164 C.
2 Thus, Iulius Severus had connections in his ancestry with the nobility of both
   Pergamum and Ancyra. 'Iulius Quadratus' is the famous military commander under
   Trajan: below, Document No. 138. For the others see Sullivan, *loc. cit.*
3 The phrase 'great crowds' is the equivalent of 'soldiers'. Ancyra had long been the
   hub of a large network of Roman roads connecting the Euphrates frontier with the
   west, and the tombstones of many soldiers have been discovered along them.
4 For these local Greek officials see the Glossary.
5 The exact year cannot be established, although the Parthian War of Trajan is meant.

129   The Jewish revolt under Trajan. AD 115–17.

A: Eusebius, *Ecclesiastical History* 4.2. Cf. Dio 68.32.1–3. **B**: Orosius, *Against the Pagans*
7.12.6–8. **C**: *P. Mil. R. Univ.* 6; H. A. Musurillo, *The Acts of the Pagan Martyrs* (Oxford 1954)
IX C; Tcherikover–Fuks, *CPJ* II 435; Smallwood, *Documents Nerva 55; Hengstl,
Griechische Papyri 17. Edict (?) of the prefect of Egypt concerning a Jewish revolt in
Alexandria. AD 115 (?). Papyrus from Tebtynis. [Greek] **D**: *P. Giss.* 19; Tcherikover–
Fuks, *CPJ II 436. A private letter from Aline to her brother the strategos of
Apollinopolis-Heptakomias in Upper Egypt. August of AD 115 (?). Papyrus from
Hermoupolis. [Greek] **E**: *P. Bremen* 40; Wilcken, *Chrestomathie* 16; Tcherikover–Fuks,
CPJ II 438; Smallwood, *Documents Nerva 57. Jewish victories in the district of
Hermoupolis. AD 116 (?). Papyrus from Hermoupolis, Egypt. [Greek] **F**: *P. Giss.* 41;
Wilcken, *Chrestomathie* 18; Tcherikover–Fuks, *CPJ* II 443; Smallwood, *Documents Nerva
58. September–November, AD 117. Apollonios requests leave of absence from the
prefect of Egypt. Papyrus from Hermoupolis. [Greek] **G**: G. E. Bean in *Belleten Türk
Tarih Kurumu* 22 (1958) 36–7, No. 26; *SEG XVII 584. Military colony sent to Cyrene.
Statue base set up early in reign of Hadrian, Attaleia in Pamphylia. [Greek] Cf.
Orosius, above, **B**, section 7.

See Tcherikover–Fuks, *CPJ* II, commentaries on Nos. 435–6, 438 and 443; Smallwood,
Jews 393–427; Marina Pucci, *La Rivolta Ebraica al Tempo di Traiano* (Pisa 1981).

A. Eusebius, *Ecclesiastical History* 4.2

In the eighteenth year of the current emperor (Trajan, AD 115) again a
movement of the Jews arose and it destroyed a huge number of them.
(2) For in Alexandria and the rest of Egypt and above all in Cyrene, as

if they had been fanned by some terrible spirit of seditiousness, they broke into factious strife against their Greek fellow citizens. In the next year it increased to a large uprising and they met in no small war, at the time when Lupus was in command of all Egypt.[1] In the (3) first encounter it happened that they over-powered the Greeks, who then fled to Alexandria and captured and killed the Jews in the city, but, although they had lost the alliance of these (Alexandrian Jews), the (Jews) from Cyrene continued to devastate the countryside of Egypt and to destroy the nome districts in it under their leader Lukuas. The emperor sent Marcius Turbo[2] against them with an infantry and naval force as well as cavalry. (4) In many battles and over a considerable stretch of time he prosecuted the war against them, killing many thousands of Jews, not only those from Cyrene but also those from Egypt who had attached themselves to Lukuas as their king. (5) The emperor suspected that the Jews in Mesopotamia would attack the people there, and he ordered Lusius Quietus[3] to clean them out of that province. He (Lusius Quietus), having drawn up his men in battle order, killed a huge number of them there and for this success he was appointed governor of Judaea by that emperor. The Greeks who wrote about events of this same time have transmitted the narrative in these very words.

B. Orosius, *Against the Pagans* **7.12.6–8**

Then in an incredible movement at one time, as if carried away by madness, the Jews flared up in different parts of the world. For throughout all Libya they waged the fiercest warfare against the inhabitants: the land was so desolated by the killing of the people who lived there at that time that, if the emperor Hadrian afterwards had not collected and then sent colonists there from elsewhere,[4] the country would have remained completely empty and scraped dry of inhabitants. (7) The Jews created havoc throughout all Egypt and Cyrene and the Thebaid by the actions of their bloody insurrection. However, in Alexandria they were overcome and wiped out in pitched battle. And in Mesopotamia by order of the emperor war was directed against the rebels. Thus, many thousands of them were killed in a blood-bath. (8) To be sure, they destroyed Salamis, a city of Cyprus, and killed all the inhabitants.

C. Smallwood, *Documents Nerva* **55. Egyptian papyrus**

(Col. 2, line 27)[5] [----] and fire against us | (Col. 3) and iron (weapons) they are preparing. I know that | they are few, but they are being brought in by ma|ny and are supported by the stronger, who pa|y not
5   to be harmed, not to be ro‖bbed. The hateful action among a few is not

an un|just complaint against the whole city. I know that | many are
slaves, and for | this reason their masters are reproached. To all of them
10 | I say not to pretend || anger because of desire for gain. Let them know
| that no longer are they unknown to us. Let them not tru|st in my good
nature and not [----] in the | days [----] I forced myself to [----] | as soon
15 as I could [---], *but if anyone* || wishes to charge anyone, he has a judge |
sent by the emperor[6] for this purpose. For | not even governors have the
power to execute men without a trial, | and a trial has its own proper |
20 time, as there is a proper form || for punishment. Let there be an end of
people saying – some truth|fully, some falsely – that they | have suffered
wounds and demanding forceful and | *unlawful* justice. For it was not |
25 necessary to suffer wounds. Some of the mis||takes perhaps could have
had an excuse | before the Roman | *vv* battle against the Jews. Now, |
however, *such courts of judgment* are useless and | have never before this
30 been permitted. || Year 19 *of Trajan*, Phaophi 16.

D. Tcherikover–Fuks, *CPJ* II 436. Papyrus from Hermoupolis

Aline to her brother Apollonios,[7] | *vv* very many greetings. *vv* | I am
worried about you because of the | talk of the present situation and the
5 fact that un||expectedly you left me, and neither to dr|ink nor *food* do I
turn with pleasure, | [but] I lie awake continuously night and d|ay with
10 one worry, your | safety. Only my father's || attentiveness keeps me
going, and on the first | [day] of the New Year, praying for your | *safety*,
I would have stayed in bed without eating, | [if] my *father* had not come
15 and forced | me (to eat). Please [keep] yourself safe || and all by yourself
| don't submit to danger [without] a guard, but, as | [the] strategos here
20 | [puts] the burden on his officials, you | [do] the same! My father || [----]
For the *name* | [--- of my] brother was put forward | [----] him (may) the
25 god | [----] If, my brother, | [----] affairs || [---] write to us. [----] to you
| [----] safe|ty [----]. (On the other side) To Apollonios, my brother.

E. Smallwood, *Documents Nerva* 57. Papyrus from Hermoupolis

The one hope and remaining expec|tation was the attack from our
5 district | of the whole body of villagers | against the unholy *Jews*, || the
opposite of which has now happened. | For on the twent[ieth (?)] we
en|gaged them and were defea|ted, but many of them | were killed
10 [----||----|----|---| now from some who] | have come [from ---] || we
received the message | that another legion of Rutilius[8] came to
Memphis and on the twenty-second | is expected [----]

F. Smallwood, *Documents Nerva* 58. Papyrus from Hermoupolis

(Col. 1) [To Rammius Martialis,[9] the] mightiest prefect, | [Apollonios
the strategos] of Apollonopolis-|[Heptakomias,] *vv* greetings. | [A copy

of the letter which I wrote to you, governor,] my lord, concerning my
5   leave of absence, ‖ I attach below, in order that, if in your provi|dence
[it seems good to you, you grant] me sixty days for | [setting straight
my affairs,] especially now when I think | [----] are pressuring (me?). I
10   pray that you | are well, my lord governor. ‖ [Year 1 (?) of the emperor
Caesar Traianus Ha]drianus Augustus, Choiak 2. |

    [To Rammius Martialis, the] mightiest *prefect*, | from [Apollonios the
strategos of Apo]llonopolis-He[ptakomias,] greetings. | [----|----] |
(Col. 2) [---] use. For not only be|cause of my long absence | do my
things begin to be completely in disorder, | but [also] because of the
5   unholy *Jews'* ‖ attack just about everything [which] | I have [in the]
villages of [Hermoupo]|lis and in the *metropolis* | needs *repair* from me. |
10   If you agree with this ‖ request of mine, with the ordering | of my things
as far as possible I will be a|ble in a more composed manner to turn to
| the attentions of the strategia.[10]

G. *SEG* XVII 584. Attaleia in Pamphylia

Lucius Gavius, son of Lucius Gavius Fron|to, Fronto, pri|mipilaris of
5   Legion Third Cyrena|ica and camp comman‖dant of Legion Fifteenth
Apollinari|s, the first and only one (of such distinction) from | his
native city, father of Lucius | Gavius Aelianus, quaestor with | pro
10   praetorian power of the People of the Rom‖ans, grandfather of Lucius
Gavius Clarus | of the broad stripe. | Honored with a public horse | by
15   Aug|ustus[11] and with decorations for bra‖very, entrusted by the god
Traianus with 3,000 ve|terans of the legions to | colonize Cyrene,[12] he
offer|ed of his own free will a perpetual gymnasiarchy | in his fourth
20   year (of that office,) the first (to do this.) He was high ‖ priest of all the
Augusti | for a four-year period and agonothetēs | at his own expense of
the theatrical games | as well as gymnastic (games). Lucius Gavius
Se|leukos (here dedicates this statue) to his patron ‖ and benefactor.

1 Marcus Rutilius Lupus governed Egypt AD 113–17.
2 For the career of Quintus Marcius Turbo under Trajan and Hadrian see E. Frézouls
   in *Syria* 30 (1953) 247–78; R. Syme in *JRS* 52 (1962) 87ff. (*Roman Papers* II 541ff.);
   Pflaum, *Carrières* No. 94. For his actions in Egypt: Smallwood, *Jews* 402ff.
3 Lusius Quietus, elevated from Moorish chieftain to trusted general under Trajan,
   was one of the four senators executed by Hadrian at the beginning of his reign. For
   his actions in Mesopotamia see Smallwood, *Jews* 415–21, and for his career see
   L. Petersen in *Altertum* 14 (1968) 211–17 and Strobel, *Untersuchungen* 68–71. In the
   Mishna (*Sot.* IX 14) we learn that 'during the war of Quietus they abolished the
   bridal crown, and ordered fathers not to teach their sons Greek'. Cf. Smallwood,
   Jews 424, and G. Alon, *The Jews in their Land in the Talmudic Age* II (Jerusalem 1984)
   413–14.
4 Cf. item G line 15 for Trajan sending out colonists.
5 Only separate words or short phrases remain of Cols. 1–2, but all the events in the

present document are to be related to the so-called *Acts of Paulus and Antoninus* (Tcherikover–Fuks, *CPJ* II 158a–b). For a summary see the introduction to that document in Tcherikover–Fuks as well as Smallwood, *Jews* 406–9.

6 Since someone in this document speaks in the first person and since the emperor is mentioned in the third person, the speaker would appear to be the prefect of Egypt, and if the dating at the end is correct (i.e. that Trajan and not Hadrian is the emperor) then that prefect would be Marcus Rutilius Lupus.

7 Apollonios is a well-known strategos in charge of a district in Egypt. Aline is probably his wife as well as sister.

8 The prefect of Egypt, Rutilius Lupus.

9 Quintus Rammius Martialis was prefect of Egypt at the very beginning of the reign of Hadrian.

10 The 'strategia' is the region or district he governs.

11 The grant of a public horse under the empire meant the acquisition of equestrian status by the recipient. 'Augustus' here must have been Domitian, not mentioned because his memory had been condemned.

12 Lucius Gavius Fronto (*PIR*[2] G 100) escorted veterans to colonize Cyrene as part of a general plan to keep the peace in that place after the Jewish revolt.

130   The earthquake at Antioch. December of AD 115.

Malalas 11.275.3–8 (von Stauffenberg). Cf. Dio 68.24ff.

Lepper, *Parthian War* 19ff. and 54–83; G. Downey, *A History of Antioch* (Princeton 1961) 213–15.

In the reign of the most divine Trajan the great (city) of Antioch by Daphne[1] suffered its third disaster (an earthquake) on the thirteenth day of the month Apellaios, i.e. December, on the first day, after the cock's crow, in the year called 164 according to the Antiochians, in the second year after the presence (in Antioch) of the most divine emperor Trajan on his way to the east.[2]

1 Daphne: a park near Antioch in Syria.

2 Malalas lived and wrote in the sixth century. His work, a world-chronicle with emphasis on the Christians, contains some reliable material but is full of mistakes and distorted views. The 164th year of the Antiochian reckoning (by the Julian era of autumn 49 to autumn 48 BC) is equivalent to AD 115. Thus, the earthquake took place in AD 115, and Trajan therefore came to Antioch two years before, in AD 113, to begin his Parthian War. If Malalas is right, then Trajan's offensives 'occupied not two but three campaigning seasons' (Lepper, *op. cit.* 83).

131   An Iberian prince with Trajan in the Parthian War.
Stone with metrical inscription found in Rome, but which was probably transported there from Nisibis in Mesopotamia. [Greek]

IG XIV 1374; *IGRR* I 192; W. Peek, *Griechische Vers-Inschriften*, I: *Grab-Epigramme* (Berlin 1955) 722; Moretti, **IGUR* III 1151.

Lepper, *Parthian War* 171; A. I. Boltunova in *Klio* 53 (1971) 221–2; Moretti, *op. cit.* 11–12.

Amazaspos, renowned son of a king, / brother of King Mithridates, / whose native land is by the Caspian Gates,[1] / an Iberian (son) of an
5   Iberian, he is buried here // by the holy city which Nikator built / near the olive-nurturing waters of Mygdon.[2] / He died as a companion to the leader of the Italians / when he (Amazaspos) came to do battle against the Parthians at the side of the emperor,[3] / but (he died) before he
10   bespattered his hand with blood of the enemy, // his hand, oh!, strong with the spear and the bow / and the two-edged sword, on foot [and] on *horseback*. / He himself (in his features) resembled young girls worthy of our reverence.

1 The 'Causasian Gates' seem to be meant, for the 'Caspian' were several hundred miles away from Iberia.
2 Seleucus Nicator (*c.* 358–281 BC), king of Syria, called the city Antiochia Mygdonia, but later it resumed its older name of Nisibis.
3 The reference is to Trajan and his Parthian War, when he captured Nisibis.

132   Trajan crosses the Tigris River. AD 116.

Arrian, *Parthica* frag. 67 (ed. Roos-Wirth = *FGrHist* 156 G 154). [Greek] Cf. Dio 68.28.1–4.

R. P. Longden in *CAH* 11.246–7; Lepper, *Parthian War* 129–36.

The emperor Trajan crossed the river (Tigris) with fifty ships. Four of them carried the royal flags and they led the way for the flagship furnished with long planks of wood. This ship was about the length of a trireme, its width and depth those of a merchantman, like the largest Nikomedian or Egyptian vessel, and it gave the emperor satisfactory living quarters. It displayed stem-post ornaments <of gold> and on top of the sail the emperor's name was inscribed along with the rest of his imperial titles in gold letters. The whole naval force had been divided into three groups to avoid the difficulty of a single, continuous line of ships.

133   Trajan's letter to the senate. AD 116
Extract from the Fasti Ostienses. [Latin]

I. Ital. XIII 1, p. 203 (AD 116); Smallwood, *Documents Nerva* 23, lines 8–13.

On the ninth (or tenth) day before the Kalends of March (February 20 or 21) a laureled letter (of victory) was sent to the *senate* [by Imperator]

| Traianus Augustus, because of which [he was given the title] Par[thicus,] ||[1] and for his safety a decree of the senate was passed and thanksgiving (at all the) shr|ines and games were held on the fifth, fourth, and the day before the Kalends of M[arch (February 25, 26, and 28), games of the circus,] | thirty events. On the day before the Nones of May (May 6) a *letter* [was sent to the senate] | by Imperator Traianus Augustus [----].

1 See Lepper, *Parthian War* 39–41 and 53 (Addendum), and P. Kneissl, *Die Siegestitulatur der römischen Kaiser* (Göttingen 1969) 74ff.

134   Trajan puts Parthemaspates on the throne of Parthia. AD 116.

Malalas 11.273.20–274.16 (ed. von Stauffenberg p. 45 = Arrian, *FGrHist* 156 F 49b). Cf. Dio 68.30.3.

R. P. Longden in *CAH* 11.248–9; Lepper, *Parthian War* 210–12; Garzetti, *Tiberius to Antonines* 370–1; G. Downey, *A History of Antioch in Syria* (Princeton 1961) 213 n. 58.

Trajan departed from the great (city of) Antioch[1] stirring up war (21) against the Persians, and he defeated them by force (22) in this manner: when he learned that Sanatrukes, (23) king of the Persians,[2] was envied by his own cousin Parthemaspates, (274.1) Emperor Trajan sent for him (i.e. Parthemaspates) and won him over by corruption, arranging (2) to give him the kingdom of the Persians if he would become his ally. (3) Having been corrupted, he went to him at night and took him into (4) his own area with the mass of his (soldiers), and the most divine (5) Trajan set out against Sanatrukes, king of the Persians. (6) Many Persians fell in battle and he captured Sanatrukes, king (7) of the Persians, as he was fleeing and killed him. And (8) in his place Trajan made Parthemaspates, son of Osdoroes, (9) king of the Persians over those who were left and who fell down before him according to the arrangement. (10) He wrote to the senate in Rome (11): 'So great and so boundless is this land and so immeasurable the distances that separate it from Rome (12) that we do not have the reach to administer it, but let us present them (13) with a king subject to the power of the Romans.' (14) In answer the senate wrote to him from Rome to do (15) everything he wished and as might seem to him to be in keeping with the interest of Rome. And (16) Parthemaspates was king of the Persians.[3]

1 The events described here took place in AD 116 at the beginning of the great rebellion in the Tigris–Euphrates region. Malalas has confused the chronology, for Trajan moved out from Antioch in force against Armenia and Parthia back in AD 114. Malalas must be used with caution.

2 Malalas is wrong. Sanatrukes, although of Parthian origin, was king of Armenia.
3 This passage is followed by the remark that Trajan's victory over the Persians had
   been narrated by Arrian in his *Parthica*, a work of great value but now extant only in
   fragments. By 'Persians' Malalas means 'Parthians' here and elsewhere.

135   Coins celebrating victory in Parthia. AD 116–17.

A: Mattingly, *BMC 3, No. 606 (+ photograph); Smallwood, *Documents Nerva* 49.
AD 116–17. Roman aureus. **B**: Mattingly, *BMC 3, No. 1035 (+ photograph);
Smallwood, *Documents Nerva* 50. AD 116–17. Roman sestertius. **C**: Mattingly, *BMC 3,
No. 1046 (+ photograph); Smallwood, *Documents Nerva* 51. AD 116–17. Roman
sestertius. Cf. Dio 68.30.3.

A. Mattingly, *BMC* 3, No. 606. Roman aureus

(Obverse: bust of Trajan, laureate)

IMPERATOR CAESAR NERVA TRAIANUS OPTIMUS AUGUSTUS GERMANICUS DACICUS PARTHICUS,

(Reverse: two captives on ground to left and right of weapons)

PONTIFEX MAXIMUS, HOLDING THE TRIBUNICIAN POWER, CONSUL FOR THE SIXTH TIME, FATHER OF HIS COUNTRY. SENATE AND ROMAN PEOPLE. PARTHIA CAPTURED.

B. Mattingly, *BMC* 3, No. 1035. Roman sestertius

(Obverse: bust of Trajan laureate)

IMPERATOR CAESAR NERVA TRAIANUS OPTIMUS AUGUSTUS GERMANICUS DACICUS PARTHICUS, PONTIFEX MAXIMUS, HOLDING THE TRIBUNICIAN POWER, CONSUL FOR THE SIXTH TIME, FATHER OF HIS COUNTRY.

(Reverse: Trajan, standing in center in military dress, with Armenia at his feet between two river-gods)

ARMENIA AND MESOPOTAMIA BROUGHT UNDER THE POWER OF THE ROMAN PEOPLE. BY DECREE OF THE SENATE.[1]

C. Mattingly, *BMC* **3, No. 1046. Roman sestertius**

(Obverse: IMPERATOR CAESAR NERVA TRAIANUS
bust of Trajan   OPTIMUS AUGUSTUS GERMANICUS
laureate)   DACICUS PARTHICUS, PONTIFEX
   MAXIMUS, HOLDING THE TRIBUNICIAN
   POWER, CONSUL FOR THE SIXTH TIME,
   FATHER OF HIS COUNTRY.

(Reverse: A KING GIVEN TO THE PARTHIANS.
Trajan in   BY DECREE OF THE SENATE.
military
dress, seated
on platform,
placing a
diadem on
head of Par-
themaspates,
with Armenia
kneeling and
arms out-
stretched)

1   The senatorial decree merely authorized the minting of the coin.

136   Trajan and his eastern empire.

A: Festus, *Breviarium* 20. **B**: Jordanes, *Romana* 268. See T. Olajos in *Acta Antiqua Academiae Scientiarum Hungarica* 29 (1981) 379–83.

A. Festus, *Breviarium* **20**

Trajan, who after Augustus set in motion the muscular strength of the Roman State, recovered Armenia from the Persians, took up the crown of Armenia Maior and appropriated its kingdom.[1] He gave a king to the Albanians. He received the Iberians, the Bosporans, and the Colchians into the trust of Roman control. He occupied the lands of the Osrhoenians and the Arabs. He took possession of the Cardueni and the Marcomedes.[2] He took control of Athemusia, the best region of Persis.[3] Seleucia, Ctesiphon, and Babylonia he took and held. Up to the border of India he advanced, in the footsteps of Alexander.[4] In the Red Sea he established a fleet.[5] He made provinces out of Armenia, Mesopotamia, and Assyria which, situated between the Tigris and Euphrates, are filled with well-watered streams like Egypt.[6]

B. Jordanes, *Romana* **268**

On the Red Sea, from which he might lay waste the confines of India, (Trajan) established a fleet and dedicated there his own statue.[7]

1   Dio 69.19.20.
2   The Cardueni may be the inhabitants of Gordyene, and the Marcomedes may be simply the Medes.
3   Dio 68.21.
4   Perhaps what is meant is 'toward' the borders of India.
5   Eutropius (8.3.2) adds 'that he might lay waste the confines of India with it'. By 'Red Sea' Festus means 'Persian Gulf'.
6   By 'Assyria' is meant 'Babylonia'. See A. Maricq in *Syria* 36 (1959) 254ff.
7   This statue apparently was still standing on Persian soil in AD 569, since it is mentioned in the third part of the *Ecclesiastical History* of John, Bishop of Ephesus, which is concerned with a diplomatic mission of that year. For the details see Olajos, *loc. cit.* Again, by 'Red Sea' the 'Persian Gulf' is meant.

137   Roman army withdraws from Dura-Europus. AD 116–17.
Stone tablet found near the Mithaeum, Dura-Europus in Syria.
[Written in a 'Hebraized' form of Greek]

M. I. Rostovtzeff in *CRAI* 1935, 285–90 (*AÉ* 1936, 69); Smallwood, *Documents Nerva 53.

Rostovtzeff, *loc. cit.*, and in *Klio* 31 (1938) 285–92; Lepper, *Parthian War* 148–50.

Year 428 (of the Seleucid era).[1] | I, Ale|xandros (son) of Epini|kos,
5   renewed this shrine ‖ which was built | long ago for himself by Epi|nikos
10   my father, | and I made an extension to | it of five cubits. ‖ The old doorways | were left by the Ro|mans and, after their | withdrawal from
15   there, out of the two | I made for my‖self other door|ways for the same shrine and also | outer (doors). This is the memorial of | Ammaios, the
20   same A[le]xandros, priest of [the] ‖ god and herald of the city | for the same [god].

1   The Seleucid era began on October 1 of 312 BC. Thus, the date here is between October 1 of AD 116 and September 30 of AD 117.

138   Career of Gaius Iulius Quadratus Bassus. Reign of Trajan.
Statue base, inscribed on front and right side, from the temple of Asklepios in Pergamum. [Greek]

A. von Premerstein in *SBAW* 1934, 2, pp. 1–86 (*AÉ* 1934, 176); Smallwood, *Documents Nerva* 214; Chr. Habicht, **Altertümer von Pergamum* VIII 3, No. 21 (+ photographs).

Premerstein, *loc. cit.*; Lepper, *Parthian War* 182–7; Habicht, *op. cit.* 43ff.; R. K. Sherk in *ANRW* 2.7.2, 1020–3; Halfmann, *Senatoren* 26; Strobel, *Untersuchungen* 64–6.

Gaius Iulius Quadratus Bassus, consul (AD 105),[1] | pontifex, army
commander | in the Dacian War and companion there in the | war to
5   Imperator Traianus, honored ‖ with triumphal decorations; legate with
pro | praetorian power of the province Iudaea, legate | with pro
praetorian power of Cappadocia-Galatia-|Armenia Minor-Pontus-
10   Paphlagonia-Isau|[ria-Phrygi]a,[2] legate with pro prae‖torian power of
the *province Syria-Phoenicia-Kommage* | [ne,] *legate* with pro praetorian
power of the *pro|vince* [Dacia;] tribune of Legion Thirteenth (Gemina),
15   trium|vir of the mint, | [quaestor of Cre]te and Cyrene, aedile ‖ [candi-
date,) *praetor* of the Roman People; | [legate of] Legion Eleventh
Claudia Rev|erent, and of *Legion* Fourth Scythian, and of Legion | [----,]
and of Legion Twelfth Fulmin|ata, [and of Legion] Third Gallica, and
20   of Legion ‖ [----, and of Legion] Thirteenth Gemina, and of Legi|[on
----.][3] He was a man well-born and from *vv* | [a family of kings]
(? consulars?) descended. *vv* | [*vv* Civic] *honor* was established for him by
the] People of Seleukeia *vv* | [---- at Zeug]ma through the agency of
25   legate ‖ [----] *vacat* | (on the adjacent side of the base) While still com-
manding in | Dacia and administering his province | he died, and his
30   body | was transported to Asia, carried by ‖ his soldiers drawn up under
the military standard | of the centurion | primipilaris Quintilius
Capit|o, a procession preceding him | in every city and military camp
35   ‖ by order of Imperator | god Hadrianus, and this memorial to him | was
constructed from (Hadrian's? own) treasury.

1 This Quadratus Bassus (*PIR* I 508), despite the many attempts to identify him with
   known personalities of the age, is apparently otherwise unknown.
2 During the Flavian emperors and on into the reign of Trajan this huge provincial
   complex was under the single command of a consular governor.
3 Quadratus Bassus did not command all these legions separately. They, or perhaps
   detached units of some of them, were placed under his overall command at some
   time in the course of the Dacian wars. See Strobel, *loc. cit.*

HADRIAN
(117–138)
IMPERATOR CAESAR TRAIANUS HADRIANUS AUGUSTUS

Titles: PONTIFEX MAXIMUS
FATHER OF HIS COUNTRY (128)
HOLDER OF THE TRIBUNICIAN POWER: first in
AD 117 on August 11, second time in same year on December
10, then annually
CONSUL: AD 108 (I), 118 (II), 119 (III)

Death: July 10, AD 138.

The *consules ordinarii* **under Hadrian**

AD
118	Imp. Caesar Traianus Hadrianus Augustus II	Cn. Pedanius Fuscus Salinator
119	Imp. Hadrianus III	P. Dasumius Rusticus
120	L. Catilius Severus Iulianus Claudius Reginus II	T. Aurelius Fulvus Boionius Arrius Antonius
121	M. Annius Verus II	Cn. Arrius Augur
122	M'. Acilius Aviola	Corellius Pansa
123	Q. Articuleius Paetinus	L. Venuleius Apronianus Octavius Priscus
124	M'. Acilius Glabrio	C. Bellicius Flaccus Torquatus Tebanianus
125	M. Lollius Paullinus D. Valerius Asiaticus Saturninus II	L. Epidius Titius Aquilinus
126	M. Annius Verus III	C. Eggius Ambibulus
127	T. Atilius Rufus Titianus	M. Gavius (Claudius) Squilla Gallicanus
128	L. Nonius Calpurnius Asprenas Torquatus II	M. Annius Libo

cf. Polotsky, *Israel Exploration Journal* 12, 1962, p. 259 for P. Metilius Nepos II as colleague of Libo

129	P. Iuventius Celsus T. Aufidius Hoenius Severianus II	L. Neratius Marcellus II
130	Q. Fabius Catullinus	M. Flavius Aper
131	M. Ser. Octavius Laenas Pontianus	M. Antonius Rufinus
132	C. Iunius Serius Augurinus	C. (M.?) Trebius Sergianus (or praenomen P. – cf. Polotsky, *Israel Exploration Journal*, 12 (1962) p. 259
133	M. Antonius Hiberus	P. Mummius Sisenna
134	L. Iulius Ursus Servianus III	T. Vibius Varus
135	L. Tutilius Lupercus Pontianus	P. Calpurnius Atilianus (Atticus Rufus?)
136	L. Ceionius Commodus	Sex. Vettulenus Civica Pompeianus

137   L. Aelius Caesar II   P. Coelius Balbinus Vibullius Pius
138   Canus Iunius Niger   C. Pomponius Camerinus

139   Creation of the Athenaeum in Rome by Hadrian.

Aurelius Victor, *De Caesaribus* 14.1–3.

Aelius Hadrianus was more suited to eloquence and the studies of
peacetime, and after peace had been brought to the east he returned to
Rome. There, after the fashion of the Greeks or of Numa Pompilius, he
began to devote his attention to religious rituals, to laws, to the
gymnasia, and to teachers, so much so that he established an institute
of liberal arts which was called the Athenaeum.[1]

1 It was a building in Rome that contained an auditorium in which Greek and Roman
   rhetors and poets could recite their works to an audience. It may also have contained
   rooms for study and scholarly works. It was still in use in the fifth century AD:
   Sidonius Apollinaris, *Letters* 9.14.2. See H. Bardon, *Les Empereurs et les lettres latines
   d'Auguste à Hadrien*[2] (Paris 1968) 426–8 with further details.

140   Chief secretary in Rome under Hadrian.
Marble stele now lost, preserved in a copy, Rome. [Greek]

IG XIV 1085; *IGRR* I 136; *OGIS* 679; Smallwood, *Documents Nerva* 264; Moretti, *IGUR*
I 62 (+ photograph of copy).

Millar, *Emperor* 88.

To the high priest of Alexandria and all Egy|pt, Lucius Iulius
Vesti|nus,[1] head of the Museum,[2] and in | charge of the Rom||an and
Greek Libraries, and Director of | Literary Studies for Hadrian the
emperor, and Chief | Secretary of the same emperor.[3]

1 Iulius Vestinus (*PIR*[2] I 623) was related to the eminent prefect of Egypt under Nero
   of the same name. See Pflaum, *Carrières* No. 105.
2 The Museum at Alexandria was an institution of higher learning which students and
   teachers were invited to attend. At this time its director was appointed by the
   emperor and the whole institution enjoyed imperial patronage.
3 The last three posts were all held as salaried positions in the equestrian career: *ā
   bibliothecis*, *ā studiis*, and *ab epistulis*. See Pflaum, *Carrières* No. 105. The *ab epistulis*
   ('Chief Secretary') was a very important person, across whose desk passed the
   official correspondence between emperor and all echelons of the imperial administration: see Millar, *loc. cit.*

141   Hadrian's frontier policy in Britain. AD 117–18 (?).
Two fragments of sandstone, from Jarrow, perhaps part of a war
memorial that originally stood near the eastern end of Hadrian's Wall
in Britain. [Latin]

CIL VII 498; R. P. Wright and I. A. Richmond in *Archaeologia Aeliana*[4] 21 (1943) 93ff.
(+ Figures 1–3 and Pl. III); *idem* in *JRS* 33 (1943) 78; **RIB* 1051 a–b.

Wright–Richmond, *loc. cit.* 93ff.; A. Piganiol, *Scripta Varia* III (Brussels 1973) 132–4.

(a) Son of all the [deified (emperors), | Imperator Caesar] *Traianus*
Hadr[ianus | Augustus,] when the necessity of *keeping intact* the empire
| [within its borders] had been *imposed* upon him by divine *instruction*,
5   ‖ consul for the *second* (third?) time[1] *vv* | [---- about 7 lines lost ----] | (b)
15(?)   having routed [the barbarians and | recovered] the province ‖ of Britain,
he *added* [a fortified boundary line between] | each *ocean's* [shore for 80
miles.] | The army of the *province* [built this defensive wall] | under the
care of [Aulus Platorius Nepos, legate of Augustus with pro praetorian
power.][2]

1   There may have been a third bar after *cos. II* on the stone, which would move the date
     up to AD 119.
2   Although much is restored in this inscription, it seems to have reflected Hadrian's
     policy of defense in Britain.

142   Hadrian cancels debts owed to the Treasury. AD 118–24.

A: *CIL* VI 967; **ILS* 309; Smallwood, *Documents Nerva* 64a. Fragment of marble from
Trajan's forum, Rome. [Latin] B: Mattingly, **BMC* 3, No. 1207 with Pl. LXXIX.5;
Smallwood, *Documents Nerva* 64b. Sestertius minted in Rome, AD 119–24/25. Cf. SHA,
Hadrian 7.6ff.; Dio 69.8.

Henderson, *Hadrian* 60–1; W. Weber in *CAH* 11.303–4; Garzetti, *Tiberius to Antonines* 385.

A. *ILS* 309, Rome

vv The senate *vv* and *vv* the Roman *vv* People. | (Dedicated) to Imperator
Caesar, son of the deified Traianus | Parthicus, grandson of the deified
5   Nerva, | Traianus Hadrianus Augustus, pontifex ‖ maximus, holding
the tribunician power for the second time (December 10, AD 117 to
December 9, 118), consul for the second time, | who was the first of all
our Leaders and the | only one to remit 900|000,000 sesterces owed to
the fiscus (i.e. the Imperial Treasury), | (and) not only his present
10   citizens but ‖ also their offspring he rendered | *vv* safe by this liberality.
vv

B. Mattingly, *BMC* 3, No. 1207. Sestertius from Rome

(Obverse: bust of
Hadrian laureate)

IMPERATOR CAESAR TRAIANUS
HADRIANUS AUGUSTUS.

(Reverse: lictor in
short tunic and cloak,
setting fire to a heap
of bonds on the
ground.)

900,000,000 SESTERCES IN OLD
ARREARS DESTROYED. BY DECREE
OF THE SENATE.[1]

1 This means merely that the senate approved the minting of the coin.

143 Letter of Hadrian on children of soldiers. AD 119.
Papyrus from Egypt. [Greek]

Mitteis, *Chrestomathie 373; Bruns[7] 196; *FIRA* I 78; Smallwood, *Documents Nerva* 333;
Daris, *Documents* 108.

J. H. Jung in *ANRW* 2.14.302–46 (marriage rights of soldiers).

    Copy of a letter [of the emperor] translated [into Greek which] | *was put
on public display* in | [year] 3 of Traianus Hadrianus Augustus | when
5   [Pub]lius A[elius for the third time and Ru]sticus ‖ were *consuls*
(AD 119), [in] the winter-camp | [of Legion Third] Cyrenaica | and
Legion Twenty-Second Deiotariana | on the day before the Nones of August
10 (August 4), which is Mesore | 11, in Headquarters. ‖
    I know, my Rammius,[1] that those people, whom | their parents at the
time of their military service | had accepted as their (children), have
been denied the | income of their fathers' *property*, | and this did not
15 seem to be harsh, ‖ since they had acted contrary to military | *regu-
lations*.[2] However, with the greatest of pleasure | I initiate procedures by
means of which | the more strict rule established by those who pre-
20 ceded me | as emperors may be interpreted more hu‖manely by me.
Although | they are not legal he|irs of their fathers' property – I refer to
those | children acknowledged[3] in the time of | military service – never-
25 theless it is my decision that they too can claim ‖ possession of such
property | in accordance with that section of the edict | which gives it to
kinsmen by birth. | This gift of mine you will be required to make well
30 known | to my soldiers and veter‖ans, not in order that I might appear
to gain high regard among them, | but that they might use this gift, | in
case they do not know of it.

1 Quintus Rammius Martialis, prefect of Egypt 117–19.
2 Soldiers were forbidden to marry.
3 See A. Berger in *Journal of Juristic Papyrology* 1 (1946) 28–33.

144 Plotina and Hadrian concerning the school at Athens. AD 121

Marble stone, broken at the top, Athens. [Latin]

CIL III 12283; *ILS* 7784; *FIRA* I 79; Smallwood, *Documents Nerva* 442.

(Letter of Plotina to her adopted son, Hadrian)
[--- | in the consulship of Marcus Annius Verus for the second time and Gnaeus A]rrius Augur (AD 121). | *vv* From Plotina Augusta.[1] *vv* | [How great my enthusiasm] is toward the school of Epicurus, you know very well, my *lord*. Prompt assistance from you must be given to its
5   succession, ‖ [for, because] it is only permitted Roman citizens to be successors (to head the school), [the opportunity] of choosing one is reduced to narrow limits. | Therefore, [I ask] in the name of Popillius Theotimus, who is presently the successor (head of the school) at Athens, that he be permitted by you | to write his testament in Greek[2] about the part of his (testamentary) decisions which pertain to the regulation of the succession and that | he be empowered to name as successor to himself a person of non-Roman status, if such a person's qualifications convince him; and (I ask) that what you grant to Theotimus, | the future successors (to head) the school of Epicurus thereafter may also enjoy the same legal rights. All the more (do I ask)
10   because it has been the practice, ‖ as often as an error has been made by a testator about the election of a successor, that by common consent a substitution is made by the stu|dents of the same school of the person who will be the best (successor), and that will be done more easily, if he is chosen from a greater number (of candidates). |

(Rescript of Hadrian)
Imperator Caesar Traianus Hadrianus Augustus to Popillius Theotimus: I permit testaments to be made in Greek about those matters which pertain to a suc|cessor (to head) the school of Epicurus. And since a successor will be elected more easily if he also has the right to name a substitute from among non-Romans, | I tender this to him as well and thereafter to the others [who] will hold the succession. Permission will be given for this right to be transferred to a non-Roman or
15   ‖ a Roman citizen.[3]

1 Plotina was the widow of Trajan and probably facilitated the accession of Hadrian by adoption.
2 Theotimus was a Roman citizen and therefore had to write his testament in Latin (Ulpian 22.2; Gaius, *Institutes* 2.285) and could not name as beneficiary a non-Roman citizen.
3 Hadrian's rescript is followed on the stone by another letter of Plotina (in Greek) 'to all her friends in Athens' about this favorable ruling of Hadrian.

145   Hadrian reviews troops on the Danube. AD 121.

Stone is lost, preserved in copy only, said to have been found on the bank of the Danube. [Latin hexameters]

CIL III 3676; *ILS* 2558; Smallwood, *Documents Nerva 336; *Anthologia Latina* 660 (ed. Riese). Cf. Dio 69.9.

I am the one who was formerly very well-known on the Pannonian shore, / first in bravery among one thousand Batavians, / the one who with Hadrian as judge was able across the vast / waters of the deep
5   Danube to swim in full battle gear.[1] // While an arrow from my bow was hanging in the air / and returning (to earth), I loosed another, struck it and split it in two. / No Roman or barbarian ever could beat me, / no soldier with his javelin, no Parthian with his bow. / Here is my place of
10   rest, here have I enshrined my deeds on stone that never forgets. // It remains to be seen whether anyone else will rival my deeds. / By example I am the first to have done such things.

1   Dio (69.9) gives substantially the same story, reminiscent of the military exercises Hadrian saw his African army perform (below, Document No. 148), with the addition here of 1,000 Batavians, which indicates an *Ala miliaria Batavorum*. In Dio's passage they are also said to have swum across the Danube under arms.

146   Hadrian's rescript about Christians. AD 122–3.

Justin Martyr, *Apologia* 1.69 (this passage also quoted by Eusebius, *Ecclesiastical History* 4.9). Cf. Eusebius, *op. cit.* 4.26.1;. [Greek][1]

Henderson, *Hadrian* 224–6; W. Schmid in *Maia* 7 (1955) 5ff.; P. Keresztes in *Latomus* 26 (1967) 54ff. and in *Phoenix* 21 (1967) 119ff.; T. D. Barnes in *JRS* 58 (1968) 37 (*Early Christianity and the Roman Empire* (London 1984) II p. 37).

To Minucius Fundanus. I received a letter written to me[2] by Serennius Granianus, a most brilliant man, whom you have succeeded in office.[3] It seems to me that the matter should not remain uninvestigated, in order that people may not be agitated and that the material means for malicious activity may not be furnished to informers. If the provincials clearly can rely on their petition against the Christians so that they address it before your tribunal, let them turn to this (procedure) and not to demands or angry shouts alone. For it is far more fitting, if anyone wishes to make an accusation, for you to determine this point. Then, if anyone does make an accusation and shows that they are acting contrary to the laws, make your decision without more ado according to the severity of the offense. By the gods, If anyone brings up the matter for the sake of blackmail, make your decision fit such cruel action and see to it that you exact retribution.[4]

1 The Latin original is lost. Eusebius (*op. cit.* 4.8) says that Justin printed the Latin but that he (Eusebius) translated it into Greek, which he gives us. The text of Justin, as we have it, does not include the Latin, only the Greek of Eusebius' translation. The Latin undoubtedly was omitted by late copyists of Justin because they were copying for Greek readers. The Greek translation should not be expected to reach the professional height of earlier official translations. For an analysis of the Greek style and phraseology see R. Freudenberger, *Das Verhalten der römischen Behörden gegen die Christen im 2. Jahrhundert* (Munich 1967) pp. 216–34, where he shows the essentially Latin origin of the letter.
2 Both Justin and Eusebius name Hadrian as the writer. It is not strictly a letter, but a rescript in reply to a letter.
3 Quintus Licinius Silvanus Granianus (*PIR*[2] L 247) was suffect consul in AD 106 and proconsul of Asia under Hadrian immediately before Gaius Minucius Fundanus, who was proconsul in AD 122–3.
4 Thus, Hadrian's rescript, in reply to Granianus' request for advice, parallels the correspondence between Pliny and Trajan about the Christians and shows that Hadrian made no legal modification in the Roman government's official attitude toward them.

147 Hadrian travels to Asia Minor and Greece. 123.
Extract from the Arabic translation of Polemon's *Physiognomica.*[1]
[Arabic]

Polemon, *Physiognomica* (ed. G. Hoffmann in R. Förster, *Scriptores Physiognomici* I, pp. 138ff.); G. W. Bowersock, *Greek Sophists in the Roman Empire* (Oxford 1969) *Appendix II, p. 121. Cf. SHA, *Hadrian* 13.1.

A. von Premerstein in *Klio*, Beiheft 8 (1908) 47–57; Bowersock, *op. cit.* 120–3.

Once I accompanied the greatest king (= emperor), and while we were traveling with him from Buraqah (= Thraqiyah = Thrace) to Asia with | his troops and vehicles, that man[2] mingled with them. And we passed many cities until | we reached the sea. And he sailed to Yun (= Ionia) and al-S<i>rw(i)s (= Sardis) and Lydia and Phrygia and many places. Then | we returned [from] Asia on the [islands (?)] in the sea and he went east to Ruk(i)s (= Rhodes). Then he went on the ships || to [Athens].[3]

1 The transmission of the Arabic translation of the sophist Polemon's Greek original, which is lost, has resulted in numerous corruptions of the text. The late Professor George Hourani of the State University of New York at Buffalo and Dr Neil Linley both pored over the Arabic given by Förster and Bowersock and gave me their written translations and notes. I have combined them with the suggestions by Bowersock to produce the above text.
2 This 'man' appears to have been an impudent and hateful person mentioned in the

passages just before and after the present translated text, a man who insinuated his way into their company.

3 The places mentioned agree with those found in SHA, *Hadrian* 13.1: 'Afterwards he traveled through Asia and the islands to Greece and, following the example of Hercules and Philip, was received into the Eleusinian mysteries [cf. Dio 69.11] and conferred many benefits upon the Athenians.' For Hadrian's travels see Garzetti, *Tiberius to Antonines* 386–401, 684–6, and 764, and for Hadrian in Asia Minor see Magie, *RRAM* I 613ff. with notes.

148   Hadrian addresses his army in Africa. AD 128.

Base of a monumental column broken into fragments, Lambaesis. [Latin]

CIL VIII 2532 and 18042; ILS 2487 and 9133–5; Smallwood, **Documents Nerva* 328.

R. Cagnat, *L'Armée romaine d'Afrique* (Paris 1913) 146–51; Henderson, *Hadrian* 94–8; J. Gagé in *Bulletin de la Faculté des Lettres de Strasbourg* 30 (1951–2) 187–95 and 226; J. B. Campbell, *The Emperor and the Roman Army* (Oxford 1984) 77–80.

Imperator Caesar Traianus | Hadrianus Augustus | [[to his own Legion
5   Third Augusta,]] |[1] after an inspection of their exercises, spoke || these words which are written below, | when Torquatus for the second time and [Lib]o were consuls (AD 128), on the Kalends of July (July !).
  vv To the chief centurions *vv* | [--- and] in your defense [my legate] *has told* me everything *which should ex|cuse* you as far as I am concerned, [i.e. that] | a (legionary) cohort is absent because each year in turn (one of them) is sent to the service of the *procon|sul*, that two years ago a
5   cohort and four men *from each* || of your centuries were given by you to support your companions in the Third Legion (Augusta), | and that many scattered posts keep you apart. | And in my memory not only have you changed your camp twice but have also built new camps.[2] | Because of all this I would have excused you [if the legion] had given up its exercises for some time. | However, you did not give them up
10   [----] || an excuse for you [is not needed (?)]. (Another fragment seems to belong here:) [---|--] the chief centurions were agile | [and brave] as is their custom. *vacat*
5   *vv* To the legionary cavalry. *vv* || Military exercises, in a manner of speaking, have their own rules | and if anything is added to or subtracted from them, | the *exercise* becomes too insignificant or too difficult. The more difficulties | [that are added,] the less pleasing is the result. Of all difficult (exercises) the most *diffi|cult* [was the one you
10   performed,] throwing (the javelin) in full battle dress || [----,] on the contrary, I approve of your élan | [----] (unintelligible fragment here)
  (Another fragment) [----] the Kalends of July (July 1), the Second Cohort of Spaniards [was addressed (?) --]

(Another fragment) [----- fortifications, which] others | [over] several days distribute, you have completed in one day: a wall requiring *much* | work, and one that is usually made for permanent winter quarters, you constructed in not *mu|ch* longer a time than it takes to build one of turf.
5   Turf in regu‖lation size is cut and carried and handled easily, and without trouble | the construction is completed, since it is soft and level by its own nature. You (worked) with stones | that were big, heavy, and of unequal shape, which nobody could (easily) carry | or lift or place in position unless their unequal shapes fit together. | A ditch, rough and
10   coarse with gravel, ‖ you dug out in a straight line and then raked it smooth. After your work was appro|ved, you entered the camp quickly, took your rations and arms, | followed the cavalry that had been sent out, and shouting very loudly on your return through | [----]

(Another fragment) I commend [Catullinus, my legate, the most illustrious,][3] | because he directed you to this exercise, [which] | took on the appearance of a [real] battle and which has trained you in such a way that I can (also) *pra|ise* you. Your prefect Cornelianus (also) has performed [his duties] very well. However, the cavalry skirmish did not
5   please me [----] ‖ is the person responsible (?). A cavalryman should ride across from cover and [pursue with caution, for if he cannot] | see where he's going or if [he cannot restrain] his horse when he wishes, | it can happen that he will be exposed to hidden traps [---|---] you ought
10   to ride out together [---|---] against whatever the enemy has [----] ‖
[---] the Nones of July (July 2 (?) at Zarai,[4] the cohort [----|----]

(New fragment) [---] the Ides of July (July 8 (?), up to the 15th). The Ala of Pannonians. | You have done everything in good order. You have filled the plain with your maneuvers. | You have thrown the javelin with some gracefulness, although you [used] javelins that were sho|rt and
5   hard. Many of you threw your lances equally well. You mou‖nted your horses just now with agility, and yesterday with speed. If anything had been missing, I would have noticed it, (and) | if anything had stood out (as bad), I would have pointed it out. In the entire exercise you have plea|sed me uniformly. Catullinus, my most illustrious legate, in the activities (another fragment fits here) over which he is in command, displays his attention in equal measure, [and ----] your *pre|fect* seems to look after you carefully. Accept this largess | for a journey.[5] In the camp of the Commagenians you will be going through your paces.
5   The cavalrymen of the Cohort VI of Commagenians. ‖ It is difficult for cavalrymen of cohorts to give a pleasing (exhibition) by themselves, and more difficult, after | an exercise by an auxiliary ala, (for them) not to give a displeasing (exhibition): the dimensions of the area are different, the number of men throwing the javelin is different, | the right-wheeling is tight, the Cantabrian maneuver[6] is in closed ranks, | and

the beauty of their horses and the smartness of their equipment are in proportion to their (lower) scale of pay. However, | because of your zeal you kept us wide awake by doing enthusiastically what had to be done. 10 || In addition you hurled stones from slings and threw projectiles in your atta|ck. You mounted your horses everywhere with speed. My most illustrious legate, Catullinus, | [is a man of outstanding diligence,] (as) is clear from the fact that such men as you under him [----]

(Two other fragments give no consecutive sense.)

1 The Third Legion Augusta was disbanded in disgrace from AD 238 to 253 for its alleged responsibility in the deaths of Gordian I and Gordian II, but thereafter it continued its legionary garrison duties at Lambaesis.
2 The Third Augusta was stationed first at Ammaedara, then at Theveste, and finally at Lambaesis.
3 Quintus Fabius Catullinus (*PIR*² F 25) was consul ordinarius in AD 130. His post at this time is commander of the legion.
4 A city in Numidia. Numidia did not become a province until the reign of Septimius Severus. Under Hadrian it formed part of the province of Africa, although as a military territory it was actually controlled by the commander of the Legion Third Augusta.
5 On the practice of the emperors giving gifts of money to the soldiers in this fashion see Campbell, *op. cit.* 182–5.
6 For the maneuver see Arrian, *Tactics* 40.

149   Hadrian and Antinous. AD 130–8.

A: Aurelius Victor, *De Caesaribus* 14.6–9. **B**: A. Erman in *Abhandlungen der königlichen preussischen Akademie der Wissenschaften* 4 (1917) 10–46; P. Derchain in **Le Monde grec: Hommages à Claire Préaux* (Brussels 1978) 808–13. See E. Iversen, *Obelisks in Exile*, Vol. I *The Obelisks of Rome* (Copenhagen 1968) 161–4 (history). Hieroglyphic text on an obelisk erected in Rome, the text apparently composed in Rome by local scholars (Egyptians? Romans?), the engraving done in Rome by craftsmen unfamiliar with Egyptian. **C**: *IG* V 2.281; **SIG*³ 841; Smallwood, *Documents Nerva* 164. Inscription on an epistyle, Mantinea.

Cf. Dio 69.11.1–4; SHA, *Hadrian* 14.5–7; Pausanias 8.9.7–8. See R. Lambert, *Beloved and God* (London 1984). For the city of Antinoöpolis in Egypt see below, Document No. 160.

A. Aurelius Victor, *De Caesaribus* 14.6–9

Hadrian, as is the custom among the fortunate rich, erected palatial mansions, turned his attention to banquets, statues, paintings. Finally, he looked forward most carefully to everything connected with luxurious living and self-indulgence. (7) Hence arose the evil rumors that he had committed sexual perversions on adults, that he was aflame with passion for Antinous, his famous servant, and that for no other reason had a city been founded with his name or statues erected for the

young man. (8) Some indeed wish these things to be acts of devotion
and religious adoration: the reason for this is that Hadrian wanted to
prolong his life, and when magicians asked for a volunteer (to die) in
his place, the story goes that while everyone drew back, Antinous
offered himself. (This explains) the acts of (Hadrian's) obligation
toward him, mentioned above. (9) We remain neutral in the controversy, although estimating that in the case of a person of free and
easy nature the society of a wholly dissimilar age is suspicious.

B. Derchain in *Le Monde grec: Hommages à Claire Préaux*, 813. **Obelisk in Rome**

Antinous, deceased, the one who rests in this tomb in the country-
estate (?) of the Emperor of Rome.[1]

C. *SIG*³ 841. **Mantinea in Greece**

Gaius Iulius Eurykles Herc(u)lanus Lucius Vibullius Pius built this
stoa with │ the seats in it for the city of Mantinea and for our fellow-
countryman,[2] god Antinous. By his heirs.

1 For discussion of the various interpretations of the very difficult hieroglyphic text
   see Lambert, 155–60 and Derchain. The chief difficulty is caused by the composer's
   problem of translating Latin phrases into Egyptian. In a forthcoming monograph
   E. Grzybek re-examines the hieroglyphs and the linguistic problems, translating,
   'qui repose en ce lieu qui est en milieu du territoire du nome du maître de Rome' and
   interpreting this to mean that Antinous was buried in Antinoöpolis, not in Tibur.
   His monograph is entitled *L'Obélisque d'Antinoüs: Mémoire presenté à la Faculté des Lettres
   de l'Université de Genève en mars 1980*.
2 Pausanias (8.9.7) explains that Antinous was born in Bithynion and that the inhabitants there were Arcadians and Mantineans in origin.

150   Hadrian visits Palmyra in the Syrian desert. AD 131.
Inscription on a stone from the little temple, broken at top, right side
and bottom, Palmyra. [Greek and Aramaic]

IGRR III 1054; Smallwood, **Documents Nerva* 77; C. Dunant, *Le Sanctuaire de Ballshamin à
Palmyre* III: *Les Inscriptions* (Rome 1971) No. 44.

[The Boule and] the *People* │ (honor) Males also known as Agrippa, │
(son) of Iaraios, (grandson) of Rhaaios, secretary │ for the second time
5   ‖ during the visit of the god Hadri│anus, providing oil │ for guests and
10 citizens, │ in all matters being of service │ for the army's ‖ entertainment,
[and he ----] the temple │ of the god *with* its fro│nt hall [and with its]
other [roofed colonnades at] *his own expense* [----][1]

1 There is an Aramaic version of the Greek on the stone. It gives the date: year 442 of
   the Seleucid era, an era that began in 312 BC.

151   The Jewish revolt under Hadrian. AD 132–5.

A: Eusebius, *Ecclesiastical History* 4.6.1–4 (Ariston of Pella, *FGrHist* 201 F 1). Cf. Dio 69.12–14. **B**: P. Benoit, J. T. Milik and R. de Vaux, *Les Grottes de Murabba'at* II (Oxford 1961) No. 24, Col. E, p. 131 (+ photograph); Y. Yadin in **Israel Exploration Journal* 11 (1961) p. 51. Hebrew papyrus from Murabba'at on the western side of the Dead Sea. See Yadin, *Bar-Kokhba* 182 (+ photograph). **C**: B. Lifshitz in **Aegyptus* 42 (1962) 241; G. Howard and J. C. Shelton in *Israel Exploration Journal* 23 (1973) 101–2. Greek papyrus, slightly damaged, from the desert of Juda in Nahal Hever. Cf. Yadin, *Bar-Kokhba* 130ff. (+ photograph). **D**: Y. Yadin in *Israel Exploration Journal* 11 (1961) 44, No. 8. Aramaic papyrus from Nahal Hever. Cf. Yadin, *Bar-Kokhba* 128. **E**: **BMC, Palestine* p. 304, no. 14; Smallwood, *Documents Nerva* 80b. Bronze coin from Palestine. Cf. Yadin, *Bar-Kokhba* 24–5 (+ photographs).

Smallwood, *Jews* 428–66; Yadin, *Bar-Kokhba, passim*; L. Mildenberg in *HSCP* 84 (1980) 311–35; G. Alon, *The Jews in the Talmudic Age*, Vol. II (Jerusalem 1984) 592–637.

A. Eusebius, *Ecclesiastical History* 4.6.1–4

When the revolt of the Jews again progressed to great size and extent, Rufus the governor of Judaea,[1] with the military forces sent to him by the emperor, marched out to the attack against their madness without mercy, destroying tens of thousands of men, women, and children and in the law of warfare enslaving their lands. (2) At that time Bar-Chochebas was the leader of the Jews. His name means 'star', and in other respects he was a man murderous and given to a bandit life, but on the basis of his name, as if speaking to slaves, he spoke as if he had come to them from heaven as a celestial light, a miracle-worker to shed light upon the oppressed. (3) The war reached its zenith in the eighteenth year of the rule (of Hadrian) at Beththera (Bethar), a certain small town, most secure, not very far distant from Jerusalem. There was a long siege, the rebels driven by famine and thirst to their final destruction, the man responsible for their madness paying a worthy penalty. From that time the whole nation was prevented by order of law and by imperial command altogether from entering the land around Jerusalem, Hadrian ordering that not even from afar should it look upon its ancestral foundation. Ariston of Pella[2] gives its history. (4) When the city had thus come to be bereft of the Jewish nation and when the destruction of its old inhabitants had been complete, it was colonized by a foreign race and the Roman city that then was formed there changed its name and was called Aelia to honor the ruler Aelius Hadrianus.

B. Yadin in *Israel Exploration Journal* 11 (1961) 51, Murabba'at

On the 20th of Shevat, year two of the liberation | of Israel by Shim'on Ben Kosiba, Prince of Israel. | In the camp which is at Herodium,[3] Yehuda son of | Rabbah has said to Hillel son of Garis | (etc.)[4]

C. Lifshitz in *Aegyptus* 42 (1962) 241, Naḥal Ḥever

Sou[mai]os to Ionathes | son of Baianos, and to Ma|[s]abala,[5] greetings.
 5 | Since I have sent ‖ A[g]rippa to you, make | haste to send to me *stems*
(of palms) and citrons[6] | and they will be set up | for the Festival of the
10 Tabernacle of the ‖ Jews. Don't do | anything else. (This) was written |
15 in Greek because | [----][7] could not be fou|nd to write it ‖ in Hebrew. Let
him (i.e. Agrippa) | return quickly | because of the Festival. | Don't do
20 anything | else. ‖ *vv* Soumaios. | Farewell.

D. Yadin in *Israel Exploration Journal* 11 (1961) 44, No. 8, Naḥal Ḥever

Shim'on Bar Kosiba | to Yehonatan son of Ba'ayan, | and to Masabala
son of Shim'on, that you will send to me El'azar[8] ‖ son of Ḥitta immediately, before the Sabbath.

E. *BMC, Palestine*, p. 304, No. 14. Bronze coin

(Obverse: wreath around the edge, legend in center)	SHIM'ON, PRINCE OF ISRAEL
(Reverse: Greek amphora in center)	FIRST YEAR OF THE REDEMPTION OF ISRAEL

1 Q. Tineius Rufus (cos. 127) was consular legate of Judaea in the period of the
  Hadrianic revolt, perhaps surrendering the governorship in AD 134 to Sextus Iulius
  Severus.
2 Nothing else is known of Ariston.
3 Herodium was a fortress built by Herod the Great about seven miles south of
  Jerusalem. Rebel headquarters, however, was at En-gedi on the western edge of the
  Dead Sea.
4 The remainder concerns the leasing of land to various persons.
5 Ionathes (Yehonatan) and Masabala are known to have been highly placed officers
  under Bar-Kokhba, apparently the military commanders of En-gedi.
6 These are needed for the Festival.
7 The restoration here is uncertain, perhaps the name of a person who could have put
  the letter into Hebrew.
8 Eleazar is known to have been a wealthy landowner in En-gedi who did not
  co-operate very fully with Bar-Kokhba. The products of his orchards as well as his
  livestock would have been important to the rebel cause.

152 Edict of prefect of Egypt about circuit court. AD 133–7.
Papyrus from Egypt. [Greek]

P. Rylands 74; **FIRA* III 166.

U. Wilcken in *Archiv für Papyrusforschung* 6 (1920) 373–6.

[Mar]cus Petronius Mamertinus, [prefect] | of Egypt, declares: | I [had it in mind] to go up to the (towns) beyond Koptos [and] | to complete
5   the circuit court of the nomes[1] [---‖---][2] However, when I estimated that [there was not sufficient] time | *for* both things and since many of those things that require a circuit court already have received the necessary judicial inquiry | through the local (authorities), | I am now holding court in [the | Thebaid] and the Heptanomia[3] according to my [usual practice. | Year -- of Imperator Caes]ar Tr[aianus] Hadria[nus
10 Augustus ‖ ----].

1 One of the most important duties of every governor was to hold circuit court in the main cities of each district of his province: see the Glossary. For Egypt see Reinmuth, *prefect*, Ch. 10, and G. Foti Talamanca, *Ricerche sul processo nell' Egitto greco-romano* I: *L'organizzazione del 'conventus' del Praefectus Aegypti* (Rome 1974).
2 Wilcken: '*as* [I announced (previously)]'.
3 See below, Document No. 156 n. 1.

153 Colonists in the new city of Antinoöpolis. AD 135.
Papyrus, Egypt. [Greek]

Wilcken, *Chrestomathie* 26, I; Abbott–Johnson, *Municipal Administration* 170, I; *P. Würzburg* 9 (in *Abhandlungen der preussischen Akademie der Wissenschaften, Phil.-hist. Klasse* 1933, Heft 6); Smallwood, **Documents Nerva* 507b. Cf. below, Document No. 156.

Abbott–Johnson, *op. cit.* 518–19; H. Braunert in *Journal of Juristic Papyrology* 14 (1962) 73–88.

53 Petronius Mamertinus[1] to Horion, strategos of the Thinite Nome, greetings. | A copy of the letter written to me by Demetrios [----,] one
55 of those ‖ chosen by lot for the city of Anti[nou]s from the city of Ptolemais, | I have attached to this letter of mine, wishing you to see to it that the people the|re and the others who have been sent *to colonize* the city of Antinous | shall live without being insulted or molested in your nome. Year 19 of the god [Ha]drian, Pharmou|this 19.

1 Marcus Petronius Mamertinus was prefect of Egypt in the period AD 135–7. Stein, *Präfekten* 68–72.

154 Roman power in the Black Sea under Hadrian.

A: Constantine Porphyrogenitus, *De Themat.* 2.12 (Phlegon of Tralles, **FGrHist* 257 F 17). B: Arrian, *Periplus Ponti Euxini* 17.1–3 (Roos). C: *IGRR* I 877; **CIRB* 47. Stone base (now lost) Panticapaeum in the Crimea.

Cf. SHA, *Hadrian* 21.10; Dio 69.15.1. See B. Nadel in *Rivista Storica dell' Antichita* 12 (1982) 175–215.

A. Phlegon of Tralles *(FGrHist* 257 F 17)

In Book 15 of his *Olympiads* Phlegon is witness to the fact that the
Bosporos was ruled by King Kotys.[1] The emperor issued the order for
him to wear the diadem and he subjected the cities to him, among
which he also included Cherson itself.[2]

B. Arrian, *Periplus Ponti Euxini* 17.1–3

Altogether, from Trapezus to Dioskourias, now called Sebastopolis,
there are 2,260 stades.[3] (2) Such are the places one sails past on his
right from Byzantium to Dioskourias, at which fort Roman control
ends for one sailing into the Pontus (Euxinus) on his right. (3) When I
learned that Kotys, the king of the Cimmerian Bosporos, had died, I
took care to inform you (i.e. Hadrian) of my decision to sail up to the
Bosporos, so that, if you had any wishes concerning the Bosporos, you
could make plans with knowledge of my trip.

C. *CIRB* 47, Panticapaeum

[Imper]ator Caesar Traia[nus, son of the god, | Hadrian]us Augustus,
of the [---- | benefactor] and his own founder,[4] to him T[iberiu]s
Iu|[lius,] *King* Rhoimetalkes, friend of *Caesar* and || [friend to Romans,]
pious and grateful [for] | being *enrolled* among [the friends (of Rome),]
has dedicated (this statue) [under the care | of Iu]lius F[lav]ianus [---.
| Year] 430 and [the -- of the month] Apellaios.[5]

1 Phlegon of Tralles was a contemporary of Hadrian. The king is Kotys II.
2 'Cherson' is the Byzantine short form for 'Chersonesus'.
3 The Greek *stadion* was 600 feet.
4 King Rhoimetalkes calls Hadrian 'his own founder' because Hadrian had made him
   king of the Bosporos. In line 2 Nadel has restored 'of the [whole Bosporos | the
   benefactor]'.
5 The 'year 430' refers to the 430th year of the local era, equal to AD 133.

155   Roman order of battle against the Alani.[1] About AD 135.

*Arrian, *Expedition Against the Alani* 1–31 (ed. Roos-Wirth); *FGrHist* 156 F 12. [Greek]

E. Ritterling in *Wiener Studien* 24 (1902) 359–72; A. B. Bosworth in *HSCP* 81 (1977)
217–55; E. L. Wheeler in *Chiron* 9 (1979) 303–18.

A (Marching formation of the army in Cappadocia)[2]

At the head of the whole army shall be the mounted scouts, arranged
in two groups with their own commander. Next shall come the mounted
Petraean bowmen also in two groups, led by their decurions. Then
shall come in the formation the men from the Ala of the Aurianians.

And with them in formation shall be the men of Cohort IV of Raetians under the command of Daphne the Corinthian. Next shall come the men from the Ala of Colonists, and with them in formation shall be the Ituraeans, Cyrenaicans, and the men from Cohort I of Raetians. (2) Demetrius shall command all these troops. Next shall come the German horsemen, also in two groups, commanded by the centurion in charge of the camp.[3]

(3) The infantry shall be drawn up next in line, holding their standards out before them, the Italians and a detached unit of the Cyrenaicans. Pulcher shall command them all, the commander of the Italians. The Bosporan infantry shall follow, with their commander Lamprokles, and then the Numidians under their commander Verus. (4) The formation shall be four heavy-armed infantrymen abreast, led by their bowmen. Their own cavalry shall guard the flanks on each side of the formation. Next shall march the mounted guards (of the commander of the legion), and next the legionary cavalry followed by the catapults. (5) Then shall come the standard of the Legion fifteenth (Apollinaris) with Valens, legionary commander,[4] and his second in command, followed by the tribunes of the soldiers who have been posted to this expedition, and then the <five> centurions commanding the first cohort (of the legion).[5] In front of the infantry standard (of the front-line troops) shall be drawn up the javelin-men. The infantry-men shall march four abreast. (6) After the Legion Fifteenth (Apollinaris) the standard of the Legion Twelfth (Fulminata) shall be formed up, its tribunes and centurions around it. This phalanx[6] formation likewise shall march four abreast.

(7) After the heavy infantry the provincial militia shall follow, heavy infantrymen from Armenia Minor and Trapezus, and spearmen from Colchis and Rhizion.[7] Following them in line shall be the infantrymen of the [Apulans].[8] The commander of all the provincial militia shall be Secundinus, commander of the [Apulans]. Then shall follow the baggage-train. (8) The rearguard shall be led by the Ala of the Dacians and its prefect. (9) Centurions shall keep the infantry flanks in line and shall be posted for this purpose. For security the Ala of the Gauls shall ride alongside each flank in one column, and also the cavalrymen of the Italians, whose prefect shall make the rounds of the flanks.

(10) The commander of the whole army shall be Xenophon (i.e. Arrian himself, governor of Cappadocia),[9] generally at the head of the infantry standards, and he shall make the rounds of the whole formation. He shall also see to it that they march in formation, restoring the disorderly soldiers to their ranks and praising the orderly. (11) Such shall be the order of march.

B (Battle formation)

When the army reaches the designated area (of combat), the entire cavalry force shall wheel round in a circular maneuver to a square formation and the scouts shall be sent out to high ground to reconnoitre the enemy. Then preparation for battle shall begin by silent signals from the standards, and, once prepared, position shall be maintained in the formations. The battle formation shall be as follows. (12) Each wing of the (auxiliary) infantry shall hold the high ground, because that will be their deployment in such terrain. The Armenians under Vasakes and Arbelos shall be deployed on the right wing, holding the highest ground of that wing, because all of them are bowmen. (13) In front of them shall be positioned the infantrymen of the cohort of the Italians. Pulcher shall be in charge of all, he who is commander of the cohort of the Italians. Vasakes and Arbelos with their cavalry and infantry shall support him. (14) On the left, holding the highest ground of that wing, shall be positioned the provincial militia from Armenia Minor, the light-armed troops from Trapezus, and the Rhizionian spearmen. In front of them shall be drawn up the 200 [Apulans] and 100 of the Cyrenaicans, their heavy-armed men to be a guard for the javelin-men and to shoot over their heads from the high ground. (15) The Fifteenth infantry phalanx shall hold the entire central area on the right beyond the middle of the whole terrain, because these troops are far greater in number, while the rest of the left side shall be filled out by the infantry of the Twelfth phalanx up to the extreme limit of the left wing.[10] The (two legionary phalanxes) shall be formed eight ranks deep, tight together. (16) The first four ranks shall be of lancers, whose lances will end in long, thin iron tips. The men in the first rank shall hold theirs on the ready, so that if the enemy comes upon them, they can jab the iron of the lances into the breasts, especially, of the horses. (17) The men <of the second rank shall strike their lances against the horsemen themselves>[11] while the posterior ranks of the third and fourth shall hold their lances forward for jabbing, when they get the chance, to wound horses and to kill horsemen. When the lance has been stuck into the shield body armor, because of the softness of the iron it will bend (on impact) and render the rider ineffective. (18) The next ranks (fifth to eighth) shall be of spearmen. Behind them shall be the ninth rank, the infantry bowmen: Numidians, Cyrenaicans, Bosporans, and Ituraeans. (19) The artillery shall be placed on each wing, to discharge their missiles as far away as possible from the advancing enemy, and behind the whole phalanx.

(20) The entire cavalry corps organized by alae and companies, eight of them, shall stand by the infantry on each of the wings, having the

infantry and bowmen as a protective screen in front of them, two companies of them, while in the middle of the phalanx six companies [---]. (21) Whatever of these forces are mounted bowmen shall take their stand near the phalanx, so that they can shoot over it. Spearmen, lancers, knifemen, and battleaxe-men shall keep watch over the flanks from each side and await the signal. (22) The mounted guards (of the legionary commander) shall be around Xenophon (Arrian) himself, including up to 200 of the phalanx infantry – special bodyguards – and the centurions attached to the mounted guards or the commanders of the special bodyguards, and the cavalry officers of the mounted guards. (23) They shall be around him [----] 100 light-armed spearmen, as he makes his rounds of the whole phalanx wherever he may learn of some fault, there he shall go and correct it. (24) Valens, commander of the Fifteenth phalanx (Legion) shall be the commander of the whole right wing along with the cavalry. The tribunes of the Twelfth (Legion) shall command the left.

(25) Thus organized, silence shall be the rule until the enemy comes within range. All shall then advance as loudly and as fiercely as possible shouting the war-cry and discharging their missiles and rocks from the artillery and arrows from bows. Spearmen shall hurl their spears, both light-armed troops and those with shields. Stones shall be thrown down upon the enemy by the provincial militia from the heights, and there shall be a general discharge of weapons at one time from every direction as closely together as possible to cause confusion among the horses and to destroy the enemy. And because of the indescribable mass of the missiles there is a chance that the advancing Scythians (Alani) will (26) not get very close to our infantry phalanx. But if they do, then the first three ranks shall bring their shields closely together, stand firm shoulder to shoulder to receive the attack with all possible resistance in the most tightly closed formation possible, locked together as strongly as possible. The fourth rank <shall hold their lances up, so that they may slay any enemy horsemen, but not extend them straight up so as to make the spearmen> overshoot (the enemy with their) spears,[12] while the first rank shall strike or hurl with their lances unsparingly against horses and enemy. (27) Once the enemy has been thrust back, if there develops a clear rout, the infantry formations shall open up and the cavalry shall advance, not all the companies but only half of them. The first of this formation shall be composed of those who advance first. (28) The other halves shall follow those who advance, but in orderly lines and not pursuing all the way, so that if the rout becomes a full one, the first pursuit can be relieved by fresh horses, and if there is a sudden turning-about of the enemy, they can be attacked as they turn. (29) At the same time the Armenian bowmen

shall advance and shoot, so as not to allow the fleeing enemy to turn back, and the light-armed spearmen shall follow on the run. The infantry formation shall not remain in the area but shall advance more swiftly than a walk, so that if there is any stiffening of resistance on the part of the enemy, it may again be a protective shield in front of the cavalry.[13]

(30) That is what will happen if a rout of the enemy occurs at the first attack, but if they should wheel around and wish to go around our wings, the wings of our light-armed archery forces shall extend their position onto the higher ground. I do not believe that the enemy, having seen our wings weakened by this extension, would push through them and cut through the infantry. (31) But if they should overwhelm one wing or both of them, it is inevitable that their cavalry will be at right angles to us, and their lances at right angles. Then our cavalry shall attack them, not by shooting at them, but with swords and battle-axes. The Scythians (Alani) are [nowhere] unprotected with armor, as also their horses, [except for their thighs and bellies ----].[14]

---

1 The Alani were a nomadic people of the Russian steppes who in this period lived to the north of the Caucasus. From Dio (69.15.1) we learn that soon after the Hadrianic war with the Jews the Alani were incited to war by Pharasmenes, king of the Iberians. Pharasmenes permitted the Alani to cross the Caucasus Mountains through the Darial Pass and they then devastated the countries of Albania and Media Atropatene to the south. They were deflected away from Cappadocia by the army of that province under the command of its governor, Lucius Flavius Arrianus (*PIR*[2] F 219). On Arrian see Halfmann, *Senatoren* 56, and the Introduction to A. B. Bosworth, *A Historical Commentary on Arrian's History of Alexander* (Oxford 1980).

2 For other accounts of the Roman army on the march see Josephus, *Bell. Jud.* 3.6.115 and 5.47–50.

3 With the exception of the mounted scouts, who formed a separate unit called a *numerus exploratorum*, the military troops mentioned thus far were part of the *auxilia* under the command of the governor of Cappadocia. All of them were mounted. The cohorts mentioned must have been *equitatae*, i.e. infantry units which included units of cavalry. All the *auxilia* of Arrian's treatise have been identified with units known from other sources to have been part of Cappadocia's army: see Ritterling, *loc. cit.* for the details.

4 Headquarters of the Fifteenth Legion were at Satala in Armenia Minor, where the whole operation seems to have been co-ordinated. For the career of Marcus Vettius Valens see Birley, *Fasti* 215.

5 The first centurion of the first cohort was the senior centurion of the whole legion and was called the *primipilus* or *primipilaris*. He served on the legionary staff.

6 Since Arrian writes in Greek and was a devout student of Greek military tactics from the time of the great Alexander's campaigns, he frequently calls the Roman legion a 'phalanx'.

7 These 'provincial militia', called by Arrian in Greek the 'allied force', are not an official part of the Roman army.

8 The manuscript here has 'Aplanoi', people who cannot be identified. Since, how-

ever, a 'Cohort Apula' is known from other sources, the manuscript has been emended. See Bosworth, *op. cit.* 232–3.

9 Xenophon was a famous Greek soldier and author in the late fifth century BC who, in his *Anabasis*, described a famous feat in Greek military history. Arrian thought of himself as Xenophon, but cf. P. A. Stadter, *Arrian of Nicomedia* (Chapel Hill, NC 1980) p. 2.

10 This makes it clear that the Fifteenth Legion is present in full strength, while the Twelfth has sent only detached units, its commander and the rest of his troops remaining back in its headquarters at Melitene.

11 There seems to be a lacuna in the accepted text. The suggestion of Bosworth (*op. cit.* 238–9, n. 92) is followed.

12 For the lacuna and the interpretation see Bosworth (*op. cit.* 240).

13 Note that the infantry plays the dominant role, with the cavalry placed to the rear. Arrian, thus, does not use his forces in the classic patterns established by Julius Caesar at the close of the Republic. See the comments of Wheeler, *loc. cit.* Arrian does not go on the offensive in the opening phase of his tactics. He is content to deflect the massed horsemen of the enemy.

14 Bosworth (*op. cit.* 235–6) suggests that Arrian's troops were instructed to aim at the unprotected thighs and bellies of the horses. Here the text breaks off. The actual battle was described in the lost section.

156   Hadrian grants a moratorium on taxes in Egypt. AD 136.

Three papyrus copies of the same edict, Egypt. [Greek]

P. Cairo 49359 + 49360 (P. Jouguet in *RÉG* 33 (1920) 376–80) and *P. Oslo* 78; *SB* 6944; *FIRA* I 81; Smallwood, **Documents Nerva* 462. Cf. Pliny, *Nat. Hist.* 5.58.

Jouguet, *op. cit.* 375–402.

Imperator Caesar, son of the god Traianus Parthicus, the god Nerva's | grandson, Traianus Hadrianus Augustus, pontifex maximus, | holding the tribunician power for the twentieth time (AD 136), imperator
5 for the second time, | father of his country, declares: ‖ Whereas I have learned that at the present time the Nile has risen quite inadequately – as also last year – | and not fully, even though in former years in succession not only a full but also | somewhat more than ever it produced a ri|se and, having covered over the [whole] land, was itself the cause of the gre|atest and most beautiful of harvests, nevertheless I thought it
10 was nec‖essary to make some beneficent concession to the farmers, | although I anticipate – let it be said with the god's wish – that in the coming years, even if | now it has failed, the Nile itself and the earth will fill out the deficiency | [--- in accordance with (?)] the nature of things that from | abundance and fertility there is a change to famine, and
15 from ‖ poverty to prosperity, – with Good Luck, know that the tax for th|is year in money will be deferred | for those in the Thebaid, who have probably been harmed the most from the scar|city, for payment in five

annual installments, for those in the | Seven Nomes in four (annual
20 installments), and for those in Lower Egypt || three (annual install-
ments).[1] Those who so wish may use semi-annual pay|ments, the fixed
due-date remaining in effect: for those in the Thebaid five years, those
in the [Seven Nomes] four years, and those in Lower Egypt | three
years.[2] *Published* at Alexandria in the twenty-first year (AD 137), Pauni
16.

1 Roman Egypt was divided into three major administrative districts: the Seven
   Nomes (Heptanomia) with the Arsinoïte Nome, the Thebaid, and Lower Egypt (the
   Delta region) with an official called the epistrategos at the head of each. Cf. above,
   Document No. 80, n. 8, and No. 152, line 8.
2 *P. Cairo* at this point inserts: 'I [Ma]r[cus Pe]t[ronius] [M]amerti[nus,] prefect of
   Egypt, have written | (this) *copy* of the edict of our greatest *emperor* in order that it may
   be known to everybody.'

157   New road from Berenike to Antinoöpolis. AD 137.
Stone base, Antinoöpolis in Egypt [Greek]

OGIS 701; *IGRR* I 1142; Smallwood, *Documents Nerva* 423; A. Bernand, **Pan du désert*
(Leiden 1977) No. 80.

J. Lesquier, *L'Armée romaine d'Égypte d'Auguste à Dioclétien* (Cairo 1918) 436–7; G. W.
Murray in *JEA* 11 (1925) 149–50 (with good map); M. G. Raschke in *ANRW* 2.9.2.648–
50; Bernand, *op. cit.* 216–32.

Imperator Caesar, son of god | [Traian]us Parthicus, | grandson of god
5 Nerva, Traianus | Hadrianus Augustus, pontifex || maximus, holding
the tribunician power | for the twenty-first time (AD 137), imperator
for the second time, | consul for the third time, father of his country, |
opened up the new Hadrianic Road from | Berenike to Antinoöpolis
10 through || safe and level countryside | by the Red Sea. | With wells that
are always full and | with resting places and with garrisons | he provided
15 it from place to place. || Year 21, Pharmenoth 1.

158   The tax law of Palmyra. AD 137.
Inscription on stone in both Greek and a dialect of Aramaic, Palmyra
in the Syrian desert. At the top is the titulature of Hadrian and a dating
by the consuls for AD 137, while below it, arranged in four groups are,
from left to right, (1) the decree of the Boule (Council) of Palmyra in
Palmyrene Aramaic and in Greek; (2) three columns of Palmyrene text;
(3) three columns of the Greek version; (4) two final columns of the
Greek.

OGIS 629; J.-B. Chabot in *Corpus Inscriptionum Semiticarum* II 3, No. 3913 (+ photographs); Smallwood, **Documents Nerva* 458.

J. F. Matthews in *JRS* 74 (1984) 157–80; M. Zahrnt in *ZPE* (1986) 279–93.

(The decree)[1] Year 448, (day) 18 of the (Seleucid) month Xandikos,[2] decree of the Boule. | When the presiding officer (of the Boule) was Bonnes son of Hairanos, when Alexandros son of Alexandros son | of Philopater was secretary of the Boule and the People, and when Malichos son of Olaies and Zebeidas son of Nesa were the ar|chons, at a regular meeting of the Boule it was decreed as follows: Since [in the]
5   past ‖ most of the dues were not included in the tax law but were only exacted by custom | – because it had been written into the contract that the person collecting the tax should do so according to the law and | the custom – and (since) it frequently happened in this matter that quarrels arose between the merchants | and the tax collectors, it has been decreed that the archons in office and the dekaprotoi[3] should decide | upon the dues that had not been included in the law and should write them into the next contract and should apply to each kind of goods the
10   ‖ customary tax; and that, after this has been approved by the contractor, they should be written down, along with the original | law, on the stone stele which is opposite the temple called Rabaseire; and that care should be taken by the | archons and dekaprotoi and syndikoi[4] who happen to be in office that the contractor does not exact any additional amount. (The Palmyrene Aramaic version is given next, and then in both Greek and Palmyrene:)

A wagon-load of any kind: the tax (on this) was exacted (at the rate) of four camel-loads.

(The new tariff law appears next, beginning with a heading that is extant in the Palmyrene only. The heading is followed by the listing of the separate items and the dues for each. A selection only is given here, translated from the Greek which can be restored by reference to the Palmyrene.)

The Tax Law of the Customs District of Hadriana Palmyra and of the Wells of Aelius Caesar:

From *those who bring* [slaves into Palmyra] or into the [borders of Palmyra (the tax collector) will exact 22 denarii for each.] [A donkey-load of] *myrrh* in [alabaster vessels:] import tax will be [13 denarii, export tax 7 denarii.] A donkey-load of *myrrh in* goat-*skins*: import *tax will be* [7 denarii,] export tax 4 denarii. A load of olive-oil in *4 goat-skins*: imported on a camel, [13 denarii;] exported, [13 denarii.][5]

(The old tariff law is also extant)

1 Only fragments of the preceding heading are extant, but sufficient for the date.
2 The Seleucid era began in 312 BC, on October 1.
3 The dekaprotoi were members of a board of local officials in charge of local taxes and finances.
4 The syndikoi were legal representatives of a city to aid it and its citizens in relations with the central government.
5 Other items in the list include purple-dyed fleece, animal fat, dried fish, and other dried products.

159   The horoscope of Pedanius Fuscus (April 6, AD 113).

Catalogus Codicum Astrologorum Graecorum, Vol. VIII, part 2, ed. C. E. Ruelle (Brussels 1911) pp. 85–6; *Hephaestion of Thebes, *Apotelesmatica*, Vol. II, ed. D. Pingree, Epitoma 4.26.52–5 (Pingree p. 236). Cf. SHA, *Hadrian* 23.1–9; Dio 69.17.1–3.

F. H. Cramer, *Astrology in Roman Law and Politics* (Philadelphia 1954) 165ff., 175ff., 268; O. Neugebauer and H. B. van Hoesen, *Greek Horoscopes* (Philadelphia 1959) 108–9 (No. L113, IV); T. D. Barnes in *Phoenix* 30 (1976) 76; E. Champlin in *ZPE* 21 (1976) 79–89.

(Antigonus)[1] says concerning (this person's) birth that he was born to his own destruction and to that of his parents about his twenty-fifth year. The theme of his nativity was the following: the Sun and the Horoskopos[2] were in (the sign of) Aries, the Moon in Taurus three days after making its appearance at the evening rising, Mercury and Saturn in Aries at the morning setting, Jupiter in Pisces at morning rising, and the Lot of Fortune[3] was falling into Taurus. In this situation, he says, the star of Mars will predominate at such a nativity. After the seventh day the Moon will be in <Leo>, after the fortieth in Libra. (= April 6, AD 113)[4]

   This person came of an illustrious family of the highest level – I speak of his father and mother, both of high repute and both meeting violent deaths. Having been born with great expectations and thinking he was coming into the imperial power, he was given bad advice and fell from favor about his twenty-fifth year. He was denounced to the emperor and was destroyed along with a certain old man of his own family, who was himself slandered because of him. In addition, all members of his family because of him were done away with in a lowly manner.[5]

1 This Antigonos was an astrologer who made a collection of horoscopes in the late second or early third century AD. Three of them are preserved by Hephaestion of Thebes.
2 The Horoskopos was the sign or degree rising at the time of birth.
3 The 'Lot of Fortune' is an area in certain degrees of the zodiac.
4 Neugebauer and van Hoesen, using the astronomical data given in this section, have calculated the exact date of the nativity.

5 The young man is certainly the (Pedanius) Fuscus mentioned by Dio (69.17.1–3) and the writer of SHA, *Hadrian* (23.1–9). However, the fact that his horoscope includes the information that he was twenty-five and not eighteen (so Dio) years old at his death changes the traditional view of modern scholars about the events leading up to Hadrian's selection of his successor. See Champlin, *loc. cit.*

PART II
SOCIETY IN THE ROMAN WORLD

---

160 Rescript of Hadrian on social status in legal penalties.

Callistratus in the *Digest* 47.21.2.

P. Garnsey, *Social Status and Legal Privilege in the Roman Empire* (Oxford 1970) Ch. 5.

The deified Hadrian issued the following rescript: It cannot be doubted that most mischievous is the action of those who have moved boundary markers, which have been positioned for the sake of indicating borders. Nevertheless, concerning the penalty a limit can be instituted based on the status of the individual and the motive for his action: for if they are individuals of the higher (social) order who are convicted, without a doubt they did it for the sake of occupying someone else's land, and they can be banished[1] for a length of time, as the age of each one permits, i.e. a younger man for a longer time, an older man for a reduced period. However, if other men[2] did the deed and performed it as a service, they ought to be punished and given over to hard labor for two years. If they stole the stone markers out of ignorance or by chance, it will be sufficient to decide the matter by a beating.

1 The word (*religari*) signifies a form of exile but with less severe restrictions than *exilium* proper.
2 Garnsey shows that 'individuals of the higher (social) order' are the *honestiores* ('higher classes') and 'other men' are the *humiliores* ('lower classes') of a later age. The distinction antedated Hadrian, beginning to harden in the first century, leading eventually to this double standard.

161   A Roman jurist on medicines and abortifacients.

A: Paulus, *Sententiae* 5.23.19. On the Cornelian Law on murderers and poisoners.
B: Paulus, *Sententiae* 5.23.14.

A. Paulus, *Sententiae* 5.23.19

If a person dies because of the medicine which was given for the health of a person or, if you like, for a remedy, then he who gave it, if he belongs to the upper social ranks, is banished to an island, but if (he belongs) to the lower social ranks, he is punished with death.[1]

B. Paulus, *Sententiae* 5.23.14

Those who give a drink to induce an abortion or sexual passion, even though they do not do so to deceive, nevertheless, because it is an act of bad example, people of the lower social ranks are banished to a mine, those of the higher social ranks to an island, after being deprived of part of their property. But if, as a consequence, a woman or a man should die, such persons are punished with the supreme penalty.[2]

1 See Karl-Heinz Below, *Der Artzt im römischen Recht* (Munich 1953) 126.
2 See S. K. Dickison in *Arethusa* 6 (1973) 159–66, a review of E. Nardi, *Procurato aborto nel mondo greco romano* (Milan 1971).

162   Greek prejudice against the Roman West.

Aulus Gellius 19.9.7.

Then a number of Greeks who were at the dinner party, men of charm and quite well acquainted with our (Latin) literature, began to harass and attack the rhetorician Iulianus[1] on the grounds that he was absolutely barbarous and backward, a fellow who came from Spain, was a big loud-mouth with a wild and quarrelsome manner of speaking, and taught exercises in that language (i.e. Latin) which had no charm and none of the soothing qualities of Venus and the Muse. Several times they asked him what he thought of Anacreon and other (Greek) poets of that sort and whether any of our (Latin) poets had created such flowing and delightful poems. 'Exceptions made', they said, 'of a few poems by Catullus and a few by Calvus. For those created by Laevius are involved, those by Hortensius without charm, those by Cinna without refinement, those by Memmius dull, and those by all the others crude and in bad taste.'

1 In the preceding passage Aulus Gellius explains that Antonius Iulianus spoke Latin with a Spanish accent and that he had introduced a number of musicians and singers who presented a variety of pieces from Anacreon and Sappho.

163   Roman citizenship, open to all in the empire.

Aelius Aristeides, *To Rome* 59–60 (Oliver, based on Keil).

J. H. Oliver, The Ruling Power (*Transactions of the American Philosophical Society* 43.4) (Philadelphia 1953) 871–1003.

Far more worthy of examination and wonder than all else is your citizenship and the magnificence of its concept, for there is nothing like it anywhere. Having divided into two groups all peoples in your empire – having used this word, I mean to say the whole inhabited world – you have defined the more accomplished, the more high-minded, and the more powerful civic body, or (one might say) everything that is of the same breed as yourself, while the rest (of the empire) is a mere subject under your rule. (60) The sea is not a hindrance to becoming a citizen, nor is the mass of the intervening land, nor is any distinction made here between Asia and Europe. Everything lies within reach of everyone. Nobody is a stranger who is worthy of magistracy or trust,[1] but a free republic,[2] in which the whole world shares, has been established under one excellent ruler and director, and everyone meets as if in a common assembly, each to receive his just reward.

1 Oliver (*op. cit.* 927) takes 'magistracy or trust' to mean that non-Italians are being admitted to equestrian and senatorial careers.
2 The word here is literally 'democracy', but in this age it means a government in which the civil rights of citizens are protected.

164   The rise of provincials in service to Rome.

A: Plutarch, *Moralia* 470C (*De Tranquillitate Animi* 10). **B**: West, **Corinth* No. 68 (+ photograph); Smallwood, *Documents Gaius* 264. Limestone base, Corinth. [Latin] See West, *op. cit.* pp. 50–3; K. M. T. Chrimes, *Ancient Sparta* (Manchester 1949) 183–7; G. W. Bowersock in *JRS* 51 (1961) 117–18. **C**: *IGRR* III 174; **OGIS* 543; *ILS* 8826; Smallwood, *Documents Nerva* 216; Bosch, *Quellen* 156. Cf. Dio 69.14.4. Stone block from the city wall of Ancyra in Galatia. [Greek] See Magie, *RRAM* I 626 with n. 54; Bosch, *Quellen* 199–203. **D**: *CIL* II 4212; McCrum–Woodhead, *Documents* 344; Alföldy, **Tarraco* No. 272 (+ photograph). Statue base of limestone. Reign of Domitian. **E**: **ILS* 9485; McCrum–Woodhead, *Documents* 315. Stone found in Antioch toward Pisidia. [Latin] See Halfmann, *Senatoren* No. 13; Levick, *Colonies* 62–3 and 112ff. **F**: *CIL* III 384; **ILS* 1018; Smallwood, *Documents Nerva* 235. Statue base, Alexandria Troas. [Latin] See M. N. Tod in *Anatolian Studies Presented to William Hepburn Buckler*, edited by W.M. Calder and J. Keil (Manchester 1939) 333–44, and Halfmann, *Senatoren* No. 40. **G**: *CIL* XVI 4; *ILS* 1987; Smallwood, **Documents Gaius* 296. Bronze tablet, first part of a diptych, Vindobona. [Latin] July 2, AD 61 (?).

See also, in the present collection, Nos. 44 and 97.

Cf. Suetonius, *Augustus* 35 and *Vespasian* 9.2; Dio 52.19; Tacitus, *Histories* 2.82.

See A. Stein, *Der Römische Ritterstand* (Munich 1927) Chs. 3–4; R. Syme, *Tacitus* 2.504–19 and 783–95; *idem* in *Proceedings of the Massachusetts Historical Society* 72 (1957–63) 3–20 (*Roman Papers* II 566–81); G. W. Bowersock in *Tituli 5: Epigrafia e ordine senatorio II (Rome 1982) 651–8; Halfmann, Senatoren* pp. 9–98; G. Alföldy in *Chiron* 11 (1981) 169ff.

A. Plutarch, *Moralia* 470C

One man is from Chios, another from Galatia, still another from Bithynia, none of them pleased with the share of reputation or power among his citizens that has fallen to his lot. Each one complains that he does not wear patrician shoes; and if he does wear them, he complains that he is not a Roman praetor; and if he is a praetor, he complains that he is not a consul; and when he is a consul, he complains that he was not announced first (in the elections) but last.

B. West, *Corinth* No. 68, Corinth

Gaius Iulius, son of Laco, | grandson of Eurycles, (of the tribe) Fabia, Spartiaticus,[1] | procurator of Caesar and Augusta | Agrippina, tribune
5   of the soldiers, ‖ awarded a public horse[2] by the deified Claudius, priest | of the deified Iulius, pontifex, duovir quinquennalis twice, agonothete of the Isthmian and Caesar|-Augustan Games, high priest
10   of the House of Augustus | in perpetuity, first of the Achaians. ‖ Because of his excellence and spirited | and all-encompassing munificence toward the | divine House and toward our colony, the tribesmen | of the
15   tribe Calpurnia ‖ (dedicate this monument) to their patron.

C. *OGIS* 543, Ancyra

5   Gaius Iulius Severus, | of kings and | tetrarchs | a descendant.[3] ‖ After holding all the | offices of distinction among his people, | he was admitted | to the rank of tribune (of the plebs) by the god | Hadrianus.
10   After serving as a lega‖te (of the governor) in Asia by a letter and | codicil of the god Hadrianus,[4] | he was commander of the Legion Fourth
15   Scy|thica and administrator of | affairs in Syria when Publi‖cius Marcellus, because of the revo|lt in Judaea, left | Syria.[5] He was proconsul of Achai|a with five fasces and sent | to Bithynia as corrector
20   ‖ and inspector of accounts[6] by the god Hadria|nus, prefect of the Treasury of | Saturn, consul (about 139), pontifex, | superintendant of
25   Public | Works in Rome, pro ‖ praetorian legate of Imperator | Caesar Titus Aelius | Hadrianus Antoninus Au|gustus Pius of Germani|a
30   Inferior. Marcus Iulius ‖ Euschemon (here honors) his own | benefactor.

D. Alföldy, *Tarraco* No. 272, Tarraco in Spain

Gaius Egnatuleius, | son of Gaius, (of the tribe) Galeria, | Seneca of
5   Tarraco, | aedile, quaestor, duovir, priest ‖ of the deified Titus; the

public horse being given to him,[7] | prefect of Mounted Cohort Four of
Thracians, | priest of the province of Hispania Citerior. | Egnatuleia
10   Sige ‖ (erected this monument) to her patron most indulgent. |

E. *ILS* 9485, Antioch toward Pisidia

Gaius Carista|nius, son of Gaius, F[ron]|to, tribune of the soldiers,
prefect of cavalry of the Ala of Bosporani, | admitted into the (Roman)
5   senate with rank of ‖ tribune (of the plebs), promoted to rank | of
praetor, legate with pro | praetorian power of the province of Pontus-
Bithynia, legate of Imperator | deified Vespasianus Augustus of Legion
10 | Ninth Hispana in Britain, ‖ legate with pro praetorian power of
Imperator deified Titus | Caesar Augustus and Imperator Domitianus
| Caesar Augustus of the province of Pam|phylia-Lycia, patro|n of his
15   colony.[8] ‖ Titus Caristanius Cal|purnianus Rufus | (erected this monu-
ment) | because of his merits, for the sake of honor.

F. *ILS* 1018, Alexandria Troas

Sextus Quinctilius, | son of Sextus, (of the tribe) Aniensis, Valerius |
Maximus, adorned with the broad purple stripe[9] by the deified
5   Augustus | Nerva, quaestor of Pontus‖-Bithynia, patron | of his colony,
pontifex, duo|vir, prefect of fabri,[10] | honored with duoviral and priestly
ornaments by decree of the decurions. | (This monument was erected
by) the Tenth District.[11]

G: Smallwood, *Documents Gaius* 296, Vindobona

Nero Claudius, son of the deified Claudius, – grandson of Germanicus
Caesar, | great-grandson of Tiberius Caesar Augustus, great-great-
grandson of the deified Augustus, – Caesar | Augustus Germanicus,
pontifex maximus, holding the tribunician power for the 7th time (AD
60–1), imperator for the 7th time, | consul for the 4th time: to the infan-
5   trymen and cavalrymen who served in ‖ the 7 cohorts called (Cohort)
One of Astures and Cal|laecians, (Cohort) One of Hispani, (Cohort)
One of Alpines, (Cohort) One of Lusi|tanians, (Cohort) Two of
Alpines, (Cohort) Two of Hispani, (Cohort) Five of Lucenses | and
Callaecians, which are in Illyricum under the command of Lucius
Sal|vidienus Salvianus Rufus, and are men who have each served
10   twenty-five ‖ years or more, whose names | are written below, to them,
to their children and their descendants | he has given (Roman) citizen-
ship and legal marriage with | the wives which they had at the time
when | (Roman) citizenship was given to them, or, if any were
15   unmarried, ‖ with those women whom afterwards they married, pro-
vided only | one to each.
    On the 6th day before the Nones of July (July 2), when Gnaeus

Pe|danius Salinator and Lucius Velleius Paterculus | were consuls (AD 61?).

    From Cohort Two of Hispani, commanded by Gaius Caesius | Aper:
20 the cavalryman Iantumatus, son of Andedunes, || Varcianus. Copied and certified from the tablet | of bronze which is attached on the Capitolium to the left side | of the Building of Treasures, on the outside.

1 Cf. Pflaum, *Carrières* No. 24 *bis*, and *PIR*² I 587.
2 I.e. 'awarded equestrian rank'.
3 The tetrarchs were the old tribal leaders of the Galatians before Galatia became a Roman province. His career: *PIR*² 573 and Halfmann, *Senatoren* No. 62.
4 Ordinarily the governor of a province chose his own legates to accompany him to assist in various posts in the province. For the emperor to do so was a mark of honor for the recipient.
5 C. Publicius Marcellus, governor of Syria, brought a legion with him to Judaea from Syria in AD 132 or 133.
6 This is the office of *corrector* or *curator reipublicae*: see G. P. Burton in *Chiron* 9 (1979) 465–87, and above, No. 126.
7 See n. 2.
8 I.e. Antioch toward Pisidia. For the career of Caristanius Fronto see *PIR*² C 423.
9 I.e. 'granted senatorial rank'. Equestrians wore a narrow stripe on the toga, senators a broad stripe.
10 He was an aide to a high official, like a consul or praetor.
11 Colonies as well as cities were divided into *vici*, i.e. 'Districts', each one numbered.

165 Inns and accommodations.

See also Document No. 66.

See L. Friedlaender, *Darstellungen aus der Sittengeschichte Roms*⁹, Vol. I (Leipzig 1922) 345–52 (English edn, Vol. I, 289–94); T. Kleberg, *Hôtels, restaurants et cabarets dans l'antiquité romaine* (Uppsala 1957); Balsdon, *Life and Leisure* 152–4, 215ff., 227ff.; L. Casson, *Travel in the Ancient World* (Toronto 1974).

A: *CIL* XIII 2301; **ILS* 6037. Plaque which once was affixed to the outside of an inn in Lugdunum. [Latin] **B**: *CIL* IV 807; **ILS* 6036. Painted letters on the outside wall of a building, Pompeii. [Latin] **C**: *CIL* II 4284; *ILS* 6039; Alföldy, **Tarraco* 801 (+ photograph). Limestone tablet, perhaps affixed to a private house, Tarraco in Spain. [Greek elegiac couplet] **D**: Appendix Vergiliana, *Copa* 1–6 [Latin elegiacs] **E**: *IG* XIV 24; **SIG*³ 1251. Syracuse. [Greek] **F**: *CIL* IV 1679. Next to the picture of a girl on the wall of a tavern in Pompeii. [Latin]

A. *ILS* 6037, Lugdunum

Mercury promises you money, | Apollo your health,[1] | (the manager) Septumanus a room | with lunch. He who comes in here | will live better afterwards. | Visitor, look carefully where you stay.

B. *ILS* 6036, Pompeii

Accommodations here for rent: | dining-room with three couches.

C. Alföldy, *Tarraco* 801

If you are shiny clean, here's a house all neat for you. / If you're dirty, I'll put up with you too, I'm ashamed to say.

D. Appendix Vergiliana *Copa* 1–6

The tavern dancing-girl Surisca, her head bound with a Greek head-dress, / skillful in moving and swaying her upper body in rhythm with her castanets, / drunkenly dances and teases within the smoky tavern,
5 / shaking her noisy castanets against her elbow: // 'What good is it to stay outside, tired from the dust of summer, / rather than to lie down here on a soft bed?'[2]

E. *SIG*[3] 1251, Syracuse in Sicily

Dekomia, the good Syrian hostess. Greetings!

F. *CIL* IV 1679, Pompeii

Hedonē[3] declares: Drinks cost one ās. If you pay double, you'll drink better. If you pay quadruple, you'll be drinking Falernian wine (the best).

1 The name of the inn may have been 'Mercury and Apollo'.
2 The poem continues to line 38 with a description of the tavern's gardens and surroundings in a suggestive manner designed to create a feeling of pleasure and comfort.
3 In Greek her name means 'Pleasure'.

166   Entertainers and actors of the imperial theater.

A: *CIL* III 372; **ILS* 5180. Stone found at Parium in Asia Minor. **B**: *CIL* IV 3867; **ILS* 5181a. Painting on a wall in Pompeii. **C**: Lucian, *On the Dance* 67–8. **D**: *CIL* X 1946; **ILS* 5183. Stone from Puteoli. **E**: *CIL* VI 10115; **ILS* 5197. Small, round piece of earthenware, Rome. **F**: *CIL* XIV 2988; **ILS* 5209a. Stone from Praeneste. **G**: *CIL* VI 10106; **ILS* 5211. Tombstone, Rome.

See also, in the present collection, Nos. 35 and 54.

Cf. Balsdon, *Life and Leisure* 270–88; M. Bonaria, *Romani Mimi* (Rome 1965); C. Garton, *Personal Aspects of the Roman Theater* (Toronto 1972).

A. *ILS* 5180, Parium

The colony (erects this monument to) | Publius | Ingenuus, | comic
5 actor, || because of his outstanding | proficiency in the art | and because of his moral uprightness.

B. *ILS* **5181a, Pompeii**

Paris, pearl of the stage.[1]

C. Lucian, *On the Dance* **67–8**

Taken as a whole, the dancer (i.e. the pantomime) professes to present
and act out delineations of character and emotion: he introduces a
lover, then an angry man, a madman, a man stricken with grief, and all
of the action in a measured manner. Most striking of all is the fact that
on the same day there is a showing of the mad Athamas, then a terrified
Ino, and at another time the same (pantomime) is Atreus, a little later
he is Thyestes, then Aegisthus or Aerope. And one man is all of these.
(68) Performances other (than pantomime) that are concerned with
sight and sound have a display of only one single action, for there is
either a flute or a lyre or vocal singing or dramatic action of tragedy or
laughter of comedy. The dancer (i.e. the pantomime), however, has all
of these in himself, and one can see that his equipment is a variety, a
blend of everything: flute, pipe, tap-dancing, sound of cymbals, the
fine voice of an actor, the harmony of singers.

D. *ILS* **5183, Puteoli**

Gaius Ummidius | Actius | Anicetus, | pantomime.[2]

E. *ILS* **5197, Rome**

(On the front) Gaius | Theoros, shining-light | and victorious over the
pantomimes. | If the lord (emperor) himself is captivated now by your
art, Theoros, | do *men* doubt that he wishes to imitate you?

    (On the back, in the middle) Theoros, | victorious over | the panto-
m|imes: (along the edge) Pylades | from Cilicia, Pierus | from Tibur, |
Hylas from Salmacis, | Nomius | from Syria.[3]

F. *ILS* **5209a, Praeneste**

Marcus Iunius, freedman of Marcus, | Maior, | archimimus,[4] | member
of the Association of Apollo.[5]

G. *ILS* **5211, Rome**

Sleep on. | To Claudia | Hermiona, first archimima of her | time, (this
monument was erected by her) | heirs.

1 He is the celebrated tragic actor L. Domitius Paris (*PIR*[2] D 156) who was put to death
   by Nero: Suetonius, *Nero* 54; Dio 63.18.1. Cf. Tacitus, *Ann.* 13.21.3 and 13.27.3.
2 Perhaps he was the freedman of Ummidia Quadratilla mentioned by Pliny, *Epist.*
   7.24.1.
3 These were all celebrated pantomimes who had been active in the early first century
   AD.

4 An archimimus was the head of a troop of mimic actors.
5 This association, the *parasiti Apollinis*, was composed of freedmen actors of all types
   in Italy, probably modeled after the Greek Dionysiac Artists. See A. Müller in
   Philologus 63 (1904) 342–61.

167   Appuleius Diocles, most eminent of all charioteers.
Marble tablet, four feet high and eight feet wide, left edge broken off,
very large letters lines 1–5, Rome. [Latin]

CIL VI 10048; **ILS* 5287.

F. Drexel in L. Friedlaender, *Darstellungen aus der Sittengeschichte Roms*[9], Vol. IV (Leipzig
1921) 185–96 (English translation, Vol. IV, 154–64, but based on earlier editions);
H. A. Harris, *Sport in Greece and Rome* (Ithaca, NY 1972) 198–201.

[Gaius Appu]leius Diocles, charioteer of the Red Faction,[1] | Lusitanian
Spaniard by *birth*, 42 years old, 7 months, 23 days. | His first chariot race
was in the White Faction when Acilius Aviola and Corellius Pansa were
consuls (AD 122). | He won his *first* victory in the same Faction when
Manius Acilius Glabrio and Gaius Bellicius Torquatus were consuls
5   (AD 124). ‖ His first chariot race in the Green Faction was when
Torquatus Asprenas for the second time and Annius Libo were consuls
(AD 128). His first victory | in the Red *Faction* was when Laenas
Pontianus and Antonius Rufinus were consuls (AD 131).
      Summary: He drove teams of chariot-horses for 24 years, started in
4,257 races, | [and won] *1,462* times, 110 of them in first races after the
parade.[2] In singles (one chariot from each Faction) he won 1,064 times,
in which he won 92 major prizes: 32 prizes of 30,000 sesterces each,
three being from races with six-horse teams; 28 prizes of 40,000
sesterces each, | two being *from races with six-horse teams*; 29 prizes of
50,000 sesterces each, one being from a race with a seven-horse team;
and three prizes of 60,000 sesterces each. In doubles (two chariots from
each Faction) he won 347 times, four of them with three-horse teams
for 15,000 sesterces each. In triples (three chariots from each Faction)
he won 51 times. He placed *2,900* | times; second place, 861 times; third
place, 576 times; fourth place, once for 1,000 sesterces; he failed to
place 1,351 times. He tied a Blue for first place 10 times and a White 91
10   times, two of these for 30,000 sesterces each. ‖ Total earnings
[received:] 35,863,120 sesterces.
      Moreover, he won three times with two-horse teams for 1,000 ses-
terces each, tied a White once and a Green twice. He took the lead and
won 815 times, came from behind and won 67 times, | and [under
handicapping (?) he won] 36 times. In various combinations he won 42
times. In final dashes he won 502 times: 216 times over the Greens, 205

over the Blues, and 81 over the Whites. He made nine horses 100-time winners, and one horse a 200-time winner. |

vv His notable feats. *vv* | [----] and in the year in which for the first time in the four-horse chariot he emerged as victor twice, he came from behind twice. It stands in the Record Book[3] that Avilius Teres for the first time of all in his own Faction won 1,011 victories, of which in one year the most he won | [was ----, but Diocles, in the year in which] for the first time he reached the 100-victory mark, won 103 times, 83 in singles. In addition, increasing the glory of his career he has surpassed
15   Thallus[4] of his own Faction, who was the first in the Red Faction ‖ [to have ----, but Dio]cles, most eminent of all charioteers, in the year in which he won 134 times with a lead-horse brought in from elsewhere,[5] won in singles 118 times, and with this record he surpassed the charioteers of all the Factions who ever | took part [in the contests of the games] of the circus. It has been noted with the well-earned admiration of everyone that in one year, with his lead-horse brought in from elsewhere and with two horses under the yoke – Cotynus and Pompeianus – he won 99 times: in one (race) for 60,000 (sesterces), in four for 50,000, in one for 40,000, and in two for 30,000. | [----, charioteer] of the Green Faction, won 1,025 times, first of all since the founding of Rome to make 50,000 sesterces in (each of) seven victories, (but) Diocles surpassed him with his three horses under the yoke – Abeigeius, Lucidus, Paratus – making 50,000 in (each of) eight victories. | [Likewise surpassing] Communis, Venustus, and Epaphroditus – three 1,000-victory charioteers of the Blue Faction – (who) had won 50,000 sesterces (in each of) eleven victories, Diocles with his Pompeianus and Lucidus, both of them under the yoke, made 50,000 | [(in each of) 12 (?) victories. ----, charioteer] of the Green Faction, won 1,025 times; Flavius Scorpus[6] won 2,048 times: Pompeius Musclosus[7] won 3,559 times: three charioteers with 6,632 wins who
20   made 50,000 sesterces (in each of) 28 victories. ‖ [Diocles, however, of all the charioteers] the most eminent, won 1,462 times but made 50,000 sesterces (in each of) 29 victories.

Diocles shines out with his most famous record: while Fortunatus of the Green Faction, with his victorious (horse) Tuscus winning 386 races, made 50,000 only nine times, Diocles, | [with his victorious Pompeianus winning] 152 races, made 50,000 ten times, and 60,000 in one race.[8] Diocles also is outstanding in regard to new kinds of prize-money never before recorded, because on a single day with a six-horse team, when 40,000 sesterces were put up twice, he won both of them. What is more, | [----,] with his own seven horses yoked together – that number of horses never seen before – he won the victory in that contest with (his lead-horse) Abigeius for 50,000 sesterces. And in other contests he won 30,000 sesterces without using a whip | [----.] With such novelties he was crowned with double glory.

Among 1,000-victory charioteers first place seems to be held by Pontius Epaphroditus of the Blue Faction, | [who in the age of our Imperator Anto]ninus Augustus Pius was sole victor 1,467 times, but Diocles, with (only) 1,462 victories, nevertheless surpasses him with 1,064 victories in singles. In the same age ‖ [Pontius Epaphroditus came from behind] and won 467 times, but Diocles came from behind and won 502 times. Charioteer Diocles, in the year in which he won 127 times, did so 103 times with his three horses Abigeius, Lucidus, and Pompeianus under the yoke, | [---. Among] eminent charioteers those who won the most with African horses under the yoke were: Pontius Epaphroditus of the Blue Faction, winning 134 times with Bubalus; Pompeius Musclosus of the Blue faction, | [with his horse --- winning] 115 times. Diocles surpassed them with his horse Pompeianus, winning 152 times, in singles 144 times.

His record was increased with his five in-yoke horses Cotynus, Galata, Abigeius, Lucidus, and Pompeianus | winning 445 times, 397 times in singles.

1 All chariot-racing in Rome and everywhere in the empire was organized into four major Clubs or Factions, each with its own *familia* or organization of grooms, trainers, aides, doctors, etc., as well as the charioteers themselves, and under the overall control of a *dominus* of the Faction. Fans attached themselves to these Factions in their loyalties. The Factions were named the Whites, Blues, Greens, and Reds. Domitian added two more, but they did not survive his lifetime. Charioteers moved from one Faction to another, probably as a result of personal choice at the end of contractual obligations and other considerations unknown to us. For history of the Factions see A. Cameron, *Circus Factions* (Oxford 1976) 45ff.
2 A parade preceded the circus games.
3 From the details in this inscription and from others this Record Book must have been similar to those kept today for each of the major sports, concentrating on the champions with their records and including sections on their horses.
4 Thallus the charioteer is mentioned by Martial (4.67.5).
5 Not all the horses, abreast, were yoked together. In a team of four horses (*quadriga*) the center two were under the yoke, but the outer two were only linked to it and helped to pull the chariot by 'traces'. In each team there also was a horse that acted as the 'leader' or 'captain', probably the most experienced horse of all. When a charioteer agreed to run a 'lead horse' from some other team or even Faction, the unknown horse could be a liability.
6 Flavius Scorpus is well known as a champion under Domitian from the epigrams of Martial: 10.74.5ff.; 10.50.53.
7 Musclosus, at the end of the first century, must rank as the great champion of the early Empire, at least in the number of total victories, his total number of victories not exceeded in racing circles until the twentieth century. See A. Cameron, *Porphyrius the Charioteer* (Oxford 1973) 179 n. 1.
8 Here the horses are singled out for recognition, making it clear that the Record Book included such information.

168   The Roman circus.

See also Documents Nos. 30, 33, 38, 60, 169.

[All in Latin] **A**: *CIL* XV 7254; **ILS* 5277. Lead pipe found in the Campus Martius, Rome. **B**: *CIL* VI 10067. Tombstone, Rome. **C**: *CIL* VI 10044; **ILS* 5314. Marble base, Rome. A palm of victory appears before and after the inscription. **D**: *CIL* VI 10052; **ILS* 5289. Marble stone, upper relief worn away, Rome. **E**: *CIL* VI 10061. From an old copy, Rome. **F**: *CIL* VI 10078; **ILS* 5300. Tombstone, Rome. At top is a sculptured relief: a boy on a two-horse team chariot, one hand holding the reins and the other a palm branch. The stone is now lost. **G**: *CIL* II 4314; *ILS* 5299; Alföldy, **Tarraco* 444 (+ photograph). Tombstone broken at top where the figure of a standing man is represented with a palm in his left hand, Tarraco in Spain. [Elegiac couplets, lines 6ff.] See Humphrey, *Circuses* 344 (+ photograph). **H**: *CIL* II 5166; **ILS* 5658 a. Limestone block from Balsa, found near Tavira, in Lusitania. **I**: A. Audollent, **Defixionum Tabellae* (Paris 1904, repr. 1967) No. 286; *ILS* 8753. Curse tablet of lead, text on both sides (a–b): on one side (a) is a male demon with grotesque head and the crest of a rooster, holding a long staff (smoking at the top) in one hand and in the other a large vessel or basket. He stands in a crudely pictured boat. Hadrumetum in Africa.

See the previous document, No. 167.

A.   *ILS* 5277. Rome

Faction of the Greens.[1]

B.   *CIL* VI 10067. Rome

To the departed spirits. | To Marcus Antonius, freedman, | horse-
5   trainer[2] | of the Green Faction. || Marcia Festa | made this (monument) for her husband, | well-deserving.

C.   *ILS* 5314. Rome

May victory | of the Blues | forever | remain unchanged![3] | Good luck!

D.   *ILS* 5289. Rome

Scorpus[4] was victorious with these horses: Pegasus, Elates, Andraemo, Cotynus.

E.   *CIL* VI 10061. Rome

To Tiberius Claudius, freedman of Augustus, | Epaphroditus, |
5   charioteer of the Faction | of the Greens. || (Erected by) Anicetus, charioteer | of the same Faction | to his master.

F.   *ILS* 5300. Rome

I am Florus here at rest, | a child charioteer who, while I wanted to race more swiftly, tumbled more swiftly into darkness. | Ianuarius (erected this monument) to his beloved foster son.

G. Alföldy, *Tarraco* 444. Tarraco

To the departed spirits. | To Eutyches, | charioteer, 22 years old. |
5   Flavius Rufinus and ‖ Sempronia Diofanis made (this monument) for
their well-deserving slave. |
   In this grave rest the bones of an inexperienced charioteer, / but one
who knew how to handle the reins. / I would have dared to mount the
four-horse chariots, / but could never be moved on from the two-horse
10   teams. // Cruel Fate envied me my years of life, / and nobody can move
his hands against Fate. / Glory of the circus was not granted to me by
the time of my death / – let the loyal crowd shed no tears for me! /
15   Disease burned away my body within me, // and physicians could not
cure it. / Please, traveler, sprinkle flowers on my grave. / Perhaps you
were a fan of mine while still I lived.[5]

H. *ILS* 5658 a. Balsa in Lusitania

Titus Cassius Celer | gave as a gift this podium for the circus, | 100 feet
long,[6] at his own expense.

I. Audollent, *Defixionum Tabellae* No. 286. Hadrumetum

5   (Side a) Ciugeu, | censue, | cinbeu, | perflue, ‖ diarunco, | deasta, |
10   bescu, | berebesu, | arurara, ‖ bazagra. (On the chest of the demon)
Antmo | arait|to. (In the boat) Noctivagus, | Tiberis, Oceanus.[7]
   (Side b) I charge you demon, who|ever you are, and demand of you |
from this hour, from this | day, from this moment that you torture the
15   horses ‖ of the Greens and Whites. | Kill them! The charioteers Gla|rus
20   and Felix and Primu|lus and Romanus, kill them! | Crash them! ‖ Leave
no breath in them! I charge you | by him who has released you | from
(the bonds) of time, the god of the sea and the air, Iao Iasdao. | Oorio
aeia!

---

1   The stables and headquarters of the Green Faction were located in the Campus
   Martius, as known from a late source. They were only one of the four main organiz-
   ations into which the charioteers and their personnel were grouped for business and
   administrative purposes, the others being the Blues, the Whites, and the Reds. See
   the previous document on Appuleius Diocles, n. 1. Cf. Tacitus, *Hist.* 2.94, and
   Suetonius, *Caligula* 55.
2   This appears to be the meaning of *conditor*, since in a Latin–Greek glossary it is
   equivalent to 'trainer of horses'. See J. Marquardt, *Römische Staatsverwaltung* III[2]
   (Leipzig 1885) p. 520 n. 5.
3   For this common phrase in circus chanting see A. Cameron, *Porphyrius the Charioteer*
   (Oxford 1973) 74ff.
4   This is the famous Flavius Scorpus immortalized by Martial. See the previous
   document on Appuleius Diocles, line 19.
5   P. Piernevieja in *Emerita* 38 (1970) 113ff. and 327 believes that the composer of this
   epitaph was familiar with the Epigrams of Martial.

6 The podium was the wall in the circus which formed the base of the seating arrangements. Since a second inscription from this same circus also mentions a gift of 100
   feet of the podium, Humphrey (*Circuses* 380) concludes that both of them relate to
   the original building of the structure and not some later rebuilding.
7 These appear to be the names of racehorses.

169   Theater and chariot races at Alexandria.

Dio Chrysostom, *Orat.* 32 (*To the Alexandrians*) 31–2, 35–6, 39–41. Humphrey, *Circuses*
510–11.

What would one say about the mass of the people in Alexandria, to
whom it is only necessary to offer plenty of bread and a seat at the
chariot-races, since they care for nothing else?[1] . . . (32) What a man
does privately does not concern the public or the city, but in the theater
one can see the character of people. And you especially have let down
your guard in that place and will betray the good reputation of your
city. You are like base women who, even though they do not live in their
homes with moderation, at least ought to appear in public at their best
behavior, but who actually misbehave the most on the streets.

   (35) Your city in size and location is the most superior of all and is
everywhere considered second (only to Rome) of all those under the
sun. (36) . . . You receive the (commerce of) the whole (Mediterranean)
Sea because of the beauty of your harbors, the size of your fleet, and the
abundance and distribution of things manufactured everywhere in the
world, and you also receive the (commerce of the) seas that lie far
beyond, the Red Sea and the Indian Ocean, whose name in former
times was not often heard, with the result that the commerce not only
of islands and harbors and some straits and isthmuses but of practically
the whole world has come to you. For Alexandria lies at some kind of
junction of the whole world, even of faraway nations that are most
distant, as if it were a market of a single city that brings together all
men and shows them to each other and makes them, as far as possible,
into a single people. (39) . . . What I meant just now about your city was
that I wished to show you that whatever disgrace you bring upon yourself is not done in secret, not even among a few people, but among all
people. (40) For I see in your city not only Greeks and Italians and
others from nearby Syria, Africa, and Cilicia, but also from the more
distant lands of Ethiopia, Arabia, Bactria, Scythia, Persia, and even
some from India, who join you in the audience and sit beside you on
each occasion. . . . (41) . . . (And when they return to their countries,
they will praise your city) and will add 'It is (a city) mad over music and
horse-racing and in such things the people act in a manner unworthy of

themselves. The people are moderate while sacrificing and bathing by themselves and doing other things, but as soon as they enter the theater or the stadium, just as if drugs had been buried in those places, they forget their former lives and are not ashamed to do or say anything that comes into their heads. (42) And worst of all, enthusiastic as they are about the show, they do not really see it, and, wishing to hear it, they really do not hear it, clearly out of their heads and deranged – not only the men, but also women and children. And when the fearful thing ceases and they take their leave, the higher fever of the riotous action is tamped down, but even so at the street-corners and narrow alley-ways it lingers on throughout the whole city for many days.'[2]

1   This is a clear reflection of Juvenal's (*Satires* 10.81) *panem et circenses* ('bread and the circuses').
2   For such factional riots among the fans of the theater and of the chariot races see A. Cameron, *Circus Factions* (Oxford 1976) Ch. 10, especially pp. 293ff.

170   The gladiatorial games.

See also Documents No. 26 (chapters 22–3), 35, 38, 88, 120, 172 E.

A: *Mosaicarum et Romanarum Legum Collatio* 11.7.4–5 (*FIRA* II p. 572). B: *CIL* IV 3884; **ILS* 5145. Painted letters on a building in Pompeii. [Latin] C: *CIL* X 1074 d; **ILS* 5053, No. 4. Stone now lost, found originally in the ruins of Pompeii. [Latin] D: *CIL* IX 465; **ILS* 5083. First of two tablets listing the members of a gladiatorial troop (*familia*) at Venusia in Italy. [Latin] E: *CIL* VI 10187; **ILS* 5085. Tombstone, Rome. [Latin] F: *CIL* VI 10195; **ILS* 5090. Tombstone, Rome. [Latin] G: *CIL* XII 3323; **ILS* 5095. Tombstone, Nemausus in Gaul. [Latin] H: *CIL* XII 3325; **ILS* 5101. Tombstone, Nemausus. I: Festus, *De Verborum Significatu* p. 358, 7–12 (Lindsay). J: *CIL* IV 4353; **ILS* 5142 d. Wall painting in Pompeii. [Latin] K: *CIL* VI 10175; **ILS* 5103. Tablet in a columbarium, Rome. [Latin] L: *CIL* V 5933; **ILS* 5115. Tombstone, in relief a gladiator standing with weapons and a dog, Milan. Photograph in M. Grant, *Gladiators* (London 1969) opp. p. 65, No. 34. [Latin] M: *CIL* IV 538; **ILS* 5138. Wall painting, with portrayal of two gladiators in combat, Pompeii. [Latin] N: **ILS* 6443 a–c. Scratched on three walls in Pompeii. [Latin] O: *CIL* X 1685; **ILS* 1397. Stone now lost, from Puteoli. [Latin] See Pflaum, *Carrières* 55.

L. Friedlaender, *Darstellungen aus der Sittengeschichte Roms*[9], Vol. II (Leipzig 1922) 50–76 (English translation, Vol. II, 41–62, but based on earlier editions); L. Robert, *Les Gladiateurs dans l'Orient grec* (Paris 1940); Grant, *op. cit.*; R. Auguet, *Cruelty and Civilization: The Roman Games* (London 1972); Balsdon, *Life and Leisure* 288–302; G. Ville, *La Gladiature en occident des origines à la mort de Domitien* (Rome 1981); K. Hopkins, *Death and Renewal* (Cambridge 1983) 3–30.

A.   *FIRA* II p. 572

There is a difference between those who are condemned to death by the sword and those condemned to a gladiatorial school: for those con-

demned to the sword are immediately put to death, or at least ought to
be put to death within a year, since this is included in the imperial
directives. On the other hand, those condemned to a gladiatorial school
are not inevitably put to death but can even gain freedom and receive
their discharge after an interval of time: freedom after a five-year period
is permitted, discharge (from the school) after a three-year period.[1]

B. *ILS* 5145. Pompeii

Decimus Lucretius | Satrius Valens, perpetual priest of Nero Caesar,
son of the Augustus, | (will present) 20 pairs of gladiators, and Decimus
Lucretius Valens, his son,[2] (will present) 10 pairs of gladiators, who
will fight at Pompeii on the 6th, 5th, 4th, 3rd, and the day before the
Ides of April (April 8–12). There will be the usual beast-hunt and (over-
head) awnings. | Written by Aemilius | Celer by himself | by the light of
the moon.

C. *ILS* 5053, No. 4. Pompeii

Aulus Clodius, son of Aulus, | (of the tribe) Menenia, Flaccus, duovir |
for the third time for the administration of justice, quinquennalis, |
5   tribune of the soldiers (elected) by the People. || *vv* In his final duovirate
at the Games of Apollo | in the forum (he presented) a parade, | (then)
bulls, bull-fighters, performers, men fighting on platforms – three pairs
of them – companies of boxers and Greek-style boxers, performances |
10   with a full card and | all kinds of pantomimes, including Pylades,[3] || and
a (gift of) 10,000 sesterces to the public in return for his duovirate. | In
his second duovirate as quinquennalis at the Games of Apollo in the
forum | (he presented) a parade, (then) bulls, bull-fighters, performers,
| and companies of boxers; on the second day, by himself, (he pre-
sented) athletes in the games, | 30 pairs of them, five pairs of gladiators, |
15   (then) 35 pairs of gladiators and || beast-hunts with bulls, bull-fighters,
boars, bears, | and other hunts in conjunction with his colleague (in
office). | In his third duovirate (he presented) games of the first rank,
with additional acts. Clodia, daughter of Aulus, erected this monument
at her own expense, | for herself and her own.

D. *ILS* 5083. Venusia

Gladiatorial troop of | [Gaius] Salvius Capito [----] | is located here. |
5   Mounted gladiator: || Mandatus (slave) of Rabirius, three victories and
two crowns. | Thracian gladiators: | Secundus (slave) of Pompeius, two
victories and two crowns; | Gaius Masonius,[4] seven victories and four
crowns; | Phileros (slave) of Domitius, 12 victories and 11 crowns; |
10 || Optatus (slave) of Salvius (Capito), beginner; | Gaius Alfidius,

beginner. | Murmillones: Quintus Cleppius, beginner; | [---] Iulius,
beginner. | Retiarii: [------,] beginner.[5]

E. *ILS* 5085. Rome

Thelyphus, a Samnite (gladiator), by nationality a Thracian.

F. *ILS* 5090. Rome

To the departed spirit | of Marcus Antonius Niger, veteran Thracian
5   (gladiator), | who lived 38 years | and fought 18 times. || Flavia Diogenis
| for her well-deserving husband | has made (this monument) at her
own expense.

G. *ILS* 5095. Nemausus in Gaul

Beryllus, charioteer (fighter in the arena), a free man[6] with 20 combats,
by nationality a Greek, 25 years old. His wife Nomas (made this monument) for her well-deserving husband.

H. *ILS* 5101. Nemausus

A murmillo (gladiator), | Columbus | Serenianus (fought) 25 times. | By
nationality an Aeduan (Gaul), | he rests here. | His wife Sperata (made
this monument).

I. Festus, *De Verborum Significatu* p. 358 (Lindsay)

When a retiarius[7] fights a murmillo, he is taunted with these words:
'It's not you I'm attacking, it's the fish I'm seeking. Why do you run
from me, Gaul?' (He calls him 'Gaul') because the type of armor worn
by a murmillo is Gaulic and the murmillones were previously called
'Gauls'. On their helmets was the figure of a fish.[8]

J. *ILS* 5142 d. Pompeii

Crescens the retiarius (is) the idol of young girls.

K. *ILS* 5103. Rome

Aulus Postumius | Acoemetus, | instructor of murmillones.

L. *ILS* 5115. Milan

To the departed spirit | of Urbicus, secutor gladiator | first rank,[9] by
nationality a Florentine, who fought 13 times | and lived 22 years. (This
5   monument was erected by) Olympias, || his daughter whom he left, five
months old, | and by Fortunesis (slave) of his daughter, | and by Lauricia
his wife, for her husband, well-deserving, | with whom she lived for
seven years. | I warn you to kill your vanquished (opponent in the
10   arena), whoever he may be. || May his fans cherish his departed spirit!

M. *ILS* 5138. Pompeii

(Under the painting of two gladiators are their names:)

<table>
<tr><td align="center">TETRAITES[10]</td><td align="center">PRUDES</td></tr>
<tr><td align="center">Tetraites, free man with
1[-] combats</td><td align="center">Prudes, free man with 18
combats,</td></tr>
</table>

(In the margin, at bottom) Let him who damages this (painting) incur the anger of Pompeian Venus!

N. *ILS* 6443 a–c. Pompeii

(a) You Campanians, in a single victory (over your teams), | were defeated along with the Nucerinians.[11]

(b) Down with the Nucerinians!

(c) Good luck to Puteoli! Good luck to all Nuceria! To Hell with Pompeii and Pithecusa!

O. *ILS* 1397, Puteoli

Lucius Bovius, son of Lucius, grandson of Lucius, (of the tribe) Falerna, Celer,[12] | duovir quinquennalis, augur, | prefect of fabri,[13] tribune of the soldiers of the Legion Third Cyrenaica, | procurator of
5   the gladiatorial school of Caesar ‖ at Alexandria by Egypt, admitted | among the (judges) chosen by Imperator Caesar Augustus, | (erected this monument for himself and | for his excellent wife Sextia, daughter of Lucius, Nerula, | with whom he lived from childhood | without animosity for 31 years.

1 A gladiatorial school was a training center where the gladiators were kept under strict guard and taught the use of arms for the arena. Under the Republic they were privately owned and operated, but under the emperors they were placed under imperial control and management in the person of a procurator (see above, *ILS* 1397 from Puteoli, Item O).
2 This family is well-known at Pompeii. The father was priest in the period AD 50–4: see P. Castren, *Ordo Populusque Pompeianus* (Rome 1976) 108–9.
3 The famous pantomime: Suetonius, *Augustus* 45.
4 He, like two others in this text, was a free man and either was there voluntarily or had been sent there under compulsion. The other gladiators are all slaves.
5 Gladiators fought in a great variety of armor and costumes, and they accordingly received names suited to them. And a 'Thracian' or a 'Samnite' gladiator, therefore, merely meant that the gladiator used the weapons and armor of a Thracian or Samnite. For a good list, with descriptions, see Friedlaender, *op. cit.* (German edn) 257–68 (by Drexel), (English edn) 171–81.
6 See L. Robert, *op. cit.* 287–92.
7 The retiarius carried a trident as weapon in one hand and a net in the other. His natural opponent was a murmillo.
8 The word 'murmillo' means a type of fish.

9 The secutor ('chaser') was another opponent of a retiarius. Urbicus here is not a beginner, he has attained 'first rank' (*primus palus*).

10 H. T. Rowell has shown in *TAPA* 89 (1958) 14–24 that this Tetraites is the gladiator called Petraites in the *Satyricon* of Petronius (52.3 and 71.6), where we learn that Trimalchio is a dedicated fan of the gladiator. The number of his combats was in excess of 10, perhaps even in excess of 20.

11 Riots and rowdy behavior were common at all gladiatorial games. At one given in AD 59 at Pompeii the spectators from the neighboring Nuceria were attacked by the spectators from Pompeii, and many were killed: see Tacitus, *Ann.* 14.17. The affair is pictured on a wall-painting from Pompeii and is reproduced in Balsdon, *op. cit.* p. 338.

12 For the career of Lucius Bovius Celer see Pflaum, *Carrières* No. 55. In the passage of time these imperial procurators were also in charge of recruiting gladiators as well as administering the gladiatorial schools all over the empire.

13 See above, Document No. 21, n. 2.

171 Physicians in the Roman world.

Documents in this section are in Latin unless otherwise noted.

See also Documents No. 49 B, 84, 108, 118 n. 2.

See J. Scarborough, *Roman Medicine* (London 1969).

A: *IG* XIV 1879; *IGRR* I 313; Peek, *GVI* 244; Moretti, *IGUR 1283 (+ photograph). Tombstone, Rome. [Greek] **B**: *CIL* VI 10172; *ILS 5152. Marble altar, Rome. **C**: *CIL* VI 33879; *ILS 5310. Marble tablet, Rome. **D**: *CIL* III 14216; *ILS 7150 a. Tombstone, Drobeta in Dacia. **E**: *CIL* XI 5400; *ILS 7812. Stone from Asisium in Italy. **F**: *CIL* VI 20; *ILS 2092. Votive stone, Rome. **G**: *CIL* VI 8711; *ILS 7803. Plaque, Rome. **H**: *CIL* VI 3984. Columbarium, Rome. **I**: *IGRR* III 733; *TAM II 910 (drawing). Altar from ruins of a theater, Rhodiapolis, Lycia. [Greek] **J**: *CIL* XI 3943; *ILS 7789. Marble tablet found near Capena, Italy.

A. Moretti, *IGUR* 1283. Rome

To the departed spirits. | (Metrical epigram) This stele was erected to Nikomedes by his relatives. / He was the finest physician in his lifetime, / and, having saved many people with drugs that banish pain, // his body now in death is free from pain. / (Below, in prose) I, Nikomedes, am of good cheer: | I was not and I was, I am not and I do not grieve. I lived 44 years and 23 days.

B. *ILS* 5152. Rome

Eutychus, | freedman of Augustus, Neronianus, | physician for the Ludi Matutini,[1] made this (monument) for himself | and Irene, freedwoman, his wife ‖ most dear | and well-deserving, | and for his freedmen and freedwomen | and their posterity.

C. *ILS* 5310. Rome

Hyla, physician | of the Blue Faction,[2] [made this] while still alive, | for himself | and his bones.

D. *ILS* 7150 a. Drobeta in Dacia

To the departed spirits. | Marcus Valerius, son of Marcus, | Longinus,
5 | physician of the Legion ‖ Seventh Claudia, | decorated with the
orname|nts of a decurion | by the most splendid | order of the Hadrianic
10 municipality of Drobeta.[3] ‖ He lived 23 years. | Marcus Victorius | [----]
and Victoria | [Ge]mina, | his most pious children, | erected (this monument).

E. *ILS* 7812. Asisium in Italy

Publius Decimius, freedman of Publius, Eros | Merula, clinical
5 physician, | surgeon, | eye doctor, sevir. ‖ For his freedom he gave
50,000 sesterces. | For the sevirate to the State he gave 2,000 sesterces.
| For putting up statues in | the temple of Hercules he gave 30,000
10 sesterces. | For paving roads ‖ for the public he gave 37,000 sesterces. |
On the day before he died | he left a patrimony | of [----]

F. *ILS* 2092. Rome

To Asclepius and | to the good health | of his fellow-soldiers | Sextus
5 Titius Alexander, ‖ physician of the Fifth Praetorian Cohort, | gave this
(monument) as a gift, when [[Imperator Domitianus]] Augustus for
the seventh time | and Titus Flavius Sabinus | were consuls (AD 82).

G. *ILS* 7803. Rome

Secunda, (female slave) of Livilla,[4] physician.

H. *CIL* VI 3984. Rome

Marcus Li[vius] | Boeth[us,] | foreman | of the physicians.[5]

I. *TAM* II 910, Rhodiapolis in Lycia

To Asklepios and Hygia.[6] | The Boule and People of Rhodiapolis | and
its Council of Elders have honored with con|tinuous honors year after
5 year Herakleitos, ‖ (son) of Herakleitos (son) of Oreios, citizen and | a
Rhodian (as well), patriotic, priest of Asklepios | and Hygia, (honored
him) with a gilded image and | a statue of Paideia (Education). He has
been honored similar|ly by the Alexandrians, Rhodians, Athenians,
10 the ‖ most holy Boule of Areopagos,[7] the | Epicurean philosophers at
Athens, and the | holy Thymelic Synod,[8] first | physician of his time,
15 writer and po|et of medical and philosophical works, ‖ described as the
Homer of medical poetry, | honored with immunity,[9] | a man who

practiced medicine without reimbursement, who built a temple | and erected statues of Asklepio|s and Hygia and who dedicated his writings
20 || and poems to his native city, to Alexan|dria, to Rhodes, and to Athens, a man who fa|vored his native city with distributions and | games of
25 Asklepios and with | 60,000 silver denarii. || His native city has also honored him with the privilege of front seat at public events.

J. *ILS* 7789. Capena in Italy

Gaius Calpurnius Asclepiades from Prusa-by-Olympus, physician,[10] | upon request obtained from god Traianus seven grants of (Roman) citizenship for his parents, for himself, and for his brothers. | He was born on the third day before the Nones of March (March 5) in the thirteenth consulship of Domitian (AD 87), on the same day | as his wife Veronia Chelidon, with whom he lived 51 years. Because of his studies and his good character he won the approval of most famous
5 men, associated with magi||strates of the Roman People just as he also did with others in the province of Asia, and was | one of those who watch over [the lots] in the urn (for the selection of) judges.

1 He attended to the wounded gladiators at these games. Cf. Galen 13.599–602, 18.2.56ff.
2 There were four factions or Clubs of chariot-racing in Rome and elsewhere. See above, Document No. 167 n. 1.
3 The decurion of Drobeta was a local senator of that municipality.
4 Livilla was the sister of the emperor Claudius.
5 Apparently Livius Boethus was in charge of the group of physicians in the imperial household.
6 Hygia was a goddess of Health.
7 The Boule (Council) of the Areopagos in Athens of the Roman imperial period lay at the heart of the Athenian administration, working in close co-operation with the Assembly and possessing wide judicial power.
8 This is a reference to the Guild of Dionysiac Artists, professional performers at the various games and theatrical performances in the Greek East.
9 See above, Document No. 84.
10 There was an earlier physician Asclepiades from this place in Asia Minor who lived in the age of Pompey the Great. See Pliny, *Nat. Hist.* 7.124.

172 Women at work.

These documents are in Latin, unless otherwise noted.

A: *CIL* II 497; **ILS* 7802. Tombstone, Emerita in Spain. B: *CIL* VI 6647. From the columbarium (underground burial vault) by the Porta Praenestina, Rome. C: *CIL* VI 27262; **ILS* 8536. Tombstone, Rome. D: *CIL* VI 9037; **ILS* 1788. Tombstone, Rome. E: *Greek Inscriptions in the British Museum* 911; L. Robert, **Les Gladiateurs dans l'Orient grec* (Paris 1940) No. 184 (+ photograph). Plaque showing relief of two female gladiators, provenance unknown in the Greek East. [Greek] F: *CIL* VI 8958; **ILS* 1784. Tombstone,

Rome. **G**: *CIL* VI 9540; *ILS 7397. Tombstone, Rome. **H**: *CIL* VI 33892; *ILS 7760.
Tombstone. **I**: *CIL* VI 9892; *ILS 7600. Tombstone, Rome. **J**: *CIL* VI 9980; *ILS 7428.
Tombstone, Rome. **K**: *CIL* VI 10111; *ILS 5215. Tombstone, Rome. **L**: Dio
Chrysostom, *Orat.* 7.133.

See S. Treggiari in *AJAH* 1 (1976) 76–104.

A. *ILS* 7802. Emerita

Sacred to the departed spirit | of Iulia Saturnina, 45 years old, incom-
5 parable wife, | excellent physician, | most blameless woman, ‖ (erected
by) Cassius Philippus, | husband, out of gratitude. She is buried here.
May the earth rest lightly upon her.

B. *CIL* VI 6647. Rome

vv To Hygia.[1] *vv* | To Flavia Sabina, | midwife. She lived 30 years. Marius
Orthrus, | and Apollonius, to his dearest wife.

C. *ILS* 8536. Rome

To the departed spirit | of Terentia Thisbe. | Terentia Selicia | made
(this monument) for her wet-nurse.[2]

D. *ILS* 1788. Rome

Extricata, | slave of Octavia Augusta, | seamstress, lived 20 years.

E. L. Robert, *Les gladiateurs dans l'Orient grec* No. 184

Provenance unknown. [Greek]

(Photograph shows two women in armed combat, resembling
gladiators)[3]

(At the top)   They were allowed to go free.

(Below first woman)   Amazon.

(Below second woman)   Achillia.

F. *ILS* 1784. Rome

To Juno. | (Tomb) of Dorcas, | born a slave of Iulia Augusta | on Capri,
5 ‖ her handmaid. | Lyncastus, her fellow-freedman, | (minor) official in
the imperial household, (erected this monument) to his wife, | most
dear to him.

G. *ILS* 7397. Rome

To the departed spirit | of Grapte, | amanuensis of Egnatia Ma|ximilla.[4]
5 | To his ‖ wife most | dear (this monument had been erected by) Gaius
Egn|atius Arogus.

H. *ILS* 7760. Rome

Sacred to the departed spirit. | To Hapate, | short-hand writer | in Greek,
5   who ‖ lived 25 years. | Pittosus ere|cted (this monument) to his wife |
most affectionate.

I. *ILS* 7600. Rome

Thymele, | Marcella's | dealer in silk.

J. *ILS* 7428. Rome

To Italia, | dressmaker for Cocceia Phyllis. | She lived 20 years. |
Acastus, fellow-slave, because of | her poverty, made (this monument).

K. *ILS* 5215. Rome

Luria Privata, | actress in mimes, lived 19 years. Bleptus | made (this
monument).

L. Dio Chrysostom, *Orat.* **7.133**

Concerning brothel-keepers and brothel-keeping I must not fail in my
efforts, as if it would be a point for debate, but must use all my strength
and prohibit them, saying that nobody, poor or rich, will work at such
a thing, taking a fee for wantonness and licentiousness and bringing
people together for loveless intercourse and for passion without affec-
tion for the sake of profit, exhibiting women or children – captured in
war or otherwise purchased – to their shame in filthy rooms, on display
everywhere in the city, at the very doors of our magistrates, in the
city-squares, near government buildings and temples, in the midst of
all that is holy.

1 The goddess of health.
2 For the duties of a wet-nurse see Soranus of Ephesus, *Gynecology* (translated by O.
   Temkin), Ch. 2.
3 For other examples of female gladiators see the passages collected by John E. B.
   Mayor, *Thirteen Satires of Juvenal* (London 1901, repr. 1966) p. 97. See Tacitus, *Ann.*
   15.32; Suetonius, *Domitian* 4.1; Juvenal, *Satires* 6.246–7; Petronius, *Satyricon* 45.
4 Cf. Tacitus, *Ann.* 15.71.

173   Men at work.
Documents are in Latin unless otherwise noted.
See also the document below, No. 177.

A: *CIL* IX 3028; **ILS* 7367. Tombstone, Teate Marrucinorum in Italy. **B**: *CIL* VI 9535;
*ILS 7393. Tombstone, Rome. **C**: *CIL* VI 9520; **ILS* 7401. Tombstone, Rome. **D**: *CIL* VI
9939; **ILS* 7414. Tombstone, Rome. **E**: *CIL* VI 9732; **ILS* 7420 a. Tombstone, Rome.
F: *CIL* VI 9676; **ILS* 7486. Tombstone, Rome. **G**: *CIL* V 5919; **ILS* 7545. Tombstone,

Milan. **H**: *CIL* VI 9279; **ILS* 7555. Tombstone, Rome. **I**: *CIL* VI 9494; **ILS* 7558. Tombstone Rome. **J**: *CIL* V 5928; **ILS* 7580. Tombstone, Milan. **K**: *CIL* IX 3962; **ILS* 7640. Tombstone, Alba Fucens. **L**: *CIL* VIII 12638; **ILS* 7738 a. Tombstone, Carthage. **M**: *CIL* VI 9454; **ILS* 7769. Tombstone, Rome. **N**: *CIL* VI 9718; **ILS* 7491. Tombstone, Rome. **O**: *CIL* VI 9179; **ILS* 7503. Tombstone, Rome. **P**: *CIL* VI 33886; **ILS* 7539. Tombstone, Rome. **Q**: *CIL* X 3965; **ILS* 7626. Tombstone, near Capua. **R**: *CIL* VI 9260; **ILS* 7639. Tombstone, Sena Gallica. **S**: *CIL* IV 710; **ILS* 6419 c. Painting on the wall of a building in Pompeii. **T**: L. Schumacher in **Epigraphische Studien* 11 (1976) 131ff. (+ photograph); *AÉ* 1976, 504. Plaque from Moguntiacum in Germany. **U**: *IG* XIV 1500; *IGRR* I 233; Peek, *GVI* 1042; Moretti, **IGUR* 1176 (+ photograph). Marble tombstone, decorated with gable and molding. Rome. [Greek epigram] **V**: *CIL* XI 6700, No. 688, **ILS* 8603. On decorated earthenware vases, Arretium in Italy. **W**. *IGRR* I 11. Marble tablet, Massilia in Narbonese Gaul. [Greek] **X**: *CIL* VI 5207; **IGRR* I 261 B. From a columbarium in Rome. [Greek] **Y**: *IGRR* I 417. Tombstone, Baiae in Italy. [Greek] **Z**: *CIL* VI 9822; **ILS* 7496. Tombstone, Rome.

See E. H. Brewster, *Roman Craftsmen and Tradesmen of the Early Roman Empire* (Philadelphia 1917); H. J. Loane, *Industry and Commerce of the City of Rome 50 BC–200 AD* (Baltimore, MD 1938); A. Burford, *Craftsmen in Greek and Roman Society*, Ithaca (NY) 1972; S. M. Treggiari in P. Garnsey (ed.), *Non-Slave Labour in the Greco-Roman World* (Cambridge 1980) 48ff.

A. *ILS* 7367. Teate Marrucinorum

(Erected for) Hippocr|ates, | (slave and) farm-manager of Plautius, | by
5 the farm household ‖ to whom he gave orders respectfully.

B. *ILS* 7393. Rome

Liburnus, Lucius Seius | Strabo's amanuensis.[1] | Salvilla his wife made (this monument).

C. *ILS* 7401. Rome

To the departed spirit | of Nicon, secretary and slave of Lucius Iul|ius
5 Vestinus.[2] | His mother made (this monument) for her ‖ beloved son.

D. *ILS* 7414. Rome

To Zethus, barber, slave of Aulus Plautius.[3]

E. *ILS* 7420 a. Rome

Psamate, Furia's | personal maid, who lived 18 years. | Mithridates, baker, | slave of Flaccus Thorius,[4] made (this monument).

F. *ILS* 7486, Rome

To the departed spirits. | Tiberius Claudius Docimus | made this
5 (monument) for himself and his freedmen | and freedwomen ‖ and their posterity. | He was a merchant of salt-fish | and Moorish wine.

G. *ILS* 7545. Milan

Gaius Atilius, son of Gaius, │ Iustus, │ cobbler of soldier's boots, │
5   ordered in his testament that this be erected for himself ‖ and his wife
Cornelia Exorata.

H. *ILS* 7555. Rome

To Lucius Caelius, son of Lucius, Ianuarius │ who lived 61 years. │
Cleomenes, tanner and leather-worker, saw to (the making of this
monument) for his well-deserving friend.

I. *ILS* 7558. Rome

To the departed spirit │ of Balonia Livittiana │ (this monument) was
made by the freedman of Marcus, Marcus Balonius Laris│cus, worker
5   in wool ‖ and maker of felt, │ for his well-deserving and beloved wife.

J. *ILS* 7580. Milan

5   To Publius Iulius │ Macedo, │ dealer in │ cloaks and skins. ‖ (This monument was made by) Publius Iulius Senna, │ freedman.

K. *ILS* 7640. Alba Fucens

Lucius Marcleius, son of Lucius, │ Philargurus, sword-maker.

L. *ILS* 7738 a. Carthage

Sacred to the departed spirits. │ Titus Flavius Apsens, │ land-surveyor,
│ who lived a pious life of 26 years, │ is buried here.

M. *ILS* 7769. Rome

Marcus Mettius │ Epaphroditus, │ teacher of Greek.[5] │ Marcus Mettius
Germanus, freedman, made (this monument).

N. *ILS* 7491. Rome

The bones of Lucius Cluvius, freedman of Lucius, │ Cerdon, │ olive-oil
dealer from the Carinae District (of Rome) (are buried here).

O. *ILS* 7503. Rome

Gaius Cacius, freedman of Gaius, Heracla, │ banker from the Esquiline
District, │ (made this) for himself and his freedmen │ and freedwomen.

P. *ILS* 7539, Rome

Gaius Tullius Crescens, │ dealer in the marble trade, from the Galban
Warehouse District, made this for himself in his lifetime and │ for
5   Tullia Primilla, │ his beloved fellow-freedwoman, and ‖ for their own
freedmen and freedwomen │ and their posterity.

Q. *ILS* 7626. Near Capua

Gaius Epillius, freedman of Gaius, | Alexander, | timber-merchant.

R. *ILS* 7639. Sena Gallica

Aulus Hirtius | Felix, | locksmith.

S. *ILS* 6419 c. Pompeii

Gaius Cuspius Pansa for aedile! | All the goldsmiths | seek his election.[6]

T. *Epigraphische Studien* 11 (1976) 131ff. Moguntiacum

To the departed spirits. To Tiberius Claudius, | freedman of Augustus, Zosimus, procurator | of the food-tasters of Imperator | Domitianus
5 Caesar ‖ Augustus Germanicus.[7] This monument | does not pass by inheritance to an heir.

U. Moretti, *IGUR* 1176. Rome

Having left the famous city of Bithynian Nikaia as a young man, / I came to the land of the Italians, / and in the sacred city of Rome I taught mathematics and geometry. / This is the monument that I, Basileus, received, the work (paid for by living a life) of the mind.

V. *ILS* 8603. Arretium

(From the shop) of Aulus Titius, | potter.
(From the shop) of Aulus Titius, | potter from Arretium.[8]

W. *IGRR* I 11. Massilia

Athenades, | (son) of Dioskourides, | teacher | of Roman letters.

X. *IGRR* I 261 B. Rome

Aspourgos, son of Biomasos, Bosporan interpreter for the Sarmatians.

Y. *IGRR* I 417. Baiae

To the departed spirits. I, Hieron, | (slave) of Marcus, pilot | of a ship, from Nikome|dia, lived 65 years. | I, Dionysos, son of Hier|on, buried him here at my own | expense.

Z. *ILS* 7496. Rome

Gaius Iulius Epaphra, | fruit-seller at the Circus | Maximus in front of the | imperial box, (made this) for himself and ‖ for Venuleia, | freed-
5 woman of Gnaeus (son) of Gnaeus, Helena, | his wife.

1 Seius Strabo was the father of Sejanus under Tiberius and was associated with him
   in the office of praetorian prefect.
2 On Iulius Vestinus see Tacitus, *Hist.* 4.53.

3 Aulus Plautius was the first governor of Britain and was in command of the invading troops in AD 43.
4 Thorius Flaccus was governor of Bithynia under Augustus.
5 For Mettius Epaphroditos see below, Document No. 178 I, for more information about him.
6 Similar public notices from Pompeii, soliciting the support of fellow-workers for the election of city officials are very common: *ILS* 6411 a (fruit-dealers); 6412 a (mule-drivers); 6417 b (wood-workers and wagoners); 6423 (fishermen); 6426 (innkeepers); 6428 b (barbers); 6429 (porters); 6431 d (ball-players); 6418 f (petty thieves).
7 The presence of this epitaph in Germany seems to indicate that Tiberius Claudius Zosimus died there while Domitian was on the Rhine frontier with his army. Another epitaph to him has been found in Rome (*ILS* 1796), set up by his wife and daughter.
8 Throughout Italy hundreds of small pottery shops or factories existed, each shop employing slaves numbering from as few as half a dozen to as many as fifty or more. The name of the owner was stamped on his products. See H. Comfort in *Economic Survey* 5.188ff.

174 A canal for fullers in Syrian Antioch. AD 73–4.
Limestone stele found on the west bank of the Orontes River in Antioch. [Greek]

D. Feissel in *Syria* 62 (1985) 81 (stele A).[1]

Under Imperator | Titus Flavius C|aesar Augustus[2] | and Imperator
5 ‖ Titus Caesar and | Domitianus Caes|ar, sons of Augustus: | work on a
10 fullers' canal[3] | and barriers ‖ that diverted | the same watercourse, | authorized by Marc|us Ulpius Traianus the le|gate of Caesar
15 Augustus,[4] ‖ was performed by the me|tropolis of Antioch | block by block[5] | in the year 122 (AD 73–4).[6] From the Orontes | up to [the
20 opening at the foot of] (Mt) Ama‖nus [it is 14 stades] | in length and [4]1 *square feet* | (in width and depth). [Equal] | distribution of the work
25 was made among the blocks | based on the proportion of the ‖ number of people (in them) and on their length, | width, and depth, in accordance with which | each block was made responsible | for its own proper space | for the delivery (of the work).
30 There are on ‖ this stele[7] the remainder | of the people (of the block) of the high-priest Damas, | (responsible for) 33½ (and) ¼ feet in length; (the block) of Bragates, | 38¼ feet in length; (the block) of Pharnakes
35 the former gymnasi|arch, 69 feet in length; (the block) of Artas ‖ son of Thrasydemos, 25½ feet in length; (etc.).[8]

1 Two stelai were found, the first 29 lines of A being identical with the first 25 lines of B. Thus, restorations of those lines in A can be confirmed from B.
2 Note that the titulature of Vespasian and his sons is incomplete.
3 Fullers require a great amount of water in their processing of wool.

4 M. Ulpius Traianus was the father of the future emperor. Consul in AD 70, he became governor of Syria soon thereafter.

5 The word 'block' here refers to the property and apartments along the route of the canal. The owners became liable for the cost of construction.

6 The year 122 refers to the Caesarian era of Antioch, equal to October of AD 73 to September of 74.

7 Feissel (p. 92) believes that for the purpose of construction the route of the canal had been divided into sections, each section 720 feet long, and each section marked by the erection of a stele. He calculated that about a dozen stelai would be required to cover the entire route and to list the participants.

8 The list continues on to line 52 and shows a total number of 16 blocks. At the end, in line 52, the total of 720 feet is recorded. Feissel calculates that the total length for the whole canal of 14 stades (extant on line 18 of stele B) would equal 8,400 feet. Such figures can form the basis for an estimate of the density of population in Antioch. Of course, the number of blocks varied from one section to another.

175   Learning a trade by apprenticeship. Reign of Nero.
Papyrus from Oxyrhynchus, Egypt. [Greek]

PSI 871.

Copy. To Ptolemaios the royal secretary and | to Apollophanes and Diogenes the secretaries of the district | and the village, *vv* | [from
5 Pe]toseiris (son) of Petoseiris ‖ of the city Oxyrhynchus on [Egzoeu] Street. | It is my desire, | from the present 11th year of Nero | Cla[udius Cae]sar Augustus Germanicus | Imperator (AD 64), that my son
10 Pete‖chon, who is not yet of age and is *registered* | on the same Egzoeu Street, | learn the coppersmith | trade from the master Herakleides |
15 (son) of Petosorapis, coppersmith on the street ‖ of the same name. I ask that he be registered | in the class of similar (apprentices), as is fitting. |

(The signatures of state officials follow, approving the request, dated to AD 65, on lines 17–25).[1]

1 Formal request and approval were necessary because the action involved a change of address of the young boy from his father's house to that of the coppersmith. In the last lines of the papyrus (26–35), dated a year later, the father had to produce a copy of the present document to prove that his son had changed his address.

176   Wholesale dealer in food at Puteoli. AD 37.
Wax-tablets (triptych a–c) from a Roman villa at Pompeii.

C. Giordano in *Rendiconti dell' Accademia di Archeologia e Lettere e Belle Arti di Napoli* 45 (1970) 213–15 (+ photographs); *AÉ* 1972, 86.

L. Casson in *Memoirs of the American Academy in Rome* 36 (1980) 21–33 (*Ancient Trade and Society* (Detroit 1984) 86–116).

(a) In the consulship of Gnaeus Acceronius Proculus and Gaius Petronius Pontius (AD 37), | on the 4th day before the Kalends of July (June 28), | I, Gaius Novius Eunus, have written that I received on | loan
5   from Evenus, freedman of Tiberius Caesar Augustus, ‖ Primianus – in his absence through his agent | Hessychus, his slave – and that I owe him | ten thousand sesterces, which I will return to him upon demand. These ten thousand sesterces, | described above, are to be given back according to the law and without error as stipulated by Hessychus, | slave of Evenus, freedman of Tiberius Caesar Augustus, Primianus,
10   ‖ (and) as I, Gaius Novius Eunus, have promised. | As security (and) pledge for these ten thousand | sesterces I have put up: (b) | [----] Alexandrian wheat, 7,000 modii,[1] more or less, as well as chick-peas,
15   husked | wheat (?), and lentils in two hundred sacks, ‖ (total of) 4,000 modii, more or less. All these (foodstuffs) | are in my possession and held in the Bassian Warehouse | of Puteoli, under my complete legal authority | and at my own risk, as I here state and declare. | Done at Puteoli.[2]

1   A *modius* was about one-quarter of a bushel.
2   As grain ships arrive from Egypt Gaius Novius Eunus buys up whole cargoes, stores them in warehouses, and sells the products to other dealers on a local level. When he needs cash to buy new shipments, he borrows it from the freedman Evenus Primianus, who, however, has his slave Hessychus act as his agent. All these actions suggest a lively business community in Puteoli and Pompeii, where the records were kept. See Casson, *loc. cit.*, who shows that these are private dealers operating on credit in a free-enterprise system. The interest is not stated in this particular document, but in the others (almost 70 of them found together) it was 1% per month.

177   Societies of the working classes.
Documents are in Latin unless otherwise noted.

A: *Digest* 47.22.1. **B**: *CIL* VI 2193 (4416); **ILS* 4966; *FIRA* III 38. marble tablet, Rome. **C**: *CIL* X 143; **ILS* 7293. Tombstone, Potentia in Italy. **D**: *CIL* VI 6215; **ILS* 7360 a. From the great monument of the family Statilii, Rome. **E**: *CIL* VI 8686; **ILS* 1577. Small column, Rome. **F**: *CIL* VI 9034. Stone found near the Porta Capena, Rome. **G**: *CIL* IX 2686. Tombstone, Aesernia in Italy. **H**: *CIL* XII 187. Stone found at Antipolis in Gallia Narbonensis. **I**: *AÉ* 1912, 171. Stone from Koptos in Egypt. [Greek]

See J. P. Waltzing, *Étude historique sur les corporations professionelles chez les romains* I–IV (Louvain 1895–1900); F. M. De Robertis, *Storia delle corporazioni e del regime associativo nel mondo romano* I–II (Bari 1974); Meiggs, *Ostia*[2] Ch. 14. Cf. Pliny, *Epist.* 10.33–4; 10.92–3.

A. *Digest* **47.22.1**

In the imperial instructions it is enjoined on the provincial governors that permission cannot be given for the existence of societies and that soldiers may not have clubs in the camps. However, it is permitted <by decree of the senate>[1] for poor people to make a monthly contribution, provided that they meet only once a month and that no illegal society meets under a pretext of this nature. The deified (Septimius) Severus also wrote in a rescript that this was valid not only in the city (of Rome) but also in Italy and the provinces. However, they are not prohibited from meeting for the sake of religion, provided that nothing is done thereby contrary to the decree of the senate, by which illegal societies are banned.

B. *ILS* **4966, Rome**

To the departed spirits. | For the society of those who play in | bands,
5   who are available for the public | sacrifices, and to whom ‖ the senate has given permission to hold meetings, to be called to assembly, and to be mustered in accordance with the | Julian Law by authority | of Augustus[2] for the sake of the games.

C. *ILS* **7293. Potentia**

To Titus Mettius Poti|tus who lived 18 years. | (Dedicated by) the Society of Mule-and-|Ass-Drivers.

D. *ILS* **7360 a. Rome**

Statilia Ammia here | is buried. Her burial | was cared for by her | Burial
5   Society: Cerdo the caretaker of the apartment block, ‖ her husband; Bathyllus the house-servant; | Musaeus the janitor; Eros the caretaker of the apartment block; Philocalus | the masseur.[3]

E. *ILS* **1577. Rome**

Marcus Ulpius, freedman of Augustus, Aeglus, | procurator of the
5   mausoleum,[4] | gave as a gift this Corinthian | likeness ‖ of Traianus Caesar | to the Society of Hay Merchants.

F. *CIL* **VI 9034. Rome**

[Tiberius Clau]dius, freedman of Augustus, Onesimus. | He was *contractor* for the public works of Caesar | and quinquennalis (president) of the Society of Carpenters. | Lustrum 19 (AD 79–83).[5]

G. *CIL* **IX 2686. Aesernia**

Lucius Lucilius, freedman of Lucius, | Successus, quinquennalis

5   (president) of the Society | of Firemen, | made this for himself and || for his mate Fannia Lea, | while he was living.

H. *CIL* XII 187. Antipolis in Gallia Narbonensis

5   To the Society | of Boatmen | Gaius Iulius | Catullinus || erected this as a gift.

I. *AÉ* 1912, 171. Koptos

(Dedicated to) the pious Zabdalas, (son) of Salma|nos and Aneina,
5 (one) of the Hadria|nic Palmyrene | Red Sea Shipowners, || who constructed from the foundations | the propylaea and the three *stoas* (?) | and all the new things | which he built at his own expense | because of
10 his love of good deeds. || The Hadrianic Palmyrene Merchants | to their friend.[6]

1 This decree of the senate is also mentioned in the regulations of a Burial Society of AD 136 (*ILS* 7212) and therefore must date from an earlier period.
2 Cf. Suetonius, *Augustus* 32.1. See E. J. Jory in *Hermes* 98 (1970) 251.
3 All of these were either slaves or freedmen of Titus Statilius Taurus (consul AD 44). The monument served to commemorate not only Statilia Ammia and those mentioned as part of the Burial Society, but also the entire household of Statilius (*CIL* VI 6213–640), a common practice among the great Roman families.
4 Probably the Mausoleum of Augustus: Suetonius, *Augustus* 100 and Strabo 5.3.263.
5 The era of this society began in 6 BC.
6 See Rostovtzeff, *SEHRE*[2] 605.

178 Slaves in the Roman world.
Documents here are in Latin unless otherwise noted.
See also Document No. 47.

A: Gaius, *Institutes* 1.9–17. B: Justinian, *Digest* 48.8.11.2. C: Justinian, *Digest* 48.18.1. D: *CIL* VI 5195; *ILS* 1514; Ehrenberg–Jones, *Documents*[2] 158. From a columbarium in Rome. E: *CIL* III 14206.21; *ILS* 7479. Tombstone found not far from Philippi in Macedonia. F: *CIL* VI 8970; *ILS* 1831. Tombstone, Rome. G: *FIRA* I 104, lines 26–8; D'Ors, *Epigrafía Jurídica de la España Romana* (Madrid 1953) No. 6, pp. 129–30, lines 26–8. Bronze tablet from Vipasca. AD 117–38. H: *CIL* XI 137; *ILS* 1980. Tombstone, Ravenna. I: The Suda *s.v.* Epaphroditos. J: *CIL* XV 7194; *ILS* 8731; Bruns[7] 159.2; *FIRA* III 127 b. Slave collar with inscription on disc. Rome.

See R. H. Barrow, *Slavery in the Roman Empire* (London 1928, repr. 1968); Balsdon, *Life and Leisure* 106–15; H. Chantraine, *Freigelassen und Sklaven im Dienst des römischen Kaiser: Studien zu ihrer Nomenklatur* (Wiesbaden 1967); K. R. Bradley, *Slaves and Masters in the Roman Empire: A Study in Social Control* (Brussels 1984).

A. Gaius, *Institutes* 1.9–17

The principal distinction in the law of persons is this, that all men are either free or slaves. (10) Next, some free men are free-born, others are freedmen. (11) Free-born men are born free, freedmen are those manumitted from lawful slavery. (12) Next, of freedmen <there are three groups: for they are either Roman citizens or Latins or> belong among the <dediticii>. Let us consider these one by one, beginning with the dediticii. (13) By the Aelian Sentian Law it is provided that slaves who have been put in chains by their owners in the name of punishment, or those who have been branded, or those who have been subjected to torture under examination for some wrongful act and have been found guilty of that act, or those who have been handed over to fight with a weapon (as gladiators) or to fight with wild animals or have been thrown into a gladiatorial school or into prison, and have been manumitted afterwards either by the same owner or by another (owner), that they will become free men of the same status as that of foreign dediticii. (14) Those called foreign dediticii are those who formerly had taken up arms and fought against the Roman People and, after being defeated, had surrendered. (15) Slaves (guilty) of the base actions (mentioned above) and manumitted by any method or at whatever age, even though they were in the full legal power of their owners, never became Roman citizens or Latins, but are under any circumstances always numbered among the dediticii. (16) However, if a slave is not (guilty) of any such base action, after manumission he becomes sometimes a Roman citizen and sometimes a Latin. (17) In the case of a particular slave, he becomes a full Roman citizen if three conditions are met: that he is over thirty years of age, that he is the legal property of his owner, and that he is set free by legal and legitimate manumission, i.e. by being touched by his owner with a piece of straw, or by the census, or by last will and testament. If any of these conditions are lacking, he will be a Latin.[1]

B. Justinian, *Digest* 48.8.11.2

After the passage of the Petronian Law[2] and the decree of the senate pertaining to that law the power of an owner by his own decision to hand over his slaves to fight wild animals was taken away from him. Nevertheless, if a slave is brought before a court of law and if the complaint of the owner is just, he is handed over to such a punishment.

C. Justinian, *Digest* 48.18.1

To unearth crimes an investigation is regularly conducted. However, let us see when or how far in scope it is to be done. The deified Augustus ordained that it must not be started by applying torture and that no credibility should be given to (such an) investigation, but a letter of the deified Hadrian to Sennius Sabinus is preserved. The words of his rescript are as follows: The point of torturing slaves ought to be reached only when a charge is brought against a suspect and only when by other evidence the action comes so close to proof that only the confession of slaves seems to be lacking.

D. *ILS* 1514. Rome

To Musicus, (slave) of Tiberius Caesar Augustus, | Scurranus, adminis-
trator of the Gallic treasury | of the province of Lugdunensis, | from his
5   vicarii (slaves)[3] who were with him in Rome when ‖ he died, well-
deserving man: | (Col. 1) Venustus, wholesale dealer; | Decimianus, in
charge of household expenses; | Dicaeus, amanuensis; | Mutatus,
10   amanuensis; ‖ Creticus, amanuensis; | (Col. 2) Agathopus, physician; |
Epaphra, financial aide; | Primio, in charge of clothing; | Communis,
15   attached to the imperial bedroom; ‖ Pothus, manservant; | Tiasus,
cook; | (Col. 3) Facilis, manservant; | Anthus, financial aide; | Hedylus,
20   in the bedroom; ‖ Firmus, cook; | Secunda (duty not given).

E. *ILS* 7479. Near Philippi in Macedonia

Vitalis, Gaius Lavius Faustus' | slave and also his son, born a slave in
the house, | is buried here. He lived | 16 years, a clerk for the Aprian
Shop, ‖ accepted by the people, | by the gods | taken away. Please, |
travelers, if I ever gave you less | than a full measure (of food or wine)
5   to add that much more to my father, ‖ forgive me. Please, by the gods
above | and below, accept the care for the best interests of my father
and mother. | Farewell.

F. *ILS* 1831. Rome

To the departed spirits. | To Titus Flavius, freedman of Augustus,
Ganymedes, | paedagogus of the slave-boys of our Caesar,[4] (this monu-
ment) was made by Ulpia Helpis, | for her excellent and well-deserving
husband, and for her own freedmen and freedwomen.

G. D'Ors, *Epigrafía Jurídica* No. 6. Vispasca

The one who steals metal ore, if he is a slave, shall be flogged with
whips by the procurator and sold on the condition that he is to be
constantly | in chains and not remain in any mines or territories of
mines. The price of the slave shall belong to the owner. The procurator
shall confiscate the property of a free man (guilty of stealing) and
forever prohibit him from the borders of mines.[5]

H. *ILS* 1980. Ravenna

Gaius Iulius Mygdonius, | by descent a Parthian, | born free, captured
5 | in my youth, given over (to be sold as a slave) in the land ‖ of the
Romans. When I was made a | Roman citizen with the help of fate, I got
to|gether a money-chest for the time when | I would be 50 years old. My
ambition since a young | man was to reach my old age. Now receive me
10 gladly, tombstone. ‖ With you I will be free from trouble.

I. The Suda *s.v.* **Epaphroditos**

Epaphroditos of Chaironea, teacher, slave (born in the house) of
Archias of Alexandria the teacher, by whom he was educated. He was
purchased by Modestus the prefect of Egypt,[6] and after teaching his
son Pelelinus he became prominent in Rome from the reign of Nero to
that of Nerva, at which time also lived Ptolemaios son of Hephaistion
and many other famous men in education. He was always buying books
and possessed thirty thousand of them, serious and recondite books.
His body was large and dark like an elephant.[7] He lived in the so-called
(district of) Phainianokorioi[8] and had two houses there. He died in his
75th year, of dropsy. He left behind quite a number of writings.[9]

J. *FIRA* III 127 b. Rome

I am a runaway. Hold me. | When you re|turn me to my owner, |
5   Zoninus, you will receive ‖ a gold coin.

1   Gaius explains later that *dediticii* can never reside in Rome. They are free, but with
    restrictions. Latins, however, can become full Roman citizens. The Aelian Sentian
    Law was passed in AD 4. See F. Schulz in *JRS* 32 (1942) 78ff.
2   Perhaps passed in AD 61, but certainly before AD 79.
3   Slaves in the imperial household and in other great households could have slaves
    themselves, who were called *vicarii*.
4   This *paedagogus* was the director of an imperial school that specialized in training
    slave-boys for the various duties in the imperial household. See Balsdon, *Life and
    Leisure* 112–13.
5   The imperial mines were worked by both slaves and free men. In some mines an
    imperial slave or freedman was in charge of the day-to-day operations. Vipasca was
    a copper and silver mining-area in what is now Portugal. See O. Davies in *OCD*[2] *s.v.*
    Mines.
6   Marcus Mettius Modestus, prefect of Egypt about the beginning of Nero's reign:
    Stein, *Präfekten* 32–3.
7   A marble relief of him is extant in Rome, showing a seated man with beard holding
    a book-roll in his hand and identified by the accompanying inscription (*ILS* 7760):
    see above, Document No. 173 M.
8   An unknown area of Rome.
9   See Cohn in *RE s.v.* Epaphroditos (5), Cols. 2711–14, and Johannes Christes, *Sklaven
    und Freigelassene als Grammatiker und Philologen im antiken Rom* (Wiesbaden 1979) 103–4.

179   Purchase of a female slave. Reign of Hadrian or Antoninus.
Third waxed tablet of a triptych written at Ravenna but found in Egypt.
The language is Latin, but for lines 1–10 the Latin is written by the use
of the Greek alphabet.

O. Eger in *ZSS*, *Rom. Abt.* 42 (1921) 453; *SB* 6304; **FIRA* III 134; Cavenaile, *CPL* 193.

When Gaius Curtius Iustus and Publius Iulius Nauto | were consuls
(date ?), on the sixth day before the Nones of October (October 2), | I,
Aischines, (son) of Aischines, Flavianus of Miletus, wrote | that I
received from Titus Memmius Montanus, soldier of the Augustan fleet
5   (at Ravenna), six hun‖dred and twenty-five denarii as the price of a
young woman of Mar|marica, old (slave)[1] whom I sold and handed over
to him at double price with the best | conditions (of the sale). After
examinatio|n of the sealed tablets, | done in the camp of the Praetorian
10   Fleet at Raven‖na.[2] | (Latin alphabet) When the same men were con-
suls, on the same day, I, Domitius The|ophilus, wrote that I appeared
as second witness to the sale of the young woman of Marma|rica,
mentioned above, on behalf of Aischines, (son) of Aischines, |
15   Flavianus. ‖ Done.

1 Here 'old' is used in the legal sense of 'not new', i.e. not a new slave. For the age of
   female slaves see K. R. Bradley in *Arethusa* 11 (1978) 243ff.
2 The remains of a seal are visible here, another after line 15.

180   Gift of gardens to freedmen and freedwomen.
Limestone tablet, Tarraco in Spain. [Latin]

CIL II 4332; *ILS* 8271; *FIRA* III 81 f; A. D'Ors, *Epigrafía Jurídica de la España Romana*
(Madrid 1953) No. 32; Alföldy, **Tarraco* 368 (+ photograph).

To the departed spirits. | For Antonia Clementina, his wife, Publius
Rufius Flavus, | husband, made this (monument and also for himself
while still living. For her perpetual memory | he handed over their
5   gardens, adjacent and suburban,[1] ‖ to the freedmen and freedwomen of
his wife's household – Marullus, Antrocles, | Helena, and Tertullina –
with the stipulation that nobody | may sell them, but that possession
will descend through their offspring | or male blood relatives or their
manumitted male (slaves).

1 SHA, *Hadrian* 12.5, relates how Hadrian, while strolling through flower gardens at
   Tarraco, was attacked by a crazed slave.

181   An imperial freedman in charge of elephants in Italy.
Tombstone from Rome. [Latin]

CIL VI 8583; *ILS* 1578.

J. M. C. Toynbee, *Animals in Roman Life and Art* (London 1973) 46–9; H. H. Scullard, *The Elephant in the Greek and Roman World* (Ithaca, NY 1974) 199–200.

To the departed spirits. To Tiberius Claudius Speclator, | freedman of Augustus, procurator | of the Formian Estate at Caieta, | procurator at Laurentum of | the elephants.[1] | Cornelia Bellica to her husband, | well deserving.

1 Elephants were kept in Italy to be used by the emperors for parades and shows, but we also learn that Claudius in AD 43 had assembled elephants for use in his invasion of Britain: Dio 60.21.

182   Public activities of a prominent patron at Ostia.
Funerary altar richly decorated, the inscription framed at right and left by pilasters, with lions above, Ostia. [Latin]

CIL XIV 409; *ILS* 6146.

R. Meiggs, *Roman Ostia*[2] (Oxford 1973) 200ff. and *passim* (+ photograph of top of stele, Pl. XXXIV b), with text of inscription p. 559, No. 5.

(Dedicated) to Gnaeus Sentius, son of Gnaeus, | grandson of Gnaeus, (of the tribe) Teretina, Felix: | by decree of the decurions admitted to the rank of aedile, by decree of the decurions admitted to the decurion-ate, | quaestor of the Ostian treasury, duovir, quaestor of the Youth,[1]
5 ‖ – he was the first of all (our citizens), in the very year in which he became a decurion, | to be made also a quaestor of the treasury and for the next year designated to be duovir | – quinquennalis (i.e. chief officer) of the treasurers of marine ships, without giving or receiving payment admitted | among the shippers of the Adriatic Sea and (likewise among those meeting) at the Chariot (statue?) | of the Forum of Wine Merchants; (also) patron of the ten-man group[2] of secretaries
10 ‖ and book-keepers and lictors[3] and messengers; likewise (patron) of the heralds and | bankers and wine merchants from the city (of Rome); | likewise (patron) of grain-measurers of Ceres Augusta; likewise (pat-ron) of the Corporation | of small boats and skiffs[4] of the ferry-service of Lucullus,[5] and of | timber-workers, and of the toga-clad of the forum
15 (?), and of the public weighers, ‖ and of the public freedmen and slaves, and of the olive-oil merchants, and of the young men | who drive two-wheeled carriages, and of the veterans of Augustus; likewise (patron) of the military aides | of procurators of Augustus, and of the fish

retailers; and he was superintendent of the Parade of Youth. | Gnaeus
Sentius Lucilius | Gamala Clodianus (dedicated this monument), a son
20 || to a most indulgent father.[6]

1 The institution of the Youth spread throughout all Italy and the western provinces.
  It represented the young men of prominent families and had headquarters in most
  of the cities.
2 The 'ten-man group' (*decuria*) in the municipalities was a pool of service personnel
  for the executive magistrates and the local senators. See Meiggs, *op. cit.* 181–2.
3 Lictors, like those in Rome, were the attendants of the executive magistrates,
  accompanying them in public.
4 For the operators of small craft see Meiggs, *op. cit.* 296–7.
5 The ferry-service operated at the mouth of the Tiber, for Ostia had no bridge near
  its mouth.
6 Gnaeus Sentius Felix is the greatest known patron of guilds or societies we know.

183 Construction of a synagogue in Jerusalem. Before AD 70.
Limestone tablet, from a cistern in Jerusalem. [Greek]

R. Weil, *Revue des Études Juives* 71 (1920) 30–4; *SEG* VIII 170 (with further references).

H. Shanks, *Judaism in Stone* (New York and London 1979) 18–20 (+ photograph);
B. Mazar, *The Mountain of the Lord* (New York 1975) 87 (+ photograph).

Theodotos, son of Vettenus,[1] priest and | synagogue director, son of a
synagogue director, | grandson of a synagogue director, con|structed
5 this synagogue for re||ading of the Law and for instruction in the Com-
mandments. And | (he also constructed) the guest-house and (sleeping-)
rooms and the | water facilities for the shelter for the | needy people
from foreign lands. | The foundation (of the synagogue) was laid by his
10 fathers and the El||ders and Simonides.[2]

1 It has been suggested that Theodotos may have been the grandson of a Jew who had
  been captured by the Romans and later given his freedom. 'Vettenus' is an Italian
  name.
2 The phrase 'and Simonides' was added later.

184 A son delivers the funeral oration for his mother.
Large marble tablet inscribed with good letters of the Augustan age,
Rome.[1] [Latin]

CIL VI 10230; *ILS* 8394; *FIRA* III 70 (lines 1–13).

F. Vollmer in *Jahrbücher für classische Philologie, Supplement-Band* 18 (1892) 484ff.; J. P. V. D.
Balsdon, *Roman Women* (London 1962) 206–8; W. Kierdorf, *Laudatio Funebris: Interpret-
ationen und Untersuchungen zur Entwicklung der römischen Leichenrede* (Meisenheim am Glan
1980) *passim*, with bare text on pp. 145–6.

(Heading) [To the departed spirit (?)] of Murdia, daughter of Lucius, my mother. | [----]² but by their own strength they exalt other things so that they are stronger | and more admirable. *vv* | She made all her sons
5 equally her heirs, after giving a share to her daughter. ‖ Her motherly love consists of affection for her children and equality of their portions. | To her husband³ she bequeathed a fixed amount of money so that the right of the dowry might be increased by the honor of her good judgment. | She recalled the memory of my father, kept it before her in her plans, remained loyal to it | and, upon making an evaluation, made specific prior bequests in her testament: | it was not in her character to prefer me to my brothers with some kind of insulting behavior toward
10 them,⁴ ‖ but, remembering my father's kindliness, | she decided to give me what, by the judgment of her (first) husband, she had received from my father's estate, | so that by her order whatever had been placed in her custody was res|tored to my ownership. *vv* |

Therefore, she decided in this way that the marriages given to her by
15 her parents to worthy men ‖ would be kept by her with obedience and honorableness, that after marriage she would become more pleasing by her merits, | that she would be considered more precious because of her trustworthiness, that she would be left more distinguished by her good judgment, | and that after death she would be praised by the consensus of her citizens, since the distribution | of her (inherited) allotment would imply her grateful and loyal feelings toward her (two) husbands, her fair|ness toward the children, and the justice in the correctness of
20 her action. *vv* ‖

For these reasons, since praise for all good women is customarily simple and sim|ilar – because their own naturally good qualities and the preservation of a place for their safe-keeping | do not need great varieties of verbal description – and since sufficient is the fact that | they all have done the same good deeds worthy of the reputation, and because | it is difficult to discover new ways to praise a woman – their
25 lives are shaken up by fewer vici‖ssitudes – by necessity the characteristics they share must be cherished by us, so that whatever | of their just precepts have been lost might not damage the remainder. *vv* |

My dearest mother deserved all the greater praise, because | in modesty, uprightness, purity, obedience, wool-working, diligence, and faithfulness | she was equal and similar to other good women, and she
30 did not yield to any ‖ of the dangers that can threaten vir|tue, work, and wisdom, [----].

---

1 At least one block preceded and another followed the present one. The heading
   began on the missing first block and continued on at the top of the second.
2 Nothing can be restored with confidence.

3 This is her second husband.
4 When Murdia's son speaks of 'my brothers', he means the sons of Murdia by her
   second husband.

185   Marriage contract.[1] 13 BC.
Papyrus from Egypt. [Greek]

BGU 1052.

    [----] | To Protarchos[2] | from Thermion (daughter) of Apion, with her
5 guardian | the [----] Apollonios (son) of Chaireas, and from Apo‖lonios
(son) of Ptolemaios. Agreement has been made by Thermion | and
Apollonios (son) of Ptolemaios that they have joined | together for a
partnership in life, and | Apollonios himself, (son) of Ptolemaios,
10 (agrees) that he has recei|ved from Thermion by hand from her ho‖use
a dowry, a pair of gold earrings | (weighing) three quarters and silver
drachmas [----;] | and from the present time Apollonios (son) of
Ptolemaios | will provide Thermion everything she needs, | including
15 clothing, as his wedded wife ‖ according to his existing means and will
not | mistreat her nor throw her out nor | insult her nor introduce
another woman, | or he will pay back the dowry in full | with an
20 additional *half*, the transaction taking place ‖ upon Apollonios *himself*,
(son) of Ptolemaios, | and upon all his property | as if by judgment of a
court; and Ther|mion [will do] what is just and right toward her hus-
25 band and | their common life and will not ‖ sleep away from home nor
be absent for a day | [from the] house without the knowledge of
Apollon|ios (son) of Ptolemaios nor destroy | [nor] damage their com-
30 mon home | [nor] consort with another man, or she too, ‖ if she has
done any of these things, will be judged and | deprived of her dowry,
quite apart from the | guilty party being liable also to the | prescribed
fine. | Year 17 of Caesar (Augustus), Pharmouthi 20.

1 For the marriage contract in the Greek East see J. Modrzejewski in *Scritti in onore di
   Orsolina Montevecchi* (Bologna 1981) 231–68. For marriage in Italy and the Roman
   West see Balsdon, *Life and Leisure*, Ch. 7, and, for the legal aspects, F. Schulz, *Classical
   Roman Law* (Oxford 1951) Ch. 3.
2 Protarchos is the person in authority to whom the contract had to be submitted for
   proper registration in this area of Egypt.

186   Apartment building for rent. Before AD 79.
Painted letters on a building in Pompeii. [Latin]

CIL IV 138; *ILS* 6035; Bruns[7] 167.1; **FIRA* III 143 a.

Apartment building 'Arriana | Polliana' of Gnaeus Alleius Nigidius Maius: | for rent from the next [Kalends] of July (July 1) are shops | with open frontages, high-class upper lodgings, || and a house. A renter | should contact Primus, slave of Gnaeus Alleius Nigidius Maius.

5

187   Auxiliary soldier declares birth of a daughter. AD 131.
Wax tablet, originally part of a diptychon, Philadelphia in Egypt. [Latin with Greek resumé]

BGU 1690; *FIRA* III 5.

(Latin) Epimachus (son) of Longinus, soldier of Cohort Two of Thebans in the century of Octavius Alexan|der [--- has testified] that a daughter | Longina has been born to him on the 7th day before the Kalends of January (December 26), | just preceding, from his hostess[1]

5   Arsus, daughter of Lucius. || He said that he resorted to this provisional report | because of his enforced military presence elsewhere (i.e. in camp). Done at Philadelphia | in the winter quarters of Cohort Two of Thebans on the 7th (?) day before the Kalends of Ja[nuary (December 26),[2] when Sergius Octavius] Laenas | Pontianus and Marcus Antonius Rufinus were consuls (AD 131), in the 16th year of Imperator Caesar | Traianus Hadrianus Augustus, on the 30th day of the month Choeac.

10 || (Greek) I, Epimachos (son) of Longinus, soldier | mentioned above, have testified | that a daughter Longina has been born, | just as written above.

1   This word seems to be used in the sense of *focaria*, i.e. 'kitchen-maid' or our word 'housekeeper'.
2   A mistake in date appears to have been made here. Instead of '7th day' in this line it is more likely that '6th day' should have been written, i.e. December 27, the daughter having been born on the preceding day. See Viereck and Zucker in *BGU*.

188   Exposure of children in the Graeco-Roman world.

A: Musonius Rufus, *Reliquiae* XV B (ed. Hense) (Stobaeus, *Florilegium* 4.84.21).
B: Plutarch, *Moralia* (*On Love of Offspring*) 497E. **C**: *P. Oxy.* 744. Papyrus from Oxyrhynchus, Egypt. 1 BC. **D**: *BGU* 1210 (Gnomon of the Idios Logos) 41 and 92. **E**: *CIL* VIII 12879; *ILS* 1486. Tombstone, Carthage.

Cf. Juvenal, *Satires* 6.602–9; Suetonius, *Caligula* 5; Pliny, *Epist.* 10.65–6 (on which see A. Cameron in *Anatolian Studies Presented to William Hepburn Buckler*, ed. W. M. Calder and Josef Keil (Manchester 1939) 48–59); Suetonius, *De Grammaticis* 7 and 21; Tacitus, *Germania* 19 and *Hist.* 5.5.

Balsdon, *Life and Leisure* 82–8; Brunt, *Manpower* 148–54; W. V. Harris in *Classical Quarterly* 32 (1982) 114–16 (with further references).

A. Musonius Rufus, *Reliquiae* XV B[1]

What seems most strange to me is not that some people who have poverty to offer as an excuse, but that those who have an abundance of things and some who are even wealthy nevertheless have the boldness not to rear children born to them, in order that those previously born might be more prosperous.

B. Plutarch, *Moralia* 497E

Poor people do not bring up their children, because they are afraid that they, having been brought up less well than is proper, will become servile and uneducated and will lack all the good qualities. Considering poverty to be the worst evil, they cannot bear to share it with their children, as if it were a dangerous, serious disease.

C. *P. Oxy.* 744, Oxyrhynchus

Hilarion to Alis my sister (and wife), many greetings, | also to Berous my lady and Apollo|narion. Know that even now we are still in
5   Alexan|dria. Do not worry. If they g‖o their way, I will remain in Alexandria. | I beg and call upon you: take | care of the little child and the minute we receive our | pay, I will send it up (river) to you. If | you
10   give birth – the best of everything to you! – and it is a ‖ boy, let it alone, but if it is a girl, expose it. | You told Aphrodisias, 'Don't | forget me.'
15   How can I forget you? | I beg you not to wo|rry. ‖ Year 29 of Caesar (1 BC), Payni 23. | (Verso) Hilarion to Alis. Deliver it.

D. Gnomon of the Idios Logos 41 and 92

(41) If an Egyptian brings up a child exposed on a dung heap and adopts him, a fourth of his estate is confiscated at death. (92) A child exposed on a dung heap cannot become a priest.

E. *ILS* 1486, Carthage

Sacred to the departed spirits. | Devoted Hypnus lived | 23 years, buried
5   here. | Asiaticus, freedman of Augustus (and) procurator ‖ of the Assuritanian region, to his devoted (and) well-deserving foster-son[2] made (this monument).

---

1 The rubric in Stobaeus reads: 'Musonius, from his (work): Whether One Should Rear All Children Born to Him'. It is not clear whether this is the Gaius Musonius Rufus who was a Stoic philosopher of Nero's time or a Musonius who lived under Trajan and Hadrian. See Parker in *HSCP* 7 (1896) 123–37.
2 This word, *alumnus* ('foster-son'), is frequently used to denote an exposed child

rescued and brought up by foster parents. It is especially common on the tombstones of Roman Africa.

189   Deed of divorce. 13 BC.
Papyrus, Egypt.

BGU 1103.

[---] | To Protarchos[1] | from Zois (daughter) of Herakleides, with her
5   guardi|an, her brother Eirenaios (son) of Herakleides, ‖ and from
Antipater (son) of Zenon. | Zois and Antipater agree that they have
separated | from each other (and) from their union of marriage | accord-
ing to the agreement through the sa|me tribunal in the present 17th
10   year of Caesar (13 BC), ‖ (month of) Hathur, and Zois (agrees) that she
has received from | Antipater by hand from the house that which he
received for her | dowry: clothing worth | one hundred and twenty
drachmas and a pair of gold earrings. | (They agree) that immediately the
15   ‖ agreement of marriage will be invalid, that no steps | will be taken by
Zois or any|body else on her behalf against Antipater | to demand back
the dowry, that neither | one of them (will take steps) against the other
20   concerning their living ‖ together or concerning anything | else, right
up to the present | day, that from (the present) day it will be permitted
| Zois to join another man in wedlock | and Antipater another woman,
25   ‖ neither being accountable to the other, | and that, quite aside from
these arrangements being valid, | liability will belong to the one who |
transgresses them for damages | and the penalty determined by law.
30   ‖ Year 17 of Caesar, Pharmouthi 2.

1   A state official in charge of a tribunal in Alexandria.

190   Recall of a will. AD 135.
Papyrus from Oxyrhynchus, Egypt. [Greek]

P. Oxy. 106.

To the agoranomoi[1] of the city of Oxyrhynchus. | I, Apolloni|os (son)
5   of Ptolemaios, assistant, | have (hereby) announced to you ‖ that the
strategos of the nome, Deme|trios, has ordered me | to return to
Ptolema, | daughter of Straton and Diony|sia from the city of Oxyrhyn-
10   chus, ‖ the will which was drawn up by you | in the 9th year of the god
Trajan | in (the month of) Mecheir under seals, | since she requested
15   the return. | Through me ‖ she has received the will. Year | 9 *vv* | of

Imperator Caesar | Traianus Hadrianus | Augustus (AD 135),
20   Pharmouthi 25. ||
      (In a different hand) I, Ptolema, daughter of Straton, have received |
my above-mentioned will under the | same seals. I, Pedon (son) of
Kalli|kornos, am registered as her guardian | and have signed for her,
25   since she is illiterate. || Same date.

1 The agoranomos was a notary for the drawing up of public papers in Egypt.

191   Official notification of death in the family. AD 37.
Papyrus from the Fayûm in Egypt. [Greek]

P. Fay. 29.

To Herakleides, village-secretary | of Euhemeria, | from Mysthes, son
5   of Pene|ouris, of [Eu]he||meria in the Themistian | district. My brother
Peneouris, | son of Peneouris, a registered in|habitant of the land
10   around the | village in question, has || died in the month of Mesore | in
the first year of Gaius | Caesar Augustus | Germanicus (AD 37). Where-
15   fore I sub|mit to you this notification || in order that *his name* may be put
| in the register of the decea|sed [according to] the custom. | (Signature)
[Mythes, son of Peneouris,] | about 42 years old with a scar on his right
20   forearm. || Year 1 of Gaius Caesar Augustus |Germanicus, Mesore 14. |
(Date then repeated in a second hand with the signature of an official).

192   Letter of recommendation to a tribune of soldiers.
Papyrus from Oxyrhynchus, Egypt. [Latin]

P. Oxy. 32 (+ photograph); Cavenaile, **CPL* 249.

To Iulius Domitius, tribune of soldiers of the legion, | from Aurelius
Archelaos, his beneficiarius (i.e. aide), | greetings. | Already previously
5   to you have I recommen||ded Theon, a friend | of mine, and now also do
I ask, | my lord, that you consider him in your eyes | as if he were me.
10   For he is | a man such as to be esteemed || by you. He has left his own
(relations) and | property and past life and | has followed me, and
through everything he has | made me secure. Thus, I ask | from you that
15   he have access || to you, and he can tell you everything | about our
common actions of the past. Whatever he said [----] I esteemed the
man [-----]¹

1 Seven following lines are unintelligible. The last lines (27–34) contain stylized
   phrases of courtesy, and the verso of the papyrus has the address to Iulius Domitius.

193   Roman senator asked to be town's patron. AD 101 or 102.
Bronze tablet, beautifully engraved, Rome. [Latin]

CIL VI 1492; *ILS* 6106; A. Bartoli in *Atti della Pontificia Accademia Romana di Archeologia, Rendiconti* 25–6 (1949–50) 89 ff.; Smallwood, *Documents Nerva* 437; R. K. Sherk, **Municipal Decrees of the Roman West* (Buffalo 1970) No. 9; Gordon, *Epigraphy* 54 (pp. 133–5 + photograph).

Bartoli, *loc. cit.*; P. Garnsey in *Historia* 17 (1968) 381; A. Soffredi in *Epigraphica* 19 (1957) 157ff. (patronage in Italy); R. Duthoy in *L'Antiquité Classique* 53 (1984) 145–56 (institution of patronage); John Nicols in *ANRW* 2.13.535–61.

When Lucius Arruntius Stella and | Lucius Iulius Marinus were consuls (AD 101 or 102), | on the fourteenth day before the Kalends *vv* of November (October 19), *vv* | Manius Acilius Placidus and Lucius
5   Petronius Fronto, ‖ the quattuorviri for the administration of justice, consulted the senate of Ferentinum in the hall of the temple of Mer|cury. (Witnesses) present at the writing (of the decree) were: Quintus Segiarnus Mae|cianus and Titus Munnius Nomantinus. *vv* | Whereas they all said that Titus Pomponius Bassus, most illus|trious
10   man,[1] was performing the charge given to him by ‖ our most considerate Imperator Caesar Nerva Traianus | Augustus Germanicus,[2] by which means (Trajan) has looked forward to the continuance forever of his Italy, | (and was performing it) in accordance with his generosity | in such a way that our whole generation | ought to give thanks for his meritorious performance, and (whereas they all said) it could happen
15   that ‖ a man of such excellent character would be of assistance to our municipality, | in regard to their pleasure about what should be done about it, concerning it they decreed as follows: | it pleased the senators (of Ferentinum) that envoys from their order | be sent to Titus Pomponius Bassus, most illus|trious man, and that (those envoys)
20   should obtain his acquiescence ‖ in thinking it fit to receive our municipality into | the patronage of his most esteemed house, | and to permit himself to be selected as our patron, with a tablet | of hospitality
25   engraved with this decree placed in his house. | Decreed. ‖ *vv* The envoys who performed (this task) were: *vv* Aulus Caecilius, son of Aulus, Quirinalis, and Quirinalis *vv* his son. *vv*

1 Pomponius Bassus (cos. suff. AD 94) was a most prominent Roman senator and experienced administrator of the period: see Sherk in *ANRW* 2.7.2.1014–16.
2 The 'charge' or 'public office' given to him by Trajan was membership in a senatorial commission to supervise the *alimenta* or Child Assistance Program in Italy: see below, No. 197.

194 Honorarium for a speaker. AD 110.
Papyrus from Egypt. [Greek]

P. Brem. 46; Hengstl, **Griechische Papyri* No. 153.

Mnesitheos (son) of Mnesitheos to Epagathos | holding the [----] bank, *greetings.* | Pay to Licinnius Dr[---,] | the rhetor, the amount due him for
5   the speeches [in] ‖ which Aur[elius ---] was honored | on the 12th day of the month Pha[ophi] | in the *gymnasium* | in the Great Serapeion, |
10 four hundred drachmas of silver: 400 drachmas. Year four‖teen of Imperator | Caesar Nerva Traianus | Augustus Germanicus Dacicus (AD 110), | Phaophi 23. (Second hand) I, Licin[nius D]r[---,] have
15 received | [the four hundred drachmas of silver:] ‖ 400 drachmas, *as specified.*

195 Receipts of various kinds.

A: *CIL* IV 3340.XL; Bruns[7] 157; *FIRA III 129 b. Waxed tablet from Pompeii. Receipt for money realized from an auction. [Latin] **B**: *P. Ryl.* II 189. Papyrus from Socnopaei Nesus, Egypt. Receipt for manufacture of clothing for the army in Judaea. [Greek] **C**: *P. Fay.* 67. Papyrus from the Fayûm, Egypt. Receipt issued at a customs-house. [Greek] **D**: G. Plaumann in *Archiv für Papyrusforschung* 6 (1920) p. 219, No. 4; *SB 7398. Ostracon from Elephantine, Egypt. Receipt for contribution toward a statue of Hadrian. [Greek] **E**: *O. Fay.* 10. Ostracon from the Fayûm, Egypt. Receipt for payment of tax on the making of beer. Reign of Nero. [Greek]

A. *FIRA* III 129 b. Pompeii

8,562 sesterces is the amount of money which, reaching the sum promised by Lucius Caecilius Iucundus, came to him from the auction of (the property of) Tullia Lampyris after his commission. Tullia Lampyris declared that she was paid in full by Lucius Caecilius Iucundus.[1] Done at Pompeii on the 10th day before the Kalends of January (December 23) in the consulship of Nero Caesar for the second time and Lucius Caesius Martialis (AD 57).
    (Signatures follow of eight men who acted as witnesses.)

B. *P. Ryl.* II 189. Socnopaei Nesus

Dionysios, son of Socrates, and the associate receivers | of public clothing for the guards have received from wea|vers of the village of Socnopaei Nesus [----] | nineteen tunics – 19 – and for the soldiers' needs ‖ of those serving in Judaea white cloaks, | five of them – 5. Year 13 of Imperator Caesar Traianus Hadrianus | Augustus (AD 128), Choiak 22. (Signature in second hand) Diogenes accepted delivery. |

(Third hand) Onesas also accepted. (Fourth hand) Philoxenos | also accepted.

C. *P. Fay.* 67. The Fayûm

Tax paid (for passage) through the gate (of the village) Bacchias by Ibia, (son) of Pt(olemaios?): | three donkeys (carrying) wheat. Year 2 of Titus, lo|rd (AD 80), Mesore the thirteenth. | (Second hand) I, Epios, signed this.

D. *SB* 7398. Elephantine

Samnous the dealer. Payment received from Psen|chnoubis, son of Pelaios, for joint | contribution[2] toward a bronze statue *and* a silver bust
5 of lord Hadrian ‖ {lord}: 4 silver drachmas. Year 2 (of Hadrian), | [Pa]chon 28.

E. *O. Fay.* 10. The Fayûm

[Year --] of Nero Claudius Caesar | [Augustus] Germanicus Imperator, [Phame]noth 4. Kopithon and Saty|[ros] (paid the tax) for making beer, individually assessed, at Euhemeria: *four* [drachmas of silver] – 4 drachmas.

1 Line-dividers could not be used in translating this document. Caecilius Iucundus was a Pompeian auctioneer and businessman in whose house was found a very large number of receipts on waxed tablets which recorded the sale of various properties by him or his agents at auctions.
2 The usual word in this context (*merismos*) means 'share of assessment'. The statue and bust are to be purchased by the whole city, its citizens being assessed a tax to pay for them. See U. Wilcken, *Griechische Ostraka* I (Munich 1899) 152–4.

196 Tenant farmers on an imperial estate. AD 116–17.
Marble block inscribed on four sides, from the ruins called Henchir Mettich, Africa. [Latin]

CIL VIII 25902; Abbott–Johnson, *Municipal Administration* 74; *FIRA* I 100; Smallwood, *Documents Nerva* 463; D. Flach in *Chiron* 8 (1978) 441–92; D. Kehoe in *ZPE* 56 (1984) 198.

Abbott–Johnson, *op. cit.* 394–6; R. M. Haywood in *Economic Survey* 4.89–94 and 98–101; Mario De Dominicis in *RIDA* 7 (1960) 389–98 (+ photograph); Kehoe, *op. cit.* 201ff. and in *ZPE* 59 (1985) 156–8.

(Col. 1) [For] the *safety* | of our Augustus Imperator Caesar Traianus, Leader, | and his whole divine family, | Optimus Germanicus Parthicus.
5 Published by Licinius ‖ [Ma]ximus and Felicior, freedman and the procurators of Augustus, based on | the Mancian Law.[1]
   To those who <live (?)> within the estate of the Villa Mag|na

Variana, that is, Mappalia Siga, to them it is permitted by the Mancian Law to cultivate those lands which are not yet sur|veyed, | [----] with the result that he who cultivates them may have the right to their use.

10 || From the products which will be grown on this land they will be required to give to the owners or | lessees or overseers of the estate a proportional amount in accordance with the Ma|ncian Law under the following terms: the tenant farmers | will be required to transport to the threshing floor whatever crops of any sort they have produced | and to thresh them, and, by their own estimate, they will report the total

15 amount || to the lessees [or] overseers of the estate; and if the less|ees or overseers of the estate answer that they will give *renters'* shares in full, | the tenant farmers under [sealed (?)] *statements* (?) will take ca|re that, in regard to the shares of the products which they are required [to

20 give,] | they will give these tenant shares || to the lessees or overseers of the [estate.] Those who have or will have domain farms on the estate of Villa Mag|na or Mappalia Siga | will be required to give to the <owners> of the estate or to their lessees or overseers | full shares of the products and wines, in accordance with | the usage of the Mancian

25 (Law), whatever ki||nd of (such products) it lists: of the wheat from the threshing | floor, a third share; of the barley from the threshing floor, | a third share; of the beans from the threshing floor, a f[ourth (?) fifth (?)] | share; of the wine from the vat, a third share; of the pressed |

30 olive-oil, a third part; of the honey in the hi||ves, a sextarius (about a pint) from each one.[2]

1 This law 'seems to have been a regulation issued by an earlier owner of a large tract in the region': Haywood, *op. cit.* 99.
2 The inscription continues at great length, laying down the rules for various other crops and farm animals.

197   Child Assistance Program in Italy. Between AD 102 and 114.
Large bronze tablet inscribed in seven columns, the heading in larger letters than elsewhere and extending over the tops of all seven columns, Veleia in Italy. [Latin]

CIL XI 1147; *ILS* 6675; Bruns[7] 145; *FIRA* III 116; Smallwood, *Documents Nerva* 436.

R. Duncan-Jones, *The Economy of the Roman Empire* (Cambridge 1974) 288ff.; W. Eck, *Die staatliche Organisation Italiens in der hohen Kaiserzeit* (Munich 1979) 146–89.

(The heading) Mortgages on estates for 1,044,000 sesterces, in order that through the indulgence of our best and greatest Leader, Imperator Caesar Nerva | Traianus Augustus Germanicus Dacicus, boys and girls may receive assistance: legitimate boys to the number of 245 at 16

sesterces each (per month), making a total of 47,040 sesterces; legitimate girls to the number of 34 at 12 sesterces each (per month),
making a total of 4,896 sesterces; illegitimate boy, 1 at 144 sesterces
(per year); illegitimate girl, 1 at 122 sesterces (per year). | Total: 52,200
sesterces, which equals interest of 5% of the principal listed above.[1]

(Details of one mortgage from this area of Italy)

(Col. 1) Gaius Volumnius Memor and Volumnia Alce, through the
agency of Volumnius Diadumenos, their freedman, put up (for
mortgage) | their Quintiacus-Aurelianus farm (and) the Hill of Muletas
with its forest, which is in the territory of Veleia | in the Ambitrebian
district, bounded by (the properties of) Marcus Mommeius Persicus,
Satrius Severus, and the public (road), (valued at) 108,000 sesterces. |
They are to receive 8,692 sesterces and to put up the above-mentioned
farm as security.[2]

1 Perhaps beginning with Nerva, assistance for indigent children in Italy was obtained
   by government loans to the districts in which children were to receive the assistance.
   Landowners who accepted such loans received about 8% of the value of their property, on which they paid a cheap rate of interest of only 5% per year. That interest
   was given to the children. In this first mortgage – of many dozens from the region –
   5% of 1,044,000 sesterces amounts to 52,200 sesterces, which was distributed to the
   children.
2 Some 48 other descriptions of mortgages follow in complete form. For discussion
   and breakdown of the statistics see Duncan-Jones, *loc. cit.* For the working and
   organization of the whole system see Eck, *loc. cit.*

198   Market days and the seven-day week.

A: Festus 177 (Lindsay). **B**: Nonius Marcellus (Lindsay) *s.v.* Nundinae. From Varro's
Marcipor, Frag. 279 of his *Menippean Satires*. **C**: *CIL* IV 8863; **I. Ital.* XIII 2 pp. 301ff.,
No. 53. Scratched on the wall of a shop in Pompeii. Before AD 79.

See L. Halkin in *Revue Belge de Philologie et d'Histoire* 11 (1932); 121–30; Balsdon, *Life and
Leisure* 59–65.

A. Festus 177 (Lindsay)

The ancients wished market-day to be a holiday, on which the country
folk could come into the city to trade.

B. Nonius Marcellus (Lindsay) *s.v.* **Nundinae**

'Which are more the boys? These dark little fellows who wait for the
market-days, so the schoolmaster can send them out to play?'

C. *I. Ital.* XIII 2 pp. 301ff., no. 53, Pompeii

Days for market:[1]

Saturn's day	Pompeii
Sun's day	Nuceria
Moon's day	Atilla
Mars' day	Nola
Mercury's day	Cumae
Jupiter's day	Puteoli
Venus' day	Roma
	Capua

1   At some time in the Hellenistic period the days received names, taken from the sun and the planets, for a total of seven. The Pompeian document lists the days on which the markets were held in various towns and cities as a reminder to the shopkeeper and his customers. There are seven days but eight towns or cities mentioned because markets were held in the same town or city only every eighth day (ninth day in the Roman count). Thus, market-day fell one name-day later from week to week. It was always a day of great social and economic significance in every Italian town: see Balsdon, *loc. cit.*

199   Italian Farmer's Almanac.[1] First century AD.

Square marble block inscribed on all four sides, each side divided into three columns, each column headed by a figure representing a sign of the zodiac. Found in Rome [Latin]

CIL VI 2305; *ILS* 8745; **I. Ital.* XIII 2.47 (+ photographs). A. Degrassi in *I. Ital.* XIII 2, pp. 286–90.

(Col. 1, figure of Capricorn)
Month: | January.
Days: 31
Nones on the 5th.
5 || Day: 9¾ hours.
Night: 14¼ hours.
Sun | in Capricorn.
10   Protector: || Juno.
Stakes | are sharpened.
Willows and | reeds
15 || are cut.[2]
Sacrifice made
to the gods | Penates.[3]

(Col. 2, figure of Aquarius)
Month: | February.
Days: 28
Nones on the 5th.
5 || Day: 10¾ hours.
Night: 13¼ hours.
Sun in Aquarius.
Protector: Neptune.
10   Crops || are weeded.
Vines | above ground tended.
Reeds | are burned.
15 || Parentalia, | Lupercalia,
Cara Cognatio, |
Terminalia (are celebrated).[4]

(Col. 3, figure of Pisces)
Month: | March.
Days: 31.
Nones on the 7th.
5 || Day: 12 hours.
Night: 12 hours.
Equinox | on the 25th.
Sun in Pisces.
10 || Protector: Minerva.
Props for vines, which
on prepared soil | are pruned.
Three-month wheat is sown.
15 || Ship of Isis, sacrifice to
Mamuris.[5]
Liberalia, Quinqua|tria,
Lavatio.[6]

(Col. 4, figure of Aries)
Month: | April.
Days: 30.
5 Nones || on the 5th.
Day: | 13½ hours.
Night: | 10½ hours.
10 || Sun in Aries.
Protector: | Venus.
Sheep | are lustrated.
15 || Sacrifice | to Pharian Isis
and likewise
to Sarapis.[7]

(Col. 5, figure of Taurus)
Month: | May.
Days: 31.
Nones on the 7th.
5 || Day: 14½ hours.
Night: 9½ hours.
Sun in Taurus.
Protector: Apollo.
Grain fields weeded.
10 || Sheep are shorn. | Wool
washed.
Young bullocks are tamed.
Vetch fit for fodder | is cut.
15 || Grain fields | are lustrated.
Sacrifice to Mercury | and
Flora.[8]

(Col. 6, figure of Gemini)
Month: | June.
Days: 30.
Nones on the 5th.
5 || Day: 15 hours.
Night: 9 hours.
Solstice | on the 24th.
Sun in Gemini.
10 || Protector: | Mercury.
Mowing of hay.

Vines | are harrowed.
15 || Sacrifice | to Hercules
and Fors Fortuna.[9]

(Col. 7, figure of Cancer)
Month: | July.
Days: 31.
5 Nones || on the 7th.
Day: | 14¼ hours.
10 Night: || 9¾ hours.
Sun in Cancer.
Protector: | Jupiter.
15 Harvesting || of barley
and beans.

(Col. 8, figure of Leo)
Month: | August.
Days: 31.
Nones on the 5th.
5 || Day: 13 hours.
Night: 11 hours.
Sun in Leo.
Protector: Ceres.
Stakes made ready.
10 || Harvesting | of grain,

Apollinaria
and Neptunalia.[10]

(Col. 9, figure of Virgo)
Month: | September.
Days: 30.
Nones on the 5th.
5 || Day: 12 hours.
Night: 12 hours.
Equinox | on the 24th.
Sun in Virgo.
10 || Protector: | Vulcan.
(Wine) jars | smeared with
     pitch.
Fruits are gathered.
15 || Ground around trees
cultivated.
Feast of Minerva.

(Col. 11, figure of Scorpio)
Month: | November.
Days: 30.
Nones on the 5th.
5 || Day: 9½ hours.
Night: 14½ hours.
Sun | in Scorpio.
10 Protector: || Diana.
Sowing | of wheat | and barley.
15 Trenching || of trees.
Jupiter's | feast.
Finding Out.[13]

15 also | of wheat. | Coarse stalks
|| are burned. | Sacrifice to
     Hope, |
Safety, Diana. | Volcanalia.[11]

(Col. 10, figure of Libra)
Month: | October.
Days: 31.
5 Nones || on the 7th.
Day: | 10¾ hours.
Night: | 13¼ hours.
10 || Sun | in Libra.
Protector: | Mars.
15 || Gathering of grapes.
Sacrifice
to Liber.[12]

(Col. 12, figure of Sagittarius)
Month: | December.
Days: 31.
Nones on the 5th.
5 || Day: 9 hours.
Night: 15 hours.
Sun in Sagittarius.
Protector: Vesta.
10 Winter begins, || solstice
of winter.
Vines manured. | Beans sown.
15 Wood-cutting. || Olives
     gathered.
Likewise, hunting. | Saturnalia.

1 For a more detailed description of work to be done and the climatic conditions to
   be expected by Italian farmers month by month see Columella, *On Agriculture*
   11.2.1–101.
2 See Columella 4.32.1–5.
3 The Household gods were prominent in every farmer's cottage.
4 The Parentalia were largely rituals for the family dead. The Lupercalia were
   celebrated at the Lupercal, a cave in the Palatine Hill, connected with goats and
   wolves. Cara Cognatio ('Dear Relatives') was a celebration at which relatives of the
   family joined in a banquet. The Terminalia were annual sacrifices and feasts,
   occasioned by the digging and placement of boundary markers.

5 The Ship of Isis was a festival which symbolized the beginning of the navigation
   season, the worship of Isis having come to Italy from Egypt. The sacrifice to
   Mamurius is obscure, but seems to refer to a certain Mamurius Veturius, an
   ancient smith.
6 The Liberalia was a day of feasting when boys put on the *toga virilis* ('toga of man-
   hood'). The Quinquatria was a festival to Minerva, falling on the 'Fifth Day' after
   the Ides. Lavatio ('Bathing') seems to have been a purificatory ceremony in which
   the Mother of the Gods, Magna Idaea, was symbolically bathed in a small stream
   that emptied into the Tiber.
7 The worship of both Isis and Sarapis came to Italy from Egypt, and Pharos was the
   famous lighthouse by Alexandria.
8 Flora was an Italian goddess of flowers and flowering plants, whose festival was
   celebrated at the end of April and early May.
9 Fors Fortuna originally seems to have been a 'Bringer' of fertility.
10 The Apollinaria were held on July 13 for Apollo, the Neptunalia on July 23.
11 The Volcanalia were held on August 23.
12 Liber was an Italian god of fertility, especially a god of wine and identified with the
   Greek Bacchus.
13 Heuresis ('Finding Out' or 'Discovery') was a festival or ceremony of Isis and Osiris
   performed by their priests, as mentioned in *CIL* X 3759 (*ILS* 6340), on November
   15. Apparently in the Graeco-Roman world it was a part of the 'Mysteries' of Osiris
   worship: see H. H. Schmitt in *RE* Suppl. IX *s.v.* Osiris, Cols. 512–13.

200   The philanthropy of Pliny the Younger.

Originally a large marble tablet erected at Comum and then later
transported to Milan, where four parts of it were found. Copies were
made of the text before three of the four parts were lost. [Latin]

CIL V 5262; *ILS 2927; Smallwood, *Documents Nerva* 230.

Gaius Plinius, son of Lucius, (of the tribe) Oufentina, Caecilius
[Secundus,[1] consul (AD 100),] | augur, legate with pro praetorian
power of the province Pontus [and Bithynia,] | in consequence [of a
decree of the senate having been sent with] consular power into that
province [by] | Imperator Caesar Nerva Traianus Augustus
5 Germanicus [Dacicus, father of his country;] || superintendent of the
channel of the Tiber and its banks and [of the sewers of the city (of
Rome);] | prefect of the treasury of Saturn; prefect of the *military*
treasury; [praetor; tribune of the plebs;] | quaestor of the emperor;
sevir of a squadron [of Roman] Knights; | tribune of the soldiers of
Legion [Third] Gallica; [decemvir concerning decisions] | on civil
status. (He ordered the construction of) *baths* [costing ---- sesterces,]
10 with an addition of 300,000 sesterces || for their decoration [---- and
further,] for their upkeep, | 200,000 sesterces, as ordered in his testa-
ment. [Likewise, for the support] of his 100 freedmen | [be bequeathed]
1,866,666 sesterces to his city, the interest [of which amount] | he

wished to go later to [feeding] the plebs of his city [----.] Likewise, in
his lifetime, for the support of the boys | and girls of the plebs of his city
he gave [500,000] sesterces,[2] [and also a library and] for the upkeep of
the library | 100,000 sesterces.

1 He is Pliny the Younger, well-known for his correspondence with Trajan and other
   notable figures of the age. For his career see R. Syme, *Tacitus* I, Ch. 7, and A. N.
   Sherwin-White, *The Letters of Pliny* (Oxford 1966) 72–82.
2 Restorations here and elsewhere are supported by Pliny's own remarks in his *Letters*:
   T. Mommsen in *Hermes* 3 (1869) 31ff. (*Gesammelte Schriften* 4 (1906) 366ff.). See *Letters*
   4.8 (augur); 10.3a (treasury of Saturn); 7.16 (military service and quaestorship); 1.10
   (tribune of soldiers in Syria); 7.18 (500,000 sesterces for support of boys and girls);
   1.8 (library at Comum). The use of private funds for the good of city and town was a
   common practice in all areas of the empire: see S. Mrozek in *Acta Antiqua Academiae
   Scientiarum Hungarica* 29 (1981) 369–77, and D. Johnston in *JRS* 75 (1985) 105ff.

Administrative District. Each Roman province was divided into administrative districts called *conventus* (*dioikeseis* in Greek). The civil jurisdiction of the governor, based on an edict, required his presence (or that of his delegate) in these districts on an annual basis. In each of them the governor held court and also conducted whatever other business might be required. See Reinmuth, *Prefect*, Ch. 10 and G. Foti Talamanca, *Ricerche sul processo nell' Egitto greco-romano. I: L'organizzazione del 'conventus' del Praefectus Aegypti* (Rome 1974).

Advisory Board. Under the Republic Roman magistrates had regularly sought the advice of the senate before making important public decisions. Thus the senate acted as a *consilium publicum* ('Public Advisory Board'). Magistrates away from Rome and promagistrates formed smaller boards from the members of their staff and entourage. Sometimes the senate supplied a magistrate with such a board for use on a particular occasion. Augustus also instituted a different kind of board for his own use, consisting of senators who served as a standing committee for six months and whose main business was the preparation of agenda for presentation to the senate. This latter type of board was discontinued under Tiberius. Under the Empire the earlier type of Advisory Board was continued on the imperial level: unofficial at first, it was a body of advisors called by the emperor from among his *amici* ('friends') to act as advisors in various ways. It became a standing institution. See J. Crook, *Consilium Principis* (Cambridge 1965).

Aediles. Many of the old duties of the Republican aediles, such as the supervision of the grain supply and most of their police functions, passed into other hands with the beginning of the Principate, although they retained the duty of keeping the streets of Rome clean and inflicting certain fines. As Roman magistrates, they retained their usefulness also in the senatorial career structure. Outside of Rome the title refers to minor administrative officials in the municipalities of Italy and in the western provinces.

Agoranomos. He was superintendent of the market in a Greek city. See No. 32 n. 2.

Ala. See *s.v.* Auxilia.

Archon. The chief magistrate of a Greek city.

Association (or League) of Asia. Associations or Leagues (*koina* in Greek) were assemblies of delegates from the constituent cities within a Roman province (such as Asia) or of several associated provinces. The nature and function of these provincial associations varied from province to province, but their delegates ordinarily met once a year in some central city and their primary function under the Empire came to be the worship of Roma and Augustus. Games and festivals were often combined with the religious ceremonies. These associations also played a political and diplomatic role, serving as avenues of communication between Rome and the provinces. See J. Deininger, *Die Provinziallandtage der römischen Kaiserzeit* (Munich 1965).

Associations (Societies). Members of the working classes in cities throughout the empire were regularly organized into associations (or clubs or societies), many of them in connection with some god. They were controlled by the state and enjoyed certain advantages of a social nature, but were not at all similar to modern labour unions. Most were burial societies. See Alföldy, *Social History* 134ff.

Augur. The *augures* ('diviners', 'interpreters') formed a college of fifteen Roman priests, increased by Caesar to sixteen. They sought to discover the will of the gods by observation of signs in nature called *auspicia*. After Augustus they were elected in the senate and the majority of them were patricians.

Augustales. See *s.v.* Sodales Augustales.

Aureus. Augustus standardized the gold coin called *aureus* at 42 to the pound, fixing its value at 25 *denarii*.

Auxilia. These were provincial military units established by Augustus as a permanent part of the imperial army out of earlier formations. They were either cavalry units (*alae*) or infantry (*cohortes*), although some infantry units also had some mounted men, and they bore numbers and names that reflected the tribes or geographic areas from which they originated. Some were named after their founders. Each was nominally 500 (*quingenaria*) or 1,000 (*milliaria*) strong, although the actual number was somewhat less. Their commanding officers were drawn from the equestrian class and were called prefects, while the main body of the units was composed of non-citizens from the provinces. Lower officers (e.g. *decuriones*) could be promoted from the ranks. After discharge, men of the ranks received Roman citizenship. See P. A. Holder, *Studies in the Auxilia of the Roman Army from Augustus to Trajan* (Oxford 1980), and D. B. Saddington, *The Development of the Roman Auxiliary Forces from Caesar to Vespasian (49 BC–AD 79)* (Zimbabwe 1982).

Beneficiarius. See *s.v.* Legion.

Boule. Best known is the one at Athens, which in classical times consisted of 500 members selected by lot from the townships of Attica. The chief task of this 'Council' was to prepare the agenda for the Assembly of the People. Outside Athens most of the Greek cities had a Boule or an equivalent institution as long as they remained democratic. The duties and functions were similar to those of the Athenian Boule, although the number of members, the length of their tenure, and other details varied considerably.

Capitolium. One of the hills of Rome, with two summits. On one of them, overlooking the Tiber to the west and the Forum to the east, was the temple of Jupiter, Juno, and Minerva. It was the very heart and soul of Rome, where the consuls took their vows, and triumphant generals climbed its heights to approach the temple. On its northern summit was the temple of Juno Moneta with an adjoining building that served as the mint.

Censor. The old Republican censors, elected once in each five-year period, not only prepared the census but also made out the list of senators. The powers of the office, but not the office itself, were offered to Augustus, but he refused them. Claudius, Vespasian, and Titus assumed the office in its old form, and Domitian accepted it as a permanent part of his rule, but subsequent emperors declined to continue his precedent. With or without holding the office itself, all emperors used its powers to control access to the senate. For the censorial powers of Augustus see A. H. M. Jones in *JRS* 41 (1951) 112–19 (*Studies* 1–17).

Centurion. See *s.v.* Legion.

Century. For the military *centuria* see *s.v.* Legion. In the old Republic the *centuria* was also a voting unit of the citizen body, each century having a single vote that was determined by the majority of voters within it. In the age of Augustus ten of the total of 193 voting centuries were named for members of the imperial house (Gaius and

Lucius Caesar), and in AD 19 five more were named for Germanicus. See the Tabula Hebana (No. 36 B). For the whole system see L. R. Taylor, *Roman Voting Assemblies* (Ann Arbor 1966) 89ff.

Circuit Court. See *s.v.* Administrative District.

Client. See *s.v.* Patron.

Consul. Although many of the powers of the consuls had been diminished or lost by the triumviral period of the late Republic, their military power remained undiminished. Under the Empire the office of consul became primarily an honorary function, marking out senators for higher command or else rewarding them for loyal service. During the triumviral period and then from the later period of Augustus' reign the suffect consulship became a regular institution. The first pair of consuls (the *consules ordinarii*), whose names were used for dating the year, held the office for a few months and then were replaced by another pair (called *consules suffecti*). This permitted a larger number of consulars to be created each year to command the many administrative posts created by the growing size and complexity of the empire.

Conventus. See *s.v.* Administrative District.

Corrector. See *s.v.* Curator rei publicae.

Curator rei publicae. Also called *corrector*, this 'superintendent of city government' was appointed by the emperor from either the senatorial or the equestrian class to supervise the administration of a city which had fallen into financial trouble. Because of his local power he tended gradually to assume more and more control over the city. See G. P. Burton in *Chiron* 9 (1979) 465–87.

Decemvir concerning civil status. See *s.v.* Vigintiviri.

Decurion (of military unit). Cavalry officer in the auxilia.

Decurion (in a city). He is a member of a municipal senate in Italy and the provinces, elected for life. Like the senators in Rome, such individuals were regularly recruited from the ex-magistrates and formed an aristocratic circle.

Denarius. A Roman silver coin that was the standard silver piece of the empire and weighed about one-seventh of an ounce (3.9 gm).

Dioiketēs. In Roman Egypt he was the head of the financial administration. From Augustus to Hadrian he was – apparently – appointed by the prefect of Egypt and, thus, had only limited competence. See No. 67 A, line 8. Beginning with Hadrian, however, he was an official of higher rank, appointed by the emperor as a procurator of centenarian salary scale (i.e. 100,000 sesterces per year). See D. Hagedorn in *Yale Classical Studies* 28 (1985) 167–210.

Dionysiac Artists. These were professional actors and musical performers who presented the great dramas and comedies everywhere in the Greek world, traveling from place to place to perform at the local festivals. Each had its own headquarters in a Greek city, and all of them enjoyed a wide variety of privileges and immunities. Since they lived in or side by side with Greek cities, each of the guilds or associations into which they formed themselves was a kind of state within a state. See Sir Arthur Pickard-Cambridge, *The Dramatic Festivals of Athens*[2] (Oxford 1968) Ch. 7.

Drachma. A standard of Greek weight as well as of silver coinage. Under the Roman Empire it came to be regarded as equivalent to the Roman denarius.

Duoviri. Local magistrates in cities outside of Rome. Their functions varied from place to place, but generally they were the heads (two in number) of the municipal administration and were elected by the local assemblies. Together with the *duoviri aediles* they formed a body of four called the *quattuorviri*.

Ephors. Local officials in Greek cities of Dorian origin.

Glossary

Epistrategos. See *s.v.* Nome.

Equestrian Career. No equestrian career structure existed in the old Republic, but the victory of the Caesarian party and the subsequent measures taken by Augustus to satisfy equestrian ambitions created the foundation on which one was to be constructed. It was a gradual process and all the parts did not emerge fully until the reign of Hadrian, and thereafter it continued to grow until finally in the third century the equestrians superseded the senators in controlling the positions of power almost everywhere. The young equestrian began his career with the necessary military service, either by holding one or more 'praetorian' posts (*primipilus*, tribune of a cohort of *vigiles*, tribune of an urban cohort, tribune of a praetorian cohort, and then *primipilus* for a second time) or else by service in the so-called *militia equestris* as prefect of an auxiliary cohort, prefect of an *ala*, and equestrian tribune of soldiers in a legion. Thereafter, he became eligible for the various procuratorial posts, the number of which steadily increased from about 23 under Augustus to about 84 under Trajan and about 103 under Hadrian. By the age of Trajan and Hadrian these equestrian procurators had become differentiated into salary classes: *sexagenarii* (60,000 sesterces annually), *centenarii* (100,000 sesterces annually), and *ducenarii* (200,000 sesterces annually). Thus, by Hadrian's reign an equestrian hierarchy had already emerged as a parallel to the senatorial career. The most capable and most acceptable to the emperor of these procurators then became eligible to hold the higher equestrian prefectures: prefect of all the *vigiles* ('The Night Watch' for fire protection), prefect of the grain supply, prefect of Egypt, and prefect of the praetorian guard. These posts formed the pinnacle of the equestrian career. See A. Stein, *Der römische Ritterstand* (Munich 1927); H. G. Pflaum, *Les Procurateurs équestres sous le haut-empire romain* (Paris 1950); E. Birley, *Roman Britain and the Roman Army, Collected Papers* (Kendal 1953) 133–71; Alföldy, *Social History* 122–6. See also below, *s.v.* Procurator.

Equites (Equestrians, Knights). By the age of Augustus these men were a social order second only to the senators in prestige and influence. Under the Empire they served as army officers and then held higher administrative posts (see above, *s.v.* Equestrian Career). They were required to have a census evaluation of 400,000 sesterces or more and to be of free birth. Their power grew steadily until eventually they replaced most senators in positions of authority in the government. See No. 37.

Exegetēs. He was a municipal official in Roman Alexandria, one of whose main duties was concerned with the enrollment of ephebes (young boys) in the Greek gymnasium, which was a necessary step in the acquisition of Alexandrian citizenship. This made him an official of great respect and influence. Cf. No. 34 n. 1.

Fellows of the priesthood of (the deified) Augustus. See *s.v.* Sodales Augustales.

Fiscus. This denoted the private funds of the emperor as well as the provincial or departmental 'chest' into which poured the provincial revenues. In time, the word came to mean the whole financial administration of the Empire, whether public or private, under the control of the emperor. Thus, the distinction between *aerarium* (the old Republican treasury of a public nature) and *fiscus* (originally the private 'chest' of the emperor) gradually disappeared in the first two centuries of the Empire, and *fiscus* became a mere equivalent for *aerarium*. For details and the controversial nature of the evidence see A. H. M. Jones in *JRS* 40 (1950) 22–9 (*Studies* 101–14) and P. A. Brunt in *JRS* 56 (1966) 75–91. Cf. No. 84 n. 4.

Freedmen. They were originally slaves who had been 'set free' (*liberti*) by their masters or through testamentary action of their masters. They followed the civil status of their former masters and, thus, generally became Roman citizens, but they enjoyed fewer rights than free-born citizens. They were excluded from holding public magistracies and from becoming members of the senate. The emperors employed them in a variety of positions, some of great importance. However, the majority were ordinary people engaged in business, industry or farming. See Weaver, *Familia Caesaris*, *passim*, and A. M. Duff, *Freedmen in the Early Roman Empire* (Oxford 1928, reissued 1958).

Gnomon. This was a code of regulations which guided the activities of the Egyptian administrator called the Idiologos. A papyrus copy of it from about the middle of the second century has been preserved (*BGU* V 1210). Originally established by Augustus, its regulations were concerned with various legal situations and conditions that brought in revenues for the imperial 'special account' (*idios logos*) in Egypt. See W. G. Uxkull-Gyllenband, *Der Gnomon des Idios Logos*, in *BGU* V, Heft 2, and also below, *s.v.* Idiologos.

Gymnasiarch. He was the director of the gymnasium in Greek cities and was generally one of the wealthiest citizens. He was responsible for the education and training of the young men ('ephebes') enrolled in it. In Alexandria completion of this training was necessary to obtain Alexandrian citizenship and, thus, was a much coveted privilege.

Ides. See Appendix II.

Idiologos. Of equestrian status, this Roman official was directly subordinate to the prefect of Egypt and was responsible for the collection of irregular or occasional sources of revenue. He was also in charge of Egyptian temples and priesthoods. Cf. above, *s.v.* Gnomon, and see G. Plaumann, *Der Idioslogos. Untersuchungen zur Finanzverwaltung Ägyptens in hellenistischer und römischer Zeit* (*Abhandlungen der Preussischen Akademie der Wissenschaften, Phil.-hist. Klasse* (1918) Heft 17) (Berlin 1919); P. Swarney, *The Ptolemaic and Roman Idios Logos* (*American Studies in Papyrology*, 8) (Toronto 1970).

Imperator. After a victory in the field, a Republican general was hailed as *imperator* by his soldiers and held the title until the end of his magistracy or until his triumph in Rome. Occasionally the senate seems to have given or confirmed the title. The growing power of the army in the late Republic made the title a symbol of military authority. Caesar was the first to use it permanently, and Augustus adopted it as a *praenomen* (part of his official name). It then became part of the nomenclature of every Roman emperor and no one outside the imperial family was permitted to hold it. See R. Syme in *Historia* 7 (1958) 172–88 (*Roman Papers* I 361–77). Cf. Dio 53.17.4.

Kalends. See Appendix II.

Latin Rights. Having its origin in the early Republic, the *ius Latii* ('Latin Rights') of the Empire was a favorable legal status enjoyed by foreigners which raised them up from an alien status and made them eligible for the acquisition of Roman citizenship. Provincials belonged to such a status when, generally, their community was recognized as a *municipium*, i.e. a Roman-style city government, and a charter was composed to spell out the regulations and rights of the new community. See No. 97. Vespasian, as censor in AD 73–4, gave the Latin Rights to all of Spain (Pliny, *Nat. Hist.* 3.30). The citizens of such communities who were elected to the local magistracies then received Roman citizenship, and, beginning with Hadrian, members of the local municipal senates were also given Roman citizenship. See Sherwin-White, *Citizenship*[2], Ch. 15.

Leader. The word *princeps* was used to describe a leading personage within the old Republican ruling class. Augustus adopted it to describe his own role within his new order, i.e. as 'first man' or 'Leader', distinguishing him from any ordinary magistrate in office. It continued to be applied to later emperors. See M. Hammond, *The Augustan Principate* (Cambridge, Mass. 1933); L. Wickert in *RE s.v.* Princeps, Cols. 1998ff.; *idem* in *ANRW* 2.1.3ff.

Legate of Augustus with Pro Praetorian Power. He was an official appointed directly by the emperor to perform certain functions on his behalf, regularly as governor of one of the 'imperial' provinces (see No. 4). As governor he served at the emperor's pleasure, the average length of service being 3–5 years. All such men were of senatorial status: those of praetorian rank were used in provinces that required no more than one legion, while those of consular rank were sent out to provinces with two or more legions.

Legion. Composed of ten tactical units called cohorts, each of which was broken down into six *centuriae*, the legion was the backbone of the Roman military establishment. No special officer commanded a cohort, but a *centurio* was in charge of each century and each cohort had its senior centurion. The manpower of each century was about 80, except in the first cohort, which was of double strength but had only five centuries. The chief centurion of the first cohort was the most experienced officer in the whole legion and was called the *primus pilus* (*primipilaris*). Lower-ranking officers (like a *beneficiarius* or aide to a senior officer) were largely specialists, technicians, or clerks, as well as standard-bearers and aides. The commanding officer of the legion was a legate ('deputy') of the emperor and regularly of praetorian rank. He served an average of 3–4 years and had a staff under him composed of the *primus pilus* and six *tribuni militum* ('tribunes of soldiers'), one of the six being of senatorial and the other five of equestrian status. The legions in Egypt differed in their command personnel, for their commanders were equestrian prefects and there were no senatorial tribunes. Augustus fixed the number of legions at 28, which was reduced to 25 after the Varian disaster of AD 9; under Vespasian there were 29; Domitian added one more; under Trajan, after losses and replacements, there were probably 30. See Webster, *Army*; G. R. Watson, *The Roman Soldier* (Ithaca, NY 1969); L. Keppie, *The Making of the Roman Army from Republic to Empire* (London 1984).

Liturgies. Compulsory public service (*leiturgia* in Greek, *munus* in Latin) was the method by which citizens and inhabitants of Greek and Roman cities were obligated to perform certain jobs or tasks at their own expense or free labor: repair and care of aqueducts, local roads, temples, public buildings, etc.; service as local judges, envoys, advocates, scribes, etc. They differed from place to place and from time to time. They were burdens (*munera*) imposed on the local population in accordance with an individual's ability to pay or, lacking wealth, to contribute physical labor for prescribed periods of time. Exemption or immunity from such service was a highly coveted privilege. See Abbott–Johnson, *Municipal Administration*, Ch. 8; Magie, *RRAM* I 61–2 and 651–8. Cf. *Digest* 50.4–6.

Munera. See *s.v.* Liturgies.

Nome. Roman Egypt was divided into three administrative districts called *epistrategiai*: the Delta, the Thebaid, and the Heptanomia. Each was administered by an *epistrategos*, a Roman of equestrian status. Separate from these districts were the 'Greek cities' of Naukratis and Ptolemais Hermiou, and, later, also Antinoöpolis. Alexandria was technically not considered a part of Egypt. Each of the three districts in turn was divided into nomes (*nomoi*), a total of 46 or 47, and each nome was administered by a *strategos*. Each nome was divided into toparchies, within each of which the smallest administrative unit was the village. See H. I. Bell in *CAH* 10.284ff.;

Glossary

V. Martin, *Les Épistratèges* (Geneva 1911); N. Hohlwein, 'Le stratège du nome' in *Musée Belge* 28 (1924) 125ff.; J. D. Thomas in *Proceedings of the Twelfth International Congress of Papyrology* (Toronto 1970) 465–9; *idem, The Epistrategos in Ptolemaic and Roman Egypt*, Part 2: *The Roman Epistrategos* (Opladen 1982).

Nones. See Appendix II.

Ornamenta triumphalia. Under the Empire the triumph was a prerogative of the emperor, and victorious generals were merely permitted to have the honor of the insignia of a triumph but not the triumph itself.

Ostracon. A small piece of broken pottery on which was written a great variety of information: tax receipts, military passes, short letters, even scraps of poetry.

Patron. From Rome's early history the weak or deprived had turned to the strong or wealthy for protection. When such a 'client' found such a 'patron' to satisfy his need, a series of strong mutual duties bound them together, each pledged to help the other in his own way. The relationship became hereditary. During the last two centuries of the Republic this institution spread to the provinces, when Roman senators became patrons not only of individuals outside of Italy and especially in the Greek East but also of whole cities or communities. Even foreign kings and potentates became clients of Roman senators. The whole system continued on into the Empire. Cf. No. 198. See Syme, *Roman Revolution, passim*, and Bowersock, *Augustus, passim*.

Pontifex Maximus. He was the chief priest of the Roman state religion. As head of the college of priests called *pontifices* in Rome, the *pontifex maximus* was considered the judge and the arbitrator over all things divine and human (Festus p. 200 L). Beginning with Caesar and Augustus, the emperors regularly held this office and included it among their official titles. The whole college supervised the public and private sacrifices, were responsible for the calendar, and watched over funeral rites and wills. They were frequently consulted on points of religious law.

Praetor. Under the Empire the office of praetor was almost completely jurisdictional and largely ornamental. The number of posts as praetor rose from 12 in AD 14 to 18 at the end of the first century, and the most favored were the 'candidates of the emperor'. Holding the post opened up a great variety of military and administrative positions. See *s.v.* Senatorial Career.

Praetorian Guard. Building upon Republican precedents, Augustus established what amounted to a military garrison at Rome, the most important part of which was the Praetorian Guard. It consisted of nine cohorts, three of them stationed in the city and the rest in nearby towns. They were an elite body of infantry, recruited from civilian life on the whole, for sixteen years of service and at a higher pay than that in the legions. Under Tiberius they were all quartered in a single building by the Porta Viminalis of Rome. Caligula raised their number to 12 cohorts; Vitellius reorganized them and raised them to 16 cohorts of 1,000 men each; Vespasian reduced them to nine, but then sometime later they were raised to ten. Their command was usually vested in two prefects of high equestrian status, although occasionally only one prefect was in charge. Their closeness to the imperial family and their presence in Rome and Italy gave them extraordinary power, which was sometimes abused. Cf. No. 40. See M. Durry, *Les Cohortes prétoriennes* (Paris 1938).

Primus Pilus (Primipilaris). See *s.v.* Legion.

Proconsul. The governor of a senatorial province was called *proconsul*, whether he had been formerly a consul or not.

Procurator. In Republican private law a procurator was a person authorized to administer someone's affairs for him, and thus he was a deputy or agent for that person. Augustus put procurators in charge of various aspects of his personal property, but with the growth of empire procurators soon came to be used also in matters not directly connected with imperial property. Many were originally freedmen but later the majority were appointed from equestrian status. Certain provinces were put under their administration, such as Judaea and Noricum. In the senatorial provinces they were in charge of the emperor's property, while in the imperial provinces they collected the various revenues. Among the numerous other duties they performed were those connected with gladiatorial supervision and the recruitment of gladiators, the water supply in Rome, the grain shipments coming in to Ostia, directorship of libraries, etc. In the passage of time these procuratorial posts became the central feature in the public service of equestrians, and by the time of Hadrian they were grouped in a graduated scale of salaries: see above, *s.v.* Equestrian Career. Cf. Pflaum, *Carrières, passim,* for the multiplicity of posts and the salary scale, and A. H. M. Jones, *Studies* 117ff. for their appearance under Augustus as provincial governors.

Quaestor. Under Augustus the number of quaestors reached 20 and they retained the financial duties of the old Republican quaestors, supervising the treasury and financial administration in Rome, and administering the finances abroad for the senatorial provinces. See below, *s.v.* Senatorial Career.

Quattuorvir. See *s.v.* Duoviri.

Quindecimvir of Sacred Affairs. As *quindecimvir sacris faciundis* this person was a member of the college of fifteen priests who were originally in charge of the Sibylline Books and their interpretation: see Livy 5.13.5–6 for background. Later, such priests also supervised the sacrifices of the many foreign cults recognized in Rome. Caesar increased the number of the priests to 16, but the old title was retained. Cf. No. 11, *passim.*

Quinquennalis. In two senses: a municipal magistrate appointed for five years, or a title conferred on a municipal magistrate every fifth year to conduct the local census.

Senate (Roman). The old Republican senate had lost its dominant role in affairs of state and politics when it was transformed by Julius Caesar and Augustus into an institution that reflected and implemented the policies of its new masters. The old aristocracy had largely disappeared from its ranks and a new one was taking its place, based on different ideals and backgrounds. New blood flowed into it from the municipalities of Italy and then of the provinces. General elections were transferred from the People to the senate (cf. No. 36), which acquired legislative power through the issuance of *senatus consulta* ('decrees of the senate'). Nevertheless, the senate lost its independence to the emperors, its only real freedom returning to it for brief moments at the death of an emperor when it played a role in choosing or approving a new one. It became an hereditary body, a pool of potential administrators and officers to fill the growing needs of the empire. See below, *s.v.* Senatorial Career. Despite its general subservience to the emperors, in strict theory it was still the seat of authority, granting *imperium* to each emperor (see No. 82). Cf. Syme, *Roman Revolution, passim,* and R. J. A. Talbert, *The Senate of Imperial Rome* (Princeton 1984).

Senatorial Career. The senatorial career of imperial times was a continuation and refinement of Republican practices, adapted by Augustus to fit the demands of his new order and gradually perfected. Its framework was the old Republican *cursus honorum,* the ladder of promotion from one office to the next in an established order, each office of a year's duration: one of the posts called collectively the vigintivirate (see below, *s.v.* Vigintiviri) and held by young sons of senators between the ages of

18 and 20; the quaestorship (minimum age 25); office of tribune of the plebs or that of aedile (may be omitted by patricians); the praetorship (minimum age 30); the consulship (minimum age 42 but sometimes held by men as young as 32 or 33 who had shown exceptional military ability). As a senator reached and held each of these offices, which were largely ornamental in their duties, he became eligible for an increasingly large variety of administrative positions in the Empire at large. After the vigintivirate the young son of a senator would ordinarily seek appointment as tribune of the soldiers and serve in one of the legions, two or three years on average. Once he had become quaestor, he was given a seat in the senate. After a pause of a few years he was eligible for one of the ten posts of tribune of the plebs or one of the six posts of aedile, or could omit them if he were a patrician. It was the praetorship which gave him the chance to hold a large number of important appointments. As an ex-praetor (*praetorius*) he could become the commanding officer of a legion (*legatus legionis*) and then praetorian governor of one of the less important provinces (*e.g.* Cilicia). As praetorian he could also become superintendent of highways (*curator viarum*) or prefect in a number of capacities (grain supply, military treasurer, etc.) in Rome or Italy. Finally, the consulship gave him access to the highest and most sensitive posts in the empire: governor of the emperor's consular provinces (*e.g.* Britain, Syria, etc.) or governor of the higher senatorial provinces (Asia or Africa). As consular he might command great armies or be placed in charge of such things as the banks of the Tiber River, the aqueducts of Rome, sacred temples, etc., and eventually, if highly successful, he might hold a second or even third consulship and become Prefect of the City of Rome (*praefectus urbi*) as a final honor. For most senators, however, the consulship itself represented the pinnacle of their careers, and only a minority reached the very highest levels beyond it. See Alföldy, *Social History* 115–22; A. R. Birley, *The Fasti of Roman Britain* (Oxford 1981) 1–35; W. Eck in *ANRW* 2.1.158–228; K. Hopkins, *Death and Renewal* (Cambridge 1983) 149–75.

Septemvir for Religious Banquets. He was a member of a college of seven priests whose principal duty was the organization of the banquet of Jupiter and other banquets at various festivals. Under Caesar these *septemviri epulones* were increased to ten, but their old title remained. Tiberius was the only emperor to have been a member, and thereafter the office was largely held by plebeians, many of them having been previously the partisans of the emperor.

Sestertius. A Roman silver coin and unit of account, four of which were equal to a *denarius*.

Sodales Augustales. These 'Fellows of the priesthood of (the deified) Augustus' ranked below the major priestly colleges and were first instituted by Tiberius after the death of Augustus. They were in charge of the cult of the late emperor. Similar 'Fellows' were later entrusted with the cults of Titus, Hadrian, and Antoninus Pius. Their relationship to the *seviri Augustales* is controversial.

Stele. A square or rectangular slab of stone, placed in an upright position for public viewing, with a smooth front surface for the engraving of epitaphs, decrees, laws or other material of a public or private nature. A stone stele often reproduces in miniature the architrave of a temple with acroteria, pediment and molding, and may contain engraved reliefs of various kinds. Like the lettering itself, these stelai show patterns of style and development along geographical and chronological lines. See Möbius in *RE s.v.* Stele, Cols. 2307–20.

Toparchy. See *s.v.* Nome.

Tribe (Roman). The Roman tribes were territorial divisions of the citizens. They were thirty-five in number and were originally confined to Rome and Italy, but with the acquisition of provinces and the gradual extension of Roman citizenship they also came to include provincial land. Registration in a tribe was a necessity for voting privileges and other civic advantages. It was also a necessary part of a Roman citizen's name. Under the Empire the Roman tribe became the organization through which poor members were entitled to help in the form of grain and food from the government. See W. Kubitschek, *De Romanorum tribuum origine ac propagatione* (Vienna 1882), and, for the Republic, L. R. Taylor, *The Voting Districts of the Roman Republic* (Rome 1960).

Tribune of Soldiers. See *s.v.* Legion.

Tribunician Power. The 'power of the (plebeian) tribune' included all the rights enjoyed by the tribunes of the plebs. Augustus, who (as a patrician) could not be tribune of the plebs, recognized its political potential within the structure of his new order, and in 23 BC his possession of it became annual by a law of the People (*Res Gestae* 10.1). Thereafter it was found to be a convenient way of dating documents and coins. In 18 BC Augustus used the tribunician power to introduce a series of Julian Laws, and in that same year he caused the senate to grant that power to Agrippa. It was also granted later to Tiberius as his designated successor. Subsequent emperors held and used it as a means to express their imperial position and to date the years of their reign. See W. K. Lacey in *JRS* 69 (1979) 28–34.

Triumvir. The title was given by the Romans to each member of a board of three men who exercised certain functions. See *s.v.* Vigintiviri for examples.

Vestal Virgins. Priestesses of Vesta, Roman goddess of the hearth. Chosen from among girls of six to ten years of age by the pontifex maximus, they served for 30 years. Thereafter they were allowed to leave and marry.

Vigintiviri. A collective term for 20 men who were broken down into smaller groups to perform certain functions of the Roman government: *decemviri stlitibus iudicandis* (ten-man board concerning civil status, i.e. to judge whether a person was free or a slave); *triumviri monetales* (three-man board to preside over the mint); *triumviri capitales* (three-man board responsible for prisons and executions); *quattuorviri viis in urbe purgandis* (four-man board in charge of cleaning and repairing the streets of Rome). See also *s.v.* Senatorial Career.

APPENDIX I

Roman names

A Roman citizen's official name had five parts, arranged in a particular order: praenomen, nomen, filiation, tribe, and cognomen. The praenomen was given to infants by their parents on the ninth day after birth, and there were not many of these praenomina to choose from. Among the Roman ruling class only the following were in common use:

A.	= Aulus	M.	= Marcus	Sex.	= Sextus
Ap.	= Appius	M'.	= Manius	Sp.	= Spurius
C.	= Gaius	Mam.	= Mamercus	T.	= Titus
Cn.	= Gnaeus	P.	= Publius	Ti.	= Tiberius
D.	= Decimus	Q.	= Quintus		
L.	= Lucius	Ser.	= Servius		

This praenomen, regularly abbreviated in official documents, was followed by the nomen, which was the clan name. The clan (gens) was a group of families linked together by a common name and their belief in a common ancestor, and the nomen is thus the single most important part of a Roman citizen's name, a link to his origins.

After the nomen comes the filiation, always abbreviated in official documents: f(ilius) = 'son' and sometimes n(epos) = 'grandson'. Thus: L.f. (L.n.) = 'son of Lucius (grandson of Lucius)'. In the case of a freedman, the word lib(ertus) = 'freedman' was preceded by the praenomen of the patron who had freed him: C.lib. = 'freedman of Gaius'.

Since every Roman citizen had to belong to a tribe, the tribal affiliation regularly became part of his official name and stood at this point in it. It was followed by the fifth and last part of his name, the cognomen. These cognomina were personal names and had specific meanings, concerned with physical peculiarities (e.g. Laevinus = 'left-handed'), individual characteristics (Cato = 'sagacious'), occupations (Pictor = 'painter'), etc. These were normally, but not always, hereditary. To their own cognomina the emperors frequently added a 'triumphal' name, such as Germanicus or Dacicus, when victories warranted them. In cases of adoption, when a man received his adoptive father's name, he officially added his old nomen in an adjectival form after his new cognomen: e.g., when C. Octavius was adopted by the dictator C. Iulius Caesar in Caesar's will, he became officially C. Iulius Caesar Octavianus.

The names of women were different. Under the Republic they had, almost without exception, only one name. Sisters, thus, had the same name and, for convenience, were distinguished by a phrase such as 'the younger' or 'the second', etc. After marriage each retained her own name but added her husband's in the genitive for greater identification.

Under the Empire several changes took place. Women commonly had two names, the first her original name and a second taken from her father's cognomen, but sometimes taken from her mother's name. Men often had more than one cognomen, and in the course of the second and third centuries there were men with a great multiplicity of them. When a foreigner acquired Roman citizenship, it was the custom for him to take the praenomen and nomen of the Roman who was responsible for granting it to him or sponsoring it. This often meant the praenomen and nomen of the reigning emperor. The new citizen then added his own native name as a cognomen. Slaves, as always, had only one name. For the imperial title see R. Syme in *Historia* 7 (1958) 172–88 (*Roman Papers* I 361–77). For a brief account of Roman names as a whole, with bibliography, see Gordon, *Epigraphy* 17–30.

Roman imperial chronology

The pre-Julian calendar was lunar with a total of 355 days. To keep the months in line with the seasons it had been the practice to add (intercalate) an extra month during February every few years, but the Romans, like the Greeks, never did this with regularity. Each month was divided into three parts by means of special days called the Kalends, Nones, and Ides. Since the frame of reference was always one of looking forward to the arrival of these days, each of the other days was given a number reflecting how many days had to pass before they did arrive. The Kalends were always the first day of each month, the Nones were either the seventh day (of March, May, July, and October) or the fifth (of all the rest), while the Ides were either the fifteenth day (of March, May, July, and October) or the thirteenth (of all the rest). The Roman method of counting these days was inclusive. Thus, e.g., the Roman date 'on the third day before the Ides of January' is by our method of counting actually the second day before the Ides of that month (January 11).

This calendar was changed by Julius Caesar in 45 BC to one based on the sun, following the Egyptian model, but with proper intercalation. Thereafter the number of days in the months were: September, April, June, and November had 30 days; February had 28; all the rest had 31. This Julian calendar had 365 days, with one intercalated day to be added in February every fourth year. See A. K. Michels, *The Calendar of the Roman Republic* (Princeton 1967).

Under the Republic the usual method of dating events in past history was by naming the two consuls of the year in question. The list of these consuls had been available to the public in Rome by its publication on stone on the Arch of Augustus for the period prior to Augustus. Thereafter historians had copies to which additions could be made. Under the Empire the same method of dating the years continued, except that, since there were then more than two consuls in office each year, only the names of the first two (called *consules ordinarii*) were used to date the year. Our list of such consuls extends to the seventh century AD. Another method of dating can be seen in the imperial documents by means of the tribunician power of the emperor: since this power was renewed each year, the simple addition of a numeral to it in his titulature became a convenient way of dating a document. And sometimes, especially in shorter documents and in those emanating from the officials of small towns or from minor functionaries throughout the many provinces, the date might appear in the form 'in the first (or second, etc.) year' of the reigning emperor.

In the provinces, of course, and especially in the Greek East, the old calendars and the old methods of chronology also remained in use. For example, in Egypt under the Empire the old Macedonian month names were simply alternative names for the Egyptian months. And since the rotation of the months through the seasons in Egypt was regular and predictable, modern tables have been constructed to account for the rotation. Thus, modern dates can be determined for Egyptian dates (see T. C. Skeat,

Appendix II. Roman imperial chronology

The Reigns of the Ptolemies (Munich 1954). The names of the Egyptian months, with their Macedonian names in brackets, are as follows:

Thoth (Dios)   Phamenoth (Artemisios)
Phaophi (Apellaios)   Pharmouthi (Daisios)
Hathyr (Audnaios)   Pachon (Panemos)
Choiach (Peritios)   Payni (Loios)
Tybi (Dystros)   Epeiph (Gorpiaios)
Mecheir (Xandikos)   Mesore (Hyperberetaios)

These equivalents, beginning in 119/18 BC, continued on into the Roman imperial period, the first day of Thoth being the beginning of the Egyptian year.

For all details see A. E. Samuel, *Greek and Roman Chronology* (Munich 1972), and E. J. Bickerman, *Chronology of the Ancient World* (Ithaca, NY 1980).

INDEXES

All references are to numbers of items and, where applicable, to lines or sections. References to explanatory notes are marked 'n.' or 'nn.'.

I. Personal names

A. GREEKS, NON-ROMANS

Acastus, 172 J 4
Achillia, 172 E
Acratus, 75 n. 1
Aedemon, 50.6 n. 3
Aegisthus, 166 C
Aerope, 166 C
Agathopus, 178 D 11
Aischines, 179.3,12
Aischines Flavianus, 179.3,12
Aiakidas, son of Ptolemaios, 62.25
Aiolos, 42 B 2
Albiorix, 38.30
Alexander (the Great), 34 n. 4; 81 n. 3; 136 A; 155 n. 6
Alexandros (King), 128.9
Alexandros (envoy from Alexandria), 25.40,57
Alexandros, son of Alexandros, 158.2
Alexandros, son of Epinikos, 137.2,18
Alexandros, son of Philopater, 158.2
Aline, 129 D 1, n. 7
Alis, 188 C 1,16
Amazaspos, brother of Mithridates, 131.2,8
Amazon, 172 E
Amyntas (king of Galatia), 4; 38
Amyntas, son of Brigatos, 128.3
Amyntas, son of Dry(?)ialos, 128.4
Amyntas, son of Gaizatodiastos, 38
Anacreon, 162 n. 1
Andendunes, 164 G 19
Aneina, 177 I 2
Antenor, 62.26
Anthus, 178 D 18
Antigonos, 43.17
Antigonos (astrologer), 159 n. 1
Antinous, 149 A–C
Antiochus (king of Commagene), 109.23, n. 7
Antiochus Epiphanes (IV), 42 D
Antipater, son of Zenon, 189.5,6,11,17,24
Antrocles, 180.5
Aphnius, 47 A 3
Aphrodisias, 188 C 11

Apion, 185.3
Apollonarion, 188 C 2
Apollonides, son of Lucius, 2 B 13,20, C 23, n. 11
Apollonios, son of Ptolemaios, 190.2
Apollonios, son of Ptolemaios, husband of Thermion, 185 *passim*
Apollonios (strategos), 129 D 1,28, F col. 1,2
Apollonios, son of Chaireas, 185.4
Apollonios of Tyana, 72
Apollonios, father of Hermaiskos, 44 col. 2.20
Apollonios (of Rome), 172 B 4
Apollonios, son of Ariston, 44 col. 2.19
Apollonios, son of Artemidorus, 44 col. 2.16
Apollonios, son of Diopeithes, 48.20
Apollophanes (district secretary), 175.2
Arbelos, 155 B 12,13
Archias (teacher), 178 I
Areios, 7 II D 10, n. 8
Ariobarzanes (King of the Medes), 26 col. 6.12
Ariobarzanes, son of Artavazdes, 26 col. 5.29, col. 6.11
Aristogenes, 7 II C 3
Aristokles, father of Aspasios, 43.19
Aristokles, son of Albiorix, 38
Ariston, father of Apollonius, 44 col. 2.19
Ariston of Pella, 151 A, n. 2
Ariston, son of Philokles, 49 B 18
Artas, 174.34
Artavazdes, son of Ariobarzanes, 26 col. 6.11
Artavasdes I, 26 col. 5.26
Artavasdes III, 26 col. 5.30, col. 6.1,11
Artaxares, 26 col. 6.1
Artaxes, 26 col. 5.25
Artemidoros, 44 col. 2.16
Artemidoros, 43.17
Artemon, 43.12
Artiknos, 38
Asandrochos, 42 A 1, n. 2
Asandros, 42 n. 1
Asclepiades of Prusa, 171 n. 10

Index of personal names

Iunius Silanus Torquatus, M., 35.4

Laberius Maximus, L. (prefect of Egypt), 98.2,11
Lacutanius Phileros, P., 13 II 43
Laelius Balbus, D. (cos. 6 BC), 11.151; 26 col. 3.29
Laenas Pontianus (cos. AD 131), 167.6
Laevius, 162
Lappius Gallus, L., 19.1
Lartia, 5 G
Lauricia, 170 L 7
Lavius Faustus, C., 178 E 1
Lentulus, L. (*PIR*² C 1384), 20 B–C
Lepidus Nepos, M., 126.13
Licinius Calvus, C. (poet), 162
Licinius Calvus Stolo, C. (*PIR*² L 171), 11.150
Licinius Crassus, M. (cos. 30 BC), 5 A–B
Licinius Crassus Frugi, M. (cos. 14 BC), 26 col. 3.23
Licinius Maximus, 196 col. 1.4
Licinius Mucianus, A. (identity?), 108.2
Licinius Nerva, A. (cos. AD 65), 70 B 7
Licinius Silvanus Granianus, Q. (cos. AD 106), 146 n. 3
Livia Ocellina, 80 n. 1
Livilla (sister of Emperor Claudius), 171 G
Livius Boethus, M., 171 H 1
Lollius, M. (cos. 21 BC), 111.107 and 151
Longina, 187.3,12
Longinus, 187.1,10
Longinus, son of Sdapezematygus, 49 D 1
Lucilius Successus, L., 177 G 1
Lucius, father of Arsus, 187.4
Lucius, father of Murdia, 184.1
Lucius, father of Vitellius, 79 F 1
Lucretius Vespillo, Q. (cos. 19 BC), 26 col. 1.37, col. 2.32,35
Lucretius Eros Mudianus, Q., 7 (I) D
Lucretius Satrius Valens, D., 170 B 1
Lucretius Valens, D., son of Decimus, 170 B 3
Lucterius Cadurcus Leo, M., 7 (I) A 1
Lucullus, 182.13
Luria Privata, 172 K 1
Lusius Quietus (Trajan's general), 129 A 5

Mamurius, 199 col. 3
Mandatus, 170 D 5
Manilius Vopiscus, P. (cos. AD 114), 126.22
Mannius Secundus, C., 49 F 1
Marcella, 172 I 2
Marcia Festa, 168 B 5
Marcius Censorinus, C. (cos. 8 BC), 26 col. 2.6
Marcius Turbo, Q. (under Trajan and Hadrian), 129 A 3
Marcleius Philargurus, L., 173 K 1
Maria Galla, 20 A 4

Marius Orthrus, 172 B 3
Marullus, 180.5
Masonius, C., 170 D 8
Memmius, C., 162
Memmius Montanus, T., 179.4
Messalina (Nero's wife), 71.52
Messalina, Valeria (Claudius' wife), 47 n. 1; 55, n. 4
Messius Campanus, P., 101.9
Metilius (governor), 38
Mettius Epaphroditus, M., 173 M 1; 178 I
Mettius Germanus, M., 173 M 4
Mettius Modestus, M. (prefect of Egypt), 178 I
Mettius Potitus, T., 177 C 1
Mettius Rufus, M. (prefect of Egypt), 105.23; 106 B 1
Minicius Italus, C., 116.1
Mommeius Persicus, M., 197 col. 1.3
Mucianus Fundanus, C. (proconsul of Asia), 146 n. 3
Mucius Scaevola, C., 11.107,150
Munnius Nematinus, T., 193.7
Murdia, 184.1
Musaeus, 177 D 6
Musicus Scurranus, 178 D 1
Musonius Rufus, C. (the stoic philosopher?), 188 n. 1
Mutatus, 178 D 9

Ninnius Hasta, Q. (cos. AD 114), 126.22
Nonius Calpurnius Asprenas Torquatus II, L. (cos. AD 128), 148
Nonius Calpurnius Torquatus Asprenas, L. (cos. AD 94), 103 col. 2.1
Norbanus Balbus, L. (cos. AD 19), 35.4
Norbanus Flaccus, C. (cos. 38 BC), 11.151
Norbanus Flaccus, C. (cos. AD 157), 30.2; 36 A frag. 1.1
Norbanus Ptolemaios, 67 A 5
Novicius, 49 E 3
Novius Eunus, C., 176.3,10
Numidius Eros, C., 16 B

Octavius Alexander, 187.1
Octavius Fronto, 35.3
Oppius Sabinus, C. (cos. AD 84), 102 B,E; 121, n. 2
Optatus, 170 D 10
Otacilius Sagitta (procurator), 87.4

Papirius Pastor, 67 A 7
Passienus Rufus, L. (cos. 4 BC), 13 V 74,84; 20 A 2; 26 col. 3.29
Paullus Fabius Maximus (cos. 11 BC), 26 col. 1.38
Pedanius Fuscus, 159 n. 5
Pedanius Salinator, Cn. (cos. AD 61?), 164 G 16

C. EMPERORS (arranged chronologically)

Index of gods and goddesses

D. IMPERIAL FAMILIES

Germanicus (the Elder, *PIR*² C 857), brother of Emperor Tiberius, 21.10; 36 A 19,27,31, frag. II col. b 10, col. c 15,16; 36 B 2; 53.7; 55.35; 70 B 1

Germanicus (the Younger, *PIR*² I 221), son of Germanicus, brother of Emperor Claudius, 28 B–C; 32.10; 33.1; 34 A–C; 36 A–B and *passim*; 44 col. 2.27

Drusus Iulius Caesar (*PIR*² I 219), son of Emperor Tiberius, 25.3; 28 D–E; 30.1; 32.11; 36 A 7

Lucius Caesar (*PIR*² I 222), grandson of Augustus, 1 H; 7 nn. 12,16

Gaius Caesar (*PIR*² I 216), grandson of Augustus, I (I); 7 nn. 12,16; 17; 18.20,15–16, 18; 19.7,25,37; 26 col. 2.45, col. 5.28;

36 A frag. II col. a 5, col. c 19; 36 B *passim*

Ulpius Traianus, M., father of Emperor Trajan, 85a 11; 174.7

Iulia Agrippina (*PIR*² I 641), sister of Emperor Gaius (Caligula), and mother of Nero, 60

Iulia Livilla (*PIR*² I 674), sister of Emperor Gaius, 60

Livia Augusta, wife of Augustus, 20 A 1; 25.45; 36 A frag. I 7 and frag. II col. b 10; 57.6

Antonia minor, mother of Germanicus the Younger, 36 A 20

(Vipsania) Agrippina, wife of Germanicus the Younger, 36 A frag. I 20

Plotina Augusta, widow of Trajan, 144 (letter of)

II. Gods and goddesses

Ammon, 81.13 (Vespasian, son of), 16, n. 3

Aphrodite, 7 n. 11; 32.11; 42 B 12 (New A. = Drusilla)

Apollo, 11.139; 25.32; 26 col. 4.1,22,24,54; 35.2; 36 A frag. II col. b 22, col. c 13,17, B 1,4; 71.50,57; 78.3 (Nero, the New A.); 165 A 2; 166 F 4; 170 C 5; 199 col. 5.8

Artemis, 55 n. 7

Asklepios, 32.35; 49 B 15, n. 8; 73.16; 84.2; 171 F 1, I *passim*

Bacchus, 199 n. 11; *see also* Dionysos

Castor, I K; 26 col. 4.12

Ceres, 182.12; 199 col. 8

Concord, 36 n. 12

Diana, 7 I C B 22; 11.103,139; 199 col. 8.11

Dionysos, 2 B 14, C 25; 7 II E 12,18; 11 n. 11

Earth, 15.8

Epione, 49 B 16

Fates, 11.90,92

Flora, 199 col. 5

Fors, 199 col. 6

Fortune, 1 C–D; 25.61; 26 col. 2.29; 32.10

Great Mother, 26 col. 4.8

Health, 32.25; 49 B 16; 171 I 1,7,19; 172 B 1

Hercules, 112 B 1; 147, n. 3; 171 D 8; 199 col. 6

Honor, 26 col. 2.29

Hope, 199 col. 8

Ianus Quirinius, 26 col. 2.41

Ilithyia, 11.115

Isis, 67 B col. 1.3; 199 col. 3, col. 4

Janus, 8.11

Juno, 7 I E; 11.103,119; 20 A 1; 26 col. 4.6; 172 F; 199 col. 1

Jupiter, 11.103,105; 26 col. 4.5, col. 4.6; 41.14; 70 B 8; 79 A 1; 84.8; 97.30,46; 103 col. 3.12; 159; 199 cols. 7,11

Lares, 26 col. 4.7

Liber, 199 col. 10

Mars, 20 E 1; 26 col. 4.21, col. 5.43, col. 4.38; 30.5; 36 B 52; 121.2; 126.4; 159; 198 C; 199 col. 10

Mercury, 159; 165 A 1; 193.5; 198 C; 199 cols. 5–6

Minerva, 26 col. 4.6; 56.1; 70 B 9; 111.28; 199 cols. 3,9

Mother Earth, 11.134

Muse, 162

Neptune, 56.1; 199 col. 2

Noctivagus, 168 I a 12

Oceanus, 168 I a 13

Osiris, 199, n. 13

Peace, I E; 26 col. 2.39; 44 col. 2.35

Penates, 26 col. 4.7; 97.31; 199 col. 1

Pollux, 1 K

Quirinus, 26 col. 4.5

Roma, 7 I B, II A–B, C 10, D 1; 26 n. 1; 38

Sarapis, 81.15; 199 col. 4
Saturn, 26 col. 4.12; 159; 164 C 22; 198 C; 200.6
Sun, 15.8; 63.17,24; 198 C

Tiberis, 168 I a 13

Venus, 103 col. 2.8; 162; 170 M; 198 C;
199 col. 4
Vesta, 26 col. 4.25; 199 col. 12

Victory, 32.10; 79 B
Virtue, 26 col. 2.29
Vulcan, 99, n. 2; 199 col. 9

Youth, 26 col. 4.8

Zeus, 7 II E 46; 15.8; 33.5; 70 A 4;
71.41,48–9,51,56; 127.1

III. Geographical names

Listing is by geographical designation, but no attempt is made to distinguish between country and inhabitants.

Achaea, 4 with n. 3; 26 col. 5.35; 47 F 7; 60;
71.12; 73.1; 164 B 9, C 16
Actium, 5, n. 3; 26 col. 5.4, nn. 6–7; 32 n. 5
Adiabenians, 26 col. 6.1
Adramyttion, 43.17
Adriatic Sea, 26 col. 5.12,32; 72; 182.8
Aeduans, 170 H 4
Aegean Sea, 72
Aegina, 72
Aelia (Capitolina), 151 A (4)
Aethiopia, 26 col. 5,19,21
Africa, 9 B; 20 A 2, C–E; 26 col. 4.40,
col. 5.5,35; 77; 109.7; 145, n. 1; 148, n. 4;
167.26; 169.40; 188, n. 2
Agrigentum, 60
Akarnania, 4
Albania, 26 col. 5.53; 136 A; 155, n. 1
Alele, 9 B
Alexandria, 25.33; 34 A 3,20; 44 col. 2.15,
col. 3 *passim*; 45 *passim*; 47 D 6; 49 C 14,
61, n. 1; 103 col. 2.3; 129 A–B; 140.1; 156.22;
169.31,36; 170 O 5; 171 I 9,20; 176.13; 178 I;
188 C 3,5; 189, n. 1; 199 n. 1
Alexandria Troas, 21 n. 3
Allia R., 19.25; 40 D
Allobroges, 55 n. 7
Alps, 26 col. 5.12; 53.8; 74 n. 1; 106 n. 1
Altinum, 53.10
Amanus Mt, 36 A frag. I 22
Ambitrebian District, 197 col. 1.3
Ammaedara, 148, n. 1
Anartii, 5 D
Anas R., 4
Anauni, 52.22
Ancyra, 26 n. 1; 38; 128, n. 2
Anio Novus, 59.4
Anthemusia, 136 A
Antinoöpolis, 157
Antinous (city), 153.55,57
Antioch, 26 n. 1; 43.15; 49 C; 85 a 18, n. 2;
107 col. 2.5,11,14,24; 130, nn. 1–2; 134, n. 1;
174.16, n. 6

Antioch toward Pisidia, 164, n. 8
Antiochia Mygdonia, 131.6, n. 2 (*see* Nisibis)
Apamea, 22.10, n. 4; 43.16
Aphrodisias, 3.3, nn. 1,3
Apollonopolis-Heptakomias, 129 F col. 2
Apulia, 21.3; 60
'Aqaba, Gulf of, 124, n. 1
Aquileia, 116.11
Aquitania, 116.10
Aquitanian Bay, 8.4
Arabia, 16 A; 26 col. 5.19,22; 106 A; 115, n. 2;
124.6; 169.40
Arar R., 7 I A 8, n. 1
Arcadia, 149, n. 2
Ariminum, 6 n. 1; 26 col. 4.19
Aritium, 41.4,18
Armenia, 10 C; 18 n. 2; 26 col. 5.24,31;
36 A frag. I 17; 64.15; 65 A 2; 118 B; 134, n. 1;
135 B; 136 A; 138.8; 155 A 7, B 12,14,29, n. 4
Arsinoe, 114, n. 2
Arsinoite Nome, 156, n. 1
Asia, 4; 7 II B E 41; 26 col. 4.49, col. 5.35;
36 A frag. I 15; 43.5; 64.8; 116.8; 128.6;
138.29; 146 n. 3; 147.1,4; 163; 164 C 10;
171 J 5
Assuritania, 188 E 5
Assyria, 117 n. 2; 118 B; 136 A, n. 6
Astura R., 8.9
Athens, 7 n. 7; 24 A–D; 75; 146.6, n. 3; 147.5;
171 I 9,11,21
Athesis R., 53.2
Atilla, 198 C
Attenia, 9 A
Attica, 8.5
Auriania, 155 A 1
Astures, 8.9,10
Aventine, 26 col. 4.6; 28 n. 5; 40 A 5
Azov, Sea of, 42 n. 3

Babylonia, 138 A
Bacchias, 195 C 1
Bactria, 169.40

IV. Subjects and terms

V. Translated passages

INSCRIPTIONS

AE

Bruns[7]

CIL II

CIL III

CIL IV

CIL V

CIL VI

Index of translated passages

PAPYRI

BGU
  1052: 185
  1103: 189
  1199: 14
  1210: 188
  1690: 187
P. Bremen
  40: 129 E
  46: 194
P. Cairo
  49359–60: 156
P. Edfou I
  ostr. 120: 83 G
P. Fay.
  ostr. 10: 195 E
  29: 191
  67: 195 C
P. Fouad I
  8: 81
  21: 67 A
P. Giss.
  19: 129 D
  41: 129 F
P. Köln
  10: 12
P. London
  904, col. 2: 114
P. Mil. R. Univ.
  6: 129 C
P. Oslo
  78: 156

P. Oxy.
  32: 192
  106: 190
  237, col. 8: 105
  744: 188 C
  1021: 61
  2435 recto: 34 A
P. Rylands
  74: 152
  189: 195 B
PSI
  871: 175
P. Yale
  1528: 67 B
SB
  3924: 34 B
  6304: 179
  6944: 156
  7398: 195 D
  8303: 63
Aegyptus 50 (1970)
  6–7: 62
Wilcken, *Chrestomathie*
  16: 129 E
  26 I: 153
  113: 61
  192: 105
  373: 143
  413: 34 C
  439: 46
  463: 103

COINS

BMC Galatia
  p. 106, no. 1: 42 D
BMC Palestine
  p. 230, no. 10: 42 E
  p. 304, no. 14: 151 E
Mattingly, *BMC*
  1, 10: 10 A
  1, 18: 10 C
  1, 63: 79 C
  1, 122: 68
  1, 293: 79 B

  1, 548: 7 I A
  1, 705: 7 II A
  1, p. 364, 1: 79 D
  1, p. 388, 99: 79 E
  2, p. 131, 604: 83 E
  3, 16: 110 C
  3, 606: 135 A
  3, 1035: 135 B
  3, 1046: 135 C
  3, 1207: 142 B

PERIODICALS AND BOOKS

AUTHORS

SCHOLIA